THE CELTIC HEROIC AGE

CELTIC STUDIES PUBLICATIONS I

The Celtic Heroic Age

Literary Sources for Ancient Celtic Europe & Early Ireland & Wales

THIRD EDITION

edited by
JOHN T. KOCH

in collaboration with
JOHN CAREY

CELTIC STUDIES PUBLICATIONS, INC.
ANDOVER, MASSACHUSETTS, & ABERYSTWYTH

2000

First published 1994
Second edition published 1995
Fist hardcover edition 1995
Second edition reprinted with corrections 1997
Third edition published 2000

Typeset in the Cynrhan type family by Celtic Studies Publications, Inc.

Cover illustration by Stephen Conlin, a reconstruction of the '40-metre structure' at Navan Fort,
Co. Atrmagh, (the Emain Macha of the Ulster Cycle tales), as it would have appeared c. 95 BC.
Published by and used with kind permission of the Navan Research Group/Department of
Archaeology, Queen's University Belfast, NI.

Cover design by Celtic Studies Publications, Inc.

ISBN 1-891271-04-0

Celtic Studies Publications, Inc.

business office:
P. O. Box 639
Andover, MA 01810–0011
USA

CelticSP@aol.com
www.celticstudies.com

editorial correspondence:
Celtic Studies Publications
Centre for Advanced Welsh and Celtic Studies
National Library of Wales
Aberystwyth, Ceredigion SY23 3HH
Wales

CONTENTS

[v]

[vii]

PREFACE

THE aim of the present volume is to make available, in English translation, a fairly extensive survey of the primary literary materials relevant to the introductory study of the early Celtic-speaking peoples. The target readership is tertiary students and, more particularly, university undergraduates engaged in one- or two-term courses in Celtic civilisation, as now taught at a number of leading institutions around the world. This book is in fact an outgrowth of such a course.

Though a great deal of effort has been put into every component of the book, we have not delayed until all the translations could be brought to a uniformly high standard. I am thinking here particularly of my own contributions. Accessibility and tolerable accuracy have been taken as the preferred goals. Future editions are anticipated, and I would be grateful to anyone drawing my attention to remaining errors and infelicities.

I wish to acknowledge the help of the following individuals who assisted in various aspects of this book's production: Nancy Breen, Michael J. Connolly, James Donohoe, Patrick K. Ford, Katherine Stuart Forsyth, Pamela S. Hopkins, Janice Koch, Anne Lea, Peter McQuillan, William J. Mahon, J. P. Mallory, Philip O'Leary, Roxanne Reddington-Wilde, William Witt, Kellie Wixson, Donna Wong.

— J. T. Koch, December 1994

PREFACE TO THE 2000 EDITION

FIVE years on, *The Celtic Heroic Age* remains, in essence, a work in progress. Material has been added to Part I, thanks mostly to Philip Freeman. Consequently, the numbering of pages and sections does not match those of the earlier editions. Several of the translations in Part III have been revised to reflect work done since the appearance of the second edition, and a few maps have been added in that section. A short Breton Latin text, the original of which we owe to Gwenaël Le Duc, has been added to the end. A new and fuller Index is provided.

Because of the obsolescence of the computer hardware and software (word processing programme, operating system, and font formats) used in creating the earlier editions, it has been necessary to undertake the production of this book more-or-less from scratch. Therefore, though it has been possible to correct some errors, many remain, and new ones have no doubt been introduced. A further reprint is anticipated for later this year or the next. The editors would thus be most grateful for *corrigenda* brought to the attention of the publisher.

— JTK, January 2000

PART I

Ancient Celtic Europe

§§1–2. Two Gaulish Religious Inscriptions
TRANS. J. T. KOCH

¶ **Note.** Though the ancient Celtic languages offer little in the way of 'literature', as the term is usually understood, archaeologists have recently uncovered some fairly long inscriptions relevant to pagan cult practices. In a number of ways, these texts illuminate survivals of pagan myth underlying vernacular literature of Early Christian Ireland and Britain.

The following inscriptions were written in a Roman cursive script on lead. The first tablet was deposited in a sacred spring—with a great quantity of other ritual depositions, including many carved wooden figurines—to communicate with gods thought to be accessible through openings to the underworld. The date was *c.* 50 AD. The gods Lugus and Maponos correspond to the Irish Lug (§81 ¶48, §71, §108 ¶¶60 69 70 72 74 79 96 98) and Welsh Lleu (§117 B².24 B¹.18) and Welsh Mabon, respectively. The tablet is written on behalf of a group of men seeking beneficial action from the gods: victory in battle and healing of a variety of medical ailments have both been suggested.

The second inscription was deposited in a woman's grave (*c.* AD 90) and has to do with the activities of a coven of sorceresses. The Gaulish word *uidluā* 'seeress' is the exact equivalent of Old Irish *Fedelm*, the name of the seeress of the *Táin*. The leading interpretation of the inscription proposes that the family relationships are part of the cult sisterhood and not actual. This is roughly one quarter of the inscription. Since some of the names seem to change gender, it is possible that cult sisters can be father and daughter, husband and wife. In the continuation of the text (which is very hard to translate) there are several third person imperative verbs, apparently injunctions concerning the grave and perhaps two rival covens.

The Gaulish texts are supplied just to give the beginner in Celtic studies some idea of what that language looked like, which is (speaking very impressionistically) more like Greek or Latin than like latter-day Irish or Welsh.

§1. The Tablet of Chamalières

¶ 1. ['THE PRAYER']

Andedion	uediiu	-mi	diiiuion	risu	naritu	Maponon
great-god(?)	beseech	I	divine	tablet	magic(?)	Maponos

Aruernatin:	lotites	sni	eθθic	sos	briχtia	Anderon:
Arvernian	quicken(?)	us	& it is	them	spell	infernal beings

¶ 2. ['THE LIST']

C. Lucion, Floron Nigrinon adgarion, Aemilion Paterin, Claudion Legitumon,
invoker
Caelion Pelign[on], Claudion Pelign[on], Marcion Uictorin Asiaticon   AθθedilIi
son of Aθθedillos

¶ 3. ['THE OATH']

Eti-c Segoui		toncnaman toncsiiont	-io:	meion,	pon-c
& it is Strong One/Victor	oath/destiny swear/destine	that	centre(?)	(&) when	

sesit,	buet-id	ollon; regu -c	cambion (;)	exsops (;)	pissiiu -mi
sows(?)	be it	whole straighten &(?)	crooked/evil	blind	see I

iso-c	canti	rissu	ison	son	bissiet.	Luge
thus/this-&(?)	with/song(?)	tablet	this/him	what(?)	be	Lugus

dessu-m	-mi	-iis; Luge dessu-mi-is; Luge dessu-mi-is Luχe.
prepare/set right	I	them Lugus

TENTATIVE TRANSLATION

¶ 1. I beseech the very divine, the divine Maponos Avernatis by means of the magic tablet: quicken(?) us, i.e. those (named below) by the magic of the underworld spirits(?):

¶ 2. C. Lucios, Floros Nigrinos the invoker, Aemilios Paterinos, Claudios Legitumos, Caelios Pelignos, Claudios Pelignos, Marcios Victorinos, Asiaticos son of AΘΘedillos.

¶ 3. And it is the destiny of the Victor to which they shall be destined (*or* and it is the oath of the Strong One that they shall swear); the centre— when he sows it—(it) shall be whole; (and) I right the wrong (:) blindly (;) thus (?) by means of this tablet (of incantation ?) I shall see what shall be. By Lugus I prepare them; by Lugus I prepare them; by Lugus I prepare them, by Lugus.

§2. The Tablet of Larzac[1]

[1A]

'In-sinde se—:   bnanom   bricto²n,— eianom anuana san-
  in this   women   magic   their   names special

  ander³na;— brictom   uidluias uidlu[. .] ⁴tigontias   so.
    underworld   magic   seeress   see-(?)   weave   this

  Adsagsona   Seuer[im] ⁵Tertionicnim   lidssatim liciatim⁶
  [fem.divine name]   Severa   daughter of Tertiū   artificer   offerer

eianom uo -dui-uoderce -lunget. ⁷ utonid ponc ni-tiχsintor   si[es],
their   two manifestation maintain below   where press down   they

⁸ duscelinatia int(-)eanom anuan[im] ⁹ esi andernados   brictom:
bad-omen-poem this their   names   is   underworld-group magic

  Bano[na] (duχtir) ¹⁰ Flatucias, Paulla   dona   Potiti[. .], ¹¹
  Banona   daughter Flatucia   Paulla   ?wife Potitos

    <i>Ai[i]a duχtir   Adiegias,   Poti[tos?] ¹²   atir
      Aia   daughter   Adiega   Potitos   father

  Paullias, Seuera   du[χtir] ¹³ Ualentos dona   Paulliu[..],
  Paulla   Severa   daughter   Valens   ?wife Paulla

---

1 One only of a total of four panels. The superscript numbers signify division into lines in the original.

[14] Adiega matir	Aiias, [15]	Potita	dona Prim[i] (*duχtir*) [16]	Abesias.
Adiega mother	Aiia	Potita	? wife Primus daughter	Abesa

TENTATIVE TRANSLATION

Herein—:

— a magical incantation of women,

— their special infernal names,

— the magical incantation of a seeress who fashions this prophecy.

The goddess Adsagsona maintains Severa daughter of Tertiu in two cult offices, (as) their scribe(?) and offering maker.

Below, where they shall be impressed, the prophetic curse of these names of theirs is a magical incantation of a group of practitioners of underworld magic: Banona daughter of Flatucia, Paulla wife of Potitos, Aiia daughter of Adiega, Potitos father of Paulla, Severa daughter of Valens [and] wife of Paullos(?), Adiega mother of Aiia, Potita wife of Primos daughter of Abesa.

The Classical Authors on the Ancient Celts²

§§3–16. Pre-Posidonian³ Authors
TRANS. PHILIP FREEMAN

§3. Hecatæus of Miletus [late 6th century BC; s.v. Stephan of Byzantium]
¶ Fragment 54.

NARBON: trading centre and city of the Celts . . . Hecataeus calls them Narbaioi.
¶ Fragment 55. Massalia: a city of Ligurians near Celtica, a colony of Phocaeans. [According to] Hecataeus in his *Europa*.

¶ Fragment 56. Nyrax: a Celtic city. [According to] Hecataeus in his *Europa*.

§4. Herodotus *History* 2.33 [5th century BC].

THE NILE flows out of Libya, cutting through the middle of that country. And as I reason, calculating unknown things from known, it begins at the same distance as the Ister [Danube]. For the Ister, beginning in the land of the Celts and the city of Pyrene,⁴ flows through the middle of Europe. The Celts live beyond the Pillars of Hercules [Straits of Gibraltar] and border on the Cynetes, who are the westernmost inhabitants of Europe. The Ister then flows through all of Europe and empties into the Euxine [Black Sea] at Istria, which colonists from Miletus inhabit.

---

2 What is perhaps the earliest reference to Celtic-speaking peoples is the reference to the inhabitants of Britain and Ireland in the *Ora Maritima* of Avienus (§50 below).

3 **Posidonius** was a Greek writer, Stoic philosopher, and historian of the earlier 1st century BC, whose firsthand description of Gaul has not survived directly, but was an important source for the surviving accounts of Diodorus (§18), Athenaeus (§17), Strabo (§19), and, to a disputed extent, Cæsar (§20). He proved so influential for subsequent Greek and Roman writings on the Celts that his career provides a convenient milestone according to which we may subdivide the classical accounts of the Celts that preceded him from those which follow. See further, J. J. Tierney, 'The Celtic Ethnography of Posidonius', *Proceedings of the Royal Irish Academy* lx, Section C, No. 5 (1960) 189–275.

4 **Pyrene.** The location is unknown, but the name may be connected with that of the Pyrenees Mts. of present-day Spain and France, in which case Herodotus has mislocated the source of the Danube.

§5 Plato *Laws* 1.637d–e [4th century BC].

I AM NOT discussing the drinking of wine nor drinking in general, but out-right drunkenness, and whether we ought to follow the custom of the Scythians and Persians, and also the Carthaginians, Celts, Iberians, and Thracians, all very warlike peoples, or be like you Spartans, who, as you claim, abstain totally from drink.

§6. Aristotle [4th century BC]. ¶ *Politics* 2.6.6

THE INEVITABLE result is that in such a state wealth is esteemed too high-ly, especially if the men are dominated by women as it is with most military and warlike cultures, except the Celts and certain other groups who openly approve of sexual relations between men.

¶ *Nicomachean Ethics* 3.7.6–7 On account of honour the virtuous man stands his ground and performs brave deeds. But the one who is fearless with excessive bravery, who fears nothing at all, not even earthquakes or waves (as they say of the Celts), has no name, unless we call him mad or insensible.

¶ *Eudemian Ethics* 3.1.25 Therefore no one is brave if he endures formidable events on account of ignorance, such as a madman who taunts thunderbolts, or if someone knows the dangers involved but is carried away by reckless passion, as the Celts who take up arms against the waves. The bravery of barbarians in general is based in passion.

§7. Ephorus [4th century BC; s.v. Strabo *Geography* 4.4.6].

EPHORUS, IN HIS ACCOUNT, says that Celtica is so large that it includes most of Iberia, as far as Gades [mod. Cadiz, near Gibraltar]. He also reports that the Celts are great admirers of the Greeks and says many things about them that are not true for current times. For example, they are very careful to avoid becoming fat or potbellied, and if any young man's belly sticks over his belt he is punished.

§8. Theopompus [4th century BC; s.v. Athenæus *Deipnosophistae* 10. 443b–c].

THE CELTS, knowing this weakness when making war on them [the Illyrians], announced to all the soldiers that a wonderful banquet had been prepared for them in their tents. They put a certain medicinal herb in the food which attacked and purged their bowels. Then some were captured and slain by the Celts, while others, unable to stand the pain, threw themselves into the rivers.

§§9–10. The Celts of the Balkans and Alexander the Great

§9. Ptolemy I [4th century BC; s.v. Strabo 7.3.8]

PTOLEMY, THE SON OF LAGUS, says that during this campaign some Celts living near the Adriatic arrived seeking good will and friendship. Alexander received them warmly and while they were sharing a drink asked them what they feared the most, thinking they would say him. They answered that they feared nothing except that the sky might fall down on them, but that they honoured the friendship of a man like him more than anything. And the following are signs of the candour of the barbarians: . . . that the Celts said that they feared no one, and yet valued above all else the friendship of great men.

§10. Arrianus Flavius [2nd century AD] *Anabasis of Alexander* 1.4.6–5.2 [TRANS. J. T. KOCH]

AT THIS POINT AMBASSADORS came to Alexander from the other autonomous tribes from the region of the Ister [Danube] and from Syrmus, King of the Triballi; others from the Celts settled on the Ionian gulf [Adriatic]. The Celts were big in stature and haughty in their bearing; however, all of them expressed their wishes for Alexander's friendship. And he gave the fitting guarantees to everyone and received these likewise. He asked the Celts what living things they feared most, hoping that his own great renown had extended as far as the Celts and beyond, and that they would confess that they feared him more than anything. However, their answer was surprising to him. Since they lived in rugged country far from Alexander and judging that his invasion was aimed in another direction, they said that they feared most that the sky might fall upon them. [Alexander] proclaimed that they were his friends, agreed to a treaty, and sent them home, making the offhand remark, 'These Celts are such pretentious boasters!'

§11. Sopater [3rd century BC; s.v. Athenæus *Deipnosophistae* 15.160e].

AMONG THEM is the custom, whenever they win
victory in battle, to sacrifice their prisoners
To the gods. So I, imitating the Celts, have vowed
To the divine powers to burn as an offering
Three of those false dialecticians.

§12. Phylarchus [3rd century BC; s.v. Athenæus *Deipnosophistae* 4.150d–f].

IN HIS THIRD BOOK PHYLARCHUS says that Ariamnes, a Galatian of very great wealth, announced that he would give a year-long feast for all the Galatians, and this is how he accomplished it: He divided the country by marking out convenient distances on the roads. At these points he set up banqueting halls made out of poles, straw, and wicker-work, which each held four hundred men or more, depending on the size of nearby towns and communities. Inside he put huge cauldrons with every kind of meat. The cauldrons were made the year before the feast by artisans from other cities [tribes]. He then provided many oxen, pigs, sheep, and other kinds of animals every day, along with great jars of wine and an abundance of grain. And not only did the Galatians dwelling in nearby towns and villages enjoy the feast, but even strangers passing by were invited in by servants, who urged them to enjoy the good things provided.

§13. Anonymous poet *Greek Anthology* 9.125 [*c.* 200 BC].

THE BOLD CELTS test their children in the jealous Rhine
And no man regards himself as a true father
Until he sees the child washed in the holy river.
For immediately when the child has come from
The mother's womb and shed its first tears, the father picks
It up and places it on his own shield, not sympathizing,
For he does not feel for the child like a true father
Until he sees it judged in the river's bath.
And the mother, having new pains added to those
Of childbirth, even if she knows him to be the true father,
Awaits in fear what the inconstant river will judge.

§14. Polybius *History* [2nd century BC].[5]

¶ 2.28.3–10.

THE CELTS had stationed the Gaesatae ['Spearmen'] from the Alps to face Aemilius on the rear, and behind them were the Insubres. On their front they placed the Taurisci and the Cisalpine Boii to face the Romans. They placed their waggons and chariots on the edges of both wings, with the booty being on one of the hills near the road under guard. Thus the Celtic army was double-faced. Their way of arranging their forces was effective as well as designed to

---

5   The first three passages concern the Battle of Telamon, fought in Etruria (Northern Italy) in 225 BC.

inspire fear in their enemies. The Insubres and Boii were clothed in pants and light cloaks, but the Gaesatae from conceit and daring threw their clothing off, and went out to the front of the army naked, having nothing but their weapons. They believed that since the ground was covered with brambles which might catch their clothing and hinder the use of their weapons, they would be more effective this way. At first the fighting was only for possession of the hill, and the amount of cavalry from all three armies made it an impressive sight to everyone. In the middle of the battle the consul Gaius, fighting with great bravery, was killed, and his head was brought to the Celtic king.

¶ 29.5–9. But the Romans, while pleased to have trapped the enemy between two of their own armies, were greatly disturbed by the ornaments and battle noise of the Celts. For there were among them countless horns and trumpets which were being blown simultaneously from every part of the army. The sound was so loud and piercing that the clamour didn't seem to come from trumpets and human voices, but from the whole countryside all at once. Also terrifying was the appearance and rapid manoeuvring of the naked warriors in front, men at the prime of their strength and magnificence. And all the warriors in front were wearing torques and bracelets. All these sights terrified the Romans, but hope of victory encouraged them to try even harder in the battle.

¶ 31.1–2. Forty thousand of the Celts were killed, and about ten thousand were captured, including Concolitanus, one of their kings. The other king, Aneroestus, fled with a few followers and joined his people in a place of security. There he committed suicide along with his companions.

¶ 21.38.1–6. [2nd century BC]. By chance, one of the prisoners captured when the Romans defeated the Asian Galatae at Olympus was Chiomara, wife of Ortiagon. The centurion in charge of her took advantage of his soldierly opportunity and raped her. He was indeed a slave to both lust and money, but eventually his love of money won out. With a large amount of gold being agreed on, he led her away to be ransomed. There was a river between the two camps, and the Galatae crossed it, paid the ransom, and received the woman. When this was accomplished, she ordered one of them with a nod to kill the Roman as he was making a polite and affectionate farewell. The man obeyed and cut off the centurion's head. She picked it up and rode off with it wrapped in the folds of her dress. When she reached her husband, she threw the head at his feet. He was astonished and said, 'Wife, faithfulness is a good thing.' 'Yes,' she said, 'but it is better that only one man alive would have lain with me.'

§15. Pseudo-Scymnus *Periplus* 183–87 [*c.* 100 BC].

THE CELTS follow the customs of the Greeks,
Being on very friendly terms towards Greece,

On account of the hospitality of those dwelling abroad.
With music they conduct public assemblies,
Using it for its soothing effects.

§16. Nicander of Colophon [2nd century BC; s.v. Tertullian De Anima 57.10].

AND IT IS OFTEN ALLEGED because of nighttime dreams that the dead truly appear, for the Nasamones receive special oracles by staying at the tombs of their parents, as Heraclides—or Nymphodorus or Herodotus—writes. The Celts also for the same reason spend the night near the tombs of their famous men, as Nicander affirms.

§§17–20. The Posidonian Tradition

§17. Athenæus [fl. *c.* AD 200] *Deipnosophistae*, TRANS. PHILIP FREEMAN

¶ 4.36

POSIDONIUS, THE STOIC PHILOSOPHER [*c.* 135–*c.* 50 BC] collected the customs and manners of many peoples in his *Histories*, which he wrote according to the principles of his own philosophical convictions. He says that the Celts place dried grass on the ground when they eat their meals, using tables which are raised slightly off the ground. They eat only small amounts of bread, but large quantities of meat, either boiled, roasted, or cooked on spits. They dine on this meat in a clean but lion-like manner, holding up whole joints in both hands and biting the meat off the bone. If a piece of meat is too difficult to tear off, they cut it with a small knife which is conveniently at hand in its own sheath. Those who live near rivers, the Mediterranean, or Atlantic also eat fish baked with salt, vinegar, and cumin. They also use cumin in their wine. They do not use olive oil because of its scarcity and, due to its unfamiliarity, it has an unpleasant taste to them. When a number of them dine together, they sit in a circle with the most powerful man in the center like a chorus leader, whether his power is due to martial skill, family nobility, or wealth. Beside him sit the remainder of the dinner guests in descending order of importance according to rank. Bodyguards with shields stand close by them while their spearmen sit across from them, feasting together with their leaders. The servers bring drinks in clay or silver vessels resembling spouted cups. The platters on which they serve the food often are of similar material, but others use bronze, wooden, or woven trays. The drink of choice among the wealthy is wine brought from Italy or the region of Massalia [the Greek colony at Marseilles]. It is normally drunk unmixed with water, although sometimes water is added. Most of the rest of the population drinks a plain, honeyed beer, which is called *corma*. They use a common cup, sipping only a little at a time, but sipping frequently. The servant carries the cup around from the right to the left. In the same direction they honour their gods, turning to the right.

¶ 4.37 Posidonius, describing the great wealth of Lovernius ['Fox-like'], father of Bituitus who was deposed by the Romans, says that in order to gain the favour of the populace, he rode through the fields distributing gold and silver to the vast crowds of Celts which followed him. He also enclosed a square over two kilometers in length on each side, into which he put vast amounts of food and expensive drink. For many days the feast was served continuously to all who would enter. Finally when the celebration had come to an end, a Celtic poet arrived too late for the feast. He composed a song for Lovernius praising his greatness and lamenting his own tardy arrival. Lovernius was so pleased with this poem that he called for a bag of gold and tossed it to the poet as he ran beside his chariot. The bard picked up the bag and sang a new song, proclaiming that even his chariot-tracks gave gold and benefits to his people.

¶ 4.40 In the twenty-third book of his *Histories*, Posidonius says that the Celts sometimes engage in single combat during their feasts. Arming themselves, they engage in mock-fights and sparring sessions with each other Sometimes, however, wounds are inflicted and these mock-battles lead to real killing unless the bystanders restrain the combatants. Posidonius also says that in ancient times, the best warriors received the thigh portion during feasts. If another man were to challenge his right to the choicest portion, a duel was fought to the death. Others in former days would collect silver, gold, or a number of wine jars. Having received gift-pledges and distributed gifts among friends and family, they would stretch themselves out across their shields on their backs and then someone standing near would cut their throats with a sword.

¶ 6.49 Posidonius, in the twenty-third book of his *Histories*, says that the Celts have with them, even in war, companions whom they call parasites ['those who dine at another's table']. These poets recite their praises in large companies and crowds, and before each of the listeners according to rank. Their tales are recounted by those called Bards, poets who recite praises in song.

§18. Diodorus Siculus [wrote *c*. 60–*c*. 30 BC] 5.27–32, TRANS. PHILIP FREEMAN

¶ 27.

IN GENERAL, SILVER IS SCARCE throughout Gaul, but gold is abundant and freely given to the inhabitants by nature without the need for mining. This is because the rivers which flow through Gaul twist and turn, dashing against the sides of mountains in their course and breaking off large amounts of earth. Thus the rivers become full of gold-dust. This is collected by labourers who repeatedly pound and wash the material until it is pure and ready to be melted in a furnace. In this manner they accumulate a large amount of gold, men and women alike using it for decoration. On their wrists and arms they wear bracelets and on their necks thick bands of solid gold. They also wear rings on their fingers and even golden tunics. The Celts of the interior also have a peculiar custom concerning the sacred places of their gods. In temples and sanctuaries throughout the country, large amounts of gold are openly displayed as dedications to the gods. No one dares to touch these sacred depositions, even though the Celts are an especially covetous people.

¶ 28. The Gauls are very tall with white skin and blond hair, not only blond by nature but more so by the artificial means they use to lighten their hair. For they continually wash their hair in a lime solution, combing it back from the forehead to the back of the neck. This process makes them resemble Satyrs and Pans since this treatment makes the hair thick like a horse's mane. Some shave their beards while others allow a short growth, but nobles shave their cheeks and allow the moustache to grow until it covers the mouth. The result is that their moustaches become mixed with food while they eat, but serve as a sort of strainer when they drink. They do not sit in chairs when they dine, but sit on the ground using the skins of wolves or dogs. While dining they are served by adolescents, both male and female. Nearby are blazing hearths and cauldrons with spits of meat. They honour the brave warriors with the choicest portion, just as Homer says that the chieftains honoured Ajax when he returned having defeated Hector in single combat. They also invite strangers to their feasts, inquiring of their identity and business only after the meal. During feasts it is their custom to be provoked by idle comments into heated disputes, followed by challenges and single combat to the death. They do not fear death, but subscribe to the doctrine of Pythagoras that the human spirit is immortal and will enter a new body after a fixed number of years. For this reason some will cast letters to their relatives on funeral pyres, believing that the dead will be able to read them.

¶ 29. In both journeys and battles the Gauls use two-horse chariots which carry both the warrior and charioteer. When they encounter cavalry in battle they first hurl their spears then step down from the chariot to fight with swords. Some of them think so little of death that they fight wearing only a loincloth, without armour of any kind. They use free men from the poorer classes as charioteers and shield-bearers in battle. When two armies are drawn up for battle, it is their custom to step before the front line and challenge the best of their opponents to single combat while they brandish their weapons in front of them to intimidate the enemy. When an opponent accepts their challenge, they recite the brave deeds of both their ancestors and themselves, at the same time mocking the enemy and attempting to rob him of his fighting spirit. They decapitate their slain enemies and attach the heads to their horses' necks. The blood-soaked booty they hand over to their attendants, while they sing a song of victory. The choicest spoils they nail to the walls of their houses just like hunting trophies from wild beasts. They preserve the heads of their most distinguished enemies in cedar oil and store them carefully in chests. These they proudly display to visitors, saying that for this head one of his ancestors, or his father, or he himself refused a large offer of money. It is said that some proud owners have not accepted for a head an equal weight in gold, a barbarous sort of magnanimity. For selling the proof of one's valour is ignoble, but to continue hostility against the dead is bestial.

¶ 30. The Gauls wear stunning clothing—shirts which have been dyed in various colours, and trousers which they call *bracae*. They also wear striped cloaks with a chequered pattern, thick in winter and thin in summer, fastened with a clasp. They use uniquely decorated, man-high shields in battle, some with projecting bronze animals of superb workmanship. These animal-figures serve for defensive purposes as well as decoration. Their helmets have large figures on top—horns, which form a single piece with the helmet, or the heads of birds and four-footed animals—which give an appearance of added height to the warrior. Their trumpets are also of a peculiar and barbaric kind which produce a harsh, reverberating sound suitable to the confusion of battle. Some use iron breast-plates in battle, while others fight naked, trusting only in the protection which nature gives. They do not use short swords, but prefer a longer variety which are hung on their right sides by chains of iron or bronze. Some wear gold or sil-ver-plated belts around their tunics. Their spears, called *lanciae*, have iron heads a cubit [18 inches] or more in length and slightly less than two palms in width. Their swords are as long as the spears of other peoples, and their spears have heads longer than others' swords. Some of the spears have straight heads, but others are twisted in their entire length so that a blow not only cuts but mangles the flesh and withdrawal tears the wound open.

¶ 31. The Gauls are terrifying in appearance and speak with deep, harsh voices. They speak together in few words, using riddles which leave much of the true meaning to be understood by the listener. They frequently exaggerate their claims to raise their own status and diminish another's. They are boastful, violent, and melodramatic, but very intelligent and learn quickly. They have lyric poets called Bards, who, accompanied by instruments resembling lyres, sing both praise and satire. They have highly-honoured philosophers and theologians [those who speak about the gods] called Druids. They also make use of seers, who are greatly respected. These seers, having great authority, use auguries and sacrifices to foresee the future. When seeking knowledge of great importance, they use a strange and unbelievable method: they choose a person for death and stab him or her in the chest above the diaphragm. By the convulsion of the victim's limbs and spurting of blood, they foretell the future, trusting in this ancient method. They do not sacrifice or ask favours from the gods without a Druid present, as they believe sacrifice should be made only by those supposedly skilled in divine communication. Not only during peacetime but also in war, the Gauls obey with great care these Druids and singing poets, both friend and enemy alike. Often when two armies have come together with swords drawn these men have stepped between the battle-lines and stopped the conflict, as if they held wild animals spell-bound. Thus even among the most brutal barbarians angry passion yields to wisdom and Ares stands in awe of the Muses.

¶ 32. It is useful now to point out a distinction unknown by most. Those tribes that live inland from Massalia, as well as those around the Alps and on the eastern side of the Pyrenees are called Celts. But those tribes in the northern area near the ocean, those near the Hercynian mountain [probably today in the Czech Republic], and those beyond as far as Scythia [present-day Ukraine and South Russia], are called Galatae. The Romans, however, group all these tribes together as Galatae.

The women of the Gauls are not only as large as their husbands but are equal to them in strength. Gaulish children are usually born with gray hair, but this takes on the parents' colour as time passes. The most savage tribes are those in the north and those which are near Scythia. Some say they eat human flesh, just like the *Prettani* [Britons] inhabiting the land called *Iris* [probably Ireland]. The savage and war-loving nature of the Gauls is well known. Some say that in ancient times they ravaged all of Asia under the name of Cimmerians, which in time became deformed to Cimbri. From long in the past it has been their nature to ravage foreign lands and view the rest of humanity as beneath them. It was they who captured Rome and plundered the temple at Delphi, and who extracted tribute from much of Europe and no small part of Asia. It was they who occupied the lands of the people whom they had defeated, and were called Gallo-Graeci because of their connection with the Greeks, and who, last of all, destroyed many great Roman armies. It is fitting to their savage nature that they practice a particular impiety in their sacrifices: they keep criminals in custody for five years and then impale them in honour of their gods. They also construct enormous pyres and burn prisoners on them along with many first-fruits. They use war prisoners as sacrificial victims to honour their gods. Some even sacrifice the animals captured in war in addition to the human beings, or burn them in a pyre or kill them through some other means of torture.

The men of the Gauls pay little attention to their women, even though they are quite beautiful, but prefer unnatural intercourse with other men. They sleep on the ground on the skins of wild animals, rolling about with their sleeping companions on each side. The oddest custom is that without any thought towards being discreet, they gladly offer their youthful bodies to others, not thinking this any disgrace, but being deeply offended when refused.

§19. Strabo [64/63 BC–AD 21 at least] *Geography*, TRANS. BENJAMIN FORTSON

¶ 4.1.13

THE PEOPLE CALLED THE TECTOSAGES live near the Pyrenees, but touch also on small parts of the northern side of the Cevennes, and the land they inhabit is full of gold. Apparently at one time they not only were the dominant power but also abounded in men to such an extent that, when a seditious conflict arose, they drove many of their own people from their homeland; then others from other tribes joined forces with these exiles. Among these people, it is said, were also those who occupied the part of Phrygia [present-day central Asiatic Turkey] that borders on Cappadocia and the Paphlagonians. And indeed as proof of this we have the people who even today are called the Tectosages, who are actually composed of three tribes: one of them, living around the city of Ankara, is called the tribe of the Tectosages, while the remaining two are the Trocmi and the Tolistobogii. While the fact that these latter peoples are of the same stock as the Tectosages shows that they emigrated from Celtica [in Western Europe], we cannot tell from which districts they set out, for we have not ascertained whether any Trocmi or Tolistobogii now live across the Alps, or in them, or on this side of them. But due to the continuous migrations probably none are left, just as comes to pass with many other peoples. There are some who say, for example, that the second Brennus—the one that invaded Delphi— was a Prausan, but where on earth the Prausans used to live we cannot say, either. The Tectosages, too, are said to have taken part in the expedition against Delphi, and supposedly the treasure that was found on them in the city of Toulouse by the Roman general Scipio [*read* Caepio] was part of the riches from Delphi, and the men augmented it with items from their private possessions by way of invoking and propitiating their god. It was because of seizing them that [Caepio] ended his life in misfortunes: he was banished from his native land as a temple-robber and left his daughters behind as his successors, who ended up becoming prostitutes and dying in shame, as Timagenes has said. But the report of Posidonius is more trustworthy: he says that the booty found in Toulouse was worth about fifteen thousand talents, some of it lying in sacred enclosures, the rest in sacred lakes, and none of it fashioned, but merely unwrought gold and silver. The temple at Delphi, on the other hand, was already at that time empty of such things, having been robbed by the Phocians during the holy war; and if anything was left, it had been divided among many. Nor is it reasonable to suppose that they escaped to their homeland safely, since after their retreat from

Delphi they departed in misery and dispersed in various directions due to dissension. But, as that one and others have reported, the land, being full of gold and belonging to men who were pious and not extravagant in their living, contained treasures in many places in Celtica. What provided safety more than anything, however, was the lakes into which they had thrown heavy weights of silver and gold. At any rate, the Romans, once they were in power over the area, sold the lakes at public auction, and many of the purchasers found millstones of hammered silver in them. And in Toulouse the temple was hallowed as well, as it was held in exceeding reverence by the inhabitants; and because of this the treasures there were very plentiful, since many made dedications and no one dared touch them.

¶ 4.4.1. After the tribes already mentioned, the remaining ones are tribes of Belgi that live along the coast, of which the Veneti are the ones that fought a naval battle against Cæsar; for they were ready to hinder his passage to Britain because they used a trading-station there. However, he defeated them easily in the naval battle, and did not even use rams (for their beams were thick), but rather, since they bore down upon him by wind, the Romans pulled down their sails with wooden halberts, for the sails were made of leather on account of the strength of the winds, and were hoisted with chains instead of ropes. They make their ships broad-bottomed with high sterns and prows because of the ebb-tides, and out of oak wood, of which there is an abundance. For this reason they do not bring the joins of the planks together, but leave gaps which they then caulk with seaweed, lest the wood dry out for lack of moisture when the ships are hauled up, as seaweed is by nature quite moist, while oak is dry and lacks fat. These Veneti, I believe, are the colonisers of the land on the Adriatic [as namesakes of Venice], for nearly all the other Celts emigrated out of the land across the Alps, as did even the Boii and the Senones; but due to the fact that they have the same name, people call them Paphlagonians. I do not insist on this point, however, for in such matters likeliness is enough. The Osismii, whom Pytheas [c. 325 BC] calls the Ostimii, inhabit a headland that juts rather far out into the ocean [western Brittany], but not as far as he and those who believe him claim. Of the tribes between the Seine and the Loire, some border on the Sequani, others on the Arverni.

¶ 4.4.2. The whole race, which they now call both Gallic and Galatic, is warlike, both spirited and quick to go to war, but otherwise simple and not malicious. Because of this, when they are provoked, they come together in a body for the fight, openly and without forethought, so that they become easy to cope with for those who want to outwit them by stratagem. Indeed, once one irritates them (at whatever time and place and on whatever false pretext one wants), one has them ready to risk their lives, even though they have nothing to aid them besides strength and courage. But if prevailed upon, they easily give themselves over to what is useful, so that they take up education and literature. As for their strength, it is partly due to the large size of their bodies, and partly to their numbers, and because of their simplicity and frankness they easily come together in great numbers, since they always share in the anger of those neighbours of theirs whom they perceive have been wronged. Right now they are all at peace, as they have been enslaved and live according to the rules of the Romans, who captured them; but it is from early times that we take this account of them, and from the customs that obtain among the Germani still to this day: for not only do these people resemble each other in their nature and their societal institutions, but they also are kindred to one another. The territory they inhabit has a common border (it is divided by the river Rhine) and is for the most part practically the same throughout, although Germania is situated farther to the north (comparing the southern parts with the south and the northern ones with the north). Because of this it is also easy for them to migrate, for they move in bands and with their whole army, or rather set out with all their households whenever they are expelled by others who are more powerful. Again, the Romans conquered them much more easily than they did the Iberians, with whom they started war earlier and stopped later, whereas all these they defeated in the meantime (all the ones between the Rhine and the Pyrenees mountains, that is). For since the former were used to falling on their enemies in a body, they were defeated in a body, but the latter would conserve their resources and split up their fights, with different men waging war at different times and in different divisions, like pirates. Indeed all of them are fighters by nature, but they are stronger as cavalry than as foot-soldiers, and among the Romans the best cavalry-force comes from them. But the ones that live farther to the north and along the coast are more warlike.

¶ 4.4.3. Of these they say the Belgi are the best; they are divided into fifteen tribes, and live along the ocean between the Rhine and the Loire, so that they alone withstood the incursion of the Germani—the Cimbri and Teutones. Among the Belgi themselves the best are said to be the Bello[v]aci, and after them, the Suessiones. Of their populousness, the following is an indication: they say that the number of Belgi of former times that can bear arms amounted to about three hundred thousand. I have already given the population of the Elvettii [=Helvetii] and the Arverni and their allies; from these facts the size of the population is clear, as well as (as I stated above) the excellence of the women at bearing and raising children. They wear *sagi*, let their hair grow long, and wear tight trousers, and instead of normal tunics wear slit ones that have sleeves and extend as far down as the private parts and buttocks. The wool from which they weave the thick *sagi* (which they call *lainai*) is coarse and shaggy, but the Romans, even in the northernmost regions, raise flocks of sheep, clothed in skins, with quite fine wool. The war-gear corresponds in size to the size of their bodies: a long sword, hung on the right side, and an oblong shield and spears in proportion, and a *madaris*, a kind of light javelin. Some also use bows and slings. There is also a certain wooden weapon like a *grosphos*, cast by hand and not from a thong, and having a longer range than arrows; these they use most of all for hunting fowl. Even to the present day many of them sleep on the ground, and eat sitting on beds of straw. Most of their nourishment comes from milk and all kinds of meats, especially pork, both fresh and salted. Their pigs live in the open, excelling in height, strength, and speed; in fact, it is dangerous for an inexperienced person to go up to them, as it is for a wolf. They have houses made from beams and wicker, big and with a conical roof, over which they throw a lot of thatch. Their herds of sheep and swine are so plentiful that they supply an abundance of *sagi* and pickled meat not only to Rome, but to most parts of Italy as well. Most of their tribes were aristocratic, but in earlier times they elected one leader per year, just as one general was chosen by the populace for war. Now, however, they abide by the commands of the Romans most of the time. At assemblies they have a peculiar practice: if anyone should disturb the person speaking and interrupt him, an officer, approaching him with drawn sword, orders him to be silent with a threat; and if he does not cease, he does it a second and a third time, and at last cuts off enough of the man's 'sagus' as to make it useless for the future. As far as the men and women and the fact that they exchange work in an opposite manner from ours is concerned, that is common among many other barbarian peoples as well.

¶ 4.4.4. As a rule, among all the Gallic peoples three sets of men are honoured above all others: the Bards, the *Vātes*, and the Druids. The bards are singers and poets, the *Vātes* overseers of sacred rites and philosophers of nature, and the Druids, besides being natural philosophers, practice moral philosophy as well. They are considered to be the most just and therefore are entrusted with settling both private and public disputes, so that in earlier times they even arbitrated wars and could keep those intending to draw themselves up for battle from so doing; and it was to these men most of all that cases involving murder had been entrusted for adjudication. And whenever there is a big yield from these cases, they believe that there will come a yield from the land, too. Both these men and others aver that men's souls and the universe are imperishable, although both fire and water will at some times prevail over them.

¶ 4.4.5. Besides simplicity and spiritedness, there is also much senselessness, boastfulness, and love of ornament about them; for not only do they go about wearing gold—in the form of necklaces around their throats, and armlets and bracelets around their arms and wrists—but also those having an honourable rank wear garments that are brightly coloured and shot with gold. And because of this lightness of character, when victorious they look intolerable, but panicky when defeated. Besides their senselessness, there is also among them the barbaric and highly unusual custom (practised most of all by the northern tribes) of hanging the heads of their enemies from the necks of their horses when departing from battle, and nailing the spectacle to the doorways of their homes upon returning. Indeed Posidonius says that he saw this himself in many places, and that while he was unaccustomed to it at first, he could later endure it calmly due to his frequent contact with it. The heads of those enemies that were held in high esteem they would embalm in cedar oil and display them to their guests, and they would not think of having them ransomed even for an equal weight of gold. The Romans put a stop both to these customs and to the ones connected with sacrifice and divination, as they were in conflict with our own ways: for example, they would strike a man who had been consecrated for sacrifice in the back with a sword, and make prophecies based on his death-spasms; and they would not sacrifice without the presence of the Druids. Other kinds of human sacrifices have been reported as well: some men they would shoot dead with arrows and impale in the temples; or they would construct a huge figure of straw and wood, and having thrown cattle and all manner of wild animals and humans into it, they would make a burnt offering of the whole thing.

¶ 4.4.6. He also says that in the ocean there is a little island, not far out to sea, situated at the mouth of the river Loire, and this island is inhabited by women of the Samnitae who are possessed by the god Dionysus and who propitiate this god with initiations and appease him with other sacred rites. No man sets foot on the island, he says, although the women themselves sail from it, have intercourse with the men, and then return back again. He further says that it is their custom once a year to take the roof off the temple and then roof it over again on the same day by sunset, with each woman bringing a load to add to the roof; if the load falls out of a woman's hands, she is torn to pieces by the others. They then carry the pieces around the temple, and do not stop crying 'Euai!' until they cease from their frenzy; and he says it always happens that someone jostles the woman who is to suffer this. Still more fabulous is the story reported by Artemidorus about the crows: there is a certain harbour on the coast called Two Crows, as the story goes, and in this harbour one can see two crows whose right wings are part white; and so people having a dispute about certain things go there, and having put a plank on a spot of high ground, each man separately throws barley-cakes on it; and the birds fly up and eat some of them, and scatter others. The one whose cakes were scattered wins the dispute. Now although what he says about these things sounds very much like legend, his story about Demeter and Core is more believable: that there is an island near Britain on which sacrifices having to do with Demeter and Core, like those in Samothrace, are performed. The following story is also one of those that are believed: that in Celtica there grows a kind of tree resembling a fig tree, which bears fruit closely resembling the capital of a Corinthian column. When this fruit is cut into, it exudes a deadly juice that they use for smearing on their arrows. And the following, too, is one of the things commonly talked about, namely that not only do all the Celts love strife, but also it is not considered shameful among them for their youth to be lavish of their charms. . .

§20. Julius Cæsar [writing *c.* 50 × 44 BC] *De Bello Gallico* 6.11–20
TRANS. ANNE LEA[6]

¶ 11.

SINCE I HAVE REACHED THIS POINT, it would seem to be not out of place to relate the customs of the Gauls and Germans and how these peoples differ between themselves. In Gaul, not only in every tribal region and every village and every area, but even in almost every single home, there are political parties and the leaders of the parties are men who are considered to have the highest authority and power of judgement, to whom decisions and judgements of all things and councils may be brought. And this seems an arrangement from long ago. By reason of the people, no one should be in need of help against someone more powerful: for no [leader] allows his people to be oppressed or assailed, or otherwise, if it is done, he has no authority among them. This same rule is in the whole of Gaul: for all the tribes are divided into two parties.

¶ 12. When Cæsar came into Gaul, the leaders of one party were the Aedui, the others were the Sequani. These, the Sequani, were less strong, since the highest authority from long ago was in the Aedui and their clientship was large. And they, the Sequani, joined the Germans and Oriovistus who with great sacrifices and promises had persuaded them. In truth, several battles were fought successfully and all of the nobility of the Aedui were slain so that a great part of their clients were brought over from the Aedui to the Sequani, and children from their leaders were taken as hostages and they were compelled to swear publicly that they would not initiate a plan against the Sequani. And the Sequani took possession of the neighbouring land by force and held pre-eminence over all of Gaul. This necessity led Divitiacus to make for the Senate at Rome in the interest of gaining assistance but he returned with the matter unresolved. With the coming of Cæsar a change of affairs was brought about. The hostages of the Aedui were given back, old clientships were restored, and new ones were arranged by Cæsar. The Aedui, who had attached themselves to their friendship, saw better

---

6   The extent to which Cæsar utilised the account of Posidonius is more uncertain than the acknowledged attribution amongst the preceding three writers. Cæsar had first-hand experience in Gaul during his governorship, 60–50 BC.

Cæsar's discussion of Gaulish tribal politics and civilisation was motivated largely by his desire to justify is military and political intervention in Gaulish politics to his Roman readers.

For Cæsar, as for the other Greek and Roman writers, *Gallia* and *Germania* ('Gaul' and 'Germany') were primarily geographical terms, Germany being the land east of the Rhine and north of the Danube and Gaul being the land to the west. The Greek and Roman writers were not overly concerned with or knowledgeable about the languages of barbarian peoples. There definitely were Celtic-speaking tribes east of the Rhine in Cæsar's day. So we should not assume that the people he calls *Germani* were linguistically Germanic.

conditions and a more just rule, and their esteem and dignity increased in the rest of their affairs and the Sequani gave up the leadership. The Remi had succeeded in their place: who, it is understood, are equal to Cæsar in esteem. The Sequani, who because of old enmities were able by no means to join the Aedui, were dedicating themselves into clientship to the Remi. The Remi carefully guarded the Sequani: in this fashion they were holding their recently and suddenly acquired authority. At that time the state of affairs was that the Aedui were regarded as foremost by far and the Remi held second place in dignity.

¶ 13. In all of Gaul there are two classes of men who are of some rank and honour. But the common people are held almost in the condition of slaves who dare nothing by themselves and none are treated in assembly. Very many of them, hard pressed by debt or extensive taxes or powerful injustice, give themselves up in servitude to the nobility: in them are all the same rights which masters have over slaves. But these other two classes are, first, the Druids and, second, the warriors with horses. The Druids intervene in divine matters; they look after public and private sacrifices; they interpret religious matters: to them a great number of young men rush together for the sake of instruction, for the Druids are great in honour before them. For as a rule they settle all public and private disputes and, if some crime has been committed, or if a slaying done or if it concerns inheritance or a border dispute, the same Druids decide: they settle the compensation and punishment; if a private person or the public does not yield to their decision they are prohibited from sacrifices. This is among the most serious punishments. Of those who are prohibited in this fashion, they are held as godless and wicked and they are cut off from all. They are avoided in conversation and meeting, and from fear of moral infection they are not received, and penance does not restore their rights nor is any honour imparted. Moreover, of all the Druids one precedes who has the highest authority among them. When this one dies either the one who excels in dignity from the rest succeeds or if there are many who are suitable, by the vote of the Druids they contend for leadership, sometimes even contending with arms. At a certain time of the year they sit down in a consecrated place in the territory of the Carnutes [near Chartres, France] which region is believed to be the centre of all Gaul. To this place all come from everywhere who have disputes and the Druids bring forth their resolutions and decisions. It is believed the training for Druids was discovered in Britain and from there it was transferred into Gaul. And now those who wish to learn the matter carefully depart for Britain for the sake of learning.

¶ 14. The Druids retire from war nor are they accustomed to any taxes. They have immunity from military service and are exempt from all lawsuits. So greatly are young men excited by these rewards that many assemble willingly in training and many others are sent by parents and relatives. They are said to commit to memory a great number of verses. And they remain some 20 years in training. Nor do they judge it to be allowed to entrust these things to writing although in

nearly the rest of their affairs, and public and private transactions, Greek letters
are used. It seems to me there are two reasons this has been established: neither
do they wish the common people to pride themselves in the training nor those
who learn to rely less on memory, since it happens to a large extent that individuals give up diligence in memory and thorough learning through the help of
writing. The foremost tenet of which they wish to convince is that the soul does
not die but crosses over after death from one place to another and this they
believe is the greatest incentive to bravery by disregarding the fear of death.
Further, they debate concerning the heavens and their movement, concerning the
size of the universe and the earth, the workings of nature, the strength and
power of the immortal gods, and these things they hand down to the young men.

The other class are the warriors with horses. These are concerned with the
practice of war (which, before Cæsar's coming, they were accustomed to these
happening nearly every year so that either they brought them on or they drove
them back), all of them are engaged in war and their class is such that each has
troops and mercenaries so that many have *ambactī* [literally 'men sent around' i.e.
'subordinates at their command'] and clients around them. They know only this
kind of esteem and power.

¶ 16. All the people of Gaul are completely devoted to religion, and for this
reason those who are greatly affected by diseases and in the dangers of battle
either sacrifice human victims or vow to do so using the Druids as administrators
to these sacrifices, since it is judged that unless for a man's life a man's life is
given back, the will of the immortal gods cannot be placated. In public affairs
they have instituted the same kind of sacrifice. Others have effigies of great size
interwoven with twigs, the limbs of which are filled up with living people which
are set on fire from below, and the people are deprived of life surrounded by
flames. It is judged that the punishment of those who participated in theft or
brigandage or other crimes are more pleasing to the immortal gods; but when the
supplies of this kind fail, they even go so low as to inflict punishment on the
innocent.

¶ 17. Of the gods they worship Mercury most of all. Of him there are many
images: they extol him as the inventor of all the arts, the ruler of journeys and
travelling, and they judge him to have the greatest power over obtaining money
and trade. After him Apollo, Mars, Jupiter and Minerva. Concerning these they
have nearly the same opinions as the rest of people: Apollo to drive away
diseases, Minerva to teach the elements of skill, Jupiter to hold the order of the
heavens, Mars to control wars. To him, when they have decided to fight a battle,
they consecrate a large part of the plunder; when they have conquered, they
collect captured living things and the rest and burn them in one place. In many
tribal territories one is allowed to see mounds of objects erected in consecrated
places and it often happens that someone neglects religion and has dared to

remove and hide things taken in war, and the greatest punishment with torture is agreed upon for them.

¶ 18. The Gauls proclaim that they are all sprung from the same father, Dis, and they say this has been transmitted from the Druids. For this reason they define the space of time not by the number of days but of nights. They observe birthdays and the beginnings of months and years in this way so that day follows night. In the rest of the undertakings of life they differ from other peoples. They consider it disgraceful for a father to be seen with his sons in public until they have grown up so that they can sustain military duty.

¶ 19. . . . Men have the power of life and death over their wives, as with their children. When the head of an illustrious family dies, his relatives meet and if matters about the death are suspicious, they question the wives in the manner of slaves. And if certain information is discovered they do away with them by fire and excruciating tortures. The funerals, by the standards of the Gauls, are splendid and expensive. It is judged that all which was held dear while alive should be put into the fire, even living beings, and a little before our time, slaves and clients of choice were burned at the completion of the funeral.

¶ 20. Of those tribes which are considered to administer their governance properly, they have a sacred law that if anyone received any information concerning their civic affairs from their neighbours by rumour or talk, they refer it to the magistrate and do not communicate it to others for often inexperienced people are accidentally frightened by false rumours and are incited to action, and they have been known to take extreme action in conclusion. Magistrates hide many things from sight of the ordinary people and produce that which they judge proper. Talk is not permitted concerning the public affairs except in the deliberation of the council.

[CÆSAR'S FIRST INVASION OF BRITAIN (55 BC)] *De Bello Gallico* 4.33, TRANS. PHILIP FREEMAN

THIS IS THE WAY THE BRITISH fight with their chariots. First, they drive about in all directions throwing spears and spreading chaos throughout the ranks of their enemies by the terror of their galloping horses and screeching wheels. When they have worked their way into the middle of the enemy cavalry they leap down from the chariots and fight on foot. Meanwhile the chariot-drivers have moved the chariots away, but close enough to come to the aid of the warriors if they are seriously threatened by the enemy. The chariot forces thus combine the advantages of cavalry mobility and infantry stability. By constant practice they have become so adept that they can gallop with their teams down steep slopes without losing control, stop and turn them in a moment, and run along the yoke between the horses then rapidly return to the chariot.

[FROM CÆSAR'S SECOND INVASION OF BRITAIN (54 BC)] *De Bello Gallico* 5.12–17, TRANS. PHILIP FREEMAN

¶ 12.

THE INTERIOR PARTS OF BRITAIN are inhabited by tribes which by their own traditions are indigenous to the island, while on the coastal sections are tribes which had crossed over from the land of the Belgae seeking booty. Nearly all these maritime tribes are called by the names of lands from which they immigrated when they came to Britain. After their arrival, they remained there and began to till the fields. The population of the island is very large. They live in homes packed close together, like the Gauls, and have many cattle. They use bronze or gold coins, or tallies of iron of a certain weight in place of money. Tin is found in the middle of the country and iron in the coastal regions, but only in limited amounts, while they import bronze. There is every variety of timber, as in Gaul, aside from beech and pine. They believe it wrong to eat hares, fowl, and geese, but they do keep these animals as pets. The climate is more temperate than in Gaul, with warmer winters.

¶ 13. The island is shaped like a triangle and one of the sides faces Gaul. On this side one of the angles, Cantium (Kent), where almost all the ships from Gaul land, faces east, while the lower angle faces south. The length of this side is about 500 miles. The second side of the triangle faces towards Hispania and the setting sun, in which direction is Hibernia (Ireland), thought to be half the size of Britain. The separation is equal to that of Britain from Gaul. In the middle of the channel is an island called Mona [Anglesey or the Isle of Man]. Several other smaller islands supposedly lie close to land, concerning which some have written that the darkness there in midwinter lasts thirty days. We could find out no information concerning this, but using a water-clock we did discover that the nights in Britain are measurably shorter than on the continent. The natives relate that this westward-facing side is about 700 miles. The third side faces the north, but there is no land opposite it. The angle of that side in general, however, does extend towards Germania. That side is estimated at 800 miles in length. Thus the whole island is two thousand miles in circumference.

¶ 14. Of all the tribes of Britain, those inhabiting the wholly maritime land of Cantium are the most civilised, differing little from the Gauls. Most of those in the interior do not sow wheat, but live on milk and meat, clothing themselves in animal skins. But all the Britons dye their skin with woad, which gives them a blue colour and fearsome appearance in battle. They wear their hair long, but shave every part of their bodies aside from the head and upper lip. Ten or twelve men have wives together in common, particularly among brothers and between fathers and sons. The children born to these women are considered part of the house to which the bride was first led.

¶ 15. The horseman and the charioteers of the enemy fought fiercely with our cavalry as we marched, but our troops were totally superior to them and drove them into the forests and hills. But some of our cavalry were too eager and were killed in their pursuit. After a short time our troops were busy digging a trench around the camp and were off their guard when the enemy suddenly dashed out of the woods and attacked some advance troops guarding in front of the camp. The fighting was very fierce and the enemy brought through the small space between our troops, even though Cæsar had sent two cohorts forward as reinforcements. The enemy withdrew from the conflict safely even when additional cohorts were sent up, as our troops were unused to this new type of fighting. On that day a tribune, Quintus Laberius Durus, was killed.

¶ 16. The fighting took place in front of the camp where all could see, and it was clear to everyone that our infantry was badly equipped for this sort of fighting, as the heavy weight of their armament prevented them from pursuing a fleeing enemy or moving far from the protective ranks of their fellow-soldiers. The cavalry was also at a great disadvantage because the enemy would deliberately retreat a little ways to separate the horsemen from the bulk of the army, then leap off their chariots and fight on foot to our disadvantage. Moreover, the tactics of their cavalrymen threatened us with the same danger whether they were retreating or attacking. In addition, the Britons never fought close together but scattered widely apart in small groups. They also had reinforcements posted at intervals so that fresh warriors could easily replace their exhausted companions.

The Gauls' Invasion of Rome

[*c.* 390 × 387 BC]; TRANS. PHILIP FREEMAN

§21. Titus Livius (Livy) [64/59 BC–AD 12/17]; *Ab urbe condita* 5

¶ 5.35–36.

THE THREE SONS OF MARCUS FABIUS AMBUSTUS were sent by the Senate as ambassadors to the Gauls attacking their Etruscan allies at Clusium, asking them not to attack a city which had harmed them in no way and moreover was a friend and ally of the Roman people. Rome, they said, would protect Clusium by force of arms if necessary, but a peaceful solution and understanding with this new group of immigrants was preferable. The purpose of the mission was entirely peaceful, but unfortunately the ambassadors behaved more like Gauls than Romans. The council of Gaulish leaders answered them as follows: 'We have never heard of Rome before, but we believe you must be a worthy people since Clusium sent to you for help in their time of trouble. You say you prefer to aid your allies peacefully if possible and do not wish to fight with us. We are willing to accept this peace with you, but only if Clusium will yield to us a portion of their territory as we badly need more land. Truthfully, they have much more than they need. These are the only conditions for peace that we can accept. We will receive your answer in person, so that if you refuse you may see us fight and tell your allies how much the Gauls exceed all other men in courage and bravery.' When the Romans asked them how they could justly ask for land by threatening war and just what right did they have to be in Etruria anyway, the Gauls simply said that they carried justice on the point of their swords.

¶ 5.38–39. The Romans' line collapsed when the Gauls attacked, showing no trace of the old Roman courage among either officers or soldiers. They were so terrified that they fled to the once-enemy town of Veii, even though the Tiber River was in between, rather than to their own homes in Rome. The Roman reserves were temporarily in a better position than the rest of the army, but the main body of the army collapsed as soon as they heard the Gaulish war cry on their sides and behind them, not even waiting to see these strange warriors. They made no effort to resist, but fled in panic before they had lost a single man. None were killed in fighting, but many were cut down from behind as they fled through the crowds of their own countrymen. Near the left bank of the river there was a horrible slaughter, as the whole left wing of the army had flung away their weapons there in an attempt to swim across. But many didn't know how to swim and others who could were dragged down to death by the weight of their armour. Half the army reached Veii alive, but they sent no message of their defeat to Rome, let alone any aid against the Gauls. The men on the right wing had been closer to the hills and away from the river, so they all rushed to Rome and took refuge on the Citadel without even taking time to close the city gates.

The Gauls couldn't believe their good fortune in winning a battle so easily. As they stood in a daze they began to wonder if the whole thing was some sort of trap, but soon began to collect the weapons of their dead in a pile, as is their custom. When finally no sign of the enemy was to be seen anywhere, they marched on Rome and reached the city at sunset. Cavalry were sent forward to spy out the city and found the gates open with no guards on the walls. Once again they were astonished at such good fortune. But the darkness might have held unknown dangers in this strange city, so after a brief further reconnaissance of the walls to try to discover some pattern to their enemies actions, they made camp between Rome and the Anio River.

¶5.41. When the night had passed the Gauls found that their lust for battle had faded, since they had faced no serious resistance and had no need to storm the city by force. So in the morning they entered the city gates cautious but calm. The Colline Gates were wide open, so they made their way to the Forum, admiring the temples and examining the Citadel above, the only place in Rome which gave a hint of war. They posted a guard at the Citadel to prevent an ambush from behind, then dispersed in small groups in search of plunder. Some of them broke into the first house they found on the empty streets, while others went further away thinking the richer booty would be away from the city centre. But the strange silence and separation from their comrades unnerved them, making them suspicious of a trap, so they soon returned to the Forum. Here they found the common houses locked and barred but the homes of the nobility wide open. The poorer houses were quickly looted, but a sense of awe kept them for a long while from the noble's homes, especially the figures seated in the open courtyards seated in majestic robes and looking with their calm eyes like the gods themselves. The seemed to be statues in some holy temple and held these bar- barian warriors in a kind of trance. But then one of the Gauls touched the long beard of a certain Marcus Papirius, and the Roman knocked him on the head with his ivory walking stick. With the spell broken, the Gauls exploded in anger, killing him and the others where they sat. From then on no mercy was given. Houses were ransacked and the empty shells were burned.

¶ 5.48. Quintus Sulpicius met with the Gaulish chieftain Brennus and agreed to pay one thousand pounds of gold, the price of a nation that would rule the world. The Romans were insulted further when the weights which the Gauls brought for weighing out the treasure turned out to be heavier than those of the Romans. When Quintus complained Brennus flung his sword on the scale and answered with words intolerable to Roman ears—*Vae victis*, 'Woe to the conquered.'

The Gauls' Invasion of Greece

[280–278 BC]; TRANS. PHILIP FREEMAN

§22. Marcus Junianus Justinus (Justin) [3rd century AD] *Epitome of the*
Philippic History 24 of Pompeius Trogus [1st century AD]

¶ 6.

ONE OF THE GAULISH GROUPS who had invaded Greece was led by
Brennus. Now when Brennus had heard of the victory of his countryman
Belgius over the Macedonians and how such rich plunder was abandoned by him
after victory, he was furious. He brought together an army composed of 150,000
infantry and 15,000 cavalry and led them in an invasion of Macedonia. While
Brennus was plundering crops and farms, he was met by a Macedonian army
under Sosthenes. This army, however, was small and terrified, while the Gauls
were numerous and powerful, so Brennus easily won. The defeated Macedonians
then hid within the walls of their cities while the Gauls plundered the whole
countryside unopposed. Then, not satisfied with spoils of human labour, he
began to plunder temples as well, foolishly joking that the gods were rich and
should be generous to people. Setting greed before fear of the gods, he
immediately began a march to Delphi, saying the immortals needed no wealth as
they commonly wasted it on people anyway.

The Temple of Apollo at Delphi is on Mt. Parnassus, surrounded by steep
cliffs on every side. A large number of settlers had originally come here from
various lands because of admiration for the grandeur of the place. Both the
community and temple are protected by nature rather than manmade fortifications, so that it is hard to say whether the natural beauty of the place or the
presence of the god is more wonderful. The middle part of the cliff recedes to
form a natural amphitheatre. Because of this, human voices and trumpets are
greatly multiplied beyond the original volume as the cliff walls echo the sounds.
People who hear this are generally unaware of the cause, with the resulting increase in sound only adding to their awe of the place. In this recess, halfway up
the hill, there is a narrow plateau with a deep fissure in the ground from which
oracles are delivered. A gust of cold air is driven up through this crack by the
wind, sending the priests into a frenzied state and causing them to answer questions under the authority of the god. There are many rich gifts here from kings
and others who were grateful for the god's generous and reliable responses.

¶ 7. When Brennus finally saw the temple, he debated whether he should attack at once or give his weary troops a night's rest. The leaders of the Aenianes and the Thessalians urged him to launch his assault at once while the enemy was unprepared and panicked over his arrival. If he allowed them until morning, they said, the Delphians would have time to rally their spirits, receive reinforcements, and blockade the now-open road. But the Gauls had endured a long, hard journey, so when they learned that the surrounding countryside was well stocked with food and wine, they were just as happy as if they had won a great victory. They spread out through the area in an unorganised mob looting everything they could find, thus giving the people of Delphi a short time to organise a defence. The story goes that at the first rumour of the coming Gauls, the oracle of the god had forbidden the nearby farmers from removing the harvested grain and wine from their farms. The sound reason for this was unknown until the spoils had succeeded in delaying the Gauls and allowing reinforcements to arrive. In this way, the Delphians added to the number of their troops and had time to fortify their town against the invaders, who could not be recalled by any means from their drunken revels. Brennus had the best 65,000 infantrymen from his whole army at Delphi, while the Greeks numbered a mere 4,000. The Gaulish leader sneered at such a paltry resistance and urged his men on by pointing out the great spoils which awaited them. The statues and chariots which they could see in the distance, he said, were made of solid gold and weighed even more than they appeared.

¶ 8. Roused by these claims, yet suffering badly from the drinking binge of the day before, the Gauls charged into battle heedless of the dangers. The Delphians relied on the god more than their own strength, and fought the despised enemy with their whole might, hurling down spears and rocks on the Gauls attempting to climb the cliffs. When the two forces were in the thick of battle, the temple priests and priestesses suddenly rushed to the front lines with their hair in disarray and wearing their holy insignia. They cried out that they had seen the god himself leaping down into his temple from the hole in the roof and that he was young and vigorous, with a beauty far beyond that of mortals. With him were two virgins in armour who had come to meet him from the nearby temples of Diana and Minerva. Not only had they seen this with their own eyes, they shouted, but had heard the twang of the bow and the clatter of the weapons. So they declared, with fierce determination, that the Delphians were not to hold back against the enemy but were to share in the victory of the gods.

The Delphians rushed fearlessly into battle with these admonitions ringing in their ears. They themselves felt the presence of the gods, as an earthquake sheared off a side of the mountain and crushed the Gauls below. The close-packed barbarians were scattered and slaughtered by the fierce Greeks, and their wounded were finished off by freezing hail from the heavens. Even Brennus died, unable to bear the pains of his wounds, killing himself with a dagger. His second-in-command fled Greece with 10,000 wounded and weary soldiers, punishing those who had urged the invasion of Greece in the first place. But Fate was not kind even to the pitiful refugees, stalking them relentlessly with bitter nights and harrowing days and grinding them down with unceasing rain, biting snow, and hungry exhaustion. The inhabitants of the lands through which they passed constantly harassed the dwindling force, and thus the once proud and powerful army that had dared to mock the gods was destroyed, with none surviving to tell the tale of their terrible defeat.

§§23–37. The Classical Authors on the Druids[7]
TRANS. PHILIP FREEMAN AND J. T. KOCH

§ 23. Diogenes Laertius [first half of 3rd century AD] *Vitae*, Intro.

¶ 1.

SOME SAY THAT THE STUDY OF PHILOSOPHY first developed among the barbarians. For the Persians had their Magi, the Babylonians or Assyrians their Chaldeans, the Indians their Gymnosophists, while the Celts and Galatae had those called Druids and Semnotheoi, according to Aristotle in the *Magicus* and Sotion in the 23rd book of his *Successions*.

¶ 5. Those who believe philosophy arose among the barbarians explain the teachings of each group. They say the Gymnosophists [of India] and Druids instruct by means of riddles, urging worship of the gods, abstinence from evil, and the practice of manly virtue.

§ 24. Dion Chrysostom [AD 40–*c*. 112], *Orations* 49.

THE PERSIANS HAVE MEN KNOWN AS MAGI . . . , the Egyptians have their holy men . . . , the Indians have their Brahmins. For their part, the Celts have men called Druids, who deal with prophecy and every division of wisdom. Even kings would not be so bold as to make a decision or take action without [the Druids'] counsel. Thus in reality it was [the Druids] who governed.

---

7   See further T. D. Kendrick, *The Druids*, New York, 1926; N. Chadwick, *The Druids*, Cardiff, 1966; S. Piggott, *The Druids*, London, 1968.

The kings, who sat on golden thrones and lived luxuriously in their great residences, became mere agents of the decisions of the Druids.

§ 25. Cicero [106–43 BC] *De Divinatione* 1.41.90.

NOR IS THE PRACTICE OF DIVINATION neglected even among the barbarian tribes, since indeed there are Druids in Gaul. Among these was Divitiacus the Aeduan, your guest and eulogist, whom I knew personally. He claimed a knowledge of the natural world which the Greeks call *physiologia*, making predictions of the future, sometimes by augury, sometimes by conjecture.

§ 26. Ammianus Marcellinus [*c.* AD 330–*c.* 395]
¶ 15.9.4.

THE DRUIDS RECOUNT that part of the population of Gaul was indigenous, but that some of the people immigrated there from outlying islands and the lands beyond the Rhine, driven out by frequent wars and violent floods from the sea.

¶ 15.9.8 Throughout these regions, as people gradually became more civilised, study of praiseworthy doctrines grew, introduced by the Bards, Euhages [*read* Vātes], and Druids. The Bards sang the praiseworthy deeds of famous men to the melodious strains of the lyre. The [Vātes] endeavoured to explain the sublime mysteries of nature. Between them were the Druids, an intimate fellowship of a greater ability who followed the doctrine of Pythagoras. They rose above the rest by seeking the unseen, making little of human mortality as they believed in the immortality of the soul.

§ 27. Suetonius [*c.* AD 69–*c.* 140] *Claudius* 25.

CLAUDIUS destroyed the horrible and savage religion of the Druids among the Gauls, which had been forbidden to citizens under Augustus.

§ 28. Pomponius Mela [wrote *c.* AD 37–*c.* 50] *De Situ Orbis* 3.2.18–19.

THE VESTIGES OF SAVAGE CUSTOMS still remain in the drawing of a victim's blood while he is being led to the altar, though outright slaughter has been abolished. Still, they have their own eloquence and wise men called Druids. They claim to know the size of the earth and cosmos, the movements of the heavens and stars, and the will of the gods. They teach, in caves or hidden groves, many things to the nobles in a course of instruction lasting up to twenty years. One of their doctrines has become commonly known to the populace so that warriors might fight more bravely, that the spirit is eternal and another life awaits the spirits of the dead. Thus they burn or bury articles useful in life with the dead. For this reason also, in past times, they would defer business and payment of debts to the next life. There were some who would even throw themselves willingly onto the funeral pyres of their relatives so that they might live with them still.

§ 29. Pliny [AD 23/4–79] *Natural History*
¶ 16.24.

NOT TO BE OVERLOOKED is the admiration of the Gauls for this plant [the mistletoe]. The Druids—as their magicians are called—hold nothing more sacred than this plant and the tree on which it grows, as if it grew only on oaks. They choose only groves of oak and perform no rites unless a branch of that tree is present. Thus it seems that Druids are so called from the Greek name of the oak [Greek *drus*]. Truly they believe that anything which grows on the tree is sent from heaven and is a sign that the tree was chosen by the god himself. However, mistletoe rarely grows on oaks, but is sought with reverence and cut only on the sixth day of the moon, as it is then that the moon is powerful but not yet halfway in its course (it is by the moon they measure days, years, and their cycle of thirty years). In their language the mistletoe is called 'the healer of all'. When preparations for a sacrifice and feast beneath the trees have been made, they lead forward two white bulls with horns bound for the first time. A priest in white clothing climbs the tree and cuts the mistletoe with a golden sickle, and it is caught in a white cloak. They then sacrifice the bulls while praying that the god will grant the gift of prosperity to those to whom he has given it. They believe that mistletoe, when taken in a drink, will restore fertility to barren animals, and is a remedy for all poisons. Such is the dedication to trifling affairs displayed by many peoples.

¶ 24.103–4. Similar to the Sabine plant [Savin] is *selagos*. It is gathered without iron implements by passing the right hand through the left sleeve-opening of the tunic as if one were stealing it. The harvester must be barefoot and wearing white, and have offered bread and wine before the gathering. The Gaulish Druids say it is a charm against every evil, and that its smoke is a good medicine against eye disease. They also gather a plant from marshes called *samolus*, which must be gathered with the left hand during a fast. This is good against diseases of cattle, but the gatherer must not look back nor put the plant anywhere except in the drinking-trough.

¶ 29.52. There is also a sort of egg, famous in the [Roman] provinces of Gaul, but ignored by the Greeks. Innumerable snakes coil themselves into a ball in the summertime. Thus they make it so that it is held together by a bodily secretion and by their saliva. It is called an *anguinum*. The Druids say that [the snakes] hiss and cast it upwards,[8] and that it is to be caught in a cloak so that it not [fall and] touch the ground. One must immediately ride off on a horse with it, for [the snakes] will continue to pursue until the course of a stream blocks their way. If one tests it, [the *anguinum*] will float against the current of a river even when covered in gold. And, as the *magi* ['wizards'] will throw a cloak of deception over their trickery, they make out as though [the eggs] are to be taken only on a particular point in the lunar cycle, as though it was up to human beings to determine the snakes' rôle in this procedure. Nonetheless, I have seen one of these eggs myself. It was round, the size of a small apple. The shell was cartilaginous, and mottled with cups like the tentacles of a squid. The Druids value it highly: it is praised as insuring success in litigation and in going to audiences with kings. However, this is nonsense; for once a man (a Roman knight and a tribesman of the Vocontii) held one of these eggs against his body during a trial, and was condemned to death by the Emperor Claudius, for that reason alone so far as I can tell.

¶ 30.13. The [Roman provinces of] Gaul also possessed [magic] down to the time of our memory. Thus it was during the reign of the Emperor Tiberius that a decree was issued by the Senate against [the Gauls'] entire class of Druids, *Vātes*, and physicians. Why do I comment on this craft that has spread beyond the ocean to the far reaches of the earth? Nowadays, Britain continues to be held spellbound by magic and conducts so much ritual that it would seem that it was Britain that had given magic to the Persians. Peoples of the whole world are alike in this way, though they are wholly ignorant of one another. Thus the debt to the Romans cannot be overestimated, for abolishing this abomination, in which slaying a man was deemed a most religious act and eating his flesh was truly thought most beneficial.

§ 30. Lucan [AD 39–65] *Pharsalia*

¶ 1.450–58.

TO YOUR BARBAROUS RITES and sinister ceremonies,
O Druids, you have returned since weapons now lie still.

---

8   In the modern folklore of England and Wales, the idea of serpent stones persists. The editor has heard a Welsh folktale in which a young girl was pursued in the woods at Castell Coch near Cardiff by a horde of writhing snakes. When they disappeared, they left behind a small jewel-like sphere made of their congealed saliva. This object, when worn on a string around the neck, was supposed to cure *y wen* ('goiter'). After its second successful application, it had completely melted away. These magical stones are called *mân macal* ('?snare stone') and *glain y nidir* ('the snake's jewel') in South Walian dialect. When alleged serpent stones have been examined, they have sometimes turned out to be glass beads from the pre-Roman Iron Age. See further Kendrick, *The Druids* 125–28.

To you alone it is given to know the gods
And spirits of the sky, or perhaps not to know at all.
You dwell in the distant, dark, and hidden groves.
You say that shades of the dead do not seek
The silent land of Erebus or the pallid kingdom of Dis,
But that the same spirit controls the limbs in another realm.
Death, if what you say is true, is but the mid-point of a long life.

§ 31. Tacitus [*c.* AD 55 – *c.* 120] *Annals* 14.30.

[ON THE ROMAN INVASION OF THE DRUID SANCTUARY OF MONĀ,
MOD. ANGLESEY, NORTH WALES]

STANDING ON THE SHORE WAS THE OPPOSING ARMY, a dense formation of men and weapons. Women in black clothing like that of the Furies
ran between the ranks. Wild-haired, they brandished torches. Around them, the
Druids, lifting their hands upwards towards the sky to make frightening curses,
frightened [the Roman] soldiers with this extraordinary sight. And so [the
Romans] stood motionless and vulnerable as if their limbs were paralysed. Then
their commander exhorted them and they urged one another not to quake before
an army of women and fanatics. They carried the ensigns forward, struck down
all resistance, and enveloped them in [the enemy's own] fire. After that, a garrison
was imposed on the vanquished and destroyed their groves, places of savage
superstition. For they considered it their duty to spread their altars with the gore
of captives and to communicate with their deities through human entrails.

Histories 5.54. It is remembered that the Gauls once took Rome [*c.* 390 BC; see
§21 above], but as Jupiter's sanctuary remained intact, the state survived. The
Druids however proclaimed, with the prophecies of foolish superstition, that the
fateful fire [at the Capitol] was a sign of the wrath of heaven and prefigured that
humanity would come under the dominion of the tribes from beyond the Alps.

§ 32. Lampridius *Alexander Severus* 59.5.

WHILE HE [ALEXANDER SEVERUS] was departing, a woman of the
Druids shouted to him in the Gaulish tongue: 'Hurry forward, but do not
hope for victory, nor put trust in your soldiers.'

§ 33. Vopiscus
¶ *Numerianus* 14.

AS MY GRANDFATHER TOLD ME, DIOCLETIAN was once staying at an
inn in the region of the Tungri tribe in Gaul. He was at the time still at a
lesser rank in the army. He went once to settle the day's bill for his accommoda-

tion with a Druidess. This woman said to him, 'You are excessively acquisitive and stingy with your money, Diocletian.' As a joke, he replied to that, 'I shall be more generous when I am emperor.' After those words the Druidess responded, 'Don't joke, Diocletian, for you *will* be emperor when you have slain The Boar.'

¶ *Aurelianus* 63.4.5. He [Asclepiodotus] used to say that Aurelian once consulted with Gaulish Druidesses to discover whether his progeny would continue to rule the empire. These women responded that no name would be more famous in the history of Rome than the future descendants of Claudius. And it is indeed so that the present Emperor Constantius is of this man's blood. I think that his descendants will achieve the glory prophesied by the Druidesses.

§ 34. Ausonius [† *c.* AD 395] *Commem. professorum.*

¶ 4.7–10

YOU ARE SPRUNG FROM THE DRUIDS OF BAYEUX,
  If the report does not lie.
To you is a sacred lineage,
  From the temple of Belenus.

¶ 10.22–30 Nor will I forget
      The old man named Phoebicius,
  Who though servant of [the Gaulish god] Belenus
      Received no profit thereby
  Sprung, it is said, from the Druids
      Of Armorica [Brittany],
  He received a chair at Bordeaux
      Through the help of his son.

§ 35. Hippolytus *Philosophumena* 1.25.

THE CELTIC DRUIDS eagerly took up the philosophy of Pythagoras, having been introduced to the study by Zalmoxis, a Thracian slave of Pythagoras. He came to those lands after his master's death and explained to them his philosophy. The Celts hold the Druids as prophets and foretellers of future events because they can predict certain events by Pythagorean science and mathematics . . . The Druids also use magic.

§ 36. Clement of Alexandria [*c.* AD 150–*c.* 210] *Stromata* 1.15.70.1.

ALEXANDER, in his book on the symbols of Pythagorean belief, says Pythagoras was a student of Zaratus the Assyrian . . . and wants us to believe that Pythagoras listened to the Galatae and Brahmins as well.

¶ 1.15.70.3. Thus the very useful study of philosophy flourished in the past among the barbarians, enlightening the peoples of the world, and only later coming to Greece. Most important were the prophets of the Egyptians, the Chaldeans of the Assyrians, the Druids of the Galatae, the Samnaeans of the Bactrians, the philosophers of the Celts, and the Magi of the Persians.

§ 37. Valerius Maximus [wrote c. AD 35] 2.6.10.

HAVING COMPLETED MY DISCUSSION OF THIS TOWN [MASSALIA], an old custom of the Gauls should be mentioned: they lend money repayable in the next world, so firm is their belief in the immortality of the spirit. I would say they are fools, except what these trouser-wearers believe is the same as the doctrine of toga-wearing Pythagoras.

The Skull Cup — L. Postumius and the Cisalpine Boii

§ 38. Livy [c. 59 BC–c. AD 17] ¶ 23.24; TRANS. J. T. KOCH

L[UCIUS] POSTUMIUS, consul designate, was lost together with his host in [Cisalpine] Gaul [in 216 BC]. He was leading his army by way of a huge forest that the Gauls call Litanā ['The Broad One']. The Gauls had cut the trees to the right and left of the road in such a way that they stood if not disturbed but fell if lightly pushed. Postumius had two Roman legions . . . that he led into the hostile country. The Gauls surrounded the wood, and when the [Roman] force entered the wood they pushed the outermost trees that had been cut. These trees fell one against the other, each one having been unstable and barely attached, and piled up from either side crushing the armament, men, and horses, so that scarcely ten men escaped. . . Postumius died fighting with all his strength trying to avoid capture. The spoils stripped from his corpse and the severed head of the commander were taken by the Boii to their holiest temple. Then, after they removed the flesh from the head, they adorned the skull with gold according to their custom. They used it as a sacred vessel to give libations on holy days, and their priests and the custodians of their temple used it as a goblet.[9]

---

9 Livy's account of an important victory and associated religious ritual amongst the Celts of northern Italy has strikingly close analogues in the following (closely paraphrased) descrip-

The Foundation of Gaul

§39. Diodorus Siculus *The Historical Library* 5.24; TRANS. JOHN CAREY

A FAMOUS MAN, THEY SAY, FORMERLY RULED CELTICA, to whom was born a daughter of gigantic stature, far surpassing all others in beauty.

---

tions of the steppe nomads living further east, as far the north-western frontiers of China. It would seem that the ritual trophy of the skull cup was a widely shared cultural attribute of the Northern Barbarian peoples of the Eurasian Iron Age.

Analogue 1. Herodotus *History*, 4.66 [5th century BC], in the context of a detailed ethnographic description of the Iranian-speaking Scythians of present-day Ukraine and South Russia, tells of Scythian head-hunting. The skulls of the enemies whom they most hated [presumably their most formidable opponents] would be turned into drinking cups. They would first saw off the portion below the eyebrows, then clean out the inside, and cover the exterior of the cranium with leather. If the Scythian trophy taker was poor, that was the final form of the cup. But if he was rich, he would also cover the interior with gold. Either way, the skull was then used as a drinking cup. The Scythians would do the same with the skulls of their own relatives if they had feuded with them and overthrown them in the king's presence. When strangers whom the Scythians regarded as important persons came to visit them, the skulls would be passed around, and the host would tell that the heads were of his kinsfolk who had fought against him and how he had overcome them. The Scythians viewed these customs as a way of proving bravery.

Analogue 2. In the Chinese annals of the Han Dynasty, the *Shiji* of Simaa Qian (Ch. 123) and the *Qian Han Shu* of Ban Gu (Ch. 96A), we find parallel and complementary accounts concerning the western nomads for the period *c.* 209–*c.* 160 BC. The two peoples in question were the Yueji, who were probably Indo-European (Iranian or Tocharian speakers) and appear later in Indian and Persian sources as the Kushan dynasty, and the Xiongnu, who were probably Turkic speakers and have often been equated with the Huns who appeared in Europe some centuries later. According to Simaa Qian, the Yueji were nomads and roamed here and there following their herds. They had the same way of life as the Xiongnu. Their mounted bowmen numbered ten or twenty myriads. According to Ban Gu, they originally lived between Dunhuang and the mountains known as Qilian Shan in what is now Gansu province in western China. Simaa Qian tells us that they had at first been strong and could make light of the Xiongnu. However, both sources tell that when Modun became Chanyu, or ruler, of the Xiongnu (*c.* 209 BC), he attacked and defeated the Yueji. Modun's son and successor Laoshang (ruled *c.* 174–160 BC) killed the king of the Yueji and made a drinking vessel of his skull. According to Ban Gu, the Yueji then moved far away beyond a region called Dayuan (perhaps the Tarim Basin?). In the West, they defeated the Daxia (the Bactrian Greeks, Alexander's successors in Central Asia) and made them their subjects. Then the Yueji made their head-quarters north of the Wei River (= the Oxus in modern Özbekistan and Turkmenistan).

But she, glorying in her strength and her wondrous beauty, refused to marry any of her suitors, considering none of them worthy of her. During his expedition against Geryon, Heracles arrived in Celtica and stayed there in the city of Alesia.[10] Having seen him, and marvelled at his nobility and physical pre-eminence, she eagerly accepted his advances—her parents had given their consent.

After uniting with him, she bore to Heracles a son named Galates, who far outstripped his fellow tribesmen in nobility of spirit and strength of body. When he had grown to manhood and succeeded to his father's kingdom, he took possession of much of the adjacent territory and performed mighty deeds of war. The fame of his valour having spread far and wide, he called his subjects Galatae after himself; from them all Galatia was named.[11]

---

§§40–41. The Foundation of Marseilles
[Latin *Massilia*, Greek *Massalia*], TRANS. JOHN CAREY

§ 40. Athenæus *Deipnosophistae* 13.576.

ARISTOTLE, in *The Constitution of Massilia*, gives a similar account:
The Phocaeans, merchants of Ionia, were the founders of Massilia. Euxenus of Phocaea was a guest of the king Nannus (for that was his name). As Nannus was celebrating his daughter's marriage, Euxenus chanced to arrive and was invited to the feast.

The marriage took place in this way: after the meal the girl was to come in, and to give a bowl of drink which she had mixed to the man whom she preferred among assembled suitors. He to whom she offered it was the bridegroom. When she came in, the girl gave the bowl—whether by chance, or for some other reason—to Euxenus; her own name was Petta.[12]

When this happened, her father concluded that she had acted in accordance

---

10 Alesia. The oppidum of Alesia was the capital of Vercingetorix as national leader of the Gaulish resistance to Cæsar in the 50s BC.

11 Galatia here is the general Greek name for Gaul and does not signify the Celtic territory in Asia Minor about Ankara.

12 The bride's name *Pettā* is Celtic meaning, most generally, 'portion, thing', cf. Welsh *peth*, Old Irish *cuit*. A specialised meaning which may be relevant to this story is that of *Pett*, *Pitt* found in hundreds of place-names in the former territory of the Picts (i.e. present-day north-eastern Scotland), where the term was taken into Scottish Gaelic in the sense a 'holding of land'.

with divine will; Euxenus took her as his wife and lived with her, changing her name to Aristoxene. And even now there is a kindred descended from this woman in Massilia, called the Protiadae: for Euxenus and Aristoxene had a son named Protias.

§ 41. Justin *Philippic Histories* 43.3.

IN THE TIME OF KING TARQUIN the young men of Phocaea, in Asia, arrived at the Tiber's mouth and concluded an alliance with the Romans; thence they voyaged to the farthest harbours of Gaul, and founded Massilia among the Ligurians and the fierce tribes of the Gauls. . .

The leaders of the fleet were Simos and Protis. They met with Nannus, king of the Segobrigii,[13] seeking an alliance: they were eager to establish a city in his territory. It happened that on that day the king was busy with the preparations for the wedding of his daughter Gyptis: according to the custom of the people, she was to be given in marriage to a bridegroom chosen during the feast. And so, when all her suitors had been summoned, the Greek visitors were also invited to attend the banquet. The maiden was led in, and instructed by her father to offer water to the man whom she chose as her husband; ignoring all the rest, she turned to the Greeks and offered the water to Protis. He who had been a guest was now a son-in-law; and he obtained from his father-in-law the land on which to found a city.

King Catumandus and the Dream-Vision of the War-Goddess

---

§42. Justin *Philippic Histories* 43.5; TRANS. J. T KOCH

[THE GREEKS OF MASSILIA] MADE GREAT WARS against [their neighbours] the Ligurians and Gauls. This increased the eminence of their city, and made their valour, through their many victories, famous amongst all the nations around them. They also thoroughly routed the Carthaginian army in a dispute which arose over the capture of some fishing boats, and they granted the vanquished peace . . . Subsequently, when Massilia was at the zenith of its renown, for the fame of its deeds as well as for the abundance of its wealth and its reputation for might, the neighbouring tribes unexpectedly conspired to lay waste to Massilia utterly, so as to wipe out its very name, as if to quench a conflagration

---

13 The tribal name *Segobrigi* is also Celtic and means 'Dwellers in the Strong Hillfort'.

that threatened to consume them all.[14] Catumandus,[15] one of their minor tribal kings, was chosen by unanimous consensus to lead them in war. As he was besieging the city with a vast force of chosen warriors, he was terrified in his sleep with the dream of a woman with a fiercesome expression. She told him that she was a goddess. He immediately sued for peace with the Massaliots. He then asked permission to enter the city in order to worship their gods. He went to the temple of Minerva, and in the portico he saw the image of the goddess that he had seen in his sleep. He suddenly blurted out that it was she who had come to him in the night and she who had demanded that he break off the siege. With congratulations to the Massaliots (for he knew that they were favoured by the immortal gods), he offered a golden torque to the goddess and thus concluded a permanent treaty of friendship with the Greeks of Massilia.[16]

---

§§43–44. The Poisoned Libation: The Love Triangle of Sinātus, Sinorīx, & the High Priestess Cammā[17]

---

§ 43. Plutarch *On the Bravery of Women* 257–8; TRANS. JOHN CAREY

SINĀTUS AND SINORĪX, distant kinsmen, were the most powerful of the tetrarchs of Galatia. Sinātus had a young wife named Cammā, much admired for her youth and beauty, but still more remarkable for her virtues.[18] For she was

---

14 The siege described in this story took place about 390 BC.

15 The Gaulish king's name *Catumandus* probably means 'war-pony' and was a common kingly name in both Gaul and Britain. The father of the powerful 7th-century Welsh king Cadwallon (see below) was Catamanus or (in later spelling) Cadfan. The Anglo-Saxon poet Cædmon's name is a borrowing from Celtic.

16 The Roman writer Justin is here summarising the lost work of the Romanised Gaul Trogus Pompeius, who was descended from the native people of the region.

17 Features of the narrative—including a queen closely connected with a goddess, a honey drink that proves poisonous, an unnatural death instead of a wedding feast, a chieftain set in a chariot as his relatives prepare his tomb, a love triangle terminating in a fateful chariot ride, kinslaying as the prelude to the downfall of king, a woman who brings great evil to those close to her through no fault of her own—resonate widely through the Celtic literary traditions and may be viewed as elements in its inherited preliterary substance.

18 *Sinorix* means 'old king', *Cammā* probably means 'evil woman', literally 'crooked one' (fem.). Galatia here means the Celtic domain founded in Hellenistic times in central Asia Minor, about modern Ankara.

not only modest and affectionate, but also shrewd and courageous, and fervently beloved by her servants on account of her compassion and her kindness. She was further distinguished by her office as priestess of Artemis, the goddess whom the Galatae most revere, and was always to be seen at the solemn processions and sacrifices, magnificently attired.

Sinorīx fell in love with her. Unable to possess her either by persuasion or by force while her husband lived, he did a dreadful deed: he killed Sinātus treacherously. Not long thereafter he proposed to Cammā, who was now living in the temple. She was biding her time, and bore Sinorīx's crime not with pathetic weakness but with a keen and foreseeing spirit.

He was importunate in his entreaties, and proffered arguments not entirely implausible: he claimed that he was a better man than Sinātus and had killed him for no reason except his love for Cammā. Even at first, her refusals were not too harsh, and in a little while she seemed to soften. (Her relatives and friends were also pressuring and seeking to force her to accept him, hoping themselves for the favour of the mighty Sinorīx.)

At last she yielded, and sent for him so that the compact and the vows might be made in the presence of the goddess. When he arrived she received him affectionately. She led him to the altar, poured a libation from a drinking-bowl, drank some herself, and told him to drink the rest. It was a drink of milk and honey [melikraton], with poison in it. When she saw that he had drunk, she cried aloud and fell down before the goddess. 'I bear witness to you, most glorious spirit,' she said, 'that it is for the sake of this day that I have lived since Sinātus's murder, in all that time taking pleasure in none of the good things of life, but only in the hope of justice. Having attained this, I go down to my husband. As for you, most impious of men, your relatives can prepare your tomb, instead of your wedding and bridal chamber.'

When the Galatian heard this, and felt the poison at work in him and penetrating his body, he mounted his chariot as if the tossing and shaking might do him good; but forthwith he desisted, got into a litter, and died in the evening. Cammā survived through the night: learning of his death, she passed away cheerfully and gladly.

§44. Polyaenus *History* 8.39; TRANS. PHILIP FREEMAN

SINORĪX AND SINĀTUS were rulers of the Galatians. The wife of Sinātus was called Cammā, and she was a woman famous for both her beauty and fine character. She was a priestess of the goddess Artemis, whom the Galatians worship above all other gods. Whenever there was a religious procession or sacrifice to Artemis, Cammā was always present, attired in magnificent and grand robes. But Sinorīx also loved Cammā. However, no matter how hard he tried to persuade Cammā to leave Sinātus and marry him, and even when he began to make threats, she refused to betray her husband while he was alive. Sinorīx took care of that difficulty very quickly. Even after her husband's death, Cammā still resisted Sinorīx's advances, even though her family was urging her strongly to give in and marry him. And so finally she agreed. 'Have Sinorīx come to the temple of Artemis,' she said, 'and there we will be married.' So Sinorīx came and all the leading men and women of the Galatians came also as wedding guests. Cammā kindly received Sinorīx into the temple, and led him to the sacrificial altar, where she poured out a drink from a golden cup. When she had drunk from it, she handed it to him so that he might drink, too. He took the cup from her, sweetly smiling at his bride, and drank. But unknown to him, the drink was a poisoned mixture of milk and honey. When Cammā saw that he had drunk from the cup, she let out a cry of victory and praised the goddess: 'O greatly-honoured Artemis, I know that you are indeed kind, because today in your own temple you gave me justice over this man who thought he could unjustly become my husband!' When she had finished speaking, she immediately collapsed and died. And Sinorīx, who was rather surprised at this turn of events, also immediately died at the altar of the goddess.

---

§§45–49. Ancient Celtic Women Leaders
TRANS. J. T. KOCH & JOHN CAREY

Onomāris

§ 45. *Tractatus De Mulieribus Claris in Bello* [5th/6th century BC?]

ONOMĀRIS is one of those held in honour by the Galatians. When her people were oppressed by famine, and sought to flee from their country, they offered themselves as subjects to anyone who was willing to lead them. When none of the men wished to do this, she placed all of their property in a common store, and led the settlers, of whom there were many, to . . . .[19] Crossing the Danube, and conquering the natives in battle, she ruled over that land as queen.

---

19 A few letters are missing in the manuscript here; perhaps a place name?

§§46–47. Boudīcā

§ 46. Dio Cassius [wrote c. AD 190–235] *Roman History* 62.

BOUDĪCĀ,[20] a British woman of royal lineage and an uncommonly intelligent woman was the person who was most instrumental in inciting the natives and convincing them to fight the Romans, who was thought fit to be their commander, and who directed the campaigns of the entire war. This very woman brought together her martial forces, approximately 120,000 in number, then she climbed up onto a raised platform, which had been built of turf in the Roman manner.

She was huge of body, with a horrific expression and a harsh voice. A huge mass of bright red hair descended to the swell of her hips; she wore a large torc of twisted gold,[21] and a tunic of many colours over which there was a thick cape fastened by a brooch. Then she grasped a spear to strike fear into all who watched her.

. . . After that, she used a type of augury, releasing a hare from the folds of her garment. Because it ran off in what [the Britons] considered to be the auspicious direction, the whole horde roared its approval. Raising her hand to the sky, Boudīcā said: 'I thank you, Andrasta [the 'Unconquered' goddess], and call out to you as one woman to another . . . I implore and pray to you for victory and to maintain life and freedom against arrogant, unjust, insatiable, and profane men.'

§ 47. Tacitus
Annals. ¶ 14.35.

IN A CHARIOT with her daughters in front of her, Boudīcā went to tribe after tribe, arguing that it was in truth proper for the Britons to fight under the command of women. 'But now,' she said, 'it is not as a woman of aristocratic descent, but as one of the folk that I take vengeance for lost freedom, my lashed body, the violated virginity of my daughters. Roman appetite has gone so far that not even our persons, not even age or virginity, are left inviolate. But heaven is on the side of just revenge; a legion that was so bold as to fight has been extinguished; the rest are hiding themselves in their camp, or are nervously considering escape. They will not bear even the clamour and cry of as many thousands [as

---

20 Her name means 'victorious' (cf. Lóegaire *Buadach* §§65, 68). On the death of her husband Pratsotagos, she assumed the leadership of her tribe the Iceni, who lived in present-day East Anglia, England. In AD 60–61, she led a revolt against the Romans, destroying the towns of Colchester, London, and Verulamium (nr. St Albans), and killing an estimated 80,000, before she was defeated and committed suicide.

21 Many torcs of twisted gold dating from the first century BC/AD have been found in East Anglia, the largest single find spot being Snettisham, Norfolk, though that group would predate the following events by more than a century.

we are], much less our onrush and our blows. If you consider fully the power of the hosts and the grounds for the war, you will see that in this battle you must prevail or die. This is a woman's determination. As for the men, they may live and be slaves.'

¶ 14.32. At this same time, with no apparent cause, the statue of Victory at Camulodūnum [mod. Colchester, England] fell down, lying with its back turned to the [Britons], as if it had run away before them. Worked up into a furor, women foretold of imminent devastation. It is said that ravings in an unknown language were heard in the Senate-house. Their theatre reverberated with mournful outcry, and in the mouth of the Tamesa [Thames] the vision of a wasted town was seen; even the ocean had taken on a semblance of blood, and, when the tide receded, there were left behind images of human figures, wonders construed by the Britons as auspicious, by the [Roman colonists] as appalling.

¶ *Agricola* 16. Urged on by such mutual incitements, the whole island rose up under the leadership of Boudīcā, a woman of aristocratic descent (the Britons do not discrimminate by gender in selecting war leaders). They hunted down the Roman troops in their widely scattered outposts, captured the forts, and attacked the [Roman] colony itself, which they regarded as the stronghold of their enslavement. The enraged victors did not hold back from any kind of cruelty. Indeed, if [the governor] Paulinus had not speedily sought aid upon hearing of the uprising, Britain would have been lost. As it was, he re-established its previous subjugation in a single successful military engagement.

Veledā

§ 48. Tacitus *Histories* ¶ 4.61, 66.

VELEDĀ,[22] A VIRGIN OF THE TRIBE OF THE BRUCTERI, possessed vast power; for according to the long-standing tradition of the Germans, many of their women were regarded as having powers of prophecy. As the superstition grew, they might come to be deemed actual goddesses. At that time, Veledā's authority was at its height, because she had foretold the triumph of the Germans and the overthrow of the legion.

. . . [The Roman colonists proposed to their enemies the Tencteri —] 'We will have as arbiters Civilis and Veledā, under whose sanction peace will be made.' With the Tencteri appeased in this way, ambassadors were sent with gifts for

---

22 *Veledā* is probably a Celtic name meaning 'seeress', a feminine equivalent of Old Irish *file* (the highest class of professional poet), 5th-century ogam Irish genitive VELITAS. Though the Bructeri and their allies the Tencteri lived east of the Rhine and were therefore reckoned as Germans by the classical authors, it is most probable that they—or at least their rulers—were ethnolinguistically Celts. In a lengthy passage which leads to the second passage below, Tacitus tells how it was agreed that Veledā and the general Civilis were chosen as arbiters of a treaty between the Romans and revolted tribes around the Middle Rhine.

Civilis and Veledā, who then settled everything as the [Roman] Colonia Agrippensis [an important imperial town founded by veterans, around Trier, Germany, ancient Augusta Treverorum] desired. However, the ambassadors were not permitted to approach or address Veledā directly. In order to make them feel greater respect for her, they were restrained from seeing her. She herself dwelt in a high tower. One of her relatives, chosen for the purpose, went to consult with and to bring back the answers, acting like the messenger of a god.

Carti(s)manduā
§ 49. Tacitus *Annals* ¶ 12.40, 2–7.

AFTER THE CAPTURE OF CARATĀCUS, the Brigantian tribesman Venutius (as I noted above) was pre-eminent in military expertise. He had long been faithful to Rome and had been defended by its arms, so long as he remained married to Queen Cartimanduā.[23] Later, dissension broke out between them, leading immediately to war. Later on, he took a hostile attitude towards us [the Romans] as well. But at first, they fought only amongst themselves. Using wily deceits, Cartimanduā captured Venutius' brother and other relatives. The

---

23 Between *c.* 43 and *c.* AD 70, Cartimanduā was queen of the Brigantes, the most numerous and extensive tribe of late Iron Age Britain, occupying territories from the North Sea to the Irish Sea in what is now northern England and southern Scotland. Under her, the Brigantian kingdom was a Roman client state beyond the frontier of the province of Britannia. In AD 51, the chief national leader of the anti-Roman British resistance, Caratācos son of Cunobelinos of the tribe the Catuvellaunī, fell into her hands, and she gave him over to the Romans.

She had two successive consorts, Venutius and Vellocatus ('Better-in-battle'). Her divorce from Venutius triggered a civil war, with the two factions led by her two husbands.

The tribal goddess of the Brigantes was *Brigantī*, the 'Exalted One', (Romanised *Brigantia*), corresponding to the Irish goddess, later saint, Brigit. Our understanding of the origins of the cult of St Brigit is that she had originally been the tribal goddess of the branch of the Brigantes living in Co. Kildare, Ireland (shown there in the ancient Geography of Ptolemy). It is apparent that there had also been a mortal high priestess closely identified with her presiding over the cult centre at Kildare. A similar institution may be posited for pre-Roman British Brigantia, with Queen Cartimanduā holding the office of high priestess of *Brigantī there.

D. A. Binchy convincingly demonstrated that the Welsh word for king, *brenin* < *brigantinos*, originally meant consort of the goddess *Brigantī and had first arisen referring specifically to (male) leaders of the Brigantes; see *Celtic and Anglo-Saxon Kingship* (Oxford, 1970). The title actually occurs on a Continental Celtic coin legend inscribed, in Iberian script, BIRIKANTIN- (to be read *brigantin*-). Insofar as we know that the historical leaders of the Brigantes, Venutius and Vellocatus, were husbands of Queen Cartimanduā, it follows that she was considered the mortal representative of the goddess, with her rival suitors raising war over the title *brigantinos*.

A further survival of this idea is seen in a fragmentary elegy to the 7th-century Welsh king Cadwallon (§§131–132) in which the River Braint (< *Brigantī) is described overflowing in grief for its fallen consort.

anti-Roman party was infuriated at that and further stirred up as they looked ahead to submitting in dishonour to the overlordship of a woman. The best of their youths were picked out for war, and they invaded her kingdom. We had anticipated this, and some auxiliary cohorts were sent to her aid. A keen struggle followed. The outcome was in doubt as it began, but it ended successfully.

Histories ¶ 3.45. These discords and ongoing rumours of civil war put spirit into the Britons, who were under the leadership of Venutius, a man who was naturally fierce, hated the name of Rome, and was also driven on by his own personal hatred of Queen Cartimanduā. Cartimanduā. because she was of most noble descent, ruled the Brigantes. She had increased her power, when, due to her underhanded capture of King Caratācus [in AD 51], she came to be viewed as having secured the most important component of the Emperor Claudius' triumph [the conquest of Britain]. After this, there came the luxury and indolence of victory. Casting aside her husband Venutius, she took Vellocatus, his armour-bearer, in marriage and to share in governing the realm. This huge scandal rocked her household to its foundation. The tribe's sentiments favoured her rightful husband [Venutius]. Favouring the illegitimate husband were the queen's libido and her ferocious temper. So then, Venutius mustered some warbands and was helped at that same time by an uprising amongst this tribe, the Brigantes. He succeeded in putting Cartimanduā into an extremely desperate position. She requested Roman forces. Some of our infantry and cavalry auxiliary units, after fighting for a time with mixed results, rescued the queen from this dangerous crisis. [But] Venutius' power was not finished, and we were [thus] left with a war.

§§50–64. Ireland before St Patrick
TRANS. PHILIP FREEMAN

§50. Avienus *Ora Maritima* [4th century AD, believed to be based on a lost 'Massaliote Periplus' of the 6th century BC]

FROM HERE it is a two day voyage to the Sacred Isle,
for by this name the ancients called the island.
It lies rich in turf among the waves,

thickly populated by the *Hierni*.[24]

Nearby lies the island of the *Albiones*.[25]
The Tartessians[26] were accustomed to trade even
to the edge of the Oestrymnides.[27] The Carthaginian
colonists and people around the Pillars
of Hercules frequented these waters.
Four months scarcely is enough for the voyage,
as Himilco the Carthaginian proved
by sailing there and back himself.

§51. Diodorus Siculus *Bibliotheca Historica* ¶ 5.32.2–3 [see §18 above.]

§52. Julius Cæsar *De Bello Gallico* ¶ 5.13 [see §20 above.]

§53. Strabo *Geography*

¶ 2.1.13

THE VOYAGE FROM CELTICA to the north is currently said to be the most extreme. By this I mean the voyage beyond Britain to *Iernē*,[28] a wretched place to live because of the cold, beyond which the lands are considered uninhabitable. They say that *Iernē* is separated from Celtica by not more than five thousand stadia.

¶ 4.5.4 There are also other smaller islands around Britain, the largest being *Iernē* which lies to its north and is longer than it is wide. Concerning this island I have nothing certain to report, except that the people living there are more savage than the Britons, being cannibals as well as gluttons. Further, they consider it honourable to eat their dead fathers and to openly have intercourse, not only with unrelated women, but with their mothers and sisters as well. I say these things not having trustworthy witnesses, and yet the custom of cannibalism is said to be found among the Scythians, and, because of necessity during sieges, the Celts, Iberians, and others besides are said to have practised it.

---

24 Hierni 'The Irish'.
25 Albiones 'The British'.
26 Living near present-day Gibraltar.
27 Oestrymnides: possibly the same tribe later known as the *Osismii*, living in western Armorica, present-day Brittany.
28 Iernē 'Ireland', home of the *Hierni* 'Irish' mentioned in §49 above; cf. the Middle Irish tribal name *Érainn*.

§54. Isidorus [c. AD 25] *De Chorographia* 3.6.53

ABOVE BRITAIN IS *Iuverna*,[29] almost the same in area, but oblong with coasts of equal length on both sides. The climate is unfavourable for the ripening of grain, but yet it is so fertile for grass, not only abundant but sweet, that livestock eat their fill in a small part of the day. Unless they were restrained from this pasturage, they would burst from feeding too long. The inhabitants of this island are unrefined, ignorant of all the virtues more than any other people, and totally lack all sense of duty.

§55. Tacitus [c. AD 98] *Agricola* 24.3.

IN THE FIFTH YEAR OF THE WAR, AGRICOLA, crossing in the lead ship, conquered tribes unknown until that time in frequent and successful engagements. That part of Britain which faces *Hibernia* he garrisoned with troops, more out of hope than fear. For *Hibernia*, lying between Britain and Spain, and placed strategically in the Gallic Sea, would unite the most robust parts of the Empire to the great advantage of both. In size it surpasses the islands of our sea, but is narrower than Britain. As for soil, climate, and the character and lifestyle of its people, it differs little from Britain. The approaches and harbours are better known due to trade and merchants. Agricola had taken in one of their tribal kings driven out by a internal discord and was keeping him under the pretence of friendship for the right opportunity. I often heard him say that *Hibernia* could be conquered and occupied by one legion and a moderate number of auxiliaries. Moreover, it would be useful against Britain as well if Roman arms were everywhere raised high and liberty, so to speak, vanished from sight.

§56. Ptolemy [c. AD 135–50] *Geography* 1.11.7

MARINUS seems to disbelieve the reports of merchants, at least the statement of Philemon that the length of the island *Ivernia* is twenty days from east to west, because Philemon said that he had heard it from traders.

§57. Solinus [c. AD 200] *Collectanea Rerum Memorabilium* 22.2–5

BRITTANIA is surrounded by many not insignificant islands, of which *Hibernia* comes closest to it in size. The latter is inhuman in the savage rituals of its inhabitants, but on the other hand is so rich in fodder, that the cattle, if not removed from the fields from time to time, would happily gorge themselves to a dangerous point. On that island there are no snakes, few birds, and an unfriendly and warlike people. When the blood of killers has been drained, the victors smear it on their own faces. They treat right and wrong as

---

29 Iuverna: this is a later Latinised form derived from the same native ethnic name *Iuerni* as earlier gave Greek *Iernē*, &c.

the same thing. There have never been bees there, and if anyone sprinkles dust or pebbles from there among the hives, the swarms will leave the honeycombs. The sea which lies between this island and *Britannia* is stormy and tossed during the whole year, except for a few days when it is navigable. Those who have made a trustworthy measurement of the distance of this passage say it is one hundred and twenty thousand paces.

§58. Anonymous [AD 297–8] *Panegyric on Constantius Cæsar* 11.4

THE BRITONS also, then a barbarous nation accustomed only to enemies as yet half-naked, such as the Picts and *Hiberni*, yielded easily to the arms and standards of Rome—nearly so easily that Cæsar should have boasted that in that one campaign he had crossed the Ocean.

§59. Anonymous [AD 310] *Panegyric on Constantine Augustus* 7.2

NOR DO I SAY THAT HE, even with so many and such great deeds accomplished, deemed worthy of conquest the forests and swamps of the Calidonians and other Picts, nor nearby *Hibernia* nor furthest Thule[30] nor, if they exist, the Isles of the Blessed.

§60. Ammianus Marcellinus [c. AD 380–95] *History* 27.8.5 [referring to AD 368]

SUFFICE IT TO SAY, however, that at that time the Picts, divided into the two tribes of the Dicalydones and Verturiones, as well as the warlike nation of the Attacotti and the *Scotti* [that is, the Irish] as well, were roaming far and wide, ravaging many lands.

§61. Pacatus [c. AD 390] *Panegyric on Theodosius* 5.2.

SHALL I TELL HOW BRITAIN was worn down by infantry battles? The Saxon defeated in naval battles is an example. Shall I speak of the *Scotti* driven back to their own bogs?

§62. Jerome [c. AD 390–415] *Adversus Jovinianum* 2.7.

WHY SHOULD I SPEAK OF OTHER NATIONS when I myself as a young man in Gaul [saw] Atticoti [other manuscripts—*Scotti*], a British people, feeding on human flesh? Moreover, when they come across herds of pigs and cattle in the forests, they frequently cut off the buttocks of the shepherds and their wives, and their nipples, regarding these alone as delicacies. The nation of the *Scotti* do not have individual wives, but, as if they had read Plato's *Republic* or

---

30 Thule: possibly Shetland here, though the name may sometimes refer to Iceland.

followed the example of Cato, no wife belongs to a particular man, but as each desires, they indulge themselves like beasts.

§63. Symmachus [c. AD 393] *Epistle 2.77.*

AS NOW THE PRESENTATION OF SEVEN *Scotti* DOGS has demonstrated, which on the day of the prelude so astonished Rome, that it was thought they were brought in iron cages.

§64. Claudian [c. AD 400]

Panegyric on the Third Consulship of the Emperor Honorius 51–58

HE CONQUERED the swift Moors and the well-named Picts, and following the *Scotti* with his wandering sword, he broke the Hyperborean waves with his daring oars.

Panegyric on the Fourth Consulship of the Emperor Honorius 8.30–33

What endless cold, what wintry air, what unknown sea
could affect him? The Orcades were soaked in Saxon
gore; Thule was warmed by Pictish blood;
icy *Hiverne* wept at the mounds of dead *Scotti.*

On Stilicho's Consulship 2.247–55

Then Britain spoke, covered in the skin of a
Caledonian beast, painted cheeks etched with tattoos,
blue cloak like the swell of the sea sweeping to her feet:
'Stilicho also defended me when I was perishing
from neighbouring tribes, when the *Scottus* roused all
Hiverne and Tethys [the sea] foamed with hostile oars.
Due to his care, I do not fear the spears of the *Scotti,*
nor tremble at the Pict, or watch along my whole coast
for the Saxon coming on uncertain winds.'

PART II

Early Irish &

Hiberno-Latin Sources

§65–72. Early Irish Dynastic Poetry

¶**Note.** The poems deal mostly with the legendary rulers of the Laigin (Leinster, South-East Ireland) in the Pre-Christian period and their ancestors. They are linguistically archaic, and most of the verses probably go back as far as the 7th century.

Several modern authorities have called these artistically poor poems. They do nonetheless highlight certain heroic values seen in some of the more ambitiously literary works.

The early poets attached to particular ruling houses — as well as praising the generosity and martial valour of the ruler — had also to praise the illustrious lineage of the patron, back to the legendary founder of the dynasty. That is what these lists are doing. A genealogy was an instrument of political propaganda for the Celts, as in many other cultures in which inheritance is a factor in determining leadership. A legitimate dynasty had to have reputable ancestors. A rival to be undermined as unrightful had to have his forebears portrayed as 'unkings' (*anflaithi*). Before the advent of full vernacular literacy, poetic genealogies were probably more easily remembered by the learned retainers of the kings than unembellished lists would have been. Poetry was also considered to be a more valid form of oral testimony in a dispute, because it was harder to make up on the spot or modify for one's own purposes.

In the Middle Irish Period (*c.* 900–1200), poems of this sort formed part of the basis for the great work of Irish legendary history, *Lebor Gabála Érenn* (§108 below).

§65. Mess-Telmann

¶ I.

Māl ad-rūalaid īathu marb,
macc sōer Sētnai,
selaig srathu Fomoire
fo doīne domnaib.

¶ 2. Dī ōchtur Alinne
ort trīunu talman
trebun trēn tūathmar,
Mess-Telmann Domnon.

¶TRANS J. T. KOCH. 1. A prince who has reached the realms of the dead | the noble son of Sétnae | laid waste the vales of the Fomoire | under the worlds of men.

2. From the heights of Ailenn [the hillfort which was the political centre of pre-Christian Leinster], the powerful tribune great in dominions Mess-Telmann of the Domnonian tribe [*Fir Domnann*] slew the mighty of the earth.

§66. Bressual Beolïach

An grēn grīssach
goires brēo: Bressual—
bress Elce, aue Luirc,
lathras bith—Bēolïach.

¶TRANS J. T. KOCH. A brilliant burning sun | that heats is the flame: Bressual—fair one of Elg [Ireland], descendant of Lorcc | who lays waste the world—Bēolïach.

§§67–72.

TRANS. JOHN CAREY drawing on the German of
Über die älteste irische Dichtung, K. Meyer (Berlin, 1913-14) = *ÄiD*.

§67. Nidu dír dermait [*ÄiD* i, 14-25]

¶ 1.

IT ILL BESEEMS ME TO FORGET the affairs of every famous king, the careers of the kings of Tara, mustered tribes on the warpath.

¶ 2.   A noble battle-hero, fair and tall was Moen, Labraid Longsech; a cruel lion, a lover of praise, a mighty lover of battle.

¶ 3.   A fair warrior was Ailill in battles against the frontiers of Crothomun; Abratchaín shook the ranks of the field of Ethomun.

¶ 4.   Dreaded master of Ireland was glorious Oengus Amlongaid. He dwelt upon the slopes of Tara: with his own will alone he conquered it.

¶ 5.   Circular Ailenn [Dún Ailinne, Co. Kildare, traditional seat of the pre-Christian kings of Leinster], Cruachu, citadels magnificent amongst strongholds, fortresses which an illustrious, powerful, spear-wielding royal host would smash.

¶ 6.   Bresal Bregom ruled the boastful world; Fergus was blood-red; Fedelmid was a seemly ruler, who reddened pure Ireland.

¶ 7.   The prince Feradach Find Fechtnach owned it; ruddy righteous Crimthann Coscrach sheltered it.

¶ 8.   Mug Airt illuminated it; Art, the old champion, laid claim to it, Alldóit ordered it, Nūadu Fuildiu was a princely champion.

¶ 9.   Feradach Foglas was an illustrious man; Ailill Glas cleansed it; the violent one seized it, Fíachra Fobrecc overpowered it.

¶ 10.   Bresal Becc smote it, a king great in blows and treasures; a lion seized it, Lugaid Lūathfḃind, a manly princely king.

¶ 11.   Like wolves the army of Sétnae Sithbacc ravaged it; he cast it down; Nūadu Necht freed it; Fergus put it in bonds.

¶ 12.   Fairrge, Rus Rūad: the thrust of his will impelled him. On the battlefield his great sons divided (it) with wild battle-fury.

¶ 13.   Find Fili, harsh Ailill, Fair Cairpre; the mighty king brought a path of destruction (even) to kings.

¶ 14.   The over-king of Macha, the mighty chariot-warrior, overcame the territories of mighty fortresses, destroyed boundary ditches.

¶ 15. Mug Corb, Cú Chorb, Nía Corb the battle-king, seemly Cormac; the ex-king Fedelmid ruled the land.

¶ 16. For fifty years Cathaír dwelt there, an enduring reign, Fíachu Aiccid, the truly brave, was a vehement prince famed for agility.

¶ 17. Bresal Bélach overcame (his adversaries), a hulking bear, a conquering champion; he broke the hosts of Conn[Cétchathach]'s descendants, a triumphant hero, a stern fighter.

¶ 18. The strong king contended for the inheritance, he triumphs, he impoverished them (?); he smote the sons of Lifechar of Liffey, he drove them to their ship.

¶ 19. Muiredach Mo-Sníthech, of noble race, pursued the great ones: a famous, distinguishing sign, the heir of fair lineages.

¶ 20. The youthful king Moenach, a strong offspring, conquered the walls of the great plain; son of Cairthenn, lover of warfare, was a nobly born lover of praise.

¶ 21. Nad Buidb was a severe hero, a victorious king, son of Erc Būadach, an aristocratic bellower of firm agreements, a stern king ordering armed encounters.

¶ 22. Blood-red heroes prevailing in combat, dominant men beyond the border army, they cast a challenge from the slope of Tara, (warriors) honourable and brilliant in battle.

◆ ◆ ◆ ◆ ◆ ◆ ◆ ◆ ◆ ◆ ◆

§68. Núadu Necht [ÄiD i. 38-50]

¶Note. Góedel Glas, who is mentioned in ¶42 of this poem, is the eponymous ancestor of the 'Gaels' or ethnic Irish (Old Irish Goídil).

¶ 1.

Núadu Necht did not endure an un-king: the overlord Etarscéle, of the race of Iär, was slain.

¶ 2. A brave king of *fiana* against a ruddy prosperous king: blood-red were the taxes of the swift grandson of Lugaid.

¶ 3. Swift in ships, he traversed the sea as a warrior of the west: a red wind, which dyed sword-blades with a bloody cloud.

¶ 4. Fergus Fairrge, Núadu Necht strong and brave: a great champion who did not love punishment from a rightful lord.

¶ 5.   As a wave does not (merely) visit the land, thunder from across the sea, an advance against a cliff.

¶ 6.   When Art's grandson struck down feeble resistance, he was not timid behind another's back in ordering the battle.

¶ 7.   Firm (?) contender against an army was Sétnae Sithbacc, enduring field of ruin, mighty horror, reaping-hook of death.

¶ 8.   Brecc's grandson has earned a victory-song; Bresal's grandson was mighty according to the harsh tale of battle.

¶ 9.   Lugaid rushed to their aid, against a lean warrior; a protracted battle, the overswearing of Sedrach.

¶ 10. Sturdy against the onslaught of champions, against the fury of champions; swift he rushed, the roar of the vast sea.

¶ 11. Deedful was battle-mighty Bresal, Fiachra the princely champion; Ailill the old champion was a deedful lord.

¶ 12. Foglas was violent, who equipped a hundred forts: a king of battles, who ruled realms with a viper's venom.

¶ 13. Núadu son of Fuildiu conquered *fiana* [war-bands], he flattened them; with red blades he made the brave kings of the world his subjects.

¶ 14. With great masses of troops he harried the land of Ethomun: troops, horror of destruction, upon the territories of Crothomun.

¶ 15. The destroyer shook worlds with his armies, Art and fierce Mug Airt, who brought ruin.

¶ 16. With great showers of blood he cleansed the swarthy world; the heaven-hued cloud flowed (?) with ruddy men.

¶ 17. Fair Crimthann Cosrach was not a holy inheritor; Feradach Find Fechtnach was no milder.

¶ 18. He left the world orphaned, the sturdy support of the host of Carmun; Fedelmid Fortrén, the savage chariot-warrior, smote a picked battalion.

¶ 19. He ploughed three hundred battlefields, nimble in the heat of conflict, when Fergus Fortamail loosed his fury upon the Britons.

¶ 20. Bresal Bregom, a contentious youth, who loved no feeble strength; fair-browed Ailill was a battle-hero, fierce and renowned was Oengus.

¶ 21. He razed eight towers of the land of Iath, he destroyed the fields of the Idrig, he ravaged eight camps of the men of Skye, he smote the armies of the Siblig.

¶ 22. Swift on the sea, good at rowing, a mighty blood-red dispenser (of booty): he fought three times fifty battles in Morc—Labraid, son of Lorc's son.

¶ 23. Every Monday he waged a bloody battle against Fergus; every Wednesday he razed a wood; every Saturday he laid waste a bog.

¶ 24. He harried the great sturdy sea-realms of the Fir Fagraig—phantoms burnt their ships—Labraid grandson of Lorc.

¶ 25. He ventured against the many Orkneys, he . . . the Sábeóin; for thousands of months he occupied Irrus, he divided the Gáileóin.

¶ 26. He cleansed the possessions of sixty kings, a manly distributor of gracious favours; he divided the south of Ireland, Labraid grandson of Lorc.

¶ 27. With broad spears, with troops, he smashed the territories of Carmun; in dire battles the ravager smote men.

¶ 28. He fettered Gaulish hostages as far as the five peaks of the Alps; scores of fierce lords, of armoured legions, go into hiding.

¶ 29. The race of the Gáileóin stormed Tara, a mighty march: Fál wails at the conquest of the troop of Fáireóin.

¶ 30. So long as he reigned, Áth Cliath asked for no aid; Labraid grandson of Lorc was like a golden door.

¶ 31. The high-hearted Loingsech, a great rich diadem, around which the princes of the stormy land of Iath arrayed their troops.

¶ 32. An occasion of fear arose (when) he bound a violent race: the reincarnation of his grandfather Lorc defied the armies of the Suidbig.

¶ 33. A noble company were Feradach, Fedelmid, Fergus Fortamail, Bresal Bregom, the lordly Oengus Ollam.

¶ 34. Fair-browed Ailill of lofty irresistible courage, Ugaine, Eochu the noble, Ailill, Lorc, Labraid.

¶ 35. Dui Ladcrai, a red goad, Fiachra Tolcrai; a . . . tumult was the wild Muiredach Bolcrai.

¶ 36. Victorious was Senén, Ethén was a bright harsh king; young and radiant was Núadu, the fierce high king.

¶ 37. Ailill Oalchloen of battles, Sírna, Dian, a brave king; Demál who was violent, Rothait, Ogamuin, a king of the plains.

¶ 38. Great was Oengus son of Fiachu, Smirgnath, Smrith, Enboth, Tigernmas—a lordly judgement.

¶ 39. Etherél was eloquent, illustrious in dispute; Éremón was great, Míl sturdy and familiar with the sea.

¶ 40. Bile was rich in treasures, with a bear's strength, noble and fair as heaven; Bregon was a sky of strength, Bráth was illustrious and handsome.

¶ 41. Deáith was powerful, bold Eirgid was a radiant one; Alldóit was a champion, Núadu a noble one.

¶ 42. Noenal, Faebur, Góedel Glas uniquely fair; Glúnfind was a radiant one, Lámfind, Etheoir was fairer.

¶ 43. Agnomain, Toi, Banb, a victorious strong one; noble Seim was a champion, Mair was a stately one.

¶ 44. Great was Ethecht, illustrious was Aurtacht, a noble fruit; Aboth, Aos, Ara, Sara, Seth, the peaceful and deft.

¶ 45. Lordly was Zru, Esru, Ethrocht, Baath was kingly (?); Ibath was a cliff of glass, Gomer was sun-like.

¶ 46. Though Japhet was fair, a famous lordly battle-warrior; more illustrious than the men of the world was the saintly Noah.

¶ 47. It was not a petty fellowship of kindred brothers, (but) a mighty splendid company of fathers and mothers.

¶ 48. Sons of the lofty God, angels of cloud-white heaven, Noah, Lamech, bright white Methuselah.

¶ 49. Enoch, Jared, Malaleel of worthy race, Cainan, Enos, nobly born (?) Seth.

¶ 50. Nobler was Adam, father of mortally descended men; a man shaped by God, a noble unique offspring.

¶ 51. Only offspring of the God of the mighty peopled earth, a hero who inhabited the dwelling of the strife-filled world.

¶ 52. Triple God, lofty single three, wondrous sole king of Heaven, infant, holy champion.

◆ ◆ ◆ ◆ ◆ ◆ ◆ ◆ ◆ ◆ ◆

§69. Móen Óen [*ÄiD* ii. 9-12]

¶ 1.

Móen, ALONE since he was an infant—it was not the custom of a high king—smote kings, a splendid spear-cast, Labraid grandson of Lorc.

¶ 2. The warriors of the Gáileóin took spears (*láigne*) in their hands: hence the valiant army of the Gáileóin are (called) Laigin.[1]

---

1 Gáileóin is an alternative name for the Laigin, the once-powerful tribal grouping who gave their name to Leinster, the south-eastern province of Ireland. Here, the tribal name *Laigin*

¶ 3.   They won wars as far as the slopes of the sea of the lands of Éremón; after exile Lóchet Loingsech of the *fíana* [extratribal warbands] took the sovereignty of the Gaels.

¶ 4.   A gryphon attacking unknown lands was the grandson of Lóegaire Lorc: exalted above men save for the holy King of Heaven.

¶ 5.   Gold brighter than the great shining sun, he conquered the worlds of men; Móen son of the sole king Aine is one god among the gods.

・ ・ ・ ・ ・ ・ ・ ・ ・ ・ ・

§70. Mára galgata [*ÄiD* ii. 17]

¶ 1.

GREAT DISASTERS: the shaking of a sword above the families of Cairpre on the slopes of Cnámros.

¶ 2,   The descendants of Conn leave corpses behind, they are slaughtered along with nine thousand; the mighty sons of a splendid king, Eochu, dear Eochaid Domlén.

¶ 3.   Ruddy Fíachu was the swift over-king of Raiphtine. Alas the news! It grieves me that Conn's valiant descendants are resting in bloody graves.

・ ・ ・ ・ ・ ・ ・ ・ ・ ・ ・

§71. Lug scéith [*ÄiD* ii. 23]

¶ 1.

LUG WITH A SHIELD, a shining phantom; under heaven none was mightier than Aine's son.

¶ 2.   A man loftier than gods, a firm acorn, the pure branching grandson of Lóegaire Lorc.

・ ・ ・ ・ ・ ・ ・ ・ ・ ・ ・

§72. Eochu art ara·chridethar cathrai [*ÄiD* ii. 22-23]

¶ 1.

EOCHU, A BEAR WHO HUGGED BATTLEFIELDS to death, who would snatch a secret from the great world; the son of Labraid led *fíana* under diadems.

---

is being explained as derived from *láigen* 'spear, lance', pl. *láigne*.

¶ 2. Bresal Bélach's grandson is an armload of valour, the hero of Ireland, a . . . prince. He smote a host of enemies, a terror to heroic rivals.

¶ 3. A shining millstone, a . . . prince, a battlefield of ruinous carnage is Eithne's contentious son, grandson of Corc of Carmun.

Tales from the Ulster Cycle

§73. *Compert Conchobuir* [*Maic Nessa*]
The Conception of Conchobor son of Nes
TRANS. JOHN CAREY

THERE WAS A KING OVER THE ULAID, EOCHU SÁLBUIDE SON OF Lóch. A daughter was born to him, Nes daughter of Eochu Sálbuide, and twelve foster fathers took her to rear her. Assa ['easy, light'] was her name at first; for she was well-behaved and mild as she was being brought up.

At that time a certain *féinnid* ['a warrior living apart from his tribe'] came from the south of Ulster, performing *féinnidecht* ['warlike deeds'] across Ireland, with a band of three times nine men: his name was Cathbad, the wondrous druid. He had great knowledge, and magic (*druídecht*), and manly strength; he was of the Ulaid by birth, but had run off from them. Once Cathbad and his three times nine men happened to be in a certain desolate place, and another *féinnid* with another three nines came into the same wilderness. At first they fought until they were weary, but at length they made peace with one another they would have destroyed each other otherwise, for their numbers were the same. Then Cathbad with his followers, and the other *féinnid* with his followers, came to Ulster and slew the girl's twelve foster fathers, for they were all feasting in a single house; and none escaped save the girl alone, and no one knew who had committed the slaughter.

The girl went to her father with great lamentation. Her father said that he could not take revenge, for it was not known who had committed the slaughter. The girl was savage and wrathful at that reply; and after that she took up *féinnidecht* with a band of three times nine men, to avenge her foster fathers. She ravaged and destroyed every region in turn. Assa had been her name up until then, for she was gentle; *Ní-assa* ['not-easy', that is *Nes*] however was her name after that, on account of the harshness [*ansatu* 'difficulty'] of her fury and her weapons. It was her custom to ask tidings of *féinnidi* from every visitor who came to her, in the hope of learning the name of the man who had carried out the slaughter.

Once when she was in the wilderness her people were preparing food for her. She went out alone to explore the wilderness, as it was her custom to explore every wilderness into which she came. When she was there she saw a fair lovely pool in the midst of the wilderness. She went into the pool to bathe, and left her weapons and her clothes on land.

Now Cathbad came, exploring the same wilderness, so that he came to the pool in which the girl was bathing. Then he went between the girl and her clothes and weapons, and bared his sword above her head.

'Grant me protection,' said the girl.

'Grant me three requests,' said Cathbad.

'You will have them,' said the girl.

'Since this is what I have decided on,' said Cathbad, 'let there be security (i.e. peace) for me, and covenants between us, and do you be my sole wife as long as you live.'

'That seems better than for you to kill me unarmed,' said the girl.

After that they and their followers met in one place. Then at an auspicious hour Cathbad came to Ulster and to the girl's father. They were made welcome, and territory was given to them: Ráith Cathbaid in the territory of the Cruithni, near the river in Crích Rois which is named Conchobor.

Once a great thirst came upon Cathbad in the night. Nes went throughout the whole stronghold seeking a drink for him, and could find no water for him to drink. Then she went to the Conchobor (that is, to the river), and strained water into the cup through her veil, and brought it to Cathbad after that.

'Let a candle be lit for us,' said Cathbad, 'so that we may see the water.' There were two worms in the water. Cathbad bared his sword above the woman's head, to slay her. 'Drink yourself,' said Cathbad, 'what you wanted me to drink: you will be dead if you do not drink the water.' Then the woman took two drinks of the water and she swallowed a worm with each of them.

The woman became pregnant after that, for the length of time that every woman is pregnant. And although according to some it was because of the worms that she became pregnant, Fachtna Fáthach was the girl's young lover, and it is he who made her pregnant in spite of Cathbad the fair druid.

Once Cathbad went to speak with the king, Fachtna Fáthach son of Rudraige, so that they came as far as Mag nInis. Labour pains seized the woman on the way. 'It would be well, wife,' said Cathbad, 'if you were able not to bear the child which is in your womb until tomorrow; for your son would be king of Ulster, or of all Ireland, and his name would be illustrious throughout Ireland forever. For on the anniversary of that same day will be born the illustrious child whose fame and power have spread across the world: Jesus Christ, Son of the ever-living God.'

'I will do that, then,' said Nes. 'Unless he comes out through my side, he will not come by any other way until that time.' Then Nes came to the water-meadow beside the river which is named Conchobor. She set herself on the slab of stone which is on the bank of the river, so that it is there that the anguish of the pangs came upon her. It is then that Cathbad recited this *retoiricc*, prophesying the birth of Conchobor; so that this is what he said:

'Nes, you are in danger:
someone arises at your giving birth,
you do not obtain solace (?),
lovely is the colour of your hands.
Daughter of Eochu Buide,
do not mourn, mortal:
your son will be chief of hundreds,
and of the troops of the world.

'Omen and portent are the same
for him and for the King of the world:
everyone will be praising him
until Doomsday of the ages.
On the same day are born
warriors will not dare defy him,
he will not be taken hostage
he and Christ.

'You bear, in Mag nInis,
on the stone in the water-meadow,
one whose tales will be famous;
he will be the king of bounty.

He will be the hound of the Ulaid,
he will take the hostages of heroes:
great will be the misfortune
when he falls at the ditch (?).

'Conchobor his name,
whoever may call him:
red will be his arms,
he will muster (?) many slaughters.
He will get his death
avenging God the Creator:
the mark of his sword will be clear
above the slope of Leitir Láim.

'The fair nimble man
will not be Cathbad's son;
not mine, who am not loved,
for you are a plain facing my court (?).
He will be Fachtna Fáthach's son,
as Scáthach knows;
he will bring hostages repeatedly
from the north and south.'

Then the girl bore the child that was in her womb, the splendid illustrious child and the prophesied son whose fame has extended throughout Ireland. And the stone on which he was born still exists, west of Airgdech. This is how the boy was born: with a worm in each hand. He went topsy-turvy into the river named Conchobor, and the river bore him backward (?), until Cathbad caught hold of him after that. And he was named after the name of the river: Conchobor son of Fachtna. Cathbad took the boy into his bosom, and was giving thanks for him and prophesying to him; so that that is when he recited the poem:

Welcome, guest who has come hither.
They tell you
he will be the red generous one,
fair Cathbad's little son.

'The little son of fair Cathbad
and of the young Nes.
Above the mighty fortress of the mantles (?),

my son and my grandson.

'My son and my grandson,
beauty of the swift world:
he will be king of Ráith Line,
he will be a poet, he will be generous.

'He will be a poet, he will be generous,
he will lead warriors across the sea:
my own self from the heat (?),
my puppy, welcome!'

Then that boy was reared by Cathbad, so that for that reason he was called
Conchobor son of Cathbad. After that Conchobor took the kingship of Ulster
by right both of his mother and his father: his father was Fachtna Fáthach son
of Rudraige king of Ireland, and it was he who begot Conchobor in spite of
Cathbad. And it is through the strength of that man's — that is, of Cathbad's
valour and magic [druídecht] that the terrible famous battle of Gáirech and Il-
gáirech was won against Ailill and Medb at the bringing of the cattle-drive of
Cuailnge (*Táin Bó Cuailnge*) out of the province of Ulster. FINIT.

• • • • • • • • • • •

§74. An Anecdote about Athairne in *Bretha Nemed*

TRANS. JOHN CAREY

'ATHAIRNE THE FIERCE': WHY WAS HE CALLED THAT? Not hard
to answer: from chanting the poem in his mother's womb. His mother
came to fetch fire from a house in which a feast was being prepared. He leapt
in her womb at the smell of the ale, so that he knocked her headlong as she
was coming out of the house. Then the woman asked three times for a drink of
the ale. The brewer refused three times, and said that though she should die of
it, and though her child should come out through her side, the ale would not
be disturbed on her account, however long she might wait before she gave birth.
And the tops of the vessels were covered until the coming of the king for
whom [the ale] had been prepared. Then something was heard: in the womb of
his mother Athairne *dixit*:

Do laith,	'For the sake of ale,
lócharn talman,	lantern of earth,
tethra mara	the expanse of the sea

mos-timchella tíre.	soon encircles the land.
Tethra tráiges /,	A sea which ebbs,
láthrach lóchet:	place of lightning:
la blae-maidm,	with bursting of the boundary,
bé tened.	a woman of fire.
Tethnatar a circuil,	Their hoops cracked,
cnómaidm.	the cracking of a nut.' [2]

Then the hoops of all the unopened vessels burst, so that people were wading in the ale throughout the house; and the woman drank three mouthfuls of it from her palm as she left the house.

If any poet recites this in the proper form after he has been refused a drink of ale, the ale will burst forth from the vessels. And it is by him, or through him, that [the vessel?] was pierced; for it is not proper that he should leave some behind without drinking of it.

§75. Athairne's Greediness ed. Rudolf Thurneysen, ZCP 12. 398–9
TRANS. JOHN CAREY

AITHIRNE AILGESACH SON OF FERCHERTNE was the stingiest man in Ireland. He went to Midir of Brí Léith and fasted against him, so that he brought away from him the cranes of refusal and stinginess (to set) beside his house, for churlishness and begrudging, lest any of the men of Ireland visit his house for hospitality or entertainment. 'Don't come, don't come,' said the first crane. 'Go away,' said the second. 'Pass by, pass by,' said the third crane. Any of the men of Ireland who saw them could not face equal combat on that day.

(Athirne) never ate his fill where anyone might see him. He went off with a fine pig and a bottle of mead, so that he could stuff himself alone. Then he saw a man approaching. 'You were going to do it alone,' he said, taking away the pig and the bottle. 'What is your name?' asked Athirne. 'It is not famous,' he said. 'Sethor Ethor Othor Sele Dele Dreng Gerce Mec Gerce Gér Gér Dír Dír, that is my name.' (Athirne) lost the pig (?), and could not make a satire on the name. It is likely that that was someone sent by God to take the pig, for from

---

2 The translation is of course only tentative. Note how the units of sense are connected by linking alliteration: the last word of each line alliterates with the first of the next in all cases except *tethra tráiges/ láthrach lóchet*, where each line alliterates internally. The main conceit in this recitation appears to be an identification of ale both with the fire for which Athairne's mother came to the house ('lantern of earth', 'place of lightning', 'woman of fire'), and with the flooding sea.

that time forward Athirne was no less hospitable than any other man.

• • • • • • • • • •

§76. Athairne & Amairgen from the *Book of Leinster*, Dublin ed., pp. 435–6
TRANS. JOHN CAREY

THERE WAS A FAMOUS BLACKSMITH AMONG THE ULAID NAMED Eccet Salach the smith. Echen was another name of his. He was an expert in every craft, so that never before or after was there a better smith. A son was born to him. Amairgen was his name. That son remained in childhood for fourteen years, without speaking. His belly swelled until it was the size of a great house (?); and it was sinewy, grey and corpulent. Snot flowed from his nose into his mouth. His skin was black. His teeth were white. His face was livid. His calves and thighs were like the two spouts of a blacksmith's bellows. His feet had crooked toes. His ankles were huge. His cheeks were very long and high. His eyes were sunken and dark red. He had long eyebrows. His hair was rough and prickly. His back was knobby, bony, rough with scabs. It was not the semblance of a comely person. He had for so long neglected to clean himself after defecating that his own excrement rose up to his buttocks. His favourite treats were boiled curds, sea salt, red blackberries, pale berries, burnt ears of grain, bunches of garlic, and 'one-eyed' nuts which he played with on the floor.

Athirne sent his servant Greth to Eccet Salach to order an ax. Greth saw that ignoble ugly monster before him on the floor of the house. He looked at him hostilely. Greth was frightened. Eccet's daughter was there, sitting in a well-made chair and wearing a handsome dress. She was alone, looking after the house, and the boy along with her. They heard the boy say something to Athirne's servant. He said, 'Does Greth eat curds?' (*In n-ith Greth gruth?*) three times. Greth made no reply, and was very frightened. Then he spoke to him again: 'A fair bush, a foul bush, bunches of garlic, hollow of a pine, apples . . . , curds. Does Greth eat curds?'

Greth fled out of the house so that he fell into the mud beyond the causeway of the fort. Then he went back to Athirne. 'You have seen warriors (?)' said Athirne; 'there is an ill look on you.' 'Well there might be,' said Greth. 'A boy who has never spoken in fourteen years spoke to me today; and that boy will deprive you of your rank unless he is destroyed.' 'What did he say to you?' asked Athirne. 'Not hard to tell,' said Greth: '"Does Greth eat curds?"' (and so forth). Athirne asked what kind of buildings were in the fort . . .

Soon Eccet returned. His daughter said to him, 'Amairgen spoke today to Athirne's servant, who came about the making of an ax.' 'What did he say to him?' ' "Does Greth eat curds?" ' (and so forth). 'This is what will come of it,' said Eccet: 'Athirne will come to kill the boy, lest he get the better of him; for the boy who said that will have great wisdom.'

Then the maiden left the fort, and the boy with her, and went to tend cattle of Sliab Mis to the south. Eccet made a clay image of the boy, and set it on his left, between himself and the bellows. He put a fine garment on it, and set it in a recumbent position, as if the boy were sleeping.

Then Athirne and his servant Greth came. They saw the boy sleeping. Their ax was made for them, and they were pleased (?), and he grasped its handle. Then Athirne brought it down upon the head of the image, as if it were the boy that was there; then they fled from the house, and an outcry was raised behind them.

The armies pursued them. Athirne gathered all his property into his fort, and then the fort was captured. The Ulaid came, and a settlement was made between them. The value of seven *cumals* ['slave women'], and his own honour-price, were given to Eccet, and agreements were made between them, and Athirne took the boy Amairgen in fosterage, and he learned expertise in poetry from him. That is how Athirne's seniority lapsed, and Amairgen became chief poet of the Ulaid.

• • • • • • • • • • •

§§77–78. Cú Chulainn & Senbecc

TRANS. JOHN CAREY

§77. Version A [ed. Kuno Meyer, *Revue Celtique* vi.182–4]

ONCE Cú Chulainn was beside the River Boyne in his chariot, and Lóeg mac Riangabra along with him, and the feat (*cles*) of nine champions was above him; he was killing the salmon in Linn Féic. They saw a little man in purple clothes, (sitting) in a bronze skiff, travelling (?) on the Boyne without rowing at all. Cú Chulainn set him and his boat on the palm of his hand. 'Here you are,' Cú Chulainn said. 'So it seems,' he said. 'I will give you my cloak and my tunic as a reward for my safety. They have a special property: they fit anyone, whether small or big. No one is drowned or burnt so long as he wears them. No deterioration will come upon them nor upon him who wears them, and every colour which anyone likes is on them.' 'I have them already,' Cú

Chulainn said. 'Take my shield and my spear, and no battle or combat will be gained against you; and you will never be wounded as long as the shield protects you.' 'I have them all,' Cú Chulainn said, 'in the hollow of my fist.' 'You are hard on me,' said Senbecc. 'What is that thing there?' asked Cú Chulainn. 'A little *timpán* (stringed musical instrument),' said Senbecc; 'shall I play it for you?' 'I would like that,' Cú Chulainn said. He drew his finger across it so that Cú Chulainn was lamenting at the wailing-strain. Then he played the laughing-strain until Cú Chulainn was carried away with laughter. He played the sleeping-strain so that Cú Chulainn fell into deep sleep and slumber from one hour until the next. Senbecc went home . . .

§78. Version B [ed. E. J. Gwynn, *Ériu* xiii.26–7]

SENBECC GRANDSON OF EBRECC, from the *síde*, came from the plain of Segais seeking *imbas* [supernatural enlightenment], and Cú Chulainn encountered him upon the River Boyne. Cú Chulainn captured him, and he explained that he had come looking for the fruit of the nuts of a fair-bearing hazel. There are nine fair-bearing hazels from whose nuts he got *imbas*: it used to drop into the wells, so that the stream bears the *imbas* into the Boyne. Then Senbecc sang to him some of his lore, and a song:

> I am not a lad, I am not a man,
> I am not a child in learning.
> The mysteries of God have made me gifted.
> I am Abcán, a sage of learning, a poet from Segais.
> Senbecc is my name, Ebrecc's grandson from the *síde*.

(These are the names of the nine hazels: Sall, Fall, Fuball, Finnam, Fonnam, Fofuigell, Crú, Crínam, Cruanbla.)

Then Senbecc offered great rewards to Cú Chulainn for letting him go free, and Cú Chulainn would not grant it. Then he stretched out his hand to his harp. He played him a wailing-strain, so that he was wailing and lamenting; he played him a laughing-strain so that he was laughing; and finally he played him a sleeping-strain so that he cast him into slumber. Then Senbecc escaped down the Boyne in a bronze boat.

§79. Cú Chulainn & Fedelm ed. Kuno Meyer, ZCP viii.120, TRANS. JOHN CAREY

CÚ CHULAINN WENT WITH HIS CHARIOTEER, LÓEG MAC RIANGABRA, to learn (?) *imbas* [supernatural enlightenment] at the Boyne. He had *fidchell* and *buanfach* [two board-games] with him in his chariot, and it was full of stones for casting; and he had a spear in his hand with a strap attached to it, for killing fish. He himself held the reins of his chariot.

Fedelm Foltchaín ['of the Lovely Hair'] and her husband Elcmaire came to the other bank of the Boyne. Elcmaire said to his wife, 'Overtake him [?], Fedelm!' Fedelm said, 'Let me see whether the man on the bench competes with his companion. Something is discovered between two men [?], with *fidchell*, with *buanfach*, with hunting birds on every slope.' Then [Cú Chulainn] spears a speckled salmon in the Boyne. Elcmaire went into the ford and cast [?] a four-sided pillar-stone so that the chariot shied at that [?]. Cú Chulainn hacked off his thumbs and big toes. Fedelm prophesied that she would be his lover for a year, and would show herself naked to the Ulaid before coming [to him]. She displayed herself a year and a day after that, so that that is what brought debility upon the Ulaid, &c.

* * * * * * * * * * * *

§80. *Scéla Muicce Meic Dá Thó*
The Story of Mac Dá Thó's Pig & Hound

TRANS. KUNO MEYER with modernisations and clarifications of language by the editor

¶ 1.

THERE WAS A FAMOUS LAND-HOLDER OF LEINSTER, MAC DÁ THÓ, Son of the Two Mutes was his byname. He had a hound that would run round all Leinster in one day. That hound's name was Ailbe, from this the Plain of Ailbe is so called. And of him it was said:

Mesroeda was Mac Dá Thó's name,
Who had the pig — no falsehood!
And Ailbe his famous cunning splendid hound,
From whom is the renowned plain of Ailbe.

Now Ireland was full of the fame and renown of that hound. Then to Mac Dá Thó came messengers from Medb and Ailill to ask him for his hound. But at the same time came messengers of Ulster and Conchobor to ask for the same hound. Welcome was made to them, and they were taken to Mac Dá Thó into the hostelry. This was one of the five hostelries of Ireland at that time, and there used to be boiling water in it always. There was the hostelry of Da Berga in Fir Cúalann in Leinster and the hostelry of Forgall Monach beside Lusk, and the hostelry of Da Reo in Brefne, and the hostelry of Da Choga in Westmeath. Seven doors there were in each hostelry, seven roads through it, and seven fireplaces in it. Seven cauldrons in the seven fireplaces. An ox and a salted pig would go into each of these cauldrons, and the man that came along the road would thrust the flesh fork into the cauldron, and whatever he brought up with the first thrust, that he would eat, and if nothing were brought up with the first thrust, there was no other for him.

¶ 2. The messengers were taken to Mac Dá Thó in the bed to be asked their pleasure before their ration was brought to them; and they said their messages. 'To ask for the hound we have come,' said the messengers of Connacht, 'from Ailill and from Medb, and in exchange for it there shall be given threescore hundred milch-cows at once, and a chariot with the two horses that are best in Connacht under it, and as much again at the end of the year besides all that.' 'We too have come to ask for it,' said the messengers of Ulster and Conchobor, 'and Conchobor is no worse friend than Ailill and Medb, and the same amount shall be given from the North, and be added to, and there will be good friendship from it continually.'

¶ 3. Mac Dá Thó fell into great silence, and was three days and nights without sleeping, nor could he eat food for the greatness of his trouble, but was moving about from one side to another. It was then his wife addressed him and said, 'Long is the fast in which you are. You have plenty of food, though you will not eat it.' And then she said:

> 'Sleeplessness was brought
> To Mac Dá Thó into his house,
> There was something on which he deliberated,
> Though he speaks to no one.
>
> He turns away from me to the wall,
> The hero of the Féni [Irish] of fierce valour,
> His prudent wife observes
> That her mate is without sleep.'

The man:

> 'Craumthann Nia Náir has said
> Do not trust your secret to women.
> A woman's secret is not well concealed,
> Wealth is not trusted to a slave.'

The woman:

'Why would you talk to a woman
If something were not amiss?
A thing that your mind will not penetrate,
Someone else's mind will penetrate.'

The man:

'The hound of Mesroeda Mac Dá Thó,
Evil was the day when they came for him,
Many fair men will fall for his sake,
More than one can tell will be the fights for him.
If to Conchobor it is not given,
Certainly it will be a churlish deed,
His hosts will not leave
Any more of cattle or of land.

If to Ailill it be refused,
All Ireland will . . . over the people,
The son of Mata will carry it off . . . .'

The woman:

'I have advice for you in this,
The result of which will not be bad,
Give it to them both,
No matter who will fall for it.'

The man:

'The advice that you give,
It does not make me glad,
. . .'

¶ 4. After that Mac Dá Thó arose, and gives himself a shake and said: 'Now bring us food, and let us and the guests who have come here be merry.' These stay with him for three days and three nights, and he went aside with them, namely, with the messengers of Connacht first, and he said to them: 'I was in great perplexity and doubt, and this is what has grown of it, that I have given the hound to Ailill and Medb, and let them come for it splendidly and proudly with as many warriors and nobles as they can get, and they will have drink and food and many gifts besides, and they will take the hound and be welcome.' Those messengers go out and were thankful.

He also went with the messengers of Ulster and said to them: 'After much doubting, I have given the hound to Conchobor, and let him and the flower of the province come for it proudly, and they will have many other gifts, and you will be welcome.'

¶ 5. But for one and the same day he had made his meeting with them all; nor was it neglected by them. So then two provinces of Ireland came and were in front of Mac Dá Thó's hostelry. He himself went to meet them and bade them welcome: 'You are welcome, warriors. Come inside into the enclosure.' Then they went beyond into the hostelry. One half of the house for the Connachtmen and the other half for the Ulstermen. That house was not a small one. Seven doors in it, and fifty beds between two doors. Those were not faces of friends at a feast, the people who were in that house, for many of them had injured another; for three hundred years before the birth of Christ there had been war between them. 'Let the pig be killed for them!' said Mac Dá Thó. Threescore milch cows had been feeding it for seven years. But on venom that pig had been reared, since on its account a slaughter of the men of Ireland was made.

¶ 6. Then the pig was brought to them, and there were sixty oxen drawing the one pig, besides their other food. Mac Dá Thó himself was attending on them. 'Welcome to you,' he said, 'and there is not to be found the like of such a quantity of food. We have many pigs and cows in Leinster, and what is lacking in our provision tonight, will be killed for you tomorrow.' 'The provision is good,' Conchobor said. There were nine men under the hurdle on which was the tail of the pig, and they had their load on it. 'The pig is good,' Conchobor said. 'It is good,' Ailill said. 'How shall the pig be divided, Conchobor?' Ailill asks. 'How would you wish to divide it,' Bricriu mac Carbaid says out of his chamber above, 'where the valourous warriors of the men of Ireland are, but by contest of arms, and let each of you therefore give a blow on the other's nose.' 'Let it be done so!' Ailill said. 'We are agreed!' Conchobor said, 'for we have lads in the house that have many a time gone round the border.'

¶ 7. 'There will be need of your lads tonight, Conchobor,' said a famous old warrior from Crúachna Conalath in the west. 'The roads of Luachair Dedad have often had their backs turned to them. Many a fat cow too have they left with me.' 'It was a fat cow you left with me,' said Munremar mac Gerrcind, 'none other than your own brother, Cruithne mac Ruaidlinde from Crúachna Conalath in Connacht.' 'He was no better,' Lugaid mac Con Roí said, 'than Ir-loth son of Fergus son of Leite, who was left [dead] by Echbél mac Dedad at Temair Luachra.' 'What sort of a man do you think he is?' said Celtchair son of Uthechar Hornskin, son of Deda, 'whom I slew myself and cut off his head!'

¶ 8. Each of them brought up his exploits in the face of the other, till at last it came to one man who beat everyone, namely Cet mac Mágach of Connacht.

He raised his prowess over the host, and took his knife in his hand and sat down by the pig. 'Now let there be found among the men of Ireland,' he said, 'one man to continue the contest with me, or let me divide the pig.'

¶ 9. There was not at that time found a warrior among the Ulstermen to stand up to him, and great silence fell upon them then. 'Prevent that for me, Lóegaire,' Conchobor said. 'It shall not be,' Lóegaire, 'Cet to divide the pig before the face of all of us.' 'Wait a little, Lóegaire,' Cet said, 'so that you may speak to me. For it is a custom with you Ulstermen that every youth among you who takes arms makes us his first goal. You too came to the border, and we met at the border, and you left charioteer and chariot and horses with me; and you then escaped with a lance through you. You will not get at the pig in that manner!' Lóegaire sat down on his couch.

¶ 10. 'It shall not be,' a tall fair warrior of Ulster said, coming out of the chamber above, 'that Cet divide the pig.' 'Who is this?' Cet said. 'A better warrior than you,' say all, 'namely Óengus son of Hand-wail of Ulster.' 'Why is his father called Hand-wail?' Cet said. 'We know not indeed,' everyone said. 'But I know,' Cet said. 'Once I went eastward. An alarm-cry is raised around me, and Hand-wail came up with me like everyone else. He makes a cast with a large lance at me. I make a cast with the same lance at him which struck off his hand, so that it was on the field before him. What brings the son of that man to stand up to me?' Cet said. Then Óengus sat down on his couch.

¶ 11. 'Still keep up the contest,' Cet says, 'or let me divide the pig.' 'It is not right that you divide it, Cet,' another tall fair warrior of Ulster said. 'Who is this?' Cet said. 'Éogan Mór son of Durthacht,' say all, 'king of Fernmag.' 'I have seen him before,' Cet said. 'Where have you seen me?' Éogan said. 'In front of your own house, when I took a drove of cattle from you. The alarm-cry was raised in the land around me. You met me and cast a spear at me so that it stood out of my shield. I cast the same spear at you, which passed through your head and struck your eye out of your head. And the men of Ireland see you with one eye ever since.' He sat down in his seat after that.

¶ 12. 'Still keep up the contest, Ulstermen,' Cet said, 'or let me divide the pig.' 'You will not divide it yet,' saith Munremar son of Gerrcend. 'Is that Munremar?' Cet said. 'It is he,' say the men of Ireland. 'It was I that last cleaned my hands in you, Munremar,' Cet said. 'It is not three days yet since out of your own land I carried off three warriors' heads from you together with the head of your first son.' Munremar sat down in his seat. 'Still the contest,' Cet said, 'or I shall divide the pig.' 'Indeed, you will have it,' a tall grey very terrible warrior of the Ulstermen said. 'Who is this? ' Cet asked. 'That is Celtchair son of Uithechar,' say all. 'Wait a little, Celtchair,' Cet said, 'unless you come to pound me to pieces. I came, Celtchair, to the front of your house. The alarm was raised around me. Everyone went after me. You came like everyone else, and going into a gap before me you threw a spear at me. I threw another spear at you which went through your loins and through the upper part of your testicles, so that you have had a urinary disability ever since, nor have either son nor daughter been born to you since.' After that Celtchair sat down in his seat. 'Still the contest,' Cet said, 'or I shall divide the pig.' 'You will have it,' Mend son of Sword-heel said. 'Who is this?' Cet said. 'Mend,' say all. 'What do you think,' Cet said, 'that the sons of churls with nicknames should come to contend with me? For it was I that was the priest who christened your father with that name, since it is I that cut off his heel, so that he carried but one heel away with him. What should bring the son of such a man to contend with me?' Mend sat down in his seat.

¶ 14. 'Still the contest,' Cet said, 'or I shall divide the pig.' 'You will have it,' said Cumscraid the Stammerer of Macha, son of Conchobor. 'Who is this?' 'That is Cumscraid,' say all. 'He has the making of a king for his figure. He earns no thanks from you,' the lad said. 'Well,' Cet said, 'you made your first raid to us. We met on the border. You left a third of your people with me, and thus you came away, with a spear through your throat, so that no word comes rightly over your lips, since the sinews of your throat were wounded, so that Cumscraid the Stammerer of Macha is your byname ever since.'

In that way he laid disgrace and a blow on the whole province.

¶ 15. While he made ready with the pig and had his knife in his hand, they saw Conall Cernach coming towards them into the house. And he sprang onto the floor of the house. The Ulstermen gave great welcome to Conall Cernach at that time. It was then Conchobor threw his helmet from his head and shook himself in his own place. 'We are pleased,' Conall said, 'that our portion is in readiness for us. Who divides for you?' 'One man of the men of Ireland has obtained by contest the dividing of it, namely, Cet mac Mágach.' 'Is that true, Cet?' Conall said, 'are you dividing the pig?' 'It is true indeed,' Cet said. Then Cet said to Conall:

'Welcome Conall, heart of stone,
Fierce glow of fire, glitter of ice,
Red strength of anger under a hero's breast,
Wound-inflicter, triumphant in battle,
I see the son of Findchoem.'

Then Conall said to Cet:

'Welcome Cet,
Cet mac Mágach, . . . of heroes,
Heart of ice, strong chariot-chief of battle,

Battling sea, fair shapely bull,
Cet mac Mágach!'

'Truly, it will be clear in our combat,' Conall said, 'and it will be clear in our-parting. There will be stories with . . . , there will be witness with . . . , for . . . the two men . . . in this house tonight.'

¶ 16. 'Get up from the pig, Cet!' Conall said. 'What brings you to it?' Cet said. 'It is so,' said Conall, 'that is to seek contest from me. Truly, I shall give you contest. I swear what my tribe swears, since I [first] took spear and weapons, I have never been a day without having slain a Connachtman, or a night without plundering, nor have I ever slept without the head of a Connachtman under my knee.' 'It is true,' Cet said, 'you are even a better warrior than I. If Anlúan mac Mágach were in the house,' said Cet, 'he would match you contest for contest, and it is a shame that he is not in the house tonight.' 'But he is,' said Conall, taking Anlúan's head out of his belt and throwing it at Cet's chest, so that a gush of blood broke over his lips. After that Conall sat down by the pig, and went from it.

¶ 17. 'Now let them come to the contest,' said Conall. Truly, there was not then found among the men of Connacht a warrior to stand up to him in contest, for they were loath to be slain on the spot. The Ulstermen made a cover around him with their shields, for there as an evil custom in the house, the people of one side throwing stones at the people of the other side. Then Conall went to divide the pig and took the end of its tail in his mouth until he had finished dividing the pig. He sucked up the whole tail, and a load for nine was in it, so that he did not leave a bit of it, and he cast its skin and membrane from him, *ut dixit poeta* [as the poet said]:

Before the hands on the body of a cart,
A load for nine its heavy tail.
While he was at the brave prosperous division,
Conall Cernach consumed it.

¶ 18. However, to the men of Connacht he gave no more but a quarter of the pig, or the to fore-legs of the pig. But their share of the pig seemed small to the men of Connacht. They rose up. Then from the other side arose the Ulstermen until each of them reached the other. Then there were blows over ear and head, so that the heap of the warriors' bodies on the floor was as high as the side of the house. For there were slain one thousand and four hundred armed men both of Ulster and Connacht, so that seven streams of blood and gore burst through the seven doors. Then the hosts burst through those doors and raised a great shout in the middle of the enclosure, and each one was striking and slaying the other. Then Fergus took the great oak that was in the middle of the enclosure to the men of Connacht, after having torn it from its roots. Others say that it was Cú Roí mac Dári who took the oak to them, and it was then that he came to them, for there was no man of Munster there before, except Lugaid, son of Cú Roí, and Cetin Pauci. When Cú Roí had come to them, he carried off alone one half of the pig with its back from Leth Cuinn. Then they broke forth from the enclosure into the field. They continued to fight in front of the enclosure.

¶ 19. Then Mac Dá Thó came out with the hound in his hand, and let him in amongst them to see which side he would choose. So the hound chose Ulster and set to tearing the men of Connacht greatly. Ailill and Medb went into their chariot, and their charioteer with them, and Mac Dá Thó let the hound after them, and they say it was in the Plains of Ailbe that the hound seized the pole of the chariot that was under Ailill and Medb. Then the charioteer of Ailill and Medb dealt the hound a blow so that he sent its body aside and the head of the hound remained on the pole of the chariot at Ibar Cinn Chon ['the Yew-tree of the Hound's Head'], from which Connacht takes its name. And they also say that from that hound Mag nAilbe ['the Plains of Ailbe'] are called, for Ailbe was the name of the hound.

¶ 20. This now is the road on which the men of Connacht went southward, namely over Belach Mugna, past Roíriu, past Áth Midbine in Maistiu, past Kildare, past Ráith Imgán into Feeguile, to Áth Mic Lugna, past Druim Dá Maige over Drochat Cairpri. There, at Áth Cind Chon ['Hound's Head Ford'] in Fir Bili, the head of the hound fell from the chariot. As they were going along Fróechmag of Meath eastward, Fer Loga, the charioteer of Ailill, lying in wait for them in the heather, jumped onto the chariot behind Conchobor and seized his head from behind. 'Conchobor', he said, 'I think you will not get out of here.' 'Your full will to you' Conchobor said. 'In truth, I do not want much from you,' said Fer Loga, 'for I want to be taken by you to Emain Macha, and the Ulster women and their maiden daughters shall sing their *cépóc* [?] around me every evening and shall all say: 'Fer Loga my darling,' &c. 'You shall have that,' Conchobor said. The maidens of Emain Macha had to do that, for they did not dare to do otherwise for [fear of] Conchobor. And on that day that a year had gone, he let him go back to the west at Athlone, and he had two horses of Conchobor's with him, with their golden bridles. But he did not get the *cépóca*, though he got the horses. And this is how Ulster and Connacht fell out about the hound of Mac Dá Thó and about his pig. FINIT.

◆ ◆ ◆ ◆ ◆ ◆ ◆ ◆ ◆ ◆ ◆

§81. *Fled Bricrenn* Bricriu's Feast[3]

INCIPIT Bricriu's Feast, & the Champion's Portion of Emain Macha, & the Ulster Women's Battle of Words, & the Hosting of the Ulstermen against the men of Cruachan Aí, and the Champion's Wager in Emain Macha.

¶ 1.   There was once a great feast held by Bricriu of the Posion Tongue for Conchobor mac Nessa and for all the Ulstermen. The preparation of the feast took a whole year. For the entertainment of the feast's guests a spacious house was built by him. Bricriu built it in Dún Rudraige so as to be like [the assembly hall] of the *Cráeb Ruad* ['Red Branch'] in Emain Macha; yet it surpassed that building for material and for artistic design, for beauty of architecture, its pillars and splendid and costly frontings, its magnificently framed carving and lintel-work, and it surpassed all building of those times.

¶ 2.   The House was made like this: on the plan of Tara's Mead-Hall, having IX compartments from the fire to the wall; each fronting of bronze was XXX feet high and all of them overlaid with gold. In the front area of the kingly house, a royal couch was set up for Conchobor above those of the whole [rest of the] house. It was set with carbuncles and other ornaments from every land that shined with a lustre of gold and of silver, gleaming with every colour, making night like day. Around it were placed the twelve couches of the twelve heroes of Ulster. The quality of the work was equal to that of the building's construction. It took a waggon team to carry each beam, and the strength of seven Ulstermen to fix each pole, and XXX of the chief artisans of Ireland were employed to assemble it and to arrange it.

¶ 3.   Then a 'sun-chamber' was made by Bricriu himself on a level with the couch of Conchobor [and as high as those] of the valorous heroes. The decorations of its fittings were majestic. Windows of glass were placed on each side of it, and one of these windows was above Bricriu's own couch, so that he could view the great house from his seat, because he knew the Ulstermen would not allow him into the house.

¶ 4.   When Bricriu had finished building his great house and its sun chamber, supplying it with quilts and blankets, beds and pillows, providing drink and food, so that nothing was lacking, neither furnishings nor food, he immediately

---

3   Based on the translation of *George Henderson*, Irish Texts Society, vol. ii, 1899, with extensive modernisations and clarifications of language by the editor. In numerous passages, the sense of the translation has been altered on the basis of Henderson's edited Irish text and the diplomatic edition of the manuscript *Lebor na hUidre* 246–77.

went to Emain Macha to meet Conchobor and the noblemen of Ulster about him.

¶ 5. It happened that on this day there was a gathering of the Ulstermen in Emain. He was then made welcome, and was seated by the shoulder of Conchobor. Bricriu addressed him as well as the body of the Ulstermen. 'Come with me,' Bricriu said, 'to share a banquet with me.' 'Gladly,' answered Conchobor, 'if that pleases the Ulstermen.' Fergus mac Róich and the nobles of Ulster also answered: 'No! For if we go our dead will outnumber our living, when Bricriu has incited us against each other.'

¶ 6. 'If you do not come, it will go worse for you,' said Bricriu. 'What then,' asked Conchobor, 'if the Ulstermen don't go with you?' 'I will stir up strife,' said Bricriu, 'between the kings, the leaders, the valorous heroes, and the free commoners, till they slay one another, man for man, if they do not come with me to share my feast.' 'We shall not do that to please you,' said Conchobor. 'I will stir up enmity between father and son so that it will come to mutual slaughter. If I do not succeed, I will make a quarrel between mother and daughter. If that does not succeed, I will set each of the Ulsterwomen at odds, so that they come to deadly blows till their breasts become loathsome and putrid.' 'Sure it is better to come,' said Fergus. 'Immediately take counsel with the chief Ulstermen,' said Sencha son of Ailill. 'Unless we take counsel against this Bricriu, the result will be misfortune,' Conchobor said.

¶ 7. Then all the Ulster nobles assembled in a council. In discussing the matter Sencha counselled them as follows: 'Take hostages from Bricriu, since you have to go with him, and put eight swordsmen about him so as to compel him to retire from the house as soon as he has laid out the feast.' Furbaide Ferbenn, son of Conchobor, brought Bricriu reply, and showed him the whole matter. 'It is happily arranged,' Bricriu said. The Ulstermen immediately set out from Emain, host, battalion and company, underking, chieftain and leader. Excellent and admirable the march of the brave and valiant heroes to the palace.

¶ 8. The hostages of the warriors had gone as security on his behalf, and Bricriu accordingly contemplated how he should bring the Ulstermen to discord. Once his deliberation and self-scrutiny ended, he went to the company of Lóegaire Buadach ['L. the Triumphant'], son of Connad mac Ilïach. 'Greetings now, Lóegaire Buadach, you mighty mallet of Brega, you hot hammer of Meath, flame-red thunderbolt, you victorious warrior of Ulster, what prevents the championship of Emain from being yours always?' 'If I choose, it shall be mine,' Lóegaire said. 'The sovereignty of the warriors of Ireland will be yours,' Bricriu said, 'if only you act as I advise.' 'I will indeed,' Lóegaire said.

¶ 9. 'Truly, if the champion's portion of my house might be yours, the championship of Emain is then yours forever. The champion's portion of my house is worth contesting, for it is not the portion of a fool's house,' Bricriu said. 'Belonging to it is a cauldron full of generous wine, with room enough for three of the valiant warriors of Ulster; furthermore, a seven-year-old boar: nothing has entered its lips since it was little except fresh milk and fine meal in springtime, curds and sweet milk in summer, the kernel of nuts and wheat in autumn, beef and broth in winter; a cow a whole seven years old: since it was a little calf neither heather nor twig-tops have entered its lips, nothing but sweet milk and herbs, meadow hay and corn. [Add to this] fivescore cakes of wheat, cooked in honey. Twenty-five bushels, that is what was supplied for these fivescore cakes, four cakes from each bushel. That is what the champion's portion of my house is like. And since you are the best hero among the Ulstermen, it is only justice to give it you, and I so wish it. By the end of the day, when the feast is spread out, let your charioteer get up, and it is to him the champion's portion will be given.' 'Dead men will be among them if it is not done in this way,' Lóegaire said. Bricriu laughed at that, because it pleased him.

¶ 10. When he was finished inciting Lóegaire Buadach to animosity, Bricriu went in to incite the company of Conall Cernach. 'Greetings to you, Conall Cernach, you are the hero of victories and of combats; the victories you have already scored over the heroes of Ulster are great. By the time the Ulstermen go across foreign frontiers you are a distance of three days and three nights in advance over many fords; you protect their rear when returning, so that [an assailant] may not spring past you, nor through you nor over you; what then would prevent the champion's portion of Emain being yours always?' Though his treachery was great dealing with Lóegaire, he showed twice as much in the case of Conall Cernach.

¶ 11. When he had satisfied himself with inciting Conall Cernach to quarrel, he went to Cú Chulainn. 'Greetings to you, Cú Chulainn, you victor of Brega, you bright banner of the Liffey, darling of Emain, beloved of wives and of maidens, for you today Cú Chulainn is no false name, for you are the champion of the Ulstermen, you ward off their great feuds and frays, you seek justice for each man of them; you alone attain what all the Ulstermen fail in; all the Ulstermen acknowledge that your bravery, your valour, and your achievements surpass theirs. Why then would you leave the champion's portion for another one of the Ulstermen, since no one of the men of Ireland is capable of contesting it against you?' 'By the god of my tribe,' Cú Chulainn said, 'whoever comes to contest it with me will lose his head.' After that Bricriu removed himself from them and followed the host as if no contention had been made among the heroes.

¶ 12. Then they entered the great house, and each one occupied his couch in it, king, prince, noble landholder, and young warrior. The half of Bricriu's hall was set apart for Conchobor and his retinue of valiant Ulster heroes; the other half [was reserved] for the ladies of Ulster attending on Mugan, daughter of Eochaid Fedlech, wife of King Conchobor. The following were those who attended upon Conchobor in the fore-part of the hall, namely, Fergus mac Róich, Celtchar son of Uthechar, Éogan son of Durthacht, and the two sons of the king, namely, Fiacha and Fiachaig, Fergna son of Findchóem, Fergus son of Leti, Cuscraid the Stammerer of Macha, son of Conchobor, Sencha son of Ailill, the three sons of Fiachach, namely, Rus and Dáre and Imchad, Munremar son of Gerrcind, Errge Echbél, Amairgene son of Ecit, Mend son of Salchad, Dubthach Dóel Ulad, Feradach Find Fechtnach, Fedelmid mac Ilair Chétaig, Furbaide Ferbend, Rochad son of Fathemon, Lóegaire Buadach [the Triumphant], Conall Cernach, Cú Chulainn, Connad son of Mornai, Erc son of Fedelmid, Illand son of Fergus, Fintan son of Nial, Cet[h]ernd son of Fintan, Fachtna son of Senc[h]ad, Conla the False, Ailill the Honey-tongued, Bricriu himself, the chief Ulster warriors, with the body of youths and artisans.

¶ 13. While the feast was being spread for them, the musicians and players performed. The moment Bricriu spread the feast with its savouries, he was ordered by the hostages to leave the hall. They immediately got up with drawn swords in their hands to expel him. Whereupon Bricriu and his followers went out to the balcony. Having arrived at the threshold of the great house, he called out, 'That Champion's Portion, as it is, is not the portion of a fool's house; give it to the Ulster hero you prefer for valour.' He left them then.

¶ 14. Then the servers rose up to serve the food. The charioteer of Lóegaire Buadach, namely, Sedlang mac Riangabra, then rose up and said to the servers: 'Assign to Lóegaire Buadach the Champion's Portion which is in your possession, because he alone is entitled to it before the other young warriors of Ulster.' Then Id mac Riangabra, charioteer to Conall Cernach, got up and spoke similarly. And Lóeg mac Riangabra spoke thus: 'Bring that to Cú Chulainn; it is no disgrace for all the Ulstermen to give it to him; it is he who is most valiant among you.' 'That's not true,' said Conall Cernach and Lóegaire Buadach.

¶ 15. They then got up upon the floor and took up their shields and seized their swords. They hacked at one another till half of the great house was an ambiance of fire with the [clash of] sword and spear edges, the other half was one white sheet from the enamel of the shields. Great alarm took hold of the hall; the valiant heroes shook; Conchobor himself and Fergus mac Róich became furious upon seeing the injury and the injustice of two men surrounding one, namely, Conall Cernach and Lóegaire Buadach attacking Cú Chulainn. There was no one among the Ulstermen who dared separate them till Sencha spoke to Conchobor: 'Part the men,' he said. (For at that period, among the Ulstermen, Conchobor was a god on earth.)

¶ 16. Then Conchobor and Fergus intervened, [the combatants] immediately let their hands drop to their sides. 'Do as I wish,' Sencha said. 'Your will shall be obeyed,' they responded. 'My wish, then,' Sencha said, 'is to divide the Champion's Portion tonight among all the host, and after that to decide about it according to the liking of Ailill mac Mágach, because it is considered un-lucky among the Ulstermen to close this assembly unless the matter is judged in Cruachan.' Then the feasting was resumed; they made a circle round the fire and got 'jovial' and made merry.

¶ 17. Bricriu, however, and his queen were in their sun balcony. From his couch the condition of the great house could be seen, and how things were going on there. He worked through his mind as to how he could contrive to get the women to quarrel as he had incited the men. When Bricriu had finished examining his mind, it just chanced as he could have wished that Fedelm of the Fresh Heart came from the great house with fifty women in her following, in high spirits. Bricriu observed her coming past him. 'Greetings to you tonight, wife of Lóegaire Buadach! Fedelm of the Fresh Heart is no false name for you because of your excellence of form and of wisdom and of lineage. Conchobor, king of a province of Ireland, is your father, Lóegaire Buadach your husband; I consider it no more than a small honour for you that any of the Ulster women might take precedence over you in entering the banqueting hall; it is only at your heel that all Ulster women should tread. If you come first into the hall tonight, you will enjoy the sovereignty of queenship forever over all the ladies of Ulster.' Fedelm then took a leap over three ridges outward from the hall.

¶ 18. After that came Lendabair, daughter of Éogan mac Derthacht, wife of Conall Cernach. Bricriu addressed her and spoke: 'Greetings to you, Lendabair; for you that is no false name; you are the darling and pet of all mankind on account of your grandeur and your radiance. As far as your spouse has outdone all the heroes of mankind in valour and in good looks, to an equal extent have you distinguished yourself above the women of Ulster.' Though the deceit he applied in the case of Fedelm was great, he used twice as much in the case of Lendabair.

¶ 19. Emer came out then with half-a-hundred women [in her following]. 'Greeting and hail to you, Emer, daughter of Forgall Manach, wife of the best mortal in Ireland! Emer of the Fair Hair is no false name for you; Ireland's kings and princes contend for you in jealous rivalry. As the sun surpasses the stars of heaven, just as much do you outshine the women of the whole world in form and shape and lineage, in youth and beauty and elegance, in good name and wisdom and eloquence.' Though his deceit in the case of the other ladies was great, in Emer's case he applied three times as much.

¶ 20. The three companies then went out till they met at one spot, that is, three ridges from the hall. None of them knew that Bricriu had incited them against each other. They returned immediately to the hall. Their carriage was even and graceful and easy on the first ridge; scarcely did one of them raise a foot past the other. But on the ridge following their steps were shorter and quicker. What's more, on the ridge next to the house it was with difficulty that each of them kept up with the other; so they raised their robes up to the curving of their buttocks competing in the attempt to go first into the hall. For what Bricriu said to each of them regarding the other was that whoever should enter first should be queen of the whole province. The amount of confusion caused then by the competition to enter the hall was at first like the noise of fifty chariots approaching. The whole great house shook and the warriors sprang to their arms and sought to kill one another inside.

¶ 21. 'Stay,' Sencha said, 'they are not enemies who have come; it is Bricriu who has set quarrelling the women who have gone out. By the god of my tribe, unless the hall is shut against them our dead will outnumber our living.' Then the doorkeepers closed the doors. Emer, daughter of Forgall Manach, wife of Cú Chulainn, because of her speed, outran the others and put her back against the door, and immediately called upon the doorkeepers before the other ladies [came], so that the men inside got up, each of them trying to open [the hall] for his own wife so that she might be the first to come in. 'Bad [look-out] tonight,' said Conchobor. He struck the silver sceptre that was in his hand against the bronze pillar of the couch and the people were seated. 'Stay,' Sencha said, 'it is not a warfare of arms that shall be held here; it will be a warfare of words.' Each woman went out under the protection of her husband, and the Ulsterwomen's war-of-words then followed.

¶ 22. Fedelm of the Fresh Heart, wife of Lóegaire Buadach, spoke:
'Born of a mother in freedom, one in rank and in race my elders;
sprung from loins that are royal, in the beauty of peerless breeding;
lovely in form I am reckoned, and noted for figure and comely,
fostered in warrior virtues, in the sphere of goodly demeanour:
Lóegaire's hand, all-noble, what triumphs it scores for Ulster!
Ulster's borderlands from foes, ever equal in strength, ever hostile
all by himself were they held: from wounds a defense and protection,
Lóegaire, more famous than heroes, in number of victories greater,
why should Fedelm the lovely not step first into the mead-hall so festive,
shapelier than all other women, triumphant and jealous of conquest?'

¶ 23. Then spoke Lendabair, daughter of Éogan mac Derthacht, wife of Conall Cernach, son of Amairgen:

'Mine is an aspect of beauty also, of reason, with grace of deportment,

finely and fairly stepping in front of the women of Ulster,
see me step to the mead-hall, my spouse and my darling Conall.
Big is his shield and triumphant, majestic his gait and commanding,
up to the spears of the conflict, in front of them always he strides:
back to me comes he proudly, with heads in his hands as his trophies;
swords he brings together for the clashing in conflict of Ulster;
guardian of every ford's way, he destroys them too at his pleasure;
fords he defends from enemies, he avenges the wrongful attack,
holds himself as a hero upon whom shall be raised a tombstone:
son of noble Amairgen, his is the courage that speaks;
many the arts of Conall and therefore he leads the heroes.
Lendabair, great is her glory, in everyone's eye is her splendour;
why not the first when she enters in such a queenly way the hall of a king?'

¶ 24. Emer, daughter of Forgall Manach, wife of Cú Chulainn, spoke:

'I am the standard of women, in figure, in grace and in wisdom;
none is my equal in beauty, for I am a picture of graces.
A presence fully noble and good, my eye like a jewel that flashes;
figure, or grace, or beauty, or wisdom, or bounty, or chastity,
joy of sense, or of loving, none has ever been likened to mine.
Ulster is sighing for me, a nut of the heart I am clearly
(now if I were welcoming or wanton, no husband would be yours
    tomorrow.)
My spouse is the hound of Culann, and not a hound that is feeble;
blood is spurting from his spear, his sword is dripping with life-blood;
his body is fashioned finely, but his skin is gaping with gashes,
there are many wounds on his thigh, but his eye looks westward nobly;
the dome he supports is always bright, and his eyes are always red,
the frames of his chariot are red, and red also are the cushions;
fighting from ears of horses and over the breaths of men folk,
springing in air like a salmon when he springs the spring of the heroes,
he performs the rarest of feats, he leaps the leap that is bird-like,
bounding over pools of water, he performs the feat of nine men;
battles of bloody battalions, he hews down the world's proud armies,
beating down kings in their fury, mowing the hosts of enemies.
Others I reckon to be deficient, shamming the pangs of women,
Ulster's precious heroes compared with my spouse Cú Chulainn.
He may be likened to blood, to blood that is clear and noble,
they to the scum and the garbage, I reckon their value to be deficient;
shackled and shaped like cattle, as cows and oxen and horses,
Ulster's precious women beside the wife of Cú Chulainn.'

¶ 25. The men in the hall behaved in the following manner after they had heard the praising speeches of the women: Lóegaire and Conall each sprang into his hero's light [a halo-like aura of heroic fury], and broke a post of the great house as tall as themselves, so that in this way their wives came in. Moreover, Cú Chulainn heaved up the great house just over against his bed, till the sky's stars were to be seen from underneath the wattlework [of the hall's wall]. Through that opening his own wife came with half-a-hundred women attendants in her following, and likewise half-a-hundred following each of the other two. Other ladies could not be compared with Emer, while no one at all was to be likened to her spouse. Then Cú Chulainn let the great house down till seven feet of the wattle entered the ground; the whole fortification [*dún*] shook, and Bricriu's balcony was laid flat to the earth, so that Bricriu and his queen toppled down till they fell into the ditch in the middle of the courtyard among the dogs. 'Woe is me,' cried Bricriu, as he hastily got up, 'enemies have come into the great house.' He took a turn round and saw how it was lopsided and all tilted to one side. He wrung his hands, then went in, so splattered that none of the Ulster folk could recognise him. It was only from his manner of speech that they knew him.

¶ 26. Then from the floor of the house Bricriu spoke: 'Alas! that I have prepared you a feast, Ulstermen. My house is more to me than all my other possessions. It is, therefore, a *geis* [a sworn tabu] not to drink, or to eat, or to sleep till you leave my house as you found it on your arrival.' Then all the valiant Ulstermen went out of the house and tried to tug it, but they did not raise it so much that even the wind could pass between it and the earth. That matter was a difficulty for the Ulstermen. 'I have no suggestion for you,' Sencha said, 'except that you ask the one who has left it lopsided to set it upright.'

¶ 27. With that the Ulstermen told Cú Chulainn to restore the house to its upright position, and Bricriu spoke then: 'O king of the heroes of Ireland, if you don't set it straight and erect, none in the world can do so.' All the Ulstermen then entreated Cú Chulainn to solve the matter. So that the participants in the feast might not be denied food or ale, Cú Chulainn got up and then tried to lift the house with a tug and failed. With that, a warp-spasm came over him, while a drop of blood was at the root of each single hair, and he absorbed his hair into his head, so that, looked on from above, his dark-yellow curls seemed as if they had been shorn by scissors. And taking on the motion of a millstone he strained himself till a warrior's foot could fit between each pair of ribs.

¶ 28. His natural capabilities and fiery vigour returned to him, and then he heaved the house up and set it so that it arrived at its previous levelness. After that, consuming the feast was pleasant to them, with the kings and the chieftains on one side around the famous Conchobor, the noble high-king of Ulster.

Further, the queens were on the other side: Mugan Aitencaetrech, daughter of Eochaid Fedlech, wife of Conchobor mac Nessa, Fedelm of the Nine-shapes, daughter of Conchobor—she could assume nine shapes, and each shape more lovely than the other—also Fedelm of the Fair Hair, another daughter of Conchobor, wife of Lóegaire Buadach; Findbec, daughter of Eochaid, wife of Cethirnd, son of Fintan; Bríg Brethach, wife of Celtchar, son of Uthichar; Findige, daughter of Eochaid, wife of Éogan mac Durthacht; Findchóem, daughter of Cathbad, wife of Amairgen of the Iron Jaw, and Derborcall (Devorgilla), wife of Lugad of the Red Stripes, son of Tri Find Emna; Emer of the Fair Hair, daughter of Forgall Manach, wife of Cú Chulainn, son of Sualdam; Lendabair, daughter of Éogan mac Durthacht, wife of Conall Cernach; Niab, daughter of Celtchar mac Uthechar, wife of Cormac Connlongus, son of Conchobor. It would be too much to recount and to detail the other noble women besides these.

¶ 29. Once more the hall became a clamour of words, the women acclaiming their men. Then Conall and Lóegaire and Cú Chulainn tried to stir up dissension. Sencha, son of Ailill, got up and shook his sceptre. The Ulstermen listened to him, and then he spoke to restrain the ladies:

'I restrain you, ladies of Ulster, noble in name and in glory;
cease your words of contention, so that the appearance of the men would
    not be paler,
striving in the keenness of conflict, amid vainglorious combat;
through guile of women, it seems to me, men's shields are liable to splinter,
in frays the hosts of the heroes are often contending in anger;
to woman's whims one may ascribe this use and habit among men folk
they bruise what will not heal and attack what they have not achieved:
gallant and glorious heroines, and noble ones, I restrain you.'

¶ 30. Then Emer spoke in answer:

'Fitting for me, it seems, to speak as the wife of a hero
who combines in natural union graces of mind and of body,
ever since his teaching was finished, and learning came easy to him.4
None will be found who will equal his age, his growth, and his splendour:
of a long-descended lineage, he speaks with grace and with order;

---

4 A list of Cú Chulainn's feats follows here. In most instances, it is uncertain what exactly the description refers to. The following are Henderson's attempts at literal renderings: over-breath-feat, apple-feat, ghost- (or sprite-) feat, screw-feat, cat-feat, valiant-champion's whirling-feat, barbed spear, quickstroke, mad roar, heroes' fury, wheel-feat, sword-edge-feat, climbing against spike-pointed things (or places) and straightening his body on each of them.

a brave and a valiant hero, he fights in the tumult like a fury,
with deft aim and so agile, and quick and sure at hunting;
and find you a man among men folk, a mould that may match with Cú Chulainn!'

¶ 31. 'Truly, lady,' said Conall Cernach, 'let that lad of feats come here that we may question him.' 'No,' Cú Chulainn said. 'I am weary and worn out today. I will not hold a duel till after I have had food and sleep.' In truth it was really so, as it was the day on which he had fallen in with [his steed] the Grey of Macha, by the side of the Grey Pool at Sliab Fuait. When it came out of the loch, Cú Chulainn crept up to it and put his two hands around the steed's neck till the two of them were wrestling, and in that way they made a circuit of Ireland, until on that night Cú Chulainn came chasing with his steed to Emain. He got the Black Sainglenn in the same manner from the Lake of the Black Sainglenn.

¶ 32. It was then Cú Chulainn spoke as follows: 'Today the Grey and I have visited the great plains of Ireland, namely, Brega of Meath, the seashore marsh of Muirthemne Macha, Mag Medba, Currech Cleitech Cerna, Lia of Linn Locharn, Fea Femen Fergna, Urros Domnand, Ros Roigne (? . . .) Eo. And more than anything I want to sleep and to eat. By the god of my tribe I swear it would be no more than fun and frolic for me to fight a duel if I had my fill of food and of sleep.' ('Well,' Bricriu said, 'this has lasted long enough. The Feast of Bricriu has to be celebrated; let food and ale be taken at once, and let the women's warfare be stopped till the feast is over.' This was done, and it was a pleasant (time) for them till the end of three days and three nights.)

¶ 33. Again it happened that they quarrelled about the Champion's Portion. Conchobor came among the nobles of Ulster trying to settle the adjudication of the heroes. 'Go to Cú Roí mac Dári, the man who will intervene,' said Conchobor. It was then he spoke: 'Ask that hardy man, because Cú Roí mac Dári is better than all other men in the advice he gives, and the judgement he gives is true. He is fair, not given to falsehood, but good and a lover of justice. He has a noble mind and is a guest-friend; he has a skilled hand like a hero and is like high king in leading; he will judge you truly. It requires courage to ask him.'

¶ 34. 'I accept that then,' Cú Chulainn said. 'I allow it then,' Lóegaire said. 'Let us go then,' Conall Cernach said. 'Let horses be brought to us and your chariot yoked, Conall,' Cú Chulainn said. 'Woe is me !' Conall cried. 'Everyone,' Cú Chulainn said, 'knows well the clumsiness of your horses and the unsteadiness of your going and of your outfit; your chariot's movement is very burdensome; each of the two wheels raises turf every way your big chariot turns, so that for the space of a year there is a well marked track easily recognised by the warriors of Ulster.'

¶ 35. 'Do you hear that, Lóegaire?' Conall said. 'Woe is me,' Lóegaire said. 'But I am not to blame or to reproach. I am nimble at crossing fords, and more, to brave the storm of spears, outdoing the warriors of Ulster. Don't put the precedence of kings on me till I practise going before kings and champions against single chariots in strait and difficult places, in woods and on confines, till the champion of a single chariot would not try to come against me.'

¶ 36. Then Lóegaire had his chariot yoked and he leapt into it. He drove over the Plain of the Two Forks, over the Gap of the Watch, over the Ford of Fergus's Chariot, over the Ford of the Mórrígan to the Rowan Meadow of the Two Oxen in the Fews of Armagh (Clithar Fidbaidi), by the Meeting of the Four Ways past Dundalk, across Mag Slicech, westwards to the slope of Brega. A dim, dark, heavy mist overtook him, confusing him so that it was impossible for him to go farther on the way. 'Let us stay here,' Lóegaire said to his charioteer, 'until the mist clears up.' Lóegaire came down from his chariot, and his gillie [subordinate, charioteer] put the horses into the meadow that was near at hand.

¶ 37. While there, the gillie saw a huge giant approaching him. His appearance was beautiful: broad[-shouldered] and fat-mouthed, with sack eyes too and a bristly face; ugly, wrinkled, with bushy eyebrows; hideous and horrible and strong; stubborn, violent, and haughty; fat and puffing; with big sinews and a strong forearm, bold and audacious and uncouth. A shorn black patch of hair on him, a dun covering around him, a tunic over it to the ball of his rump; on his feet old tattered brogues, on his back a heavy club like the wheel-shaft of a mill.

¶ 38. 'Whose horses are these, gillie?' he asked, as he gazed furiously at him. 'The horses of Lóegaire Buadach.' 'Yes! a fine fellow!' And as he spoke this way, he brought down his club on the gillie and gave him a blow from top to toe. The gillie gave a cry, with that Lóegaire came up. 'What is this you are doing to the lad?' asked Lóegaire. 'It is a penalty for damage to the meadow,' said the giant. 'I will come myself then,' Lóegaire said. They struggled together. Lóegaire then fled till he reached Emain, after having left his horses and gillie and arms.

¶ 39. Not long after that Conall Cernach took the same way and arrived at the plain where the druidical mist overtook Lóegaire. The same hideous black, dark cloud overtook Conall Cernach, so that he was unable to see either heaven or earth. With that, Conall there leapt out and the gillie unharnessed the horses in the same meadow. Not long after that he saw the same giant [coming] towards him. He asked him whose servant he was. 'I am servant to Conall Cernach,' he said. 'A good man,' said the giant, as he raised his hands till they gave a blow to the gillie from top to toe. The fellow yelled. Then Conall came, and he and the giant got to close quarters. The wrestling moves of the giant were stronger.

Conall fled, as Lóegaire had done, having left behind his charioteer and his horses, and came to Emain.

¶ 40. Cú Chulainn then went by the same way till he came to the same place. The same dark mist overtook him as had fallen upon the two before him. Cú Chulainn sprang down, and Lóeg brought the horses into the meadow. He had not long to wait till he saw the same man coming towards him. The giant asked him whose servant he was. 'Servant (companion) to Cú Chulainn.' 'A good man,' said the giant, plying him with the club. Lóeg yelled. Then Cú Chulainn arrived, and he and the giant came to close quarters, and each of them pounded the other. The giant got worsted. He forfeited horses and charioteer, and Cú Chulainn brought along with him his fellow [contestant]'s horses, charioteers, and accoutrements, till he reached Emain in triumph. He gave them to their rightful owners.

¶ 41. 'The Champion's Portion is yours,' Bricriu said to Cú Chulainn. 'I knew well from your deeds that you are not on a par with Cú Chulainn.' 'Not true, Bricriu,' they said, 'for we know it is one of his friends from the Otherworld that came to him to play us an evil trick and compete with us for the championship. We shall not give up our claim on that account.' The Ulstermen, with Conchobor and Fergus, failed to produce a settlement. They sent them either to go to Cú Roí mac Dári, or else to go to Cruachan, to Ailill and to Medb.

¶ 42. (So, in one place the Ulstermen assembled in council concerning the heroes. The three were similarly arrogant and overbearing. The conclusion the Ulster nobles in Conchobor's following arrived at was to accompany the heroes and have the difficulty judged at the habitation of Ailill mac Mágach and of Medb of Cruachan Aí) with reference to the Champion's Portion and the mutual rivalry of the women. The progress of the Ulstermen to Cruachan was fine and lovely and majestic. Cú Chulainn, however, remained behind the host entertaining the Ulster ladies, [performing] nine feats with apples, nine with javelins and nine with knives, so that one did not interfere with the other.

¶ 43. Lóeg mac Riangabra then went to the place of feats to speak with him and said: 'You sorry simpleton, your valour and bravery have passed away, the Champion's Portion has gone from you; the Ulstermen have reached Cruachan a long while ago.' 'Indeed we have not noticed it at all, Lóeg my friend. Yoke us the chariot then,' Cú Chulainn said. Lóeg accordingly yoked it and off they started on their journey. By that time the Ulstermen had reached Mag Breg. Cú Chulainn, having been incited by his charioteer, advanced with such speed from Dún Rudraige, the Grey of Macha and the Black Sainglenn racing in this way with his chariot across the whole province of Conchobor, across Sliab Fuait and across the Plain of Brega, that the third chariot arrived first in Cruachan.

¶ 44. Due to the swiftness and the reckless speed with which all the valiant Ulstermen reached Cruachan under [the lead of] Conchobor and the body of princes, a great shaking took hold of Cruachan, till the war-arms fell from the partitions to the ground, and also took hold of the entire host of the stronghold, till the men in the royal keep were like rushes in a stream. Medb then spoke: 'Since the day I took up home in Cruachan I have not until now heard thunder when there are no clouds.' Then Findabair, daughter of Ailill and of Medb, went to the sun balcony over the high porch of the keep. 'Mother dear,' she said, 'I see a chariot coming along the plain.' 'Describe it,' Medb said, 'its form, appearance and style; the colour of the horses; how the hero looks and how the chariot runs.'

¶ 45. 'Truly, I see,' said Findabair, 'the two horses that are in the chariot. Two fiery dappled greys, alike in colour, shape and excellence, alike in speed and swiftness, prancing side by side. Ears pricked, head erect, of high mettle and strongly bounding pace. Nostril fine, mane flowing, forehead broad, full dappled; very slim of girth and broad-chested, manes and tails curled, they career along. A chariot of fine wood . . ., having two black revolving wheels (and two beautiful pliant reins). Its rear shafts are hard and straight as a sword. Its swift frame is new and freshly polished, its curved yoke is silver-mounted. Two rich yellow looped reins. In the chariot a fair man with long curling hair; his tresses tri-coloured: brown at the skin, blood-red at the middle, like a diadem of yellow gold is the hair at the tips. Three halos encircle his up-turned head, each merging into the other. A soft crimson tunic is around him, having five stripes of glittering gold. A shield spotted and indented, with a bright edge of bronze. A barbed five-pronged javelin flames at his wrist. An awning of the rare plumage of birds is over his chariot's frame.'

¶ 46. 'We recognise that man,' Medb said, 'from his description.'
    'Peer of kings, an old disposer of conquest,
    a fury of war, a fire of judgement,
    a flame of vengeance; in mien a hero,
    in face a champion, in heart a dragon;
    the long knife of proud victories which will hew us to pieces;
    the all-noble, red-handed Lóegaire;
    the vigour that cuts the leek with the sword-edge is his
    the back-stroke of the wave to the land.'

'By the god of my people,' Medb said, 'I swear if it is with fury of hostile feeling Lóegaire Buadach comes to us, that like as leeks are cut to the ground by a sharp knife, so will be the intensity of the slaughter he will inflict on us, whatever our number at Cruachan Aí, unless his glowing fury, wrath and high-purpose are guarded against and soothed in accordance with his very wish.'

¶ 47. 'Mother dear,' the daughter said, 'I see then another chariot coming along the plain, not a bit inferior to the first.' 'Describe it,' Medb said. 'Truly I see,' she said, 'in the chariot, on the one hand, a roan spirited steed, swift, fiery and bounding, with broad hoof and expanded chest, taking strong vigorous strides across fords and estuaries, over obstacles and winding roads, scouring plains and vales, raging with triumph. Judge it from the likenesses of soaring birds, among which my very quick eye gets lost from their most straight coursing on a lofty course. On the other a bay horse, with broad forehead, heavy locks and wavy tresses; of light and long dashing pace; of great strength; altogether swiftly he courses the bounds of the plain, between stone enclosures and fastnesses. He encounters no obstacle in the land of oaks, coursing on the way. A swift chariot of fine wood, on two bright wheels of bronze; its pole bright with silver mounting; its frame very high and creaking, having a curved, firmly mounted yoke with two rich yellow looped reins. In the chariot a fair man with wavy hanging hair. His countenance is white and red, his jerkin clean and white, his mantle of blue and crimson red. His shield is brown with yellow bosses, its edge veined with bronze. In his hand flames a fiery, furious spear. And an awning of the rare plumage of birds over the swift frame of his chariot.'

¶ 48. 'We recognise the man from his description,' Medb said.

'A lion that groans, a flame of Lug, that diamonds can pierce;
a wolf among cattle; battle on battle,
exploit upon exploit, head upon head he heaps;
as a trout on red sandstone is cut
would the son of Findchóem cut us; should he rage against us—no peace!

By my tribe's god, as a speckled fish is cut upon a shining red stone with flails of iron, such I swear will be the small bits from the damage Conall Cernach will execute on us should he rage against us.'

¶ 49. 'I see another chariot coming along the plain.' 'Give us its description,' Medb said. 'I see, in truth,' the daughter said, 'two steeds, alike for size and beauty, fierceness and speed, bounding together, with ears pricked, head erect, spirited and powerful . . . with fine nostril, long tresses and broad foreheads, full dappled, with girth full slim and chest expanded, mane and tail curled, dashing along. Yoked in the chariot, the one, a grey steed, with broad thighs, eager, swift and fleet, wildly impetuous, with long mane and broad haunches, thundering and trampling, mane curled, head on high, breast broadly expanded. From out of the hard course he fiercely casts up clods of earth from his four hard hoofs, a flock of swift birds in pursuit. As he gallops on the way a flash of hot breath darts from him; from his bridled jaws gleams a blast of flame-red fire.

¶ 50. 'The other horse, dark-grey, head firmly knit, compact, fleet, broad-hoofed, and slender. Firm, swift, and of high mettle, with curl and plait and tress, broad of back and sure of foot, lusty, spirited and fiery, he fiercely bounds and fiercely strides the ground. Mane and tail long and flying, heavy locks down his broad forehead. Grandly he runs the country after winning the horse-race. Soon he bounds the river valleys, casts off fatigue, traverses the plains of the Mid Glen, finding no obstacle in the land of oak, coursing the way. A swift chariot of fine wood, having two yellowish iron wheels and a bright silver pole with bright bronze mounting. A frame very high and creaking, with metal fastenings. A curved yoke richly gilt, two rich yellow looped reins. The back shafts hard and straight as sword-blades.

¶ 51. 'In the chariot a sad, melancholy man, comeliest of the men of Ireland. Around him a soft crimson pleasing tunic, fastened across the breast, where it stands open, with a salmon-brooch of inlaid gold, against which his bosom heaves, beating in full strokes. A long-sleeved linen kirtle with a white hood, embroidered red with flaming gold. Set in each of his eyes eight red dragon gem-stones. His two cheeks blue-white and blood-red. He emits sparks of fire and burning breath, (with a ray of love in his look. A shower of pearls, it seems to me, has fallen into his mouth. Each of his two eyebrows as black as the side of a black spit. On his two thighs rests a golden-hilted sword, and fastened to the copper frame of the chariot is a blood-red spear with a sharp tempered blade on a shaft of wood well fitted to his hand. Over both his shoulders a crimson shield with a rim of silver, chased with figures of animals in gold. He leaps the hero's salmon-leap into the air and does many similar swift feats besides. Such a man is the chief of a royal chariot.) Before him in that chariot there is a charioteer, a very slender, tall, much freckled man. On his head very curly bright-red hair, with a fillet of bronze upon his brow which prevents the hair from falling over his face. On both sides of his head cups of gold confine the hair. A shoulder-mantle about him with sleeves opening at the two elbows, and in his hand a goad of red gold with which he guides the horses.'

¶ 52. 'Truly, it is a drop before a shower; we recognise the man from his description,' Medb said.

'An ocean fury, a whale that rages, a fragment of flame and fire;
a majestic bear, a grandly moving billow,
a beast in maddening anger:
in the crash of glorious battle
through the hostile foe he leaps,
his shout the fury of doom;
a terrible bear, he is death to the herd of cattle,
feat upon feat, head upon head he heaps:
praise the hearty one, he who is a complete victor.

As fresh malt is ground in the mill shall we be ground by Cú Chulainn.'

'By the god of my tribe,' Medb said, 'I swear if it is in fury that Cú Chulainn comes to us, unless his fury and violence are quelled, he will grind us to mould and gravel just like a ten-spoked mill grinds very hard malt. It would even be so though the whole province is around us [protecting us] in Cruachan.'

¶ 53. 'How do they come this time?' Medb said.

'Wrist to wrist and palm to palm,
tunic to tunic they stand,
shield to shield and frame to frame,
a shoulder-to-shoulder band,
wood to wood and car to car,
thus they all, fond mother, are.'

'As thunder on the roof when breaking,
the chargers dash with speed,
as heavy seas which storms are shaking,
the earth in turn they crash;
then it vibrates as they strike,
their strength and weight are like and like.
High is their name, no ill fame!'

Then Medb spoke:

'Women to meet them, and many, undressed,
full-breasted and bare and beautiful, in great number;
bring vats of cold water where they are needed, beds ready for rest,
bring forth fine food, and not scanty, but of the best,
strong ale, sound and well malted, warriors' keep;
let the gates of the stronghold be set ajar, open the enclosure.
Welcome! the battalion that's cantering won't kill us!'

¶ 54. Then Medb went out by the high door of the great house into the court, three times fifty maidens in her following, with three vats of cold water for the three valiant heroes in front of the hosts, in order to alleviate their heat. Choice was immediately given them to determine whether separate houses should be allocated them or one house among the three. 'To each a separate house,' Cú Chulainn said. After that those that they preferred of the 150 girls were brought into the house, fitted up with beds of surpassing magnificence. Findabair in preference to any other was brought by Cú Chulainn into the apartment where he himself was. On the arrival of the Ulstermen, Ailill and Medb went with their whole household and wished them welcome. 'We are pleased,' responded Sencha son of Ailill.

¶ 55. Then the Ulstermen came into the fort and the great house was left to them as recounted, that is, seven circles and seven compartments from the fire to the partition, with bronze frontings and carvings of red yew. Three stripes of bronze in the arching of the house, which was of oak, with a covering of shingles. It had twelve windows with glass in the openings. The dais of Ailill and of Medb was in the centre of the house, with silver frontings and stripes of bronze round it, with a silver wand by the fronting facing Ailill, that would reach the mid 'hips' of the house so as to contain the people inside without limit. The Ulster heroes went around from one door of the great house to the other, and the musicians played while the guests were being prepared for. Such was the spaciousness of the house that it had room for the hosts of valiant heroes of the whole province in the suite of Conchobor. Moreover, Conchobor and Fergus mac Róich were in Ailill's compartment with nine valiant Ulster heroes besides. Great feasts were then prepared for them and they were there until the end of three days and of three nights.

¶ 56. After that Ailill inquired of Conchobor with his Ulster following what was the purpose of his advancing [to Cruachan]. Sencha told the story of why they had come, that is, the rivalry of three heroes for the Champion's Portion, and the ladies' rivalry over precedence at feasts 'They could not stand being judged anywhere else than here by you.' At that Ailill was silent and was not in a happy mood. 'Indeed,' he said, 'it is not to me this decision should be given as to the Champion's Portion, unless it is being done from hatred.' 'There is really no better judge.' 'Well,' Ailill said, 'I require time to consider.' 'We really require our heroes,' Sencha said, 'for their value is great to timid folks.' 'For that then three days and three nights are what I need,' Ailill said. 'That would not forfeit friendship,' answered Sencha. The Ulstermen immediately said farewell; being satisfied, they left their blessing with Ailill and Medb and their curse with Bricriu, because it was he who had incited them to strife. They then departed from the territory of Medb, having left Lóegaire and Conall and Cú Chulainn to be judged by Ailill. The same sort of supper as before was given to each of these heroes every night.

¶ 57. One night as their portion was assigned them, three cats from the Cave of Cruachan were let loose to attack them, i.e., three beasts of magic.[5] Conall and Lóegaire made for the rafters, having left their food with the beasts. In that way they slept till the next day. Cú Chulainn did not flee from his place from the beast which attacked him. But when it stretched its neck out for eating, Cú Chulainn gave a blow with his sword on the beast's head, but [the blade] glided off as if it were striking stone. Then the cat set itself down. In the

---

5   The cave of Cruachan, nr. Connacht's court, is a place with otherworldly and, in a Christian sense, even diabolical, associations in Irish tradition.

circumstances Cú Chulainn neither ate nor slept. As soon as it was early morning the cats were gone. The three heroes were seen in such a condition the next day. 'Isn't that trial enough to judge you?' asked Ailill. 'By no means,' said Conall and Lóegaire, 'it is not against beasts we are striving, but against men.'

¶ 58. Ailill having gone to his chamber, set his back against the wall. His mind was agitated, because he took the difficulty that faced him to be filled with danger. He neither ate nor slept till the end of three days and three nights. 'Coward!' Medb called him then, 'if you don't decide, I will.' 'It is difficult for me to judge them,' Ailill said; 'it is a misfortune for one [hero] to have to do it.' 'There is no difficulty,' Medb said, 'for Lóegaire and Conall Cernach are as different as bronze and *findruini* [a pale precious metal]; Conall Cernach and Cú Chulainn as different as *findruini* and red gold.'

¶ 59. It was then, after she had pondered her advice, that Lóegaire Buadach was summoned to Medb. 'Welcome, Lóegaire Buadach,' she said; 'it is fitting to give you a Champion's Portion. We assign to you the sovereignty of the heroes of Ireland from this time forth, and the Champion's Portion, and a cup of bronze with a bird chased in white metal on its bottom. In preference to everyone else, take it with you as a token of award. No one else is to see it till, at the day's end, you have come to the Red Branch [hall] of Conchobor. When the Champion's Portion is being displayed among you, then you shall bring your cup out in the presence of all the Ulster nobles. Moreover, the Champion's Portion is in it. None of the valiant Ulster heroes will dispute it further with you. For the thing you are to take away with you shall be a token of genuineness in the estimation of all the Ulstermen.' Then the cup full of luscious wine was given to Lóegaire Buadach. There and then he drank the contents at a draught. 'Now you have the feast of a champion,' Medb said. 'I wish you may enjoy it a hundred hundred years at the head of all Ulster.'

¶ 60. Lóegaire then said farewell. Then Conall Cernach likewise was summoned into the royal presence. 'Welcome,' Medb said, 'Conall Cernach, fitting it is to give you a Champion's Portion, with a cup of white-metal besides, having a bird on the bottom of it chased in gold.' After that the cup was given to Conall full of luscious wine.

¶ 61. Conall said farewell. A herald was then sent to fetch Cú Chulainn. 'Come to speak with the king and queen,' the messenger said. Cú Chulainn at the time was busy playing *fidchell* [a board game (= W. *gwyddbwyll*)] with Lóeg, son of Riangabair, his own charioteer. 'No mocking,' he said, 'you might try your lies on some other fool.' Having hurled one of the *fidchell* men, it pierced the centre of the herald's brain. He got a mortal wound from it, and fell between Ailill and Medb. 'Woe is me,' Medb said; 'Cú Chulainn works his fury painfully when his fit of rage is on him.' Then Medb got up and came to Cú Chulainn, and put her two arms round his neck. 'Try a lie upon another,' Cú Chulainn said.

'Glorious son of the Ulstermen, on the floor of the great house, and flame of the heroes of Ireland, it is not a lie that we like where you are concerned. If all Ireland's heroes were to come, we would grant the quest to you by preference, because, concerning fame, bravery, and valour, distinction, youth, and glory, the men of Ireland acknowledge your superiority.'

¶ 62. Cú Chulainn got up. He accompanied Medb into the great house, and Ailill wished him warm welcome. A cup of gold was given him full of luscious wine, and having on the bottom of it birds chased in precious stone. With it, and in preference to everyone else, there was given him a lump, as big as his two eyes, of dragon-stone. 'Now you have the feast of a champion,' Medb said. 'I wish you may enjoy it a hundred hundred years at the head of all the Ulster heroes.' 'Moreover, it is our verdict,' Ailill and Medb said, 'just as you yourself cannot be compared with the Ulster warriors, neither is your wife to be compared with their women. Nor is it too much, we think, that she should always precede all the Ulster ladies when entering the Mead Hall.' At that Cú Chulainn drank down at one draught the full cup, and then said farewell to the king, the queen, and the whole household.

(After that he followed his charioteer. 'My plan,' Medb said to Ailill, 'is to keep those three heroes with us again tonight, and to further test them.' 'Do as you think right,' Ailill said. The men were then detained and brought to Cruachan and their horses unyoked.)

¶ 63. Their choice of food was given them for their horses. Conall and Lóegaire told them to give two-year-old oats to theirs, but Cú Chulainn chose barley grains for his. They slept there that night, and the women were apportioned among them. Findabair, with a following of fifty maidens, was brought to the house of Cú Chulainn. Sadb the Eloquent [*Sadb Sulbair*], another daughter of Ailill and of Medb, with fifty maids in attendance, was ushered into the presence of Conall Cernach. Conchend, daughter of Cet mac Mágach, along with fifty maidens, was brought into the presence of Lóegaire Buadach. Moreover, Medb herself stayed in Cú Chulainn's house and they slept there that night.

¶ 64. The next day they arose early in the morning and went into the house where the youths were performing the wheel-feat. Then Lóegaire seized the wheel and tossed it till it reached halfway up the side wall. The youths laughed and cheered him for that. It was in reality a jeer, but it seemed to Lóegaire a shout of applause. Conall then took the wheel; it was on the ground. He tossed it as high as the ridge-pole of the great house. The youths raised a shout at that. It seemed to Conall it was a shout of applause and of victory. To the youths it was a shout of scorn. Then Cú Chulainn took the wheel it was in mid-air when he caught it. He hurled it aloft till it knocked the ridge-pole off of the great house; the wheel went a man's cubit into the ground in the outside enclosure. The youths raised a shout of applause and of triumph in Cú Chulainn's case. It seemed to Cú Chulainn, however, it was a laugh of scorn and of ridicule that they expressed then.

¶ 65. Cú Chulainn then sought out the women-folk, and took three times fifty needles from them. These he tossed up one after the other. Each needle went into the eye of the other, till in that way they were joined together. He returned to the women, and gave each her own needle in her hand. The young warriors praised Cú Chulainn. Whereupon they said farewell to the king, the queen, and household as well.

¶ 66. 'Go to the house of my foster father and foster mother,' Medb said, 'namely, Ercol and Garmna, and stay as guests tonight.' They kept on their way, and after running a race at the Cruachan assembly, Cú Chulainn won the victory of the games three times. They then went to the house of Garmna and of Ercol, who wished them welcome. 'What have you come for?' Ercol asked. 'To be judged by you,' they said. 'Go to the house of Samera; he will judge you.' They went accordingly and guides were sent with them. They were welcomed by Samera, whose daughter Buan fell in love with Cú Chulainn. They told Samera that it was in order to be judged that they had come to him. Samera sent them each in turn to the Amazons of the Glen.

¶ 67. Lóegaire went first, but left his arms and clothing with them. Conall also went, and left his spears with them, but took his chief weapon, namely, his sword, away with him. On the third night Cú Chulainn went. The Amazons shrieked at him. He and they fought each other till his spear was splintered, his shield broken, his clothes torn off. The Amazons were beating and over-powering him. 'O Cú Chulainn,' said Lóeg, 'you sorry coward, you squinting savage! Your valour and your bravery are gone when it is sprites that beat you.' Then Cú Chulainn was enraged at the sprites. He turned back upon the Horrors, and cut and gashed them till the glen was filled with their blood. He brought off his company's brave banner with him and turned back in triumph to the seat of Samera, the place where his companions were.

¶ 68. Samera wished him welcome; it was then he spoke:

'Not right to share the champion's fare of the cooking pit,
fatted cows, well-fed swine, honey and bread;
through ladies' cunning do not take his share
from Culann's Hound, of name and fame.
Cleaver of shields, raven of prey,
that bravery wields, eager for fray boar of battle.
As wood takes fire, his anger strikes Emain's foes;
beloved of victory-loving plague of death.

A judge in consideration, not in appearance, eye flashing far
hostile ports where ships resort his tributes know;
his chariot rides the mountain-side,
pride of his clan, he leads the vanguard, an eagle of war.
Why to Lóegaire, lion of fences, liken him?
Why to Conall, rider of fame?
Why should not Emer, of shining mantle—it is our pleasure divining
    according to grace
of Ulster ladies high-born and all, enter first the merry Mead-Hall?
Cú Chulainn's share, I knew well,
is not just [elsewhere] to allot.'

'My verdict to you then: the Champion's Portion to Cú Chulainn, and to his wife the precedence of the ladies of Ulster Cú Chulainn's valour to rank above that of everyone else, Conchobor's excepted.'

¶ 69. After that they went to the house of Ercol, who wished them welcome. They slept there that night. Ercol challenged them to combat with himself and with his horse. Then Lóegaire and his horse went against them. The gelding of Ercol killed the horse of Lóegaire, who was himself overcome by Ercol, before whom he fled. He found his way to Emain across Assaroe, and brought a story with him of his comrades having been killed by Ercol. Conall likewise fled, his horse having been killed by Ercol's; the way he went was across Snám Rathaind [Rathand's Swim] on the route to Emain. Moreover, Conall's gillie [servant, charioteer], Rathand, was drowned in the river there, and after him Snám Rathaind takes its name since.

¶ 70. The grey of Macha, however, killed the horse of Ercol, and Cú Chulainn took Ercol himself bound behind his chariot along with him to Emain. Buan, daughter of Samera, went on the track of the three chariots. She recognised the track of Cú Chulainn's framed chariot, as it was no narrow track it used to take, but undermining walls, either enlarging or else leaping over breaches. The girl at last leapt a fearful leap, following him behind in his chariot's track till she struck her forehead on a rock, and she died from it. From this comes the name Buan's Grave. When Conall and Cú Chulainn reached Emain, they found the Ulstermen holding a keen for them, because they felt certain they were killed. This was the report Lóegaire brought. Then they related their adventures and told their news to Conchobor and to the Ulster nobles as a group. But the chiefs of chariots and the valorous men as a body were reproaching Lóegaire for the lying story he told concerning his fellows.

¶ 71. Then Cathbad spoke as follows:

'A tale inglorious!
base Outlaw, black and false,

for shame! your face from sight!
Ulster's Champion's Portion
unhappily did you dispute,
nor won it by right,
your lying upset.
Cú Chulainn has coped with Ercol,
victor in battle-fight;
tied at the tail of his car,
Hercules strong he held;
nor do men conceal his feats,
they tell his great havoc.
A champion glorious, battle-victorious,
when the fray rages,
slaughter-head of the hosts,
a lord that moves in might,
zealous of valour and stout;
with him to dispute
the Champion's Portion,
unworthy of a hero's repute.'

¶ 72. The heroes ceased their discussions and their babblings and went to eating and enjoying themselves. It was Sualtam mac Róich, father of Cú Chulainn himself, who attended the Ulstermen that night. Moreover, Conchobor's ladder-vat was filled for them. Their portion having been brought to their presence, the waiters came to serve, but at the outset they withheld the Champion's Portion from distribution. 'Why not give the Champion's Portion,' said Duach Chafer Tongue, 'to some one of the heroes; those three have not returned from the King of Cruachan, having no sure token with them, whereby the Champion's Portion may be assigned to one of them?'

¶ 73. Then Lóegaire Buadach got up and lifted on high the bronze cup having the silver bird [chased] on the bottom. 'The Champion's Portion is mine,' he said, 'and none may contest it with me.' 'It is not,' Conall Cernach said. 'Not alike are the tokens we brought off with us. Yours is a cup of bronze, whereas mine is a cup of white metal [findruini]. From the difference between them the Champion's Portion clearly belongs to me.' 'It belongs to neither of you,' Cú Chulainn said as he got up and spoke. 'You have brought no token that brings you the Champion's Portion. Yet the king and queen whom you visited did not want to intensify the strife in the midst of the distress. But you have received no less than you deserve at their hands. The Champion's Portion remains with me, as I brought a token distinguished above the rest.'

¶ 74. He then lifted on high a cup of red gold having a bird chased on the bottom of it in precious dragon-stone, the size of his two eyes. All the Ulster nobles in the chamber of Conchobor mac Nessa saw it. 'Therefore it is I,' he said, 'who deserves the Champion's Portion, provided there is fair play.' 'To you we all award it,' said Conchobor and Fergus and the Ulster nobles too. By the verdict of Ailill and of Medb, the Champion's Portion is yours.' 'I swear by my tribe's god,' said Lóegaire and Conall Cernach, 'that the cup you have brought is purchased. You have given some jewels and treasures that are in your possession to Ailill and to Medb for [the cup] in order that a loss might not be counted against you, and that the Champion's Portion might be given to no one else in preference. By my people's god, that judgement shall not stand; the Champion's Portion shall not be yours.' They then sprang up one after the other, their swords drawn. Immediately Conchobor and Fergus intervened, with that they let down their hands and sheathed their swords. 'Hold!' Sencha said, 'do as I command.' 'We will,' they said.

¶ 75. 'Go forth to the ford of *Budi* ['Yellow'], son of Fair. He will judge you.' Accordingly the three heroes went to the house of Budi. They told their wants and the rivalries which brought them. 'Wasn't a judgement given you in Cruachan by Ailill and by Medb?' said Budi. 'In truth there was,' Cú Chulainn said, 'but those fellows don't stand by it.' 'We won't stand by it,' said the other men. 'What has been given us is no decision at all.' 'It is not easy for another to judge you then,' said Yellow, 'seeing you did not stand by Medb and Ailill's arrangement. I know,' he continued, 'one who will venture it, namely, Uath mac Imomain ["Terror son of Great Fear"], at yonder loch [lake]. Off then in quest of him; he will judge you.' Terror son of Great Fear was a big powerful fellow. He used to shift his form into whatever shape he wished, to do tricks of magic and that sort of arts. He in truth was the wizard from whom Muni, the Wizard's Pass, is named. He used to be called 'wizard' from the extent to which he changed his divers shapes.

¶ 76. To Uath at his lake they went accordingly. Budi had given them a guide. To Uath they told the cause for which they had sought him out. He said that he would try to make judgement provided they would just adhere to it. 'We will adhere to it,' they said; at which point he solemnly pledged them. 'I have a covenant to make with you,' he said, 'and whoever of you fulfills it with me, he is the man who wins the Champion's Portion.' 'What is the covenant?' they said. 'I have an axe, and the man into whose hands it will be put is to cut off my head today, I to cut off his tomorrow.'

¶ 77. Then Conall and Lóegaire said they would not agree to that arrangement, for it would be impossible for them to live after having been beheaded, although he might. Therefore they declined that: (although other books narrate that they agreed to the bargain, namely, Lóegaire to cut off Uath's [Terror's] head the first day, and (on the giant's returning) that Lóegaire shirked his part of the bargain and that Conall likewise behaved unfairly). Cú Chulainn, however, said he would agree to the covenant if the Champion's Portion were given to him. Conall and Lóegaire said they would allow him that if he agreed to a wager with Uath. Cú Chulainn solemnly pledged them not to contest the Champion's Portion if he made covenant with Uath. And they then pledged him to ratify it. Uath, having put spells on the edge of the axe, laid his head upon the stone for Cú Chulainn. Cú Chulainn with his own axe gave the giant a blow and cuts off his head. He then went off from them into the lake, his axe and his head on his breast.

¶ 78. The next morning he came back on his quest. Cú Chulainn stretched himself out for him on the stone. [Uath] brought down the axe with its edge reversed three times on Cú Chulainn's neck. 'Get up,' said Terror, 'the sovereignty of the heroes of Ireland to Cú Chulainn, and the Champion's Portion without contest.' The three heroes then went to Emain. But Lóegaire and Conall disputed the verdict given in favour of Cú Chulainn and the original contest as to the Champion's Portion continued. The Ulstermen advised them to go for judgement to Cú Roí. To that too they agreed.

¶ 79. On the morning of the next day the three heroes, Cú Chulainn, Conall and Lóegaire, then set off to the Fort of Cú Roí. They unyoked their chariots at the gate of the hold, then entered the court. Whereupon Blathnat, Mind's daughter, wife of Cú Roí mac Dári, wished them warm welcome. That night on their arrival Cú Roí was not at home. But knowing they would come, he counselled his wife concerning the heroes until he should return from his oriental expedition into Scythian territory. From the age of seven years, when he took up arms, until his demise, Cú Roí had not reddened his sword in Ireland, nor ever had the food of Ireland passed his lips. Nor could Ireland contain him for his lordliness, renown and rank, overbearing fury, strength and gallantry. His wife acted according to his wish concerning bathing and washing, providing them with refreshing drinks and excellent beds. And they liked it very much.

¶ 80. When bedtime came, she told them that each was to take his night watching the fort until Cú Roí should return. 'And, furthermore, Cú Roí said that you take your turn watching according to seniority.' In whatever part of the globe Cú Roí should happen to be, every night he chanted a spell over the fort, till the fort revolved as swiftly as a mill-stone. The entrance was never to be found after sunset.

¶ 81. The first night, Lóegaire Buadach took the sentry, as he was the eldest of the three. As he kept watch into the later part of the night, he saw a giant [Scáth] approaching him far as his eyes could see from the sea westwards. Exceedingly huge and ugly and horrible he thought him, for in height, it seemed to him, he reached the sky, and the broad expanse of the sea was visible between his legs. So he came, his hands full of stripped oaks, each of which would form a burden for a waggon-team of six, at whose root not a stroke had been repeated after the first sword-stroke. One of the stakes he cast at Lóegaire, who let it pass him. Twice or three times he repeated it, but the stake reached neither the skin nor the shield of Lóegaire. Then Lóegaire hurled a spear at him and it did not hit him.

¶ 82. The giant stretched his hand towards Lóegaire. Its length was such that it reached across the three ridges that were between them as they were throwing at each other, and so he seized him in his grasp. Though Lóegaire was big and imposing, he fitted like a year-old into the clutch of his opponent, who then ground him in his grasp as a *fidchell* playing piece is turned in a groove. In that state, half-dead, the giant tossed him out over the fort, till he fell into the mire of the ditch at the hall's gate. The fort had no opening there, and the other men and residents of the stronghold thought he had leapt outside over the fort, as a challenge for the other men to do likewise.

¶ 83. There they were until the day's end. When the night-watch began, Conall went out on sentry, for he was older than Cú Chulainn. Everything occurred as it did to Lóegaire the first night. The third night Cú Chulainn went on sentry. That night the three Grey ones of Sescind Uair-béoil, the three Ox-feeders (?) of Brega, and the three sons of Big-Fist the Siren met by appointment to plunder the stronghold. This too was the night for which it was foretold that the Spirit of the Lake by the fort would devour the whole host of the fort, man and beast.

¶ 84. Cú Chulainn while watching through the night had many uneasy forebodings. When midnight came he heard a terrific noise drawing near to him. 'Hello, hello,' Cú Chulainn shouted, 'who is there? If they are friends, let them not stir; if foes, let them flee.' Then they raised a terrific shout at him. At that Cú Chulainn sprang upon them, so that the nine of them fell dead to the earth. He heaped their heads in disorder into the sitting place of the watchman and resumed sentry. Another nine shouted at him. In the same way he killed the three nines, making one cairn of them, heads and arms.

¶ 85. While he was there far on into the night, tired and sad and weary, he heard the rising upwards of the lake, sounding as if it were the booming of a very heavy sea. However deep his dejection, his spirit could not endure not to go to see what caused the great noise he heard. He then perceived the looming monster, and it seemed to him to be thirty cubits [about 15 metres] arching above the lake. It raised itself on high into the air, sprang towards the fort, opened its mouth so that one of the great houses could go into its gullet.

¶ 86. Then [Cú Chulainn] called to mind his swooping feat, sprang on high, and was as swift as a winnowing fan right round the monster. He entwined his two arms about its neck, stretched his hand till it reached into its gullet, tore out the monster's heart, and cast it from him on the ground. Then the beast fell from the air till it rested on the earth, having sustained a blow on the shoulder. Cú Chulainn then plied it with his sword, hacked it to pieces, and took the head with him into the sentry-seat along with the other heap of skulls.

¶ 87. While there, depressed and miserable in the morning dawn, he saw the giant approaching him westwards from the east. 'Bad night,' he said. 'It will be worse for you, you uncouth fellow,' Cú Chulainn said. Then the giant cast one of the branches at Cú Chulainn, who let it pass him. He repeated it two or three times, but it reached neither the skin nor the shield of Cú Chulainn. Cú Chulainn then hurled his spear at the giant, but it didn't reach him. At that the giant stretched his hand towards Cú Chulainn to grip him as he did the others. Cú Chulainn leapt the hero's 'salmon-leap,' and called to mind his swooping-feat, with his drawn sword over the monster's head. As swift as a hare he was, and in mid-air circling round the monster, till he made a water-wheel of him. 'Life for life, Cú Chulainn,' he said. 'Give me my three wishes,' Cú Chulainn said. 'At a breath they are yours,' he said. 'The Sovereignty of Ireland's Heroes should be mine henceforth. The Champion's Portion without dispute. The Precedence to my wife over Ulster's ladies forever.' 'It shall be yours,' [the giant] said at once. Then he who had been conversing with him vanished he knew not where.

¶ 88. [Cú Chulainn] then mused within himself as to the leap his fellows leapt over the fort, for their leap was big and broad and high. Moreover, it seemed to him it was by leaping it that the valiant heroes had gone over it. He tried it twice and failed. 'Alas!' Cú Chulainn said, 'my previous exertions for the Champion's Portion have exhausted me, and now I lose it through being unable to take the leap the others took.' As he thought this way, he tried the following feats. He would keep springing backwards in mid-air a shot's distance from the fort, and then he would rebound from there until his forehead would strike the fort. Then he would spring on high till all that was within the fort was visible to him, while again he would sink up to his knees in the earth due to the force of his vehemence and violence. At another time he would not take the dew from off the tip of the grass by reason of his buoyancy of mood, vehemence of nature, and heroic valour. With the fit and fury that raged upon him he stepped over the fort outside and landed in the middle at the door of the great house. His two footprints are [still] in the flagstone on the floor of the stronghold at the spot where the royal entrance was. He entered the house after that and heaved a sigh.

¶ 89. Then Mind's daughter, Blathnat, wife of Cú Roí, spoke: 'Truly, not the sigh of one dishonoured, but a victor's sigh of triumph.' The daughter of the king of the Isle of the Men of Falga knew full well of Cú Chulainn's evil plight that night. They were not long there when they beheld Cú Roí coming towards them, carrying into the house with him the standard of the 'three nines' slain by Cú Chulainn, along with their heads and that of the monster. He put the heads aside from his breast onto the floor of the dwelling, and spoke: 'The youth whose one night's trophies are these is a fit lad to watch a king's stronghold forever. The Champion's Portion, over which you have contested with the gallant youths of Ireland, truly belongs to Cú Chulainn. The bravest of them, were he here, could not match him in number of trophies.' Cú Roí's verdict on them was: 'The Champion's Portion to be Cú Chulainn's. With the sovereignty of valour over all the Gael. And to his wife the precedence on entering the Mead Hall before all the ladies of Ulster.' And he gave seven *cumals* [the value of seven female slaves] of gold and of silver him in reward for his one night's performance.

¶ 90. They immediately wished Cú Roí farewell and kept on till they were seated in Emain before the day closed. When the waiters came to deal and to divide, they took the Champion's Portion with its share of ale out of the distribution that they might have it separately. 'Truly, we are sure,' said Duach Chafer Tongue, 'do not think tonight of contending over the Champion's Portion? The man you sought out has undertaken your judging.' With that the other people said to Cú Chulainn: 'The Champion's Portion was not assigned to one of you in preference to the other. As to Cú Roí's further judgement upon those three, they did not concede to Cú Chulainn upon their arriving at Emain.' Cú Chulainn then declared he by no means coveted the winning of it. Because the loss resulting to the winner from it would be equal with the profit got from it. The championship was therefore not fully assigned until the coming of the Champion's Covenant in Emain.

THE CHAMPION'S COVENANT

¶ 91. Once upon a time as the Ulstermen were in Emain, fatigued after the gathering and the games, Conchobor and Fergus mac Róich, with Ulster's nobles as well, proceeded from the sporting field outside and seated themselves in the *Cráeb Ruad* ['Red Branch', the name of the hall] of Conchobor. Neither Cú Chulainn nor Conall Cernach nor Lóegaire Buadach were there that night. But the hosts of Ulster's valiant heroes were there. As they were seated, it being dusk, and the day drawing towards its close, they saw a big uncouth fellow of exceeding ugliness drawing near them into the hall. To them it seemed as if none of the Ulstermen would reach half his height. The churl's appearance was horrible and ugly. Next to his skin he wore an old hide with a dark brown mantle around him, and over him a great spreading tree-club the size of a winter-shed, under which thirty bullocks could find shelter. He had ravenous yellow eyes protruding from his head, each of the two the size of an ox-vat.

Each finger as thick as another person's wrist. In his left hand a stock, a burden for twenty yoke of oxen. In his right hand an axe weighing three times fifty glowing molten masses [of metal]. Its handle would require a plough-team [a yoke of six] to move it. It was so sharp that it would lop off hairs when the wind blew them against its edge.

¶ 92. Looking like that, he went and stood by the [hall's] fork-beam beside the fire . . .

¶ 93. [He said] . . . 'Neither in Ireland nor in Britain nor in Europe nor in Africa nor in Asia, including Greece, Scythia, the Isles of Gades, the Pillars of Hercules, and Bregon's Tower, have I found the quest on which I have come, nor a man to do me fair play in it. Since you Ulstermen have excelled all the folks of those lands in strength, prowess, valour; in rank, magnanimity, dignity; in truth, generosity and worth, get one among you to give me the boon I crave.'

¶ 94. 'In truth it is not just that the honour of a province might be carried off,' said Fergus mac Róich, 'because of one man who fails in keeping his word of honour. Death, certainly, is not any nearer to him than to you.' 'Not that I shun it,' he said. 'Make your quest known to us then,' said Fergus mac Róich. 'If only fair play be guaranteed me, I will tell it.' 'It is also right to give fair play back,' said Sencha son of Ailill, 'for it is not fitting for a great tribal people to break a mutual covenant with some unknown person. To us too it seems likely, if at long last you find such a person, you will find here one worthy of you.' 'Conchobor put aside,' he said, 'for sake of his sovereignty, and Fergus mac Róich also on account of his similar privilege. These two excepted, let whoever of you come who dares, so I may cut off his head tonight and he mine tomorrow night.'

¶ 95. 'Sure then there is no warrior here,' said Duach, 'after these two.' 'By my word there will be this moment,' said Fat-Neck, son of Short Head, as he sprang on to the floor of the hall. The strength then of this Fat-Neck was as the strength of a hundred warriors, each arm having the might of a hundred centaurs. 'Bend down, bachlach ['outlandish churl'],' said Fat-Neck, 'that I may cut your head off tonight that you may cut off mine tomorrow night.' 'Were that my quest, I could have got it anywhere,' said the bachlach. 'Let us act according to our covenant,' he said, 'that I cut off your head tonight, you to avenge it tomorrow night.' 'By my tribe's god,' said Duach of the Chafer Tongue, 'so death is for you no pleasant prospect should the man killed tonight attack you tomorrow. It is possible for you alone if you have the power, to be killed every night, to avenge it next day.' 'Truly I will carry out what you all as a body agree upon by way of counsel, strange as it may seem to you,' the bachlach said. He then pledged to his opponent to keep his word in this contention with regards to fulfilling his appointment for the next day.

¶ 96. With that Fat-Neck took the axe from out of the *bachlach*'s hand. Seven feet apart were its two angles. Then the *bachlach* put his neck across the block. Fat-Neck dealt a blow across it with the axe till it stuck in the block underneath, cutting off the head till it lay by the base of the fork-beam, the house being filled with the blood. Immediately the *bachlach* rose, recovered himself, clasped his head, block and axe to his breast, thus made his exit from the hall with blood streaming from his neck. It filled the Red Branch on every side. The people's horror was great, wondering at the marvel that had appeared to them. 'By my tribe's god,' said Duach Chafer Tongue, 'if the *bachlach*, having been killed tonight, comes back tomorrow, he will not leave a man alive in Ulster.' The following night, however, he returned, and Fat-Neck shirked him. Then the *bachlach* began to press his pact with Fat-Neck. 'Truly it is not right for Fat-Neck not to fulfill his covenant with me.'

¶ 97. That night, however, Lóegaire Buadach was present. 'Who of the warriors that contest Ulster's Champion's Portion will carry out a covenant tonight with me? Where is Lóegaire Buadach?' he said. 'Here,' Lóegaire said. [Lóegaire] pledged him too, yet Lóegaire did not keep his appointment. The *bachlach* returned the next day and similarly pledged Conall Cernach, who did not come as he had sworn.

¶ 98. The fourth night the *bachlach* returned, and he was fierce and furious. All the ladies of Ulster came that night to see the strange marvel that had come into the Red Branch. That night Cú Chulainn was there also. Then the fellow began to upbraid them: 'You Ulstermen, your valour and your prowess are gone. Your warriors greatly desire the Champion's Portion, yet are unable to contest it. Where is that poor mad mortal that is called Cú Chulainn? I would like to know if his word might be better than that of the others.' 'I desire no covenant with you,' Cú Chulainn said. 'That's likely, you wretched fly [*cuil*, a pun on Cú Chulainn's name], greatly you fear to die.' With that Cú Chulainn sprang towards him and dealt him a blow with the axe, hurling his head to the top rafter of the Red Branch till the whole hall shook. Cú Chulainn again caught up the head and gave it a blow with the axe and smashed it. After that the *bachlach* rose up.

¶ 99. The next day the Ulstermen were watching Cú Chulainn to see whether he would shirk the *bachlach* as the other heroes had done. As Cú Chulainn was awaiting the *bachlach*, they saw that great dejection seized him. It had been fitting if they had sung his dirge. They felt sure his life would last only till the *bachlach* came. Then Cú Chulainn said with shame to Conchobor, 'You shall not go until my pledge to the *bachlach* is fulfilled; for death awaits me, and I would rather have death with honour.'

¶ 100. They were there as the day was closing when they saw the *bachlach* approaching. 'Where is Cú Chulainn?' he said. 'Here I am,' he answered. 'Your speech is dull tonight, unhappy one; greatly you fear to die. Yet, though great your fear you have not shirked death.' After that Cú Chulainn went up to him and stretched his neck across the block, which was of such size that his neck reached only half-way. 'Stretch out your neck, you wretch,' the *bachlach* said. 'You keep me in torment,' Cú Chulainn said. 'Dispatch me quickly; last night, by my word, I did not torment you. Indeed I swear if you torment me, I shall make myself as long as a crane above you.' 'I cannot slay you,' said the *bachlach*, 'on account of the size of the block and the shortness of your neck and of your side.'

¶ 101. Then Cú Chulainn stretched out his neck so that a warrior's full-grown foot would have fitted between any two of his ribs; he distended his neck till it reached the other side of the block. The *bachlach* raised his axe till it reached the roof-tree of the hall. The creaking of the old hide that was about the fellow and the crashing of the axe—both his arms being raised aloft with all his might—were as the loud noise of a tempest-tossed forest in a night of storm. Down it came then . . . on his neck, its blunt side turned down, all the nobles of Ulster gazing upon them.

¶ 102. 'Cú Chulainn, arise! . . . Of the warriors of Ulster and Ireland, no matter their mettle, none is found to be compared with you in valour, bravery and truthfulness. The sovereignty of the heroes of Ireland to you from this hour forth and the Champion's Portion undisputed, and to your lady the precedence always of the ladies of Ulster in the Mead Hall. And whoever shall lay wager against you from now, as my tribe swears I swear, . . .' Then the *bachlach* vanished. It was Cú Roí mac Dári who had come in that form to fulfill the promise he had given to Cú Chulainn.

AND SO HENCEFORTH THE CHAMPION'S PORTION OF EMAIN,
AND THE ULSTER WOMEN'S WAR OF WORDS, AND THE
CHAMPION'S WAGER IN EMAIN, AND THE HOSTING OF THE
ULSTERMEN TO CRUACHAN.

◆ ◆ ◆ ◆ ◆ ◆ ◆ ◆ ◆

§82. *Mesca Ulad* The Intoxication of the Ulstermen[6]

¶ 1.

WHEN THE SONS OF MÍL ESPÁINE [i.e. the Soldier of Spain] came to Ireland, their cleverness prevailed over the Tuath Dé Danann: thus Ireland was left to be divided by Amairgen Glúnmár, son of Míl; for that man was a poet-king and judge-king. He divided Ireland in two, and he gave the half of Ireland that was underground to the Tuath Dé Danann, and the other half to the sons of Míl Espáine who were of his own blood-kindred.

¶ 2. The Tuath Dé Danann went into hills and the tumuli [*síd-brugaib*], so that the *síd*-beings under the earth granted hostages to them [as a token of submission]. [The Tuath Dé] left five men of their people for each province in Ireland making a proliferation of battles, conflicts, strife, and aggression amongst the sons of Míl. They left five men for the province of Ulster in particular: these are the names of these five men—Brea mac Belgain [left] in the ridges of Brega [East-central Ireland], Redg Rotbél in the flat lands of Mag n-Itha, Tinnell mac Boclachtnai in Sliab Edlicon, Grici in Cruachán Aigli [in modern Co. Mayo], Gulban Glas mac Gráci in Benn Gulbain Guirt meic Ungairb.

¶ 3. These men imposed a division upon the province of Ulster splitting it in three at the period when the province was largest, that is at the time of Conchobor son of Fachtna Fáthach. Those who divided the province with Conchobor were his own foster son, Cú Chulainn son of Sualtam, and Fintan son of Niall Niamglonnach from Dún Dá Bend. This is the division that was applied to the province: Cú Chulainn's portion of the province went from the Hill of the Summit of Forcha (which is called Uisnech Mide [i.e. the hill-top earthwork in Meath reckoned to be the geographical centre of Ireland]) to the prominence at the centre of the Strand of Baile; then Conchobor's third was from the Strand of Baile to the Strand of Tola in Ulster; Fintan's third was from the Strand of Tola to the Peak of Semne and Lathairne.

¶ 4. For a year the province was in three parts like this, until the making of the celebration of Samain by Conchobor in Emain Macha. The great magnitude of the feast included one hundred vats of every kind of drink. Conchobor's men

---

6   The translation is provisional and based on the edition of J. Carmichael Watson, Dublin: Dublin Institute for Advanced Studies, 1941.

of rank said that all of Ulster's aristocracy would not be too many to join in so excellent a feast.

¶ 5. The plan made by Conchobor was to send Lebarcham for Cú Chulainn in Dún Delga [Dundalk, Co. Louth] and Finnchad Fer Bend Uma, son of Fráeglethan, for Fintan son of Niall Niamglonnach in Dún Dá Bend.

¶ 6. Lebarcham arrived at Dún Delga and asked Cú Chulainn to come to converse with his dear foster father [i.e. Conchobor] at Emain Macha. In fact, though, it so happened that Cú Chulainn himself had assembled a great feast in Dún Delga for the tribesfolk within his own boundaries. And he said that he was not going, but would see to the upkeep of the tribesfolk dwelling within his own boundaries. Emer Foltcháin ['of the Lovely Hair'], daughter of Forgall Manach, one of the six best women to come forth in Ireland, said that he should not do so, but rather should go to converse with his foster father Conchobor. Cú Chulainn said that his horses were to be yoked for him and his chariot harnessed.

¶ 7. 'The horses are yoked and the chariot is harnessed,' said Lóeg. 'You are not to be held off until it is an inauspicious time. Don't let it restrain your valour. Step into [the chariot] when you wish.' Cú Chulainn put on his armament and leapt into his chariot. Cú Chulainn went forward directly over the roads by the shortest routes to Emain Macha. And Sencha son of Ailill came to welcome Cú Chulainn on Emain's grounds. This is the welcome he gave him:

'Your coming is welcome (to me), ever-welcome, chief of good fortune for Ulster's host, salmon of combat and valour of the Gaelic people, many-thronged, crimson-fisted son of Dechtine.'

¶ 8. 'That is the welcome of a man looking for favour,' Cú Chulainn said. 'Yes, absolutely,' said Sencha son of Ailill. 'Say what favour you ask,' Cú Chulainn said. 'Yes, I will, but only if there are sureties acceptable to me.' 'Say what sureties you request for asking your favour.' 'The two Conalls and Lóegaire, i.e. Conall Ánglonnach son of Íriel Glúnmár, and Conall Cernach son of Amairgen, and Lóegaire Londbuadach.' On these conditions the favour was agreed upon, in exchange for a counter-favour due to Cú Chulainn. 'Who are the guarantors you ask for your counter-favour?' asked Sencha. 'The three noble, young, splendid lads—Cormac Connlongas son of Conchobor, Mes Dëad son of Amairgen, Eochu Cenngarb son of Celtchair.' 'This is what I ask,' said Sencha son of Ailill, 'that the third part of Ulster that is in your possession you leave to Conchobor for a year.' 'If the province would be better for being his for a year, it is not inappropriate, for he is the spring of rightful proprietorship no one can claim against or challenge, descendant of the kings of Ireland and of Britain. So, if the province were better off for being his for a year, it is not incongruous that it be his, and if [his rule] seems no better to us than little boys squabbling, he will be put back over his own third at the end of the year.

¶ 9. Fintan son of Niall Niamglonnach arrived. The good and marvellous druid Cathbad met him. He welcomed him: 'Your coming is welcome to me, beautiful, marvellous young warrior, chief armed combatant of the superior province of Ulster, whom neither raiders nor plunderers nor pirates can conquer, man of the frontier boundaries of the province of Ulster.' 'That is the welcome of a man looking for favour,' said Fintan. 'Yes, absolutely,' said Cathbad. 'Tell it so that you may have it,' said Fintan. 'Yes, I will, but only if there are sureties acceptable to me.' 'Say what sureties you ask in exchange for a counter-favour for me?' asked Fintan. 'Celtchair son of Uithider, Uma son of Remanfisech from Fedan Cuailnge, Errge Echbél from Brí Errgi.' It was agreed on these conditions. 'Do you say now, Fintan, what guarantors you will take for your counter-favour.' 'The three sons of Uisnech of the Great Deeds, the three firebrands of armed combat in Europe, Noísiu, and Ánli, and Ardan.' These sureties were undertaken on each side.

¶ 10. They came into the house where Conchobor was, i.e. into the Téite Brecc. 'Conchobor is Ulster's king now,' said Cathbad, 'for Fintan gave his third to him.' 'It is so,' Sencha said, 'for Cú Chulainn gave his.' 'If it is so,' Cú Chulainn said, 'let him come to drink and enjoy himself with me, for it is my counter-favour.' 'Where are *my* requests and my guarantees,' said Fintan, 'if one dares to speak of such?'

¶ 11. The pledged men for each of them executed their obligations barbarously. And it was such barbarity in the upsurge that there were nine men wounded, and nine men bloody, and nine killed outright amongst the men on each side. Sencha son of Ailill rose up and brandished his peace-making branch, so that the Ulstermen were mute and silent. 'You quarrel excessively,' Sencha said, 'for Conchobor is not king of Ulster until the end of a year.' 'We will make it so,' Cú Chulainn said, 'only if you will not come between us at the end of a year.' 'No, I will not do that,' Sencha said. Cú Chulainn bound the obligation on him. They remained for three days and nights drinking that feast of Conchobor's until it was used up by them. [Then] they went separately to their houses, and strongholds, and fine residences.

¶ 12. [For] anyone who came at the end of a year, the province was as a gushing spring and [there was] rightfulness with Conchobor, so that from the Peak of Semne and Lathairne to the Hill of the Summit of Forcha and to Dub and to Drobais there was not an abandoned ring-fort, not one without the son in the place of his father and grandfather serving his legitimate lord.

¶ 13. It was then that a fine conversation between Cú Chulainn and Emer took place. 'It seems to me,' Emer said, 'that Conchobor is now high-king of Ulster.'

'If so, there is nothing wrong with that,' Cú Chulainn said. 'It is now time to make his feast of kingship for him,' Emer said, 'for he is king forever.' 'It shall be made then,' Cú Chulainn said.

¶ 14. The feast was assembled in which there were one hundred vats with every kind of drink in them. It was at the same time that Fintan son of Niall Niamglonnach had his feast made, so that there were one hundred vats with every kind of drink in them, and so that it was in time and all ready. On the same day these [feasts] were undertaken, and on the same day they were ready. On the same day their horses were yoked for them and their chariots were harnessed.

¶ 15. Cú Chulainn arrived first in Emain. He had no more than unyoked his horses when Fintan arrived and proceeded into Emain. It was at that time, as Cú Chulainn was inviting Conchobor to his feast, that Fintan arrived. 'Where are my agreed terms and my pledged men, one dares ask?' 'We are here,' said the sons of Uisnech as they rose together. 'Nor am I for my part,' Cú Chulainn said, 'without legal guarantees.' The Ulstermen rose barbarously for their weapons, for Sencha did not dare to stand between them. They were averse to peace.

¶ 16. Conchobor could not contain them at all, but rather left them in the royal great house as they were. And a son of his followed him, whose name was Furbaide son of Conchobor. It so happens that this [son] Cú Chulainn had fostered. And Conchobor skulked off from [Cú Chulainn] with [the son]. 'Good son,' said Conchobor: 'if you were willing, you could make peace among the Ulstermen.' 'How is that?' asked the boy. '. . . to cry and grieve in the presence of your dear foster father Cú Chulainn. For he would not feel the need for combat or strife if you were on his mind.' The boy turned back, and he cried and grieved in the presence of his foster father Cú Chulainn. Cú Chulainn asked what was wrong. The lad said to Cú Chulainn: 'When the province is a gushing spring, you yourself are harming and destroying it rather than trading one night.' 'I gave my word on it', Cú Chulainn said, 'and there will be no going back on it.' 'I for my part also swear my word,' said Fintan, 'that I will not let the Ulstermen hold off from coming with me tonight.' 'I will get wonderful advice for you, if I dare say so', said Sencha son of Ailill; 'the first half of the night to Fintan, and the last half Cú Chulainn, to remedy the little boy's grief.' 'I for my part shall allow that,' Cú Chulainn said. 'I shall hold to that as well,' said Fintan.

¶ 17. Then the Ulstermen rose up around Conchobor, and he sent messengers around the province to convene the tribe of the province for Fintan's feast. Conchobor himself, with the court retinue of the *Cráeb Ruad* ['the Red Branch', the name of Conchobor's hall at Emain] around him, went to Dún Dá Bend, up to the house of Fintan son of Niall Niamglonnach.

¶ 18. The Ulstermen came as called to the feast so that there was not a man left in even any half-sized settlement in Ulster that did not come there. This is how they came: each hospitaller with his wife, each king with his queen, each musician with his proper spouse, each noble warrior with his noblewoman. As though only nine people had come to the settlement, that was how well they were served. There were exquisite, ornamented, perfectly formed sleeping-houses to receive them. There were beautiful elevated sun-rooms spread with rushes and fresh reeds, and long host-lodgings; broad well-stocked cooking-houses, and a multi-coloured feasting building with a broad entryway; [this building was] broad, full of great store, great and brimming; it had had a recessed, four-doored corner room, in which Ulster's aristocrats, both women and men, found accommodation for drinking and enjoyment. The best of food and drink was served them, so that the food and drink for a hundred reached each nine of them.

¶ 19. After that, the drinking house was put in order by Conchobor according to the deeds and divisions and kindreds, according to the social ranks and arts and refined manners, for the sake of the decorous ordering of the feast. Food servers came to serve portions and drink-bearers to pour, and door-keepers for doorkeeping. Their music and their songs and their entertainments were sung. Their poems and their compositions and their panegyrics were recited. Valuables and riches and treasures were shared out amongst them.

¶ 20. It is then that Cú Chulainn said to Lóeg son of Riangabar: 'Get up and go forth, my dear kinsman Lóeg. Look to the stars of the sky. Find out when the very middle of the night will come, as you are frequently in distant foreign countries watching for me and protecting me.' Lóeg rose and went out. He busied himself with contemplating and watching the distance until the middle of the night came. When the middle of the night came, Lóeg came inside to where Cú Chulainn was. 'It is the middle of the night now, Hound of feats,' he said. As Cú Chulainn heard it, he told Conchobor, and Cú Chulainn was in the warrior's seat in [Conchobor's] presence. Conchobor rose with the stippled gleaming drinking horn from an aurochs. A mute silence fell over the Ulstermen when they saw the king standing. They were so silent that had a needle fallen from the roof-beam to the floor it would have been heard. One of the Ulstermen's *gessi* ['sworn tabus'] was for them to speak prior to their kings, and one of the king's *gessi* was to speak prior to his druids. It is then that the good and wondrous druid Cathbad said: 'What is that, superlative high-king of Ulster, Conchobor?' 'It is Cú Chulainn here: he thinks it time to go and drink his feast.' 'Would he want the unanimous affirmation of the Ulstermen and to leave our weak ones and our women and our youths [here]?' 'Yes, I would,' Cú Chulainn said, 'but only if our heroes and our champions and our fighting soldiers, and our men of music and poetry and story should come with us.' The Ulstermen rose as one man and went out onto the hard surface of the grounds.

¶ 21. 'Good, my dear kinsman Lóeg,' Cú Chulainn said, 'take the way lightly in the chariot.' The charioteer at that time had the three skills of charioteering, i.e. manipulating the goad, direct motion, and leaping over a gap. 'Good, my dear kinsman Lóeg,' Cú Chulainn said, 'seize hold of the battle goad over the horses.' Cú Chulainn's horses broke into the brilliant surge of Bodb [the war-goddess, often in crow form, a.k.a. the Mórrígain]. The Ulstermen's horse teams followed, and this is the way they went: into the green of Dún Dá Bend, to Cathir Osrin, to Lí Thúaga, to Dún Rígáin, to Olarbi, and by the edge of Olarbi into the Plain of Macha, into Sliab Fuait and Áth na Forari, to Port Nóth Con Culainn, into the Plain of Muirthemne, into the land of Saithi, across Dubid, across the stream of the Boyne, into the Plain of Brega and Meath, into Senmag Léna in Mucceda, into Claithar Cell, across the Brosnachai Bladma; with their left to the Pass of Mera daughter of Trega (called Bernán Éle today), to their right to Slíab Éblinni ingini Guaire [the Mountain of Éblenn daughter of Guaire], across Findsruth, which is called the River of the Descendants of Cathbad, into Machaire Mór na mMuman [the Great Plain of Munster], across Lár Martini [the Lowland of Martin] and into Smertaini. Their right was before the white rocks of Loch Gair, across the stream of Lind Mági, to Clíu Máil Meic Úgaine, into the borders of the Little Dési in the land of Cú Roí mac Dári. Every hillock over which they went, they would level it so that they left it as valleys. Every wood they crossed through, the iron wheels of the chariots would chop the roots of the enormous trees so that it was a country of plains after them. Every stream, and every ford, and every river-mouth they crossed over were fully dry, bare stone slabs afterwards for a long time and long distances, because of the quantity that the horses carried away before their knees from the [water] which made up the cascades, and the fords, and the river-mouths.

¶ 22. It is then that Conchobor, king of Ulster, said: 'We have not taken this road between Dún Dá Bend and Dún Delga [now Dundalk, Co. Louth].' 'Indeed we may put our word to that,' said Bric[riu]. 'For as a whisper is more evident to us than a shout to anyone else, it seems to us that we are not in the country of Ulster at all.' 'We may put our word to that,' said Sencha son of Ailill, 'not in Ulster's country at all are we.' 'We give our word,' Conall said, 'that it's true.' Then the charioteers of the Ulstermen pulled tight their bridles in their horses' bits from the first charioteer to the last. And so Conchobor said: 'Who might determine for us what territory we are in?' 'Who would find that out for you,' Bricriu said, 'other than Cú Chulainn, because he is the one who has said that there was no [territory of] thirty hundred [settlements] in which he had not already done the killing of thirty hundred [men]?' 'I can, Bricriu,' Cú Chulainn said. 'I shall go,' Cú Chulainn said.

¶ 23. Cú Chulainn went to Druim Collchaille, which is called Áne Cliach. 'Say, dear kinsman Lóeg, do you know what territory we are in?' 'No, truly, I do not.' 'Truly, I do know,' Cú Chulainn said. 'Cenn Abrat in Slíab Caín is this to the south. Sléibti Éblinni is this on the north-east. The distant huge bright water that you see is the Pool of Limerick. Druim Collchaille is this place in which we are, which is called Áne Cliach, in the territory of the Little Dési. To the south of us there is the army in Clíu Máil Meic U gaine, in the land of Cú Roí mac Dári son of Dedad.' As long as they were going on like this, an enormous and heavy snow fell on the Ulstermen, so that it reached to the men's shoulders and the shafts of chariots' frames. Large-scale work was done by the Ulstermen's charioteers who raised stone columns between them for shelters for their horses, keeping them from the snow: so that there remains 'the horse coverings of the Ulstermen's horses' [Echlasa Ech (n)Ulad] from that time onward. That is one of the tangible signs of this story.

¶ 24. Onwards, Cú Chulainn and his charioteer, i.e. Lóeg, went to where the Ulstermen were. 'A question now,' Sencha son of Ailill said, 'what territory are we in?' 'We are,' Cú Chulainn said, 'in the territory of the Little Dési, in the land holding of Cú Roí mac Dári, in Clíu Máil Meic Úgaine.' 'Then woe from it,' Bricriu said, 'and woe to the Ulstermen.' 'Don't say that, Bric[riu],' Cú Chulainn said, 'for I will give information to the Ulstermen for backtracking the same way, so that we shall have gone beyond our enemies before it is day.' 'Woe to the Ulstermen for their having been born,' said Celtchair son of Uithidir, 'a foster son who gives the counsel.' 'We have not known,' said Fergna son of Findc[háem] the royal hospitaller of the Ulstermen, 'ever to have from you before this night a counsel for the Ulstermen of decrepitude or timidity or lack of martial valour, Cú Chulainn.' 'Woe for the coming of a man who gives counsel,' said Lugaid Lámderg ['Red-Hand'] son of Léte, king of Dál nAraide [now Co. Down], 'that there is no place of spear-points and swords and metal edges made for him.'

¶ 25. 'But there is another issue,' said Conchobor: 'what is your wish?' 'It is our wish,' said Celtchair son of Uithidir, 'being for a day with a night in the territory in which we are; because to depart from it [sooner] would seem to us like a military defeat, for it is not the trail of a fox in the grassland or in the wasteland or in the woodland that is ours.' 'So say, Cú Chulainn,' said Conchobor, 'what place is suitable for us to make camp for this day and night?' 'The tribal assembly place of Senchlochar is here,' Cú Chulainn said, 'and this present rough wintry season is no season of tribal assembly. And Temair Luachra is on the slope of the Eastern Luachair, and it is there that the buildings and the provisions are.' 'Then it is going to Temair Luachra that is suitable,' Sencha son of Ailill said.

¶ 26. They went forward on the direct routes to Temair Luachra, and Cú Chulainn was in the front giving them guidance. If Temair Luachra were ever deserted before or since, it was not empty that night. That was as one might expect, for a son was born to Ailill and to Medb, who had the name Maine Mó-epert, and that son was given in fosterage to Cú Roí mac Dári, and Ailill and Medb came that night together with their province's aristocracy to drink [a feast] at the end of that son's first month. Even with all these people being there, Eochu son of Luchta was there with his province, and also Cú Roí mac Dári with all the Clanna Dedad ['Children of Dedad']. And even with all these being there, Medb, the woman warrior, the daughter of Ireland's high-king, i.e. Eochu Feidlech, was a wary woman: there were two watchers and [they were] two druids, to watch over her. Their names were Crom Deróil and Crom Darail, two foster sons of the good and marvellous druid Cathbad.

¶ 27. It is at that time that it happened that these [druids] were on the wall of Temair Luachra, watching and standing lookout, regarding and staring outwards to every side from them. It is then that Crom Deróil said: 'Did you see what I saw?' 'What is that?' Crom Darail asked. 'It seems to me that they are a great number of ruddy arms, and it is the to-ing and fro-ing of well-arrayed war-bands and of companies that I see crossing the slopes of the Eastern Luachair from the east.' 'I would not be too much in my view that gore and blood should be in the mouth that would make that claim,' said Crom Darail, 'because that is no army nor arrayed war-band, but the enormous oak-trees that we came past yesterday.' 'If that's what they were, what is it that causes the enormous royal chariots under them?' 'Those aren't chariots,' Crom Darail said, 'but rather the royal ring-forts which we came past.' 'If they were ring-forts, what causes the beautiful pure-white shields in them?' 'They are not shields at all,' said Crom Darail, 'but the stone columns that are at the gates of the royal ring-forts.' 'If they were columns,' said Crom Deróil, 'what is it that causes so many spear-points of red armament over the great black middle of the vast army?' 'Those are not spear-points at all,' said Crom Darail, 'but the deer and wild beasts of the territories, with their horns and antlers on them.' 'If they were deer and stags,' said Crom Deróil, 'what is that that causes their herds of horses to cast up sods from their hooves, so that it is very black up to the sweeping sky over their heads?' 'These are not herds of horses,' Crom Darail said, 'but rather the flocks and cattle droves and cows of the territories that have been released from their corrals and wood-fenced cow-yards; for it is on these grazing lands that the birds and fowl stay on the snow.' 'On my confession, if it's birds and fowl there, it is hardly movement of birds alone.'

¶ 28.   'If they are flocks of birds with a flock's colours,

it is not the migration of birds alone.
There is a multi-coloured cloak . . . white gold.
Consider each individual bird.

If they are sure, rough flocks of birds,
that are as spear-points would be,
the bitter spears are not few
with the war shafts.

It seems to me that it is not snow showers they are
but rather indeed little men
who are from the bountiful company
with the straight spear-points
a man under each hard purple shield.
The flock is immense.'

¶ 29. 'And don't you contradict me at all,' said Crom Deróil; 'for I am the one with the truth of it. As they were coming past the tips of the oaks of the Eastern Luachair, what would make them stoop if they were not men?' And thus he was contradicting (Crom Darail), and he sang this lay:

'Crom Darail, what do I see through the mist?
On whom is the omen of gore after the battle?'
'It is not right for you to dispute with me on every count.
You say that unmoving bushes are bent men.'

'If they are bushes that are silent there, they would not arise,
unless they needed to go away.

If they are a grove of alder wood, over the wood of a cairn,
they would not go in a deceitful way, if they were dead.

Since they are not dead, their battle is fierce, their colour is rough.
They cross plains and the barrier of woods, because they are alive.

If they were trees from the tops of hills, without any hostile action,
then they would not move such cloaks, if they were but dappled.

Since they are not trees, their din is ugly, without any lie,
men with victories and men with alder [shields], whose arms are red.

Since it is on the backs of dark horses that they are, they are drawn
    out as an arrayed host.
If they are stones, they move rapidly and are red for stones.

Where does the glimmer on each helmet come from, a certain strife

. . .

as they come past the peak what makes them stoop?'

¶ 30. Cú Roí, the exquisitely formed son of Dáre, heard the dispute of the two druids before him, outside on the wall of Temair Luachra. 'These druids outside are not in agreement,' said the king of the world, Cú Roí the exquisitely formed son of Dáre. It is then that the sun rose over the curvature of the earth. 'The army is now plain to us,' said Crom Deróil. The sun rose [shining] onto the slopes of the Eastern Luachair. And so it was that he was speaking, and he chanted this lay, and Cú Roí replied to him one stanza of the lay:

'I see Luachair of many hills, the sun's coloured face beams against it.
They are warriors that come from afar between the black moor
   and wood.

If it were a flock of crows that is off in the east, if it were a heavy
   flock of landrails,
if it were a flock of calling starlings, if it were a flock of wild-geese or
   cranes;

If it were a flock of shrieking barnacle-geese, if it were a flock of
   blaring swans,
it is a long way from them to heaven, it is a short way from them to the
   grass.

Cú Roí, dear son of Dáre, man who goes across the salty current,
tell, for best is your sense, what thing moves across the aged mountain?'

'The two watchmen, the two druids, their confusion is immense.
It is a panicked eye that sees these things. Their debate is indecisive.'

'If they were horned curly cattle, if they were hard-faced rocks,
if it were a black-green sparse woodland, if it were the wave's crash of
   the sea of Mis,

if they were cattle with cattle's colour, they are not the migration of
   cows alone.
There is a wild man who shakes a dripping spear on the back of each
   cow.

There is a sword for each cow, and its shield to its left side.
There are standards, hard against hard, I see alongside the cows.'

¶ 31. The two druids [who were] two watchmen were not long there before the first band broke into the brilliant surge of Bodb across the glen. It was so barbarously that they charged that they left no spear on its spear-butt nor shield on its peg nor sword on the weapon rack in Temair Luachra that did not fall over. On every house with a roof in Temair Luachra, the roof fell off in huge plaited sheets. It was as if the sea should come over the walls and the corners of the world towards them. The colours of faces were changed, and there were teeth chattering in Temair Luachra. The two druids fell into stupors and into senselessness and swoons, one of them [fell] over the wall to the outside, namely Crom Darail, and Crom Deróil [fell] over the wall to the inside. And despite that Crom Deróil got up and cast an eye over the first band that came into the enclosed grounds.

¶ 32. The host bounded onto the grounds [of the fort]. And they sat as a convened tribe on the grounds. The snow trickled and melted thirty feet on all sides around them from the heat of the great valorous warriors. Crom Deróil came into the house where Medb and Ailill and Cú Roí and Eochu son of Luchta were, and Medb asked: 'How did this noise of weapons occur that has come towards us? Down from the air or across the sea from the west or out of Ireland from the east?' 'It is out of Ireland from the east, without doubt, across the slopes of the Eastern Luachair,' said Crom Deróil; 'the march of a barbarous host, whether they are Irishmen or they are foreigners I do not know. If they are Irishmen and not from overseas, they are Ulstermen.'

¶ 33. 'Wouldn't Cú Roí there recognise the Ulstermen?' Medb said. 'For it is often that he is on hostile expeditions and on hostings and on journeys together with them.' 'I would recognise them,' Cú Roí said, 'if only I could get their descriptions.' 'The description of the first band of them that entered, truly I have it,' Crom Deróil said. 'Give it to us then,' Medb said.

¶ 34. 'Far off to the east of the fort outside,' said Crom Deróil, 'I have seen an immense royal band: the equal of a king every single man in the group. In the forefront of it are three—a broad-eyed regal huge warrior in their midst in the centre, comparable to the moon at her greatest, at the fifteenth day of its cycle, is his aspect and his gaze and his face. He has a forked fair narrow beard, his cropped ruddy-yellow hair caught up in a tied band to the curving of the nape of his neck. A purple, fringed cloak is about him, an inlaid golden pin in his cloak above his white shoulder; a shirt of regal satin against the surface of his white skin. There is a dark purple shield with bosses of yellow gold. He has an inlaid gold-hilted sword, a spear with blades of gleaming purple in his white illustrious right hand, and its branched short spear is along with it. There is a proper warrior to his right side; bright as snow his aspect, and his gaze, and his face. A small black broad shield is to his left side; he is more resplendent by far. A fair very radiant man plays blade-feats with swords above them. His ivory-hilted, sharp, and naked stabbing sword is in one of his hands, in the other his great soldier's slashing sword. He throws them alternately up- and downwards, so that they throw shadows against the hair and against the cheek of the great warrior in the middle. Before they can fall to the ground, the same man catches their blades by their tips and edges.'

¶ 35. 'Regal is the description,' Medb said. 'Regal is the band whose description it is,' Cú Roí said. 'What is that, who is there?' Ailill asked. 'Not difficult,' Cú Roí said: 'The great warrior over there in the middle is Conchobor son of Fachtna Fáthach, the Ulstermen's own worthy king, descendant of the kings of Ireland and Britain. On his right side is Fintan son of Níall Niamglonnach, lord of a third of Ulster, and bright as snow is his countenance and his face. Cú Chulainn son of Sualtam is the small black-browed man on his left. Ferchertne son of Corpre son of Iliach is that fair very bright man, who is performing weapon-feats above them. A royal chief-poet of the royal chief-poets of the Ulstermen is he, and rear-guard to Conchobor when he goes into the country of his foes. Whoever should wish to speak with the king, he will not dare until he has spoken with that man.'

¶ 36. 'Off there, to the east of these, outside,' Crom Deróil said, 'I have seen three handsome nimble men there, with soldier's dress about them. Two of them are young and adolescent. The third lad has a branched, ruddy-brown beard. They do not take dew from the grass, so swiftly and lightly have they travelled so that none of the great host saw them, and they see all of the host.' 'Mild and light and peaceful is the description,' Medb said. 'Mild and peaceful is the band whose description it is,' Cú Roí said. 'Who is there?' Ailill asked. 'Not hard to answer, in truth,' Cú Roí said: 'these are three noble youths of the Tuath Dé Danann, Delbaeth son of Eithliu, Óengus Óc son of the Dagda, and Cermait Milbél. They came at the end of night this day to increase battle and strife, and mingled themselves with the host; and true it is that the host does not see them, and they see the host.'

¶ 37. 'Off there, to the east of these, outside,' Crom Deróil said, 'I see there a soldierly, fully valorous war-band, with a prominent trio in precedence before them. A wrathful brown-haired warrior is there, and a fair, truly beautiful warrior, and a heroic, stout-armed, strong warrior, with cropped ruddy-yellow hair. The bright glint of his hair is like the crest of a birch at the end of autumn, or to brooches of pale gold. He has a branched brown swarthy beard, equal to the measure of a warrior's arm in length; his aspect, and his gaze, and his face are comparable to the purple of the foxglove or to embers of fresh fire. They bear three brown-red warrior-like shields. They have three great, broad spear-heads, with several points upon their spear-shafts. They have three heavy, strong slashing swords. Three fine vestments of purple are about them.' 'We are aware that the description is warrior-like and heroic,' Medb said. 'Warrior-like and heroic is the band whose description it is,' Cú Roí said. 'What is that, who is there?' Ailill asked. 'Not hard to answer: these are three prime warriors of the Ulstermen, the two Conalls and Lóegaire, that is, Conall Anglonnach son of Íriel Glúnmár and Conall Cernach son of Amairgen and Lóegaire from Ráith Immil.'

¶ 38. 'Off there, to the east of these, outside,' said Crom Deróil, 'I have seen there a frightful and unknown trio in the forefront of the host. Three linen shirts are wrapped up against their skins, three shaggy grey-brown cloaks are gathered about them. Three stakes of iron are in the cloaks above their fronts. They have three heads of hair—very brown and heather-like. They carry three bright brownish shields with hard circles of white bronze. They have three broad-bladed spears and three golden-hilted swords. The snorting bellow of each warrior's heart is like the bay of a foreign hound in the attack as they hear their enemies in this stronghold.' 'Barbarous and heroic is the description,' Medb said. 'Barbarous is the band whose description it is,' Cú Roí said. 'What is that, who is there?' Ailill asked. 'Not hard to answer,' Cú Roí said: 'these are three props of battle of the Ulstermen, Uma son of Remanfissech from Fedan Cuailnge, Errge Echbél from Brí Errgi, Celtchair Mór son of Uithidir from Ráith Celtchair, from Dún Dá Lethglass.'

¶ 39. 'Out there, to the east of these, outside,' said Crom Deróil, 'I have seen a great-eyed, great-thighed, great-shouldered man, excessively great and tall, with a fine brown cloak about him. Seven short dusky hoods of equal smoothness are around him, each upper one shorter, each lower one longer. There are nine men at each of his two sides. A dreadful iron club is in his hand. It has a rough end and a gentle end. His sports and feats are that he lays the rough end upon the heads of the nines so that he slays them in a twinkling. He lays the gentle end upon them so that he brings them back to life in the same time.' 'Wonderful is the description,' Medb said. 'Multifaceted is the one whose description it is,' Cú Roí said. 'What is that, who is there?' Ailill asked. 'Not hard to answer,' Cú Roí said: 'the great Dagda son of Eithliu, the good god of the Tuath Dé Danann. In order to increase battle and strife this morning he mingled himself wth the host, and yet none in the host sees him.'

¶ 40. 'Out there, to the east of these, outside,' said Crom Deróil, 'I have seen there a stout, broad-fronted man, powerful and dark-browed, broad-faced and gleaming-toothed without dress, without clothes, without weapons, without blades, but a well-worked brown leather apron to the crotches of his two armpits. Each limb of his is thick as a man. The stone pillar that all the Children of Dedad cannot raise he took from the earth and performed the ball-feat with it from one finger to the other. He let it down from him to the ground as a young boy would let down a thistle, for swiftness and lightness.' 'Heroic, stout-armed, strong, most valorous is the description,' Medb said. 'Very mighty is the one whose description it is,' Cú Roí said. 'What is that, who is there?' Ailill asked. 'Not hard to answer: that is Triscatail the Mighty, the champion of Conchobor's house. It is he who slays the three bands of nine men by his furious look and no more.'

¶ 41. 'Out there, to the east of these, outside,' said Crom Deróil, 'I have seen a young and childlike lad in bonds and fetters. Three chains are on each of his two legs and a chain on each of his two arms. Three chains are about his neck, and seven men upon each chain, which is equal to eleven sevens. He gives a great turn, manly and vigorous, so that he overthrows the eleven sevens, and drags them as he would drag so many puffballs, for swiftness and lightness. When he would perceive the smell of his enemies, when he would strike the head of one of them against a projecting clod of the clods of the ground or against the rock, this is what that man would say: 'It is not to accomplish prowess or valour that this turn is made, but on account of the smell of the food and drink that are in this stronghold.' A fit of shame seizes him, and he goes with them for a space quietly and silently, until the same wave of barbarousness comes to him.' 'We are aware,' Medb said, 'destructive and intractable is the description.' 'Destructive and intractable is the one whose description it is,' Cú Roí said. 'What is that, who is he?' Ailill asked. 'Not hard to answer: the son of the three champions of whom I spoke before, namely, Uma son of Remanfissech, Errge Echbél and Celtchair son of Uithidir. There is need of that cohort of his host to guard him when he goes into the country of his enemies for the sake of tempering his valour. He is Uanchend Arritech, and he has completed but his eleven years; and never has he consumed his portion, but he would offer it to each one who might be in the house.'

¶ 42. 'Out there, to the east of these, outside,' said Crom Deróil, 'I have seen a band of their troop of rabble there. One man is among them, with close-shorn black bristly hair on him; great eyes in his head, all white and bulging; he has a smooth dark Ethiopian face. A cloak of striped cloth is gathered around him; a hook of brass is in his cloak above his front; a long crook of bronze is in his hand. He has with him a sweet-sounding little bell, and waves his horse lash above the host, so that he gives hilarity and merriment to the high-king and to all the host.' 'Laughable and entertaining is the description,' Medb said. 'Laughable is everything in the description,' Cú Roí said. 'Who is there?' Ailill asked. 'Not hard to answer,' Cú Roí said: 'that is Róimid the king's jester,' he said, 'Conchobor's jester. Never was there on any Ulsterman enough loss or sorrow that he would mind it if he might see Róimid the king's jester.'

¶ 43. 'Out there, to the east of these, outside,' said Crom Deróil, 'I have seen there a purple-coloured man beginning to turn grey, in a ?compartmented chariot above a tall horse-team. A much-speckled wonderful mantle is about him, with ornament of gold thread. A bracelet of gold, too, is about each of his two arms, a ring of gold about each of his fingers. He has weapons with golden ornament. Nine charioteers are before him, and nine charioteers after him, and nine charioteers at each of his two sides.' 'Stately and regal is the description,' Medb said. 'Regal and stately is he whose description it is,' Cú Roí said. 'What is that, who is there?' Ailill asked. 'Not hard to answer,' Cú Roí said: 'that is Blad Briuga son of Fiachna from Temair na hArdda, and every path he travels there is need of these nine charioteers around him, for he listens to the speech of none other of the host but to their speech. To any but him they speak but seldom.'

¶ 44. 'Out there, to the east of these, outside,' said Crom Deróil, 'I have seen there a vast regal company. One man is in the forefront of it. He has heather-like very black hair. A mild tint is in his one cheek, a foam of red blood in his other, that is, at one time a smooth, civil answer, at another time a furious one. An open-mouthed leopard (?) is on each of his two shoulders. He bears a white-fronted shield, and has a white-hilted sword. A great warrior, his spear reaches to the height of his shoulder. When its spear-heat seizes it, he strikes the butt of the great spear across his palm, so that the fill of a sack-measure of fiery tinder-sparks bursts out over its blade and over its tip, when its spear-heat takes hold of it. Before him there is a cauldron of black blood, of dreadful liquid, prepared by night by his sorcery from the blood of dogs and cats and druids, in order that the head of that spear might be dipped in that poisonous liquid when its spear-heat comes to it.' 'We are aware that the description is destructive,' Medb said. 'Destructive is the one whose description it is,' Cú Roí said. 'What is that, who is there?' Ailill asked. 'That is Dubthach Dóel Ulad,' Cú Roí said, 'a man who never earned the thanks of anyone. When all the Ulstermen make a raid, he makes a raid alone. The swift death-dealing [sword] Lúin of Celtchair he has borrowed, and has in his hand, and a cauldron of red blood is before it, so that it would not burn its shaft or the man who carried it were it not bathed in the cauldron of poisonous blood; and it is foretelling battle that it is.'

¶ 45. 'Out there, to the east of these, outside,' said Crom Deróil, 'I have seen another band there. A sleek ancient man with white-grey hair is in the vanguard of it. A cloak of bright white is about him, with border-edges of pure white silver. A beautiful shirt of pure white is encircled around him next to his skin. A [sword with] rounded hilt [?] of bright silver he carries under its cover [?] and a bronze branch reaches to the height of his shoulder. The swiftness of a minstrel is in his voice, his speech fully loud and slow.' 'We are aware that the description is judge-like and wise,' Medb said. 'Wise and judge-like is he whose description it is,' Cú Roí said. 'What is that, who is there?' Ailill asked. 'Not hard to answer: it is the great Sencha son of Ailill son of Máelchlód from the Cairn-Plain of Ulster, the skilful speaker of the men of the earth, and the peacemaker of the host of Ulster. The men of the world from the sunrising to the sunsetting he would pacify with his three brilliant words.'

¶ 46. 'Out there, to the east of these, outside,' said Crom Deróil, 'I have seen there a keen, truly beautiful band. In the vanguard of it is a young and youthful lad with yellow ever-curling hair. The judgement that the warrior who is before him cannot give, he gives it.' 'Knowing and wise is the description,' said Medb. 'Knowing and wise is the one whose description it is,' said Cú Roí. 'Who is there?' Ailill asked. 'Not hard to answer: that is Caíni Caínbrethach ['Fair-judging'], son of Sencha son of Ailill, and the judgement that his father does not give and cannot, he gives it.'

¶ 47. 'Out there, to the east of these, outside,' said Crom Deróil, 'I have seen there a grisly outlandish trio, with heads of short hair throughout and high. Brown-grey outlandish garments are about them. Three darts of brass are in their right hands, three clubs of iron in their left. No one of them speaks to another, and none of the great host speaks to them.' 'Slave-like and outlandish is the description,' said Medb. 'Slave-like and outlandish is the band whose description it is,' Cú Roí said. 'What is that, who is there?' Ailill asked. 'Not hard to answer,' Cú Roí said: 'these are the three door-keepers of Conchobor's royal house, Nem and Dall and Dorcha.'

¶ 48. (That is the description of the first company of them that came into the grounds. The great druid did not relate their description from here on.)

'These are the Ulstermen, then,' Medb said. 'They are indeed,' Cú Roí said. 'Has the like [of them] been known before or since, or do you have it in presage or prophecy?' 'If we have, we do not know it,' Cú Roí said. 'Is there any in the stronghold who knows it?' said Medb. 'There is a senior of the Children of Dedad,' Cú Roí said, 'namely Gabal Glinne, who, being blind, has been for thirty years dutifully sustained in this stronghold.' 'Let one go to inquire of him whether they have been prepared for, and let it be asked of him, what preparation has been made for them.' 'Who will go there?' Cú Roí said. 'Let Crom Deróil and Fáenglinne mac Dedad go.'

¶ 49. They went to the house in which Gabal Glinne was sustained. 'Who is here?' he said. 'Crom Deróil and Fáenglinne mac Dedad,' they said, 'asking of you whether the coming of the Ulstermen was in prophecy or prediction, or, if it is, whether there is a preparation for them.' 'Long has their coming been in prophecy, and preparation has been made for them. The preparation is a house of iron and two houses of boards around it and an earthen house below beneath it and a firm-set slab of iron on it; and all that could be found of kindling sticks and firewood and coal has been gathered into the earthen house, so that it is quite full. This is what has been foretold to us, that the nobles of Ulster would gather on the same night in that house. There are seven chains of new iron here under the legs of this bed as a preparation for binding and closing in; let them be made firm to the seven pillars that are outside upon these grounds.'

¶ 50. They came into the house in which Medb and Ailill and the nobles of the provinces were, and related to them how the Ulstermen had been prepared for. 'Let there go to bid them welcome one from you, Cú Roí, and one from me,' Medb said. 'Who shall go there?' Cú Roí said. 'The same pair,' Medb said; 'and so let them be given welcome from me along with the nobles of the province of Connacht and from you along with the nobles of the two provinces of Munster.' 'I will indeed know the man who answers the welcome,' Cú Roí said, 'whether it is in peace or in strife (they have come). For if it is Dubthach Dóel Ulad who answers, it is in belligerence they have come; if it be Sencha son of Ailill who answers, it is in peace.' They went forward to where the Ulstermen were upon the grounds. 'Your coming is welcome (to me), ever-welcome, greatly-valorous most noble high-king of Ulster,' said Crom Deróil, 'from Medb and from Ailill and from the nobles of the province of Connacht along with them.' 'Your coming is welcome (to me), ever-welcome, greatly valorous high-king of Ulster,' said Fáenglinne mac Dedad, 'from Cú Roí son of Dáre along with the nobles of the two provinces of Munster who are over there in the stronghold.' 'We consider it loyal, and the king considers it loyal,' said Sencha son of Ailill; 'and it is not to do injury or battle that the Ulstermen have come, but enlivened by drink, from Dún Dá Bend to Clíu Máil meic Ugaine, and they thought it no distinction to them to leave the region until they should spend a night residing in it.'

¶ 51. They came along to the place where Medb and Ailill and Cú Roí and Eochu with the nobles of the three provinces were. They related the matter to them. The poets and the musicians and entertainers were sent to the Ulstermen while a house was being arranged for them, to make entertainment and music for them. Messengers were sent to them to tell them that the best warrior of the Ulstermen was to make his choice of a house for them. A . . . contention arose among the Ulstermen about that. A hundred warriors of them, of like valour, rose at once and went for their weapons, until Sencha son of Ailill placated them. 'Let Cú Chulainn go there,' Sencha said; 'for the sake of his house you came; and you will be under his protection until you reach it again.'

¶ 52. Cú Chulainn got up. The Ulstermen rose as one man after Cú Chulainn. Cú Chulainn looked at the largest house that was in the settlement. That was the iron house which had two houses of boards surrounding it. Servants came there to attend them, and a huge stack of a fire was lit for them. Choice portions of food and of drink were distributed to them.

¶ 53. As night drew on their servants and attendants one by one stole away from them until the last shut the door behind him. The seven chains of new iron were put on the house and made fast to the seven stone pillars that were outside on the grounds. Three times fifty smiths, with their smith's bellows, were brought to intensify the fire. Three circles of them were set about the house. The fire was kindled from below and from above into the house, so that the fierce heat of the fire came through the house from below. The host shouted loudly about the house, and mute silence came over the Ulstermen. Then Bricriu said: 'Ulstermen! what is the immense heat which is getting at your feet? For as a whisper is more evident to me than a shout to anyone else, it seems to me that we are being burned from below and from above, and the house is closed in on us.' 'There is a trick we can use to find out,' Triscatail the Mighty said, as he got up and gave a kick to the door of new iron that was at the entrance. The door did not creak, nor did it groan, nor did it cave in.

¶ 54. 'It is not good fortune that you made your feast for the Ulstermen, Cú Chulainn,' Bricriu said. 'You have given them into an enemy's cage.' 'Don't say that, Bricriu!' Cú Chulainn said. 'I shall do with my [sword named] Crúadín something by means of which all the Ulstermen will go out.' Cú Chulainn shoved his sword so that it reached up to the hilt through the iron house and through the two board houses. 'This is a house of iron,' Cú Chulainn said, 'between two houses of boards.' 'That is worse than any other malicious ploy,' Bricriu said. 'If this cudgel of mine falls on them, it will kill them!' 'I am the one,' Triscoth said, 'that any man of them that I look at in fury will have his lips die.' 'I am the one,' Reordae Drúth [the Jester] said. 'I am the one,' Nia Natrebuin Chró. 'I am the one,' said Dóeltenga. 'It is one of us that shall go,' said Dub and Rodub [Black and Excessively Black]. All of them rose around [those two] against one another.

¶ 55. 'Don't let any of that work you up,' Sencha said. 'The man that the Ulstermen will choose, though he may not be the best warrior, he is the one who will go.' 'Which of us is that?' asked the Ulstermen. 'Cú Chulainn over there, though he may not be the best warrior, it is he who will go.'

¶ 56. After that they rose up and entered the stronghold's enclosure, led by Cú Chulainn. 'Is it this imp who is the best warrior of the Ulstermen?' Fintan said. With that Cú Chulainn leapt up high so that he was on the upper part of the courtyard; and his weapons leapt over the fore-bridge, so that the weapons which were in the stronghold fell from their racks.

¶ 57. Then they were taken into a house of oak with a cupped roof and a door of yew on it that was three feet in thickness, and two hooks of iron through it, and an iron bolt on those two hooks. The house was spread with quilts and coverlets. Crom Deróil brought their weapons after them, and they were set in place, and Cú Chulainn's weapons were raised above them. 'Heat washing water for them,' Ailill said. And he gave them beer and food until they were drunk. Crom Deróil was visiting them still to see whether there was anything they wished for. When they were drunk, Sencha beat his fateful wooden wand. They all listened to him. 'Now give your blessing to the sovereign ruler to whom you have come!' It has been made most fine for you. No hand is a barren field. There is plenty of beer and food for you thanks to the sovereign ruler you have come to. There was no need to call for service.'

¶ 58. 'That's true', Dóeltenga said. 'I swear what my tribe swears that you will not reach your land till Judgement Day but only as much of you as the birds will carry in their talons, and the men of Ireland and Britain will settle your land and take your women and your portable valuables and smash the heads of your male children on stones.'

¶ 59. It is concerning that that Fergus, during the *Táin*, said this:

> Leave Dubthach Dóeltenga out,
> drag him behind the host;
> he has not done any good thing;
> he slew the party of maidens.
>
> He performed an infamous inauspicious act,
> the slaying of Fiacha son of Conchobor.
> There was no heroic virtue heard about him,
> [concerning] the slaying of Maine son of Fedelmid.
>
> It is not the kingship of Ulster that he contests,
> the son of Lugaid son of Casrubae.
> This is what he does to men:
> those he cannot kill he turns against one another.'

¶ 60. 'That is no lie there,' said Dubthach. 'Look at the house for its strength and look at how the house penned in all around. Don't you see that though you wanted to go out it is not possible to? May there be shame on me if I were not to say that even now they are debating outside about attacking us. And yet, it is none other than that warrior over there who is best of the armed men with the Ulstermen who will find out the story from them.'

¶ 61. Cú Chulainn moved himself to action and gave a chariot warrior's salmon-leap on high, so that he took off the top roof post from the house and was then on the house post of the other house. He saw the army below him. They mustered into a single battle formation to attack [the Ulstermen]. Ailill set his back against the door to protect them. He took in hand his seven weapons from the door. The host broke out onto the middle of the enclosure of the stronghold. Cú Chulainn came to his people, and he shoved his heel against the door so that his leg went through till it reached his knee. 'Had it been your wife who had left [the door],' said Dóeltenga, 'it would [now] be lying down.' Once again Cú Chulainn shoved his heel against the door, and then the door frame fell into the hearth under him.

¶ 62. 'Let us decide,' Sencha said. 'That is what will be now,' Cú Chulainn said. 'You have every fit thing that is wanted by young warriors for combat. Here are your opponents coming for you. What do you advise?' Sencha asked. 'Put every one of your backs against the wall, and let everyone's armament be in front of him, and order one man to make parley. If that [burden] becomes too heavy to lift, put the house aside from you.' 'Who will speak to them?' Sencha aksed. 'I shall speak to them,' said Triscoth. 'Any man of them whom I shall look at, his lips will die.'

¶ 63. The enemy was organising their counsel outside. 'A question, who shall speak to them and go first to them in the house?' the young warriors outside asked. 'I shall go,' said Lopan. After that Lopan went into the house to them, with a band of nine [or he was one of the nine]. 'That is soldierly, soldiers,' he said. 'What is soldierly is a man going for his foe,' Triscoth said. 'True, true. Triscoth is here speaking on behalf of Ulster. They have no good spokesmen except him.' Triscoth looked at him furiously so that he fell down with his soles turned up.

¶ 64. After that Fer Caille came into the house, with a band of nine. 'That is a suitable mature soldier, soldiers,' he said. 'What suits a mature soldier is a man going for his foe,' said Triscoth. Triscoth looked at him furiously so that he fell down with his soles turned up.

¶ 65. After that Mianach Anaidgned came into the house, with a band of nine. 'It is very white that those wounded men there on the floor seem to us,' he said. Triscoth looked at him. 'Look at me,' he said, 'to see whether I die from it.' His opponent seized [Mianach's] leg from under him, and then he waved him around against the three bands of nine men that were in the house so that ot one of them went out alive.

¶ 66. After that the army that was outside around the house shouted to seize it from the Ulstermen. The Ulstermen threw the house over their heads, so that three hundred men fell under the house from the army that was outside. One warband closed in with the other. After that the warbands were fighting until the middle of the next day. The Ulstermen were defeated, after all, because they were [relatively] few.

¶ 67. Ailill was atop the residential building of the stronghold looking at them. [?He said:] 'News worth telling to me was news of the Ulstermen until today. I have heard that there were not in Ireland young warriors their equal, until I saw that they could bring about only disgrace today. It has for a long time been proverbial, "battle is not won without a king." If I myself were, therefore, leading the warband, it would not be for any long time that one could withstand [me]. You see that I have no power over them. It is an injury that I am harmed because of you.'

¶ 68. With that Cú Chulainn made a leap through the host, and he struck it three times. Then Furbaide Fer Bend, son of Conchobor struck it all around. The enemy would not thrust at him, because they thought he was beautiful. 'Why is this splendid man not being wounded?' asked another man of them. 'The pretty work that he does cannot be destructive.' 'I for my part swear what my tribe swears, though it were even a head of gold that was on him,[7] I would kill him as he is killing my brother.'

¶ 69. That man stabbed a spear into him, and [Furbaide Fer Bend] died from it. Then the Érainn [a tribal group with territory near where this action is set in the South-west] were overthrown in battle, and only a third of them made it out. Then, the Ulstermen killed all of the people in the fort, but they saved Ailill and his seven sons, since they were not at war against them. From then on, Temair Lúachra has not been inhabited.

¶ 70. Craumthann Nia Nár, of the Érainn, came back out. He came upon Riches, the woman satirist, in the West at Lemain. The woman was Craumthann's foster mother. 'Was my son left behind?' she asked. 'Yes, he was,' said Craumthann. 'Come with me,' she said, 'for you to take revenge.' 'What revenge?' said Craumthann. 'For you could slay Cú Chulainn to get back for [my son],' said she. 'How will that be done?' he said. 'Not hard to answer: if you have two hands for him, there will be need for nothing else, since you will take him easily.'

---

7 'Head of gold' is the value of the life or honour of a person of highest status; cf. Part I, §18 ¶29, §19 ¶4.4.5 above, ¶73 below.

¶ 71. From there, they went after the army so that they found Cú Chulainn at a ford in front of them at Crích Uathne. Riches stripped off her clothes in Cú Chulainn's presence. Cú Chulainn averted his face towards the ground in order not to see her nakedness. 'Let him be attacked at this instant, Craumthann,' Riches said. 'There is the man [going] for you, [so defend yourself],' said Lóeg. 'Absolutely not,' Cú Chulainn said; 'while the woman is in that condition, I shall not rise.' Lóeg grabbed a stone from out of the chariot, and he threw it so that it happened to strike through her arse, causing her back to break in two and for her afterwards to die from it. Then, after that, Cú Chulainn got up to oppose Craumthann, and he fought against him until he took his head with him and his armament.

¶ 72. They went afterwards behind the army until they were in Cú Chulainn's stronghold, and they spent that night there. They were entertained till the end of forty nights in a single feast of Cú Chulainn's. They went from him after a time and left a blessing with him.

¶ 73. Later, Ailill came from the south to the Ulstermen to visit them. Ailill was given the width of his face in gold and silver, and each of his sons [were given] seven *cumals* [slave women, or equal value]. Then Ailill went back to his country in peace and in harmony with the Ulstermen. After that, Conchobor was free of any downgrading of his kingship for as long as he was alive.

◆ ◆ ◆ ◆ ◆ ◆ ◆ ◆ ◆

§83. *Echtrae Nera* The Adventure of Nera

TRANS. JOHN CAREY

ONE SAMAIN NIGHT, AILILL AND MEDB WERE IN RÁITH CRUACHAN with their whole household. They set about boiling their food. Two prisoners had been hanged by them the day before. Then Ailill said, 'Whoever puts a supple twig around the foot of one of the two prisoners who are on the gallows, that man will have from me as a reward anything he wishes.'

Now the darkness and horror of that night were great, and demons used always to appear on that night. Each of the men in turn went out to try the night; and it was soon that they came inside again.

'I will have the reward from you,' said Nera. 'I will go out.'

'You will have my gold-hilted sword,' Ailill said.

Then Nera armed himself well, and went out to where the prisoners were. He put a supple twig around the foot of one of the two prisoners. It came off afterwards—this happened three times. Then the prisoner told him that unless he put a special spike in it, even if he were there till morning, its own spike would not hold the looped twig shut. Then Nera put a special spike in it.

The prisoner said to Nera from the gallows, 'Well done, Nera!'

'Well done indeed!' said Nera.

'By your honour as a warrior, take me upon your neck so that I can drink a drink with you. There was a great thirst on me when I was hanged.' 'Come onto my neck, then!' said Nera. He climbed onto his neck. 'Where shall I take you?' said Nera. 'To the house which is nearest us,' said the prisoner.

Then they went to that house. They saw something: a lake of fire around the house. 'Our drink is not in this house,' said the prisoner. 'The hearth-fire is always raked here. Go on to the next house nearest to us,' said the prisoner.

They went there, and saw a lake of water around it. 'Do not go to that house,' said the prisoner. 'There is never any water left over from washing and bathing, nor a tub with slops, left there after bedtime. Go on to the next house,' said the prisoner.

'My drink is in this house, anyway,' said the prisoner. He let him down onto the ground. He went into the house. There was used washing-water and bathing-water there, and he took a drink from each. There was a tub of slops in the middle of the house, and he drank from it and then spat the last mouthful from his mouth into the faces of the people who were in the house, so that they all died. Hence it is not good for there to be water left over from washing and bathing, or a hearth-fire which has not been raked, or a tub with slops in it, in a house after bedtime.

After that Nera carried him back to his torture, and returned to Cruachu [i.e. Ráith Cruachan]. He saw something: the stronghold before him had been burnt, and he saw the heads of its people which had been heaped up by the warriors from the [enemy] stronghold. He followed the army into the cave of Cruachu.

'There is a man in the troop,' said the last man next to Nera. 'Heavier is the troop,' said his companion to him; and every man said those words to his companion, from the last man up to the first. After that they reached the *síd* of Cruachu, and went into the *síd*.

'What shall be done with the man who came with you?' said one of the men. 'Let him come here so that I may speak with him,' said the king. He came to him then, and the king spoke with him. 'What brought you into the *síd* with the warriors?' said the king to him. 'I was accompanying your army,' said Nera. 'Go to that house over there,' said the king. 'There is a single woman there, who will make you welcome. Tell her that I sent you to her. And come to this house every day with a bundle of firewood.'

It was done as he had been instructed. He was made welcome, and [the woman] said, 'You are welcome, if it is the king who sent you hither.' 'He did,' said Nera. Nera used to go to the court every day with a bundle of firewood. Every day he saw before him a blind man with a lame man on his back coming out of the court. They would go to the edge of the spring in front of the court. 'Is it there?' said the blind man. 'It is indeed,' said the lame man; 'let us go hence!'

Nera asked the woman about that. 'Why,' he said, 'do the blind man and the lame man visit the spring?' 'They visit the crown which is in the spring,' said the woman: 'a diadem of gold which is on the head of the king. That is where it is kept.' 'Why is it those two who go there?' said Nera. 'Because,' said she, 'it is they whom the king trusts to visit the crown. One of the men was blinded, and the other was lamed.'

'Come here now for a little,' said Nera, 'so that you can tell me something about my adventures.' 'What has appeared to you?' said the woman. Nera answered, 'When I was going into the *síd*, it seemed to me that Ráith Cruachan was destroyed, and that Ailill and Medb and their whole household had been slain.' 'That is not true,' said the woman; 'it is an army of phantoms which came to you. [But] it will become true,' she said, unless he revealed it to his comrades. 'How can I warn my people?' said Nera. 'Go to them,' she said. 'They are still around the same cauldron, and its contents have not yet been taken from off the fire.' But he had reckoned that he had been in the *síd* for three days and three nights. 'Tell them that watch should be kept on the Samain that is coming, unless they come themselves to ravage the *síd*. For that has been prophesied of them: that Ailill and Medb would ravage the *síd* and bear off Brión's crown.'

(These are the three things that were found in [the *síd*]: Lóegaire's mantle in Armagh, and Brión's crown in Connacht, and the snare (?) of Dúnlaing among the Laigin in Kildare.)

'How will it be believed that I have gone into the *síd*?' asked Nera. 'Bring the fruits of summer [*toirthe samraid*] with you,' said the woman. So he brought wild garlic with him, and primroses and buttercups. 'And I will be pregnant by you,' said the woman, 'and I will bear you a son. And send me a message, when your people come to ravage the *síd*, so that I can fetch your own people and cattle out of the *síd*.'

Then Nera went to his people, and found them around the same cauldron.

He told them his story, and the sword was given to him, and he stayed with his people after that until the year was up. (That was the very year in which Fergus mac Róich left the territory of the Ulaid to go into exile, and came to Ailill and Medb in Cruachain Aí.) 'It is the time of your meeting, Nera,' Ailill said. 'Go, so that you may bring your people and cattle out of the *síd*, so that we may ravage it.'

Nera went to his wife in the *síd*, and she wished him welcome. 'Go forth to the court,' his wife said to Nera, 'and take a bundle of firewood with you. For a whole year I have been going there every day with a bundle of firewood on my back in your stead; I have said that you have been ill. And here is your son, over there.'

He went forth to the court, with a bundle of firewood on his back. 'Welcome back alive from your sickness!' said the king. 'But I am displeased that the woman slept with you without asking.' 'Your own will will be done in that matter,' said Nera. 'It will not be any harder for you,' said the king. He went back to his house. 'Look after your cattle today,' said the woman. 'I gave one of the cows to your son, as soon as he was born.' Then Nera went out that day with his cows.

Then, as he slept, the Morrígain bore off his son's cow, so that the Donn of Cuailnge bulled it in Cuailnge in the east; after that she came back westward with the cow. Cú Chulainn overtook her as she was returning, in Mag Muirthemne. (For it was one of Cú Chulainn's *gessi* ['sworn tabus'] that cattle or women be permitted [to leave] his territory (?), unless he knew of it. It was one of his *gessi* for birds to graze in his territory, unless they left something with him; or for fish to be in the river-mouths, unless he slew them. It was one of his *gessi* for there to be warriors of a foreign race in his territory without his challenging them before morning if they came by night, or before night if they came by day. Every marriageable girl or single woman among the Ulaid was under his protection until she was entrusted to a husband. Those are the *gessi* of Cú Chulainn.) Cú Chulainn overtook the Morrígain with her cow. 'The cattle-drive must not be made!' Cú Chulainn said.[8]

Nera came home in the evening with his cows. 'I have lost my son's cow,' he said. 'It is not my due, that you should go herding in that fashion,' his wife said to him. With that the cow came. 'Strange! From where has the cow come?' 'She has come,' said the woman, 'from Cuailnge, after being bulled by the Donn of Cuailnge. Go now,' said the woman, 'lest your warriors be anxious. This warband can do nothing for a year, until the next Samain. They will come again

---

8 This is a fragmentary version of the story *Táin Bó Regamna*, which goes on to describe the conversation between Cú Chulainn and the Morrígain, and her prophecy of the events of *Táin Bó Cuailnge*.

next Samain night, for the *síde* of Ireland are always open at Samain.'

Nera came to his people. 'Where do you come from?' said Ailill and Medb to Nera, 'and where have you been since you went from us?' 'I have been in fair lands,' said Nera, 'with treasures and great riches, with abundance of clothing and food and strange treasures. They will come to destroy you on the Samain night which is coming, unless it is revealed to you.' 'We will go against them, then,' Ailill said. They remained there until the end of a year. 'If you have anything in the *síd*, Nera,' Ailill said, 'bring it out.'

On the third day before Samain, then, he brought his cattle out of the *síd*. As the bull calf came out of the *síd*, the calf of Aingen's cow—Aingen[e] was the name of his son—uttered three bellows. At that time Ailill and Fergus were playing *fidchell* [a board game]. They heard something: the bull calf's bellow in the plain. It is then that Fergus said:

> Not pleasing to me is the calf
> which bellows in the plain of Cruachu:
> the son of the Black One of Cuailnge. . .,
> the son of the bull beyond Loch Loíg.
>
> Because of him, calves will be without cows
> in Bairrche, in Cuailnge.
> The king will set out upon a great march
> because of Aingen's calf.

(Aingene was the name of the man and Bé nAingene was the name of the woman; and the appearance which Nera saw upon them was the same which Cú Chulainn saw in *Táin Bó Regamna*.)[9]

Then that calf encountered the Finnbennach in the plain of Cruachu. They fought for a day and a night, until at last the calf was beaten. The calf bellowed then, when it was beaten. 'Why did the calf bellow?' Medb asked her cowherd, who was named Buaigle.

'I know that, *popa* Fergus; it is the song which you sang in the morning,' Bricriu said. Fergus looked aside at him at that, and struck Bricriu across the head with his fist, so that the five *fidchell*-pieces which were in Fergus's fist went into Bricriu's head, which was a cause of lasting ill to him.

'He said,' said Buaigle, 'that if his father the Donn of Cuailnge were to come to fight against [the Finnbennach], he would not be seen in Aí, and he would be beaten from end to end of Mag nAí.' Then Medb made an oath: 'I swear by

---

9 Cf. the previous note. The allusion is to an elaborate and grotesque description of the Morrígain and her male companion in *TBR*; there seems to be some confusion here as to whether Aingene is the name of this mysterious figure, or of Nera's son.

the gods by whom my tribe swears that I will not lie down, nor sleep upon feathers or cushions, that I will not drink buttermilk, nor care for (?) my side, nor drink red ale or wine, nor eat any food, until I have those two bulls fighting before me.'

Then the men of Connacht and the 'black exiles'[10] went into the *síd*, so that they ravaged the *síd* and brought forth what was within, and after that brought out the crown of Brión. That is one of the three wondrous gifts (?) of Ireland, together with the mantle of Lóegaire in Armagh, and the snare (?) of Dúnlaing among the Laigin in Kildare. Nera was left in the *síd* together with his people, and he has not come out yet, and he will not come out until the end of the world.

◆　◆　◆　◆　◆　◆　◆　◆

§84. The Death of Lóegaire Buadach

ed. Kuno Meyer, 'The Death-tales of the Ulster Heroes', *Todd Lect. Ser.* 14, p. 22, TRANS. JOHN CAREY

ᕼOW DID LÓEGAIRE BUADACH'S DEATH COME ABOUT? Not hard to tell. Aed mac Aininne slept with Mugain Aittinchairchech. Mugain was Conchobor's wife. Aed was one of Conchobor's poets. Their affair was discovered. The poet was seized by Conchobor. He asked that his execution be by drowning, and Conchobor granted him that. After that he was taken to be drowned in every lake in Ireland; and he used to chant a spell above the water, so that every shore was made dry, and not a drop remained upon it. No river or lake in Ireland would drown him until he reached Loch Laí, in front of Lóegaire's house. The spell had no effect upon that lake. When they were about to drown him, Lóegaire's steward came from the courtyard. 'Alas, Lóegaire!' he said. 'In all Ireland no place for drowning the poet was found until he came here.' Then Lóegaire rose and seized his sword; and as he bounded from the house he struck the top of his head against the lintel of the door, so that the

---

10 'Black exiles', i.e. Fergus and the other exiles from Ulster.

back of his skull was knocked off and bits of his brains were strewn upon his mantle. Then he killed thirty of the men charged with the drowning, and Aed escaped from them. Lóegaire died after that. So that is the death of Lóegaire.

◆ ◆ ◆ ◆ ◆ ◆ ◆ ◆

§85. The Death of Fergus Mac Róich

ed. Kuno Meyer, 'The Death-tales of the Ulster Heroes', *Todd Lect. Ser.* 14, p. 32–4,
TRANS. JOHN CAREY

ᕼOW DID FERGUS MAC RÓICH'S DEATH COME ABOUT? Not hard to tell. Fergus was in exile in Connacht after he had been dishonoured with regard to the sons of Uisliu. (For he had been one of the three pledges for their safety, he and Dubthach Doeltenga and Cormac Connloinges.) They were all in exile in the west until the end of fourteen years; and in all that time the wailing and trembling which they brought upon the Ulaid never ceased, but they brought wailing and trembling upon them every night. It was he who killed Fiachra mac Conchobair and Geirge mac Illeda and Eógan mac Curthacht. It is by Fergus that the great cattle-raid was taken. He did many deeds in the court of Ailill and Medb, and he and his men were more often abroad in the field than they were at court. Three thousand men was the number of the exiles; and (Fergus') comrade in Ailill's court was Lugaid the blind poet. Lugaid was Ailill's brother.

After their deeds they were beside the lake on Mag nAí. They had a great encampment there where they held games and meetings. One day the whole host went into the lake to bathe. 'Go down, Fergus,' Ailill said, 'and dunk the men!' 'They are no good in water,' said Fergus. He went down all the same. Medb's heart would give her no ease until she went into the lake. When Fergus came into the lake all the gravel and stones which were on the bottom were brought to the surface. Then Medb went onto Fergus' breast, and wrapped her legs around him, so that the lake concealed them (?) then. Ailill was seized by jealousy. Afterwards Medb came up again.

'It is charming what the stag and doe are doing in the lake, Lugaid,' Ailill said. 'Why should they not be killed?' said Lugaid, who had never made a false spear-cast. 'Make a cast at them for us!' Ailill said. 'Turn my face towards them,' said Lugaid, 'and give me a spear.'

Fergus was washing himself in the lake, and his breast (*bruinne*) was towards them. Ailill's chariot was fetched to him, so that he had it beside him. Lugaid cast the spear, so that it came out on the other side, through his back. 'The cast reached its mark!' said Lugaid. 'That is true,' said everyone. 'That is the end (*bruinne*) of Fergus.'

'It is sad,' said Lugaid, 'that I should kill my comrade and foster brother without just cause.' 'Bring me my chariot!' Ailill said. The whole host fled, each man going his own way, both the exiles and the Connachta. Fergus plucked out the spear and cast it after Ailill so that it went through the hunting-dog which was between the shafts of his chariot. He came out of the lake then, and laid himself out on the hill beside the lake, and at once his soul left him. His grave is still there. So that is the death of Fergus.

◆ ◆ ◆ ◆ ◆ ◆ ◆ ◆ ◆ ◆ ◆

§86. The Death of Cú Chulainn
as related in the Book of Leinster
TRANS. JOHN CAREY

. . .The sons learned magic [*druídecht*] and hostile spells [*coimlecht*] and blighting [*admilliud*] and 'sucking forth' [*toshúgud*];[11] the daughters learned knowledge and books [*dúile*] and witchcraft [*amaitecht*]. . . . . . .And blinded [them] all, so that they were blind in the left eye. . . . . . .Great was their longing to avenge their father with the arts which they had learned. . . .

. . . 'No, it was no mere jest for my father to oppose Cú Chulainn: perhaps it will be no mere jest for me, if I undertake it. . . . '

. . . 'And when shall we go against Cú Chulainn?' Erc said. 'Not hard to answer,' said the sons of Calatín. 'When three weapons are made with which to attack him: it will be the work of a week. . . . . . .'We think it time,' said Erc and Lugaid, 'to muster to us the men of Ireland.' 'It is not yet time,' said the sons of Calatín; 'for the work of a week is the work of seven years, that is, a day every year to be spent in making the spears. . . .'

. . . Maine, a venomous man: it is he who riveted [the spears] and smoothed them thereafter. . . .

. . . The Ulaid decided on the advice to give to Cú Chulainn: that he should not go forth from Emain Macha until the Ulaid could go around him. . . .

---

11 This account of Cú Chulainn's death lacks a beginning; further fragments survive however in another manuscript, and I have given below those which come from the part of the story missing from the Book of Leinster. In the main text there are several speeches in obscure diction, and a few poems; I have made no attempt to translate these.

. . . 'Cú Chulainn will bring [it]; and be on the watch for him. . .'

◆ ◆ ◆ ◆ ◆ ◆ ◆ ◆ ◆ ◆ ◆ ◆

'. . .that I have never allowed there to be lamenting by women and boys without intervening until now.'

Then the fifty queens came before him, and bared their breasts to him. It is by them, so it is told, that women's breasts were first bared, i.e. during his boyhood deeds, and [again now] to keep Cú Chulainn in Emain Macha. And the three vats of water were brought to quench his fury; and he was not allowed to go to the battle that day.

'I see that you have not brought Cú Chulainn here today with your skill of "sucking forth", sons of Calatín,' said Lugaid. 'The men who are here from Dún Cermnai and Belach Con Glais and Temair Luachra and Commar na Trí nUisce have been a long time before Béoil Menbolg. Bad is this craft of "sucking forth" of yours; it is long till Cú Chulainn comes,' said Lugaid.

'He will come through our agency tomorrow.'

They were there next day; and the children of Calatín put a magical appearance on the hosts around Emain Macha until all the plain of Macha was one great cloud of the smoke of conflagration, and Emain Macha tumbled down upon the hosts, and the weapons fell from their racks. And the bad news was brought to Cú Chulainn.

Then Lebarcham said, 'Arise, Cú Chulainn,' &c.

So then Cú Chulainn said, 'Wait for me, girl,' &c.

Then Niam daughter of Celtchar, Conall Cernach's wife, said, 'It is right for you, Cú Chulainn,' &c.

'Woman,' Cú Chulainn said, 'though I am doomed, conscience does not overtake me (?) which has protected my honour. Loss does not frighten me; I do not avoid my wounding.'

Then Cú Chulainn leaped to his weapons, and wrapped himself in a mantle. The first mantle which he put on burst around him, so that its brooch fell from his hand. Then Cú Chulainn said, 'The brooch which brings a warning is not guilty,' &c.

After that he wrapped himself in his mantle, and took his shield with a scalloped edge. Then he said to Lóeg son of Riangabair, 'Prepare the chariot for us, *popa* Lóeg.'

'I swear by the god my tribe swears by,' said Lóeg, 'that if the whole of Conchobor's province were around the Liath Macha they could not bring him to the chariot. I never contradicted you until today; the spirits in which I have always rejoiced are not in me now. If you wish, come to speak with the Liath yourself.'

Cú Chulainn went to him; and the horse turned his left side to him three times. And the Morrígain had broken the chariot the night before; for she did not wish Cú Chulainn to go to the battle, for she knew that he would not come back to Emain Macha. So that because of that Cú Chulainn said to the Liath Macha, 'It was not usual, illustrious Liath,' &c.

Then the Liath Macha came and shed great round tears of blood on his feet. At that Cú Chulainn leaped into the chariot, and raced off southward along the road of Midluachair. He saw a girl in front of him, Lebarcham daughter of Áu and Adarc ['Ear' and 'Horn']; Áu and Adarc were a male and a female slave in the house of Conchobor. Then Lebarcham said, 'Do not leave us, do not leave us, Cú Chulainn,' &c.; and the three times fifty women who were in Emain Macha said the same thing in a great voice.

'It would be better that they not be left,' said Lóeg, 'for that is what you have never violated until today: the strength of your mother's race.'

'Alas!' Cú Chulainn said, 'keep on, Lóeg, leave it be! Maintenance is proper to a charioteer, protecting [a territory] to a chariot-warrior, counsel to a champion, manliness to men, despondency to women. Go before me to the battle. Do not nourish the compassion which does not help you.'

The chariot was drawn around on a sunwise course. At that the troop of women gave a cry of lamentation; with that the troop of women gave a cry of lamentation and mourning, and they beat their hands, for they knew that he would not come back to Emain Macha. . . .

The house of his foster mother, who had raised him, was before him on the road. He always used to visit her when he went driving past her southward or northward; she always had a drink waiting for him. He drank the drink, and went forth, and wished his foster mother farewell.

He went on along the road of Midluachair, across Mag Mugna. He saw something: three witches blind in the left eye, before him on the road. They were cooking a lap-dog, with poison and spells, on spits of holly. It was one of Cú Chulainn's *gessi* to pass a cooking-place without visiting it to eat something there. But it was also a *geis* [tabu] of his to eat the flesh of his namesake. He made haste and sought to go past: he knew that they were not there to do him good.

Then the witch said, 'Pay a visit, Cú Chulainn.'

'I will not,' Cú Chulainn said.

'The food is only a hound [*cú*],' she said. 'If it were a great roast which was here,' she said, 'you would visit; but since there is only a little you will not. He does not deserve the great who will not take the little.'

Then he approached; and the witch gave him the dog's shoulder with her left hand. Cú Chulainn took it from her hand and put it under his left thigh. The hand which took it and the thigh under which he put it were stricken from top to bottom, so that their normal strength did not remain in them.

They went on along the road of Midluachair around Sliab Fuait, heading southward. Then Cú Chulainn said to Lóeg, 'What do you see for us, *popa* Lóeg?' Lóeg said, 'Many doomed men, and great carnage.' 'Woe, alas!' Cú Chulainn said. . . .

When Cú Chulainn came southward along the road of Midluachair, he and the host encamped in Mag Muirthemne beheld one another. Then Erc son of Cairpre said: 'I behold a fair chariot coming,' &c. 'That man is coming towards us, men of Ireland! Prepare for him!'

Then a mound of sods was raised beneath Erc son of Cairpre, and an array of shields was made around him; and the men of Ireland were drawn up in three fierce equally-proficient armies. And Erc said, 'Prepare for that man (i.e., Cú Chulainn), men of Ireland!'; and he said these words: 'Arise, men of Ireland!', &c.

'How shall we make ready? How shall we stand fast against his feats?' said the men of Ireland. 'Not hard to answer. Here is my counsel to you,' said Erc: 'let the four provinces of the provinces of Ireland who are here make a single host of yourselves; and a single wall of shields beneath that host and around it and above it. And set three men at each corner of that host—two of those who are strongest in the host fighting, and a long-haired (?) satirist with them— so that they may demand his spear from him, which is named *Blad ar Bladaib*; and so that they may demand the spears which have been prepared, when these are cast at him. It is prophesied of his spear that a king will be slain by it, if it is not demanded of him. And give a cry of woe and lamentation: the man will not accept it (?) because of his fury and the greater fury of the horses, and he will not demand single combat with you as he did on the cattle-raid of Cuailnge.' It was done then as Erc had said.

Then Cú Chulainn came to the host, and he performed the three thunder-feats standing on his chariot: the thunder-feat of a hundred, and the thunder-feat of three hundreds, and the thunder-feat of three nines, to clear the hosts from Mag Muirthemne. Cú Chulainn came to the host, and set about the craft of plying his arms upon them. He plied spear and shield and sword and feats alike, so that as many as the sands of the sea, and the stars of heaven, and the dew of May, and snowflakes and hailstones, and leaves on the trees, and buttercups upon Bregmag, and grass under horses' hooves on a summer day were their cloven heads and cloven skulls and severed hands, and their red bones scattered far and wide across Mag Muirthemne; and that plain was grey with their brains after the sudden attack and plying of weapons which Cú Chulainn wrought upon them.

Then he saw two men fighting without any to separate them. 'Shame on you, Cú Chulainn, that you do not intervene between these two,' said the satirist. Then Cú Chulainn sprang at them, and gave a blow of his fist to the head of each so that their brains came out through their ears and nostrils. 'You have intervened indeed,' said the satirist; 'neither of them will do (?) ill to the other.' 'They would not be made quiet by asking it of them,' Cú Chulainn said.

'Give me that spear, Cú Chulainn,' said the satirist.

'I swear what my tribe swears: you have no more need of it than I. The men of Ireland are attacking me here, and I am attacking them.'

'I will satirise you if you do not give it,' said the satirist.

'I have never been satirised because of stinginess.' With that he hurled the spear at him, the butt-end first, so that it went through his head and killed nine men on the other side of him.

Cú Chulainn passed through the host to the far side. Then Lugaid son of Cú Roí took one of the three spears which had been prepared by the sons of Calatín. 'What will fall by this spear, sons of Calatín?' said Lugaid. 'A king will fall by that spear,' said the sons of Calatín. Then Lugaid cast the spear at the chariot so that it struck Lóeg son of Riangabair, and the entrails in the midst of his body came out onto the chariot's upholstery. It is then that Lóeg said, 'Sharply have I been wounded', &c.

Then Cú Chulainn drew out the spear, and said farewell to Lóeg; and Cú Chulainn said, 'Today I am both chariot-warrior and charioteer.'

When Cú Chulainn reached the far side of the host he saw two men fighting before him, and a long-haired (?) satirist with them. 'Shame on you, Cú Chulainn,' said one of the men, 'that you do not intervene between us.' Then Cú Chulainn sprang upon them and hurled them apart, so that he broke them into bits on a rock that was nearby.

'Give me that spear, Cú Chulainn,' said the satirist.

'I swear what my tribe swears,' Cú Chulainn said, 'that you do not need the spear any more than I do. It is my arm and my valour and my weapons which must clear the four provinces of Ireland from Mag Muirthemne today.'

'I will satirise you,' said the satirist.

'I am obliged to yield to only one demand in a day; and I have already paid for my honour today.'

'I will satirise the Ulaid on account of you,' said the satirist.

'They have never been satirised,' he said, 'because of me or because of my churlishness; however little of my life remains, they will not be satirised today.' Cú Chulainn gave him the spear butt-end first so that it went through his head and killed nine men behind him; and he went through the host as we have said before.

Erc son of Cairpre took one of the three spears which had been prepared by the sons of Calatín. 'What will this spear do, sons of Calatín?' said Erc son of Cairpre. 'Not hard to answer: a king will be slain by that spear,' said the sons of Calatín. 'I heard you say that [a king] would fall by the spear which Lugaid cast a long time ago.' 'That is true,' said the sons of Calatín: 'the king of the charioteers of Ireland fell by it, the charioteer of Cú Chulainn, Lóeg son of Riangabair.' 'I swear what my tribe swears, it does not go to strike the king whom it has struck (?)'

Then Erc cast the spear at him, so that it struck the Liath Macha. Cú Chulainn drew the spear out, and they wished each other farewell. Then the Liath Macha went off, and half of the yoke on his neck, until he went into Linn Léith ['Liath's lake'] in Sliab Fuait: out of it he had come to Cú Chulainn, and into it he went after he had been wounded. And so it is therefore that Cú Chulainn said, 'You will run today as a horse of a single yoke.'

Then Cú Chulainn put one foot under the end of the yoke, and drove through the host just as before. He saw two men fighting in front of him, and a long-haired (?) satirist with them. He parted them; and that parting was no worse than what he had done for the other four.

'Give me that spear, Cú Chulainn,' said the satirist.

'You do not need this spear any more than I.'

'I will satirise you,' said the satirist.

'I have paid for my honour,' he said.

'I will satirise the Ulaid because of you.'

'I have paid for their honour,' he said.

'I will satirise your race,' said the satirist.

'Tales of my reproach shall not go before me to the land to which I have not come; for little of my life remains.' Cú Chulainn cast the spear at him, and the butt-end towards him, so that it went through his head and through three times nine other men.

'That is a gift with anger, Cú Chulainn,' said the satirist.

After that Cú Chulainn again passed through the host to the far side. Then Lugaid took hold of one of the three spears which had been prepared by the sons of Calatín. 'What will this spear do, sons of Calatín?' 'A king will fall by it,' said the sons of Calatín. 'I heard you say that [a king] would fall by the spear which Erc cast this morning.' 'That is true,' he [sic] said: 'the king of the horses of Ireland fell by it, the Liath Macha.' 'I swear what my tribe swears, it does not go to strike the king whom it has struck (?)'

Then Lugaid cast the spear at Cú Chulainn so that it pierced him, so that what was in his midriff came out onto the chariot's upholstery. At that the Dub Sainglenn left him, with half his yoke, so that he went into Loch nDub in the territory of the Múscraige Tíre: out of it he had come to Cú Chulainn, and into it he went again, so that then the lake boiled.

After that the chariot sat alone on the plain. Then Cú Chulainn said, 'I would like to go to the lough yonder, to drink a drink from it.' 'You have our leave,' they said, 'provided that you come back to us.' 'If I do not come back,' Cú Chulainn said, 'I will call you so that you may come for me.'

Then he gathered his entrails up in his bosom, and went off to the lough. As he reached the lough he pressed his hand against his belly, so as to keep his entrails in his belly. He drank a drink then, and washed himself. From that Loch Lámraith ['hand-guarantor lough' (?)] in Mag Muirthemne is named; another name for it is Loch Tonnchuil. Then he leaped away, and called out to them to come for him.

A broad territory extended westward from the lough, and he cast his eye upon it, and went to a stone pillar which is in the plain. And he put his belt around it, so that he might not die sitting or lying down, but might die standing up. Then the men came around him, and did not dare approach him; they thought he was alive. 'Shame on you,' said Erc son of Cairpre, 'that you do not bring the man's head away with you in revenge for my father's head, which was carried off by him and buried next to the stump of the neck of Eochaid Nia Fer; his head had been carried off so that it is in Síd Nenta iar nUisciu.'

Then the Liath Macha came to protect Cú Chulainn as long as his soul remained in his body and the lon láith [?'hero's light'] still blazed from his forehead. It is then that the Liath Macha made the three 'red onsets' around him, so that fifty were slain by his teeth and thirty by each of his hooves: that is what he killed of the host. So that it is because of that that it is said 'They are not the victorious onsets of the Liath Macha after the killing of Cú Chulainn'.

After that the scald-crow alit on his shoulder. 'Birds were not accustomed to light on that pillar,' said Erc son of Cairpre. Then Lugaid arranged his hair behind him, and cut off his head. Then Cú Chulainn's sword fell from his hand so that it severed Lugaid's arm, so that it was on the ground. So Cú Chulainn's arm was cut off to avenge that.

Then the armies departed, taking with them Cú Chulainn's head and arm, and came to Tara. So that that is where the resting-place [literally 'sickbed'] of his head and arm are, and the full of his shield of earth. Concerning him Cenn Fáelad son of Ailill said in 'The Deaths of the Ulaid': 'Cú Chulainn fell, a fair hero', &c.

Then the armies went southward from there until they reached the river Liffey. When they came to the river Lugaid said to his charioteer, 'It is heavy for me, that my girdle should be full around me (?),' he said. 'I want to bathe myself.' They went off in front of the host. He bathed then. After that they went onward. A salmon came between his calves; he cast it up to his charioteer. At once he kindled a fire to prepare it.

It is then that the Ulaid came southward from Emain Macha to Sliab Fuait, after putting their debility from them. There was a compact of mutual boasting between Cú Chulainn and Conall Cernach: whichever of them was killed first, the other would avenge him. 'And if I am killed first,' Cú Chulainn said, 'how quickly will you avenge me?' 'On the day on which you are killed,' Conall Cernach said, 'I will avenge you before evening. And if I am killed,' Conall said, 'how quickly will you avenge me?' 'I will not let your blood grow cold upon the earth,' Cú Chulainn said, 'before I avenge you.'

As Conall Cernach came before the host in his chariot he saw the Liath Macha going to Linn Léith, bleeding from many wounds. Then Conall Cernach said: 'Not able to bear a yoke to Linn Léith (?)', &c. Then Conall Cernach went, and the Liath Macha before him, and they made a circuit of the battlefield. They saw Cú Chulainn by the pillar. Then the Liath Macha went and laid his head on Cú Chulainn's breast. 'That body yonder is a grief to the Liath Macha,' Conall said. Then Conall went and set his foot upon the hedge [airbe]. 'I swear what my tribe swears,' he said: 'this hedge will be the hedge of a great man [rofher].' 'You have given the place its name,' said the druid. 'The name of this region will be Airbe Rofhir forever.'

Then he set out after the army. Lugaid was bathing. 'Keep a watch on the plain for us,' said Lugaid to his charioteer, 'lest anyone come upon us unawares.' The charioteer looked past him.

'A lone horseman is coming,' he said, 'and great are the speed and swiftness with which he comes. You would think that the ravens of Ireland were above him. You would think that snowflakes cover the plain in front of him.'

'Not dear to us is the horseman who comes there,' said Lugaid: 'that is Conall Cernach, mounted upon the Derg Drúchtach. The birds which you saw above him are the clods from the hooves of the horse. The snowflakes that you saw covering the plain in front of him are the foam which comes from the horse's mouth and bridle-bit. Look again,' said Lugaid, 'to see what way he takes.'

'He is coming towards the ford,' said the charioteer, 'the way that the army went.'

'Let the horse go past us,' said Lugaid; 'we have no wish to encounter him.'

When Conall Cernach reached the middle of the ford, he looked to one side. 'The smoke of a salmon is there,' he said. He looked to the side a second time. 'The smoke of a charioteer is there,' he said. He looked to the side a third time. 'The smoke of a king is there,' he said. 'It were well for me to go thither.'

He went to them. 'Welcome is the face of a debtor,' Conall Cernach said; 'the one to whom he owes the debt demands it of him. And you are my debtor,' Conall Cernach said, 'for the killing of my comrade Cú Chulainn; and I am come to make the claim on you.'

'It is not right,' said Lugaid; 'for it will not be reckoned warrior-like in you to fight against me here, until the glory of slaying me may reach my land of Munster (?).'[12]

'I would do it, if there was a way for us not to travel on a single road, talking together and being together,' Conall Cernach said.

'There will be no difficulty in that regard,' said Lugaid. 'I will go by Belach Gabráin until I come into Belach Smechuin; do you go across Gabor and Mairg Lagen, so that we may meet in Mag Argetrois.'

Lugaid came first; his companion came after him, that is, Conall Cernach. He made a cast at him with his spear (and his foot was against the stone pillar which is in Mag Argetrois), so that he struck Lugaid; from this is Coirthe Lug-dach ['Lugaid's pillar'] in Mag Argetrois.

After that first wounding he went to Ferta Lugdach in Droichte Ossairge. They came up with one another. 'I should like,' said Lugaid, 'to have fair play from you.'

'In what way?' Conall Cernach said.

'That you use only one arm against me, for I have only one arm.'

'You will have that,' Conall Cernach said. Then his arm was bound to his side with ropes.

They were [fighting] from one hour to another, and neither got an advantage over the other. When Conall did not get the advantage he glanced aside at his

---

12 This is the best that I can do with the wording of the text. The sense seems to be that the heroic thing for Conall to do is not to fight Lugaid on ground unfamiliar to the latter, but to allow him to return to his own province and then encounter him there.

horse, the Derg Drúchtach. (A hound's head was on her; she would slay men in battles and combats.) With that the horse came to him, so that she took a piece out of his side, so that what was in his midriff came out around his feet.

'Alas!' said Lugaid. 'That is not fair play, Conall Cernach!'

'I only granted it to you,' Conall Cernach said, 'on my own account. I did not grant it to you on behalf of beasts and senseless animals.'

'I know,' said Lugaid, 'that you will not go until you take my head with you, for we took Cú Chulainn's head. Do you then put my head on your head,' he said, 'so that you may add (?) my kingship to your kingship and my prowess to your prowess. For I would prefer,' he said, 'that you were the best warrior in Ireland.'

With that Conall Cernach struck off his head.

He set out then taking the head with him, and met up with the Ulaid in Rairiu in the lands of the Laigin. The head was set upon the stone and was forgotten there. They came to Gris. Then Conall Cernach asked, 'Did any of you bring the head?' 'We did not,' said everyone. Then Conall Cernach said, 'I swear what my tribe swears, that is no small crime [mid-bine].' Hence is named Midbine in Rairiu. They returned to the head. They saw something: the head had melted the stone so that it had gone through it.

The Ulaid did not consent [to return (?)] in triumph to Emain Macha that week. But the soul of Cú Chulainn consented, so that he appeared to the fifty queens whom he had spurned on that day before going into battle. Something was seen: Cú Chulainn in his phantom-chariot in the air above Emain Macha. Then Cú Chulainn chanted to them, saying after his death: 'Emain, Emain', &c. [Two more arcane compositions follow, with the headings 'The phantom discourse of Cú Chulainn on the day of his death' and 'Cú Chulainn said, *de aduentu Christi*'.]

The Liath Macha went to bid farewell to Emer, so that he put his head in her bosom and went three times sunwise around her, and sunwise around Dún nImrith, and Dún nDelga.

This is Emer's lament: 'Liath Macha, many a sorrow', &c.

FINIT. AMEN.

• • • • • • • • • •

§§87–91. Mythological Tales of Pre-Christian Kings

§87. The Origin of Dowth[1]

TRANS. JOHN CAREY

hERE IS ANOTHER TALE that is known to me concerning the hill of Dubthach yonder: it was made, though the task was a great one, by Bresal Bódíbad.

In his time there was a plague on cattle (*díbad ar búaib*) everywhere in Ireland, except for seven cows and a bull who prevailed (?) with every hosteler during his reign.

The rough hill was raised by him in imitation of Nimrod's tower[2]: the reason why it was attempted was so that he might reach heaven from that.

He had the men of Ireland raising it for him for a single day; he levied hostages from them for that day's work.

His own sister told him that she would not permit the great sun to move: there would be no night, only clear day, until the work [of raising] was done.

His sister goes forth on a journey, she works her magic (*druídecht*) powerfully. The sun did not move above her head: it was fastened in a single spot.

Lust seized Bresal, and he went from the hill to where his sister was. The hosts were shocked at it: he found her in Ferta Cuile.

He came together with her, though it was a sin (*col*): with his sister, though it was a violation. Ever since then that hill is called 'mound of sin' (*Ferta Cuile*).

When it was no longer day for them (we think it likely that it was night) the hill was not finished: the men of Ireland went home.

The hill has been there ever since without getting any higher; nor will it get

---

1   **Dowth** (Old Irish *Dubad*) is a Neolithic burial mound located east of the more celebrated passage grave at Newgrange (Old Irish *Síd in Broga*), County Meath. The account which follows is drawn from the poem 'Búa, ingen Rúadrach rúaid' (*Met. Ds.* 3.42–6; cf. 4.270–2). The Flann named as author in the final stanza is identified in one of the manuscripts as Flann mac Lonáin (died 918), but this can scarcely be correct; a more plausible candidate is Flann Mainistrech (died 1056).

2   **Nimrod's tower**, i.e. the Tower of Babel.

any bigger henceforth until the calamitous Last Judgement.

It is Flann, bright his skill, who relates this—no false saying! A choice tale: tell it widely, women and men! May mouths commemorate it among noble things!

• • • • • • • • • • •

§88. *De Gabáil in t-Sída* The Taking of the Hollow Hill
according to the *Book of Leinster*
TRANS. JOHN CAREY

THERE WAS A WONDROUS KING OVER THE TUATHA DÉ IN IRELAND, Dagán by name [a.k.a. 'the Dagda']. Great was his power, even over the sons of Míl after they had seized the land. For the Tuatha Dé blighted the grain and milk of the sons of Míl until they made a treaty [*cairdes*] with the Dagda. Thereafter they preserved their grain and their milk for them.

Great too was his power when he was king in the beginning; and it was he who divided the *síde* among the Fir Dé ['men of the gods']: Lug son of Eithliu in Síd Rodrubán, Ogma in Síd Aircheltrai, the Dagda himself however had Síd Lethet Lachtmaige. . . , Cnoc Báine, Brú Ruair.

They say, however, that Síd in Broga [i.e. the megalithic tomb now called Newgrange] belonged to him at first. The Mac Óc came to the Dagda seeking territory when he had made the division to everyone; he was a foster son of Midir of Brí Léith and of Nindid the prophet.

'I have nothing for you,' said the Dagda; 'I have finished the distribution.'

'Obtain for me then,' said the Mac Óc, 'just a day and a night in your own dwelling.' That was granted to him then.

'Now go to your house,' said the Dagda, 'for you have used up your time.'

'It is plain,' he said, 'that the whole world is day and night, and that is what was granted to me.'

Then Dagán departed from there, and the Mac Óc remained in his *síd*. That is a wondrous land. There are three trees there perpetually bearing fruit, and an everliving pig on the hoof and a cooked pig, and a vessel with excellent liquor; and all of this never grows less.

• • • • • • • • • • •

§89. *Tochmarc Étaíne* The Wooing of Étaín

TRANS. JOHN CAREY

¶I

THE BEGINNING OF 'THE WOOING OF ÉTAÍN'—:

There was a wondrous king ruling over Ireland of the race of the Tuatha Dé, named Eochaid Ollathair. Another name of his was 'the Dagda', for it was he who used to work miracles for them, and to apportion storms and fruits: so folk used to say, and therefore he was called 'Dagda' ['good god']. Elcmar of the Bruig [na Bóinne = Newgrange] had a wife named Eithne; another name of hers was Bóand. The Dagda desired to lie with her. The woman was willing, save for her fear of Elcmar, because of the might of his magic power. The Dagda sent Elcmar away on an errand to Bres son of Elatha in Mag nInis; and the Dagda worked mighty spells on Elcmar as he set forth so that he would not soon return, and he banished the darkness of night from him, and kept hunger and thirst away from him. He sent him far astray, so that nine months passed like a single day for he had said that he would come home again between day and night. The Dagda, meanwhile, went to Elcmar's wife so that she bore him a son named Oengus. And the woman had recovered from her confinement when Elcmar came back, and he did not detect her misdeed, that is, that she had shared the Dagda's bed.

The Dagda, meanwhile, bore his son to the house of Midir, in Brí Léith in Tethba, to be fostered. Oengus was reared there until nine years had passed. Midir had a great playing field in Brí Léith: there were three times fifty boys there, of the lads of Ireland; and three times fifty girls of the girls of the land of Ireland. Oengus was first among them on account of the greatness of Midir's love for him, and the beauty of his appearance, and the nobility of his race. He was called 'the Mac Óc' ['the young son'], for his mother had said 'Young is the son [*is óc in mac*] who was begotten at the beginning of a day, and born between then and evening'.

Oengus had a quarrel with Triath, son of Febul or Gobor of the Fir Bolg: he was head of one of the two sides on the playing field, and a foster son of Midir's. It did not please Oengus to be talking to Triath, and he said, 'It distresses me that the slave's son addresses me.' (For until then Oengus had thought that Midir was his father, and that he himself was destined for the kingship of Brí Léith; and he did not know that he was related to the Dagda at that time.)

Triath answered, 'It is no more pleasing for me to be addressed by a hireling whose mother and father are not known.' Oengus went to Midir with tears and grief after his shaming by Triath. 'What is it?' said Midir. 'Triath has made fun of me and mocked me to my face, saying that I have no father and mother.' 'That is false' said Midir. 'Who is my mother,' said Oengus, 'and from where is my father?' 'Eochaid Ollathair is your father,' said Midir, 'and Eithne the wife of Elcmar of the Bruig is your mother. I have brought you up unknown to Elcmar, lest it grieve him that he was cuckolded at your begetting.' 'Come with me,' said Oengus, 'so that my father may acknowledge me, and I no longer need live in hiding and subject to the mockery of the Fir Bolg.'

Then Midir and his foster son went to speak with Eochaid, so that they came to Uisnech Midi in the middle of Ireland. For it is there that Eochaid's house was, for Ireland extended equally far from it in every direction: south and north, east and west. They came to where Eochaid was before them in the assembly. Midir called the king over to a place apart, so that he might speak with the boy. 'What is the wish of this young man, who has not come here before?' 'He wishes to be acknowledged by his father, and to have land granted to him,' said Midir; 'for it is not fitting for your son to be without territory, and you the king of Ireland.' 'He is welcome,' said Eochaid, 'since he is my son; but the territory which I desire for him is not yet empty.' 'What territory is that?' said Midir. 'The Bruig on the north side of the Boyne,' said Eochaid. 'Who occupies it?' said Midir. 'Elcmar,' said Eochaid, 'is the man who is there. I do not wish to do him further injury.'

'What advice do you give this boy?' said Midir. 'I have some for him,' said Eochaid. 'At Samain let him go into the Bruig, and let him bring weapons with him. That is a day of peace and concord among the men of Ireland: none fears his neighbor then; and Elcmar will be on the hill of Síd in Broga, bearing no arms and holding a forked stick of white hazel in his hand, with a double cloak around him, and a gold brooch in the cloak, and three times fifty in the playing field playing before him. And let Oengus go to him, and threaten to kill him; but it is best that he not kill him, provided that he promises to grant him his will. And let this be Oengus's will: kingship for a day and a night in the Bruig; and do not release his territory to Elcmar until he submits [the matter] to my decision. And let this be Oengus's plea when he does so: the territory became his permanent possession when he refrained from killing Elcmar. It is kingship for a day and a night that he demanded, and' he said, 'it is in days and nights that the world is spent.'

Then Midir went back to his own territory with his foster son, and around the next Samain Oengus took weapons and went into the Bruig; and Oengus threatened Elcmar so that in exchange for his life he promised him kingship in his territory for a day and a night. That same day, and that night, the Mac Óc remained as king of the land, with Elcmar's people doing his will. Next day Elcmar came to demand (?) his territory from the Mac Óc, and he threatened him with great threats. The Mac Óc said that he would not yield his territory until [the matter] had been submitted to the will of the Dagda in the presence of the men of Ireland.

They appealed to the Dagda; he determined that each man was bound by what he had agreed to. 'The territory belongs to the youth now, then,' said Elcmar. 'That is proper,' said the Dagda. 'You were caught off your guard on a day of peace and concord. You gave up your land to save yourself, for your life was dearer to you than your land; and you will have land from me that will be no less convenient for you than the Bruig.' 'What place is that?' said Elcmar. 'Cleittech,' said the Dagda, 'with the three lands which are around it, and your boy-troop playing before you in the Bruig every day, and the fresh fruits of the Boyne from this territory for your use.' 'It is good,' said Elcmar; 'let it be done so.' And he moved to Cleittech. Then a stronghold was made by him there, and the Mac Óc remained in his territory of the Bruig.

Midir came after that, a year from that day, to the Bruig to visit his foster - son. He found the Mac Óc standing on the mound of Síd in Broga on the day of Samain, and the two boy-troops before him at their games in the Bruig, and Elcmar watching them from the mound of Cleittech to the south. A quarrel flared up between the boys in the Bruig. 'Do not move,' said Midir, 'on account of Elcmar, lest he rush down onto the plain. I will go to separate them.' Then Midir went; and it was not easy for him to separate them. A holly javelin was cast at Midir as he was intervening, so that it brought one of his eyes out of his head. Midir came to the Mac Óc with his eye in his hand, and said to him: 'It was no good thing for me to come to get news of you, since now I am shamed. For with this blemish I cannot see the land in which I have arrived; and now I will not reach the land from which I have come.'

'That will not be true,' said the Mac Óc. 'I will go to Dian Cécht so that he may come to heal you, and you will have your own territory, and you will have this territory, and your eye will be whole without shame or blemish.'

The Mac Óc went to Dian Cécht 'so that you may come with me, to come to the aid of my foster father who had one of his eyes put out on Samain day in the Bruig.' Dian Cécht came and healed Midir, so that he was whole. 'Good is my journey now,' said Midir, 'for I have been healed.' 'That will be true,' said the Mac Óc. 'Stay here for a year, so that you may see my *fian*-troop and my followers and my household and my territory.'

'I will not stay,' said Midir, 'unless I have payment for it.' 'What payment is that?' said the Mac Óc. 'Not hard to answer. A chariot worth seven *cumals* [slave-women],' said Midir, 'and a cloak which suits my rank, and the loveliest girl in Ireland.' 'I have,' said the Mac Óc, 'the chariot, and the mantle which will be suitable for you.' 'There remains then,' said Midir, 'the girl who excels the girls of Ireland in beauty.' 'In what place is she?' said the Mac Óc. 'She is among the Ulaid,' said Midir: 'Ailill's daughter, Étaín Echraide ['of the horses'], the daughter of the king of the north-eastern part of Ireland. And she is the fairest and gentlest and most exquisite in Ireland.'

The Mac Óc went to ask for her, so that he was in Ailill's house in Mag n-Inis. He was made welcome, and stayed there for three nights. He gave his message, and named his race; he said that it was to ask for Étaín that he had come.

'I will not give her to you,' Ailill said. 'For I cannot exact any satisfaction (?) from you, because of the nobility of your race, and the greatness of your power and the power of your father. Whatever shame you may do to my daughter, nothing could be exacted from you.' 'It will not be thus,' said the Mac Óc: 'I will buy her from you now.' 'Agreed,' Ailill said. 'Let us learn your [terms],' said the Mac Óc.

'Not hard to answer,' Ailill said: 'that you clear twelve plains for me in my territory, which are now all wilderness and woodland, so that they may forever afford grazing to cattle, and dwellings to men, games and assemblies, meetings and encampments.' 'It will be done,' said the Mac Óc. He went home, and complained of his plight to the Dagda. He caused the twelve plains in Ailill's territory to be cleared in a single night. These are the names of those plains: Mag Macha, Mag Lemna, Mag n tha, Mag Tóchair, Mag nDula, Mag Techt, Mag Lí, Mag Line, Mag Muirthemne.

When that work had been done by the Mac Óc, he came to Ailill to ask for Étaín. 'You shall not take her,' Ailill said, 'until you bring twelve chief streams out of this territory to the sea, which are now in springs and bogs and marshes, to bring produce from the sea to tribes and kindreds, to dry the land and the earth.' He went to the Dagda, to complain to him of his plight. Then he caused the twelve chief waters to be directed to the sea in a single night. Until then they had never been seen there. These are the names of the waters: Find and Modorn and Slena and Nas and Amnas and Oichén and Or and Banna and Samaír and Lóche.

When those tasks were done, the Mac Óc came to speak with Ailill, to ask him for Étaín. 'You shall not take her until you pay for (?) her; for I shall get no good out of the girl after you take her, but only what I get now.' 'What do you ask of me now?' said the Mac Óc. 'I ask,' Ailill said, 'that you give me the girl's weight in gold and silver, for that is my share of her price; what you have done so far, its profit will be to her family and kindred.' 'It will be done,' said the Mac Óc. She was set in the midst of Ailill's house, and her weight in gold and silver was given to her. That treasure was left with Ailill, and the Mac Óc took Étaín with him to his house.

Midir welcomed that company. Étaín slept with Midir that night, and a mantle suitable for him, and his chariot, were given to him next day; and he was grateful to his foster son. He remained with Oengus in the Bruig for a full year.

On the day that the year was up Midir went to his own territory of Brí Léith, and took Étaín with him. On the day that he departed from him the Mac Óc said to Midir, 'Keep a watch on the woman whom you are taking with you, on account of the terrible fierce woman who awaits you, with the great knowledge and lore and power which belong to her race,' said Oengus; 'and my word and protection [are pledged] to her with respect to the Tuatha Dé Danann.' That was Fuamnach, Midir's wife, of the progeny of Bethach son of Iardanél. She was wise and shrewd and knowledgeable in the lore and power of the Tuatha Dé Danann, for it was Bresal the druid who had fostered her until she was betrothed to Midir.

She welcomed her husband Midir; and the woman spoke many words to them. 'Come, Midir,' said Fuamnach, 'so that I may show you your house and your rightful territory, lest the king's daughter think shame of me (?)' Midir went around the whole territory with Fuamnach, and she showed his entitlement to him and to Étaín; and Étaín spoke ill to Fuamnach after that.[3] Fuamnach went before them into the sleeping-house in which she used to sleep, and said to Étaín 'You have come into the seat of a good woman.' As Étaín sat in the chair in the midst of the house Fuamnach struck her with a switch of purple rowan so that she made her into a pool of water on the floor of the house. Then Fuamnach went to her foster father Bresal, and Midir left the house to the water which she had made of Étaín. After that Midir was without a wife.

The heat of the fire and the air, and the fervour of the earth, all worked together with the water until they made a worm out of the water which was on the floor of the house, and then made a purple fly of that worm, which was the size of a man's head, and the most beautiful in the land. Sweeter than pipes and harps and horn-players was the sound of her noise and the hum of her wings. Her eyes used to shine like precious stones in times of darkness. Her fragrance and her beauty would ward thirst and hunger away from anyone around whom she used to go. The sprinkling of drops from her wings would cure the afflictions and diseases and plagues of the one around whom she used to go. She used to go with Midir and accompany him throughout his territory, wherever he might journey. It used to nourish armies in assemblies and gatherings in encampments to listen to her and gaze upon her. Midir knew that it was Étaín who was in that shape, and he did not take a wife as long as that fly was in his company; and it nourished him to gaze upon her. He used to fall asleep at the noise she made, and she would wake him whenever someone who did not love him was coming.

---

3 'Étaín spoke ill . . .' This is the best that I can make of the puzzling phrase *Dobert Édain dorisi fri Fuaimnigh iar sin*; Bergin and Best conjectured 'something apparently omitted here'. I take *doris* to represent *do-* 'bad, evil, wrong' + *ris* 'report, tale, tidings'.

After a time Fuamnach came to visit Midir, and the three gods of Danann came with her as safeguards: Lug and the Dagda and Ogma. Midir reproached Fuamnach bitterly, and told her that she would not have gone from him [again] but for the strength of the safeguard she had brought. Fuamnach said that she did not repent of what she had done, for it was better in her eyes to do a good deed for herself than for her spouse; and that wherever in Ireland she might be, she would concern herself with nothing but harming Étaín for as long as she lived, whatever shape she might be in.

She brought great spells and enchantments of un-gods (?) from Bresal Etarlam the druid, to exile and banish Étaín from Midir; for she knew that the purple fly who was entertaining Midir was Étaín, for Midir did not love a woman when he did not see the purple fly, and took no pleasure in music or drinking or eating when he could not see her and could not hear her music and her sound. Fuamnach stirred up a hostile magic wind, so that Étaín was driven from Brí Léith, and could not manage to light on treetop or tree or hill or high place for seven years, but was on rocks in the sea and expanses of waves, and hovering in the air, until on the day the seven years were up she alit upon. . . in the breast of the Mac Óc as he stood on the hill of the Bruig.

It is in that place that the Mac Óc said:

'Welcome, Étaín,
travel-worn, woebegone,
driven into great perils
by the winds of Fuamnach.
You have not found rest or pleasure
befitting your side
in Midir's household.
It is I who brought about
labouring with multitudes
the clearing of the wilderness,
the digging of the deeps,
the excess of treasure.
Fruitless is the suffering
of Ailill's daughter,
so that it is your pitiful
remnant which has come to me.
After that, welcome'

The Mac Óc made the girl—that is, the purple fly—welcome, and folded her up against his bosom in the fleece of his mantle. He brought her to his house and his sun-room [*grianán*], with bright windows for going out and in, and purple clothing was put upon her, and that sun-room used to be carried by the Mac Óc wherever he went. And he used to sleep in it every night, to keep her company and entertain her until her health and good looks came back to her; and that sun-room was filled with exotic fragrant plants, so that she was being nourished by the fragrance and beauty of those rare and precious plants.

Fuamnach was told of the love and honour which the Mac Óc bestowed upon her. Fuamnach said to Midir, 'Let your foster son be summoned hither so that I may make peace between you, and so that I may go in search of Étaín.' A messenger came to the Mac Óc from Midir, and he went to speak with him; and Fuamnach went meanwhile by a roundabout route so that she was in the Bruig. And she brought the same blast against Étaín, which bore her out of the sun-room upon the same flight which she had been upon before, throughout Ireland for the space of seven years. The wind drove her, wretched and weak, until it set her on the ridgepole of a house in Ulster where folk were drinking, so that she fell into the gold cup which was beside the wife of Étar the warrior from Inber Cíchmaine in the province of Conchobor, so that she swallowed her together with the drink which was in the vessel. Then she was conceived in her womb, so that she was a girl after that. A name was given to her: Étaín daughter of Étar. It was one thousand and two years from Étaín's first birth from Ailill to the second birth from Étar.[4]

Then Étaín was brought up at Inber Cíchmaine by Étar, together with fifty girls from among the daughters of chieftains; and he fed them and clothed them so that they should be attending on Étaín always. One day all the girls were bathing in the river-mouth, when they saw a horseman on the plain coming towards where they were in the water. He was riding a brown horse with an arched neck, splendid, broad, with curly mane and tail. A great (?) green mantle was wrapped around him, and he wore a tunic with red embroidery, and a gold brooch in his mantle which reached to his shoulders on both sides. On his back was a silver shield with a gold rim; its handle was of silver, and its boss of gold. In his hand was a five-pointed spear with a gold band reaching from the butt-end to the socket. Fair yellow hair came down onto his forehead, with a twisted band of gold on his brow to keep the hair from falling over his face. He paused for a while at the harbour, looking at the girls, and all the girls loved him. Then he uttered this poem:

> 'Étaín is here today
> at Síd Ban Find west of Ailbe;
> she is among small boys
> on the bank of Inber Cíchmaine.
>
> 'It is she who healed the eye of the king

---

4   Cf. the interval of 1002 years in the story of Tuán below, §107.

in the well of Loch Dá Líg,
it is she who was swallowed in the drink
in the cup by Étar's wife.

'Because of her the king will chase
the birds from Tethba,
and drown his two horses
in the pool of Loch Dá Airbrech.

'There will be very many wars
fought because of you against Eochaid of Mide:
raids upon *síde*,
and battle for many thousands.

'It is she who was injured in the land,
it is she who seeks the king:
she is Bé Find ['white woman'], whom he summons;
she is our Étaín after that.'

The warrior went away from them after that, and they did not know from where he had come nor where he went.

When the Mac Óc came to speak with Midir he did not find Fuamnach in Midir's company, and [Midir] said to him, 'The woman has deceived us; and if she has been told that Étaín is in Ireland, she will go to do her ill.' 'Étaín has been at my house in the Bruig for a long time, in the shape in which she appeared to you; and perhaps the woman is going to her.'

The Mac Óc came back to his house, and found the glass sun-room without Étaín in it. The Mac Óc turned back upon Fuamnach's track, so that he caught up with her at Oenach Bodbgnai, at the house of Bresal Etarlam the druid. The Mac Óc attacked her and struck off her head, and took the head with him so that it was on the edge of the Bruig.

(But elsewhere the story is that the two of them, Fuamnach and Midir, were killed in Brí Léith by Manannán; from which it is said:

The foolish Fuamnach, who was Midir's wife,
[and] Sigmall, a hill with trees,
in Brí Léith, an ample scheme,
were burned by Manannán.[5]

---

5   For another version of this stanza see *Lebar Gabála*, ¶98.

¶ 2

THIS IS STILL 'THE WOOING OF ÉTAÍN'.

Eochaid Airem took the kingship of Ireland. The five provinces of Ireland, and the king of every province, gave him hostages. These were their kings at that time: Conchobor son of Nes and Mes Gegra and Tigernach Tétbannach and Cú Roí and Ailill son of Máta Muirisce. These were Eochaid's strongholds: Dún Frémainn in Mide and Dún Frémainn in Tethba. Frémann Tethbai was dearest to him among the strongholds of Ireland.

Eochaid summoned the men of Ireland to hold the *feis Temro* ['Feast of Tara', associated with the confirmation of the king] the year after he took the kingship, to adjudge their rents and taxes for the next five years. All of the men of Ireland made the same answer to Eochaid: that they would not convene the *feis Temro* for a king who did not have a queen; for there was no queen with Eochaid when he took the sovereignty.

Eochaid sent messengers forth to every province throughout Ireland to find for him the most beautiful woman or girl in Ireland; for he said that none should be with him but a woman who had never known a man of the men of Ireland. She was found for him at Inber Cíchmaine: Étaín Echraide. And Eochaid married her then, for she suited him in form and shape and race, in beauty and youth and pre-eminence.

The three sons of Find son of Findlug, the sons of the queen, were Eochaid Feidlech and Eochaid Airem and Ailill Anguba. Ailill Anguba fell in love with Étaín at the *feis Temro*, after she had slept with Eochaid. For he took to staring at her for long periods, and 'long staring is a sign of love'.[6] Ailill's spirit tormented him for what he did, but that was no help: desire was stronger than mind. Ailill fell ill because of it; for he would not allow his honour to be reproached, and he did not speak to the woman herself.

When he expected death, Eochaid's physician Fachtna was brought to examine him. The physician said to him, 'What is in you is one of the two pains lethal to man which physicians cannot cure: the pain of love, and the pain of jealousy.' Ailill did not admit it to him, for he was ashamed. Then Ailill was left in Frémann Tethbai to die, and Eochaid went on a circuit of Ireland. And Étaín was left with Ailill so that his funeral rites might be performed by her: the digging of his grave, the raising of his lament, the slaughtering of his cattle.

Étaín used to come to visit Ailill every day in the house in which he lay sick; and his sickness was the less on that account, and for as long as Étaín was

---

6 'Long staring is sign of love.' *Is descaid seirce sírshilliud.* The alliteration suggests that this statement may have been proverbial; cf. in *Briathra Flainn Fhína* the maxim *Descaid trebaire tuae* 'Silence is a sign of prudence', *Anecdota from Irish MSS* 3.15.

in that place he would be watching her. Étaín noticed that, and gave thought to it. One day when they were in the house together, Étaín asked Ailill the cause of his illness. 'It is for love of you,' he said. 'Alas that it was so long until you said so,' she said. 'You would have been whole long ago if I had known.' 'Even though it be today, I could be whole if it pleased you,' Ailill said. 'It does indeed,' she said.

After that she used to come every day to wash his head and to cut up his food and to pour water on his hands. On the day when three ninefold periods were up after that, Ailill was whole. He said to Étaín, 'And when will I have from you what is still wanting in my cure?' 'You will have it tomorrow,' she said. 'But let it not be in the dwelling of the true ruler [*fírfhlaith*] that the sin is committed. Meet me tomorrow on the hill above the court.'

Ailill sat up through the night. But he slept at the time of the tryst; he did not awake until the third hour after dawn the next day. Étaín went to meet him, and saw a man waiting for her whose appearance resembled Ailill's, and he complained of the weakness caused by his illness; he answered her as Ailill was wont to speak.

Ailill awoke at the hour of terce. He fell to grieving for a long time when Étaín came into her house. 'What makes you sorrowful?' said Étaín. 'That I sent you to meet me, and did not come for you: sleep fell upon me, so that I have only just arisen now. Plainly it is not fated that I should be healed.' 'It will not be thus,' said Étaín: 'one day comes after another.' He sat up that night, and a great fire in front of him, and water next to him to put upon his eyes. When Étaín went to meet him at the time of her tryst she saw the same man, resembling Ailill. Étaín went to the house. Ailill fell to lamenting.

Étaín went for a third time, and Ailill did not come to the tryst. She found the same man there. 'It is not with you,' she said, 'that I have arranged to meet. Who are you, who have come to meet me? It is not for sin and mischief that I go to meet the man with whom I have trysted, but to save a man fit to be king of Ireland from the illness which has assailed him.'

'It would be right for you to come to me; for when you were Étaín Echraide daughter of Ailill it was I who was your spouse, after giving in exchange for you a mighty payment of the chief plains and waters of Ireland, and gold and silver amounting to your own weight.'

'What is your name?' she said.

'Midir of Brí Léith,' he said.

'What parted us?' she said.

'The magic of Fuamnach, and the spells of Bresal Etarlam.'

Midir said to Étaín, 'Will you go with me?'

'No,' she said. 'I will not sell the king of Ireland for a man whose family and kindred I do not know.'

'It is I,' said Midir, 'who set love of you in Ailill's heart so that his blood and his flesh fell from him; and it is I who took all carnal desire from him, so that there should be no injury to your honour from it. But come with me to my country if Eochaid bids you to.'

'I am willing,' said Étaín.

After that she came to her house. 'Good is our meeting,' Ailill said: 'for I have been healed now; yet there is no damage to your honour.' 'A wondrous thing!' said Étaín.

After that Eochaid returned from his circuit, and gave thanks that his brother was alive, and many thanks were given to Étaín for what she had done before his coming.

¶ 3

'THE WOOING OF ÉTAÍN' still.

At another time, Eochaid Airem king of Tara arose on a beautiful day in summer, and went up onto the rampart of Tara to gaze upon Mag Breg. Fair was its appearance, and fair its flowers of every colour. As he looked around him, he saw a strange warrior standing before him on the rampart. He wore a purple mantle, and his golden-yellow hair reached to the tips of his shoulder-blades. Shining blue eyes in his head; a five-pointed spear in his hand; a white-bossed shield in his hand, with gems of gold upon it. Eochaid was speechless: for he did not know of his having been present in Tara the night before, and the courtyards had not been opened at that hour.

Then he came before Eochaid. Eochaid said, 'Welcome to the warrior whom we do not know.'

'It is therefore that we have come,' said the warrior.

'We do not know you,' said Eochaid.

'But I know you,' said the warrior.

'What is your name?' said Eochaid.

'It is not well known,' he said: 'Midir of Brí Léith.'

'What has brought you?' said Eochaid.

'To play *fidchell* [a board game] with you,' he said,

'Indeed,' said Eochaid, 'I am good at *fidchell*.'

'Let us test that,' said Midir.

'The queen is sleeping,' said Eochaid. 'The *fidchell*-board is in the house where she is.'

'Here,' said Midir, 'is a *fidchell*-board which is not the worst.' That was true: a silver board, and pieces of gold, and each corner of it lit up by a precious stone, and the bag for the pieces woven of bronze chains.

Midir set out the game. 'Play,' said Midir.

'I will not play except for a stake,' said Eochaid.

'What shall the stake be?' said Midir.

'I don't care,' said Eochaid.

'If you beat me,' said Midir, 'you shall have from me fifty dark gray horses, with dappled red heads, pricked ears, broad chests, round nostrils, narrow hooves: all equally bold, keen, ardent, lofty, spirited, steady, and well fitted with fifty crimson bridles. I will bring [them] here at the hour of terce tomorrow.'

Eochaid pledged the same to him. They played after that. Midir was beaten. He went from him, and took his *fidchell*-board with him.

When Eochaid arose next morning he went up onto the rampart of Tara around sunrise. He saw the other beside him, coming towards him along the rampart; he did not know where he had gone or from where he came. He saw the fifty dark gray horses with their crimson bridles.

'That is honest,' said Eochaid.

'What is declared is owed,' said Midir.7

'Shall we play *fidchell*?' said Midir.

'I am willing,' said Eochaid, 'but let there be a stake.'

'You shall have from me,' said Midir, 'fifty young boars with dappled curly coats, gray below and blue above, with horses' hooves, and a tub of blackthorn which will contain them all; together with fifty gold-hilted swords; together with fifty white red-eared cows with white red-eared calves with them, and a bronze halter on each calf; together with fifty wethers, blue with red heads, three-headed, three-horned; together with fifty ivory-hilted swords; together with fifty mantles shining with many colours. But each of those fifties will be upon its own day.' His foster father inquired of Eochaid, and asked him from where he had obtained his great wealth. He said, 'Indeed, that is a tale worth telling.' 'It is indeed. You should be on your guard with him; it is a man of great power who has come to you. Place great hardships upon him, my boy,' he said.

Then the other came to him, and Eochaid set the famous great oppressions upon him: clearing stones from Mide, laying rushes across Tethba, a causeway across the bog of the Lámraige, a wood across Bréifne. Concerning that the poet uttered these stanzas:

---

7   As Bergin and Best observed, the phrase *Is fiach ní dlomthar* is also found in the legal literature. See now D. A. Binchy, *Corpus Iuris Hibernici* (Dublin, 1978), 1237.13, 1371.26, 2007.12, 2204.32.

These are the four things
which Eochaid Airem chose
from the many manly-seeming companies,
with abundant shields and swords:

A causeway across the bog of the Lámraige,
a wood across Bréifne, without difficulty,
the fair removal of the stones of great Mide,
and rushes across Tethba.

Those were the stakes and hardships which were imposed then. 'Too great is what you put upon me,' said Midir. 'Not at all,' said Eochaid. 'Let me have a request and demand from you. So far as your power extends, let no woman nor man be outside their house until sunrise tomorrow.' 'It will be done,' said Eochaid.

No one had ever travelled upon that bog before. Eochaid instructed his steward to watch the work when they were making the causeway. So the steward went into the bog. It seemed to him that all the men in the world, from the sun's rising to its setting, had come to the bog. They all made a single heap of their garments, and Midir went upon that heap. A forest [of trees], with trunks and roots, is what they were putting in the bottom of the causeway. Midir stood calling out to the host on every side. You would have thought that all the men in the world were making a commotion because of him. Then soil and gravel and stones were put upon the bog. Until that night the men of Ireland harnessed oxen across the forehead; the people of the *síd* harnessed them across the shoulders. The same was done by Eochaid—that is why he is called Eochaid Airem ['ploughman'], for it was under him that men first put yokes upon the necks of oxen in Ireland.

This is what the host were saying, as they made the causeway:

'Put it in hand,
set it in hand,
famous oxen
in the hours after sunset.
Oppressive is the demand:
it is not known whose is the benefit,
whose the harm,
from a causeway across the bog of the Lámraige.'

There would not be a better causeway in the world, if no one had been watching; but flaws were left in it because of that. Afterwards the steward went and told Eochaid of the great work which he had witnessed, and said that there was not upon the ridge of the world power which could surpass it.

While they were speaking thus they saw Midir coming towards them, elaborately arrayed, and with an ill look upon him. Eochaid arose and wished him welcome.

'It is therefore that we have come,' said Midir. 'It is savage and senseless of you to put great labours and great hardships upon me. I would have obtained something else which would have pleased you; but my mind is wrathful against you.'

'It will not be "anger met by rage" [*bara fri búiri*] in your case, however; your desire shall be done,' said Eochaid.

'It is accepted,' said Midir. 'Shall we play *fidchell*?' said Midir.

'What will be the stake?' said Eochaid.

'Whatever stake each party chooses,' said Midir.

Eochaid was beaten that day.

'You have beaten me,' said Eochaid.

'Had I wished, I would have done so long ago,' said Midir.

'What do you want from me?' said Eochaid.

'Two arms around Étaín, and a kiss from her,' said Midir.

Eochaid was silent at that; then he said, 'Come one month from today; that will be given to you then.'[8]

The year before Midir came to play *fidchell* with Eochaid he was wooing Étaín, but she would not yield to him. The name by which Midir called her was 'Bé Find', so that he said to her:

'Bé Find, will you go with me
to a strange land where there is music?
Hair there is like the primrose flower;
on the smooth body there is the colour of snow.

There is no "mine" or "yours";
white the tooth, black the brow.
The multitude of our host delights the eye:
the colour of the foxglove is in every cheek.

---

8 The section that follows seems to come from an alternative version of the story.

Every neck ruddy as the flowers of the plain (?),
the blackbird's eggs a delight to the eye
although the plain of Fál is fair to gaze upon,
it is a wilderness after one has known the Great Plain.

Though you think the ale of the island of Fál good,
the ale of the Great Land is stronger.
A wonder among lands is the land of which I speak:
there, youth does not give place to age.

Warm sweet streams across the land,
the best of mead and wine;
splendid folk there without flaw,
conception without sin or fault.

We see everyone on every side,
and no one sees us;
it is the darkness of Adam's sin
which prevents our being counted.

Woman, if you come to my mighty people,
a crown of gold will be on your head;
honey, wine, ale, new milk to drink
you will have from me there, Bé Find.'

Étaín said, 'If you obtain me from the master of my house, I will go with
you; if you do not, I will not go.'

Then Midir came to Eochaid and yielded the game to him at first, so that
he might have a grievance against Eochaid. That is why he fulfilled the mighty
terms, and why he asked that the stake not be stated in advance, but declared
after it had been pledged. When Midir and his people were fulfilling the terms
of the night—that is, a causeway across the bog of the Lámraige, and clearing
the stones from Mide, and rushes across Tethba, and a wood across Bréifne—
this is what his followers were saying, according to the Book of Druim
Snechtai: 'Cuirthe i lland, tochre i lland,'[9] &c.

Midir made an appointment for that day next month. Eochaid summoned
the best warriors in Ireland so that they were in Tara, and the best of the

---

9   This is another version of the chant attributed to Midir's followers in the first account of
   the building of the causeway above; this one is considerably longer and more difficult. For
   the most recent attempt to translate it, and references to earlier treatments, see S. Mac
   Mathúna, *Immram Brain* (Tübingen, 1985), 452.

fianna of Ireland, ring surrounding ring around Tara, in the midst, outside, and inside, and the king and queen in the centre of the house, and the court closed and locked; for they knew that the man of great power would come. Étaín was pouring drink for the princes that night, for pouring drink was a special skill [*sain-dán*] of hers.

Then as they were speaking they saw Midir coming towards them across the floor of the palace. He was always beautiful; that night he was more beautiful. The hosts who gazed upon him were amazed. They were all silent then, and the king wished him welcome.

'It is therefore that we have come,' said Midir. 'Let what was pledged to me be given to me,' he said; 'what is declared is owed. I have given you what was pledged.'

'I have not thought about that until now,' said Eochaid.

'Étaín herself promised,' said Midir, 'to leave you.'

Étaín blushed at that.

'Do not blush, Étaín,' said Midir. 'You have not shamed your womanhood. For a year,' he said, 'I have been wooing you with the fairest gifts and treasures in Ireland; and I did not get you until I had Eochaid's permission. It is not through my *déoas* that I would obtain you (?).'[10]

'I told you,' she said, 'that I would not go to you until Eochaid sold me. For my own part, I will go with you if Eochaid sells me.'

'I will not sell you, however,' said Eochaid. 'But let him put his arms around you as you are, in the middle of the house.'

'It will be done,' said Midir. He put his weapons in his left hand, and took the woman under his right arm, and carried her off through the skylight of the house. The hosts rose up around the king after this shame had been put upon them. They saw two swans circling Tara. They headed for Síd ar Femun, that is, Síd Ban Find.

This was the counsel of the men of Ireland: that every *síd* in Ireland should be dug up until his wife came to him thence. They dug up Síd Ban Find, and someone came out to them, and told them that the woman was not there. 'The man who has come to you is the king of the *síde* of Ireland. He is with the girl in his royal stronghold: go thither until you reach it.' They went north. They began digging up the *síd*. They spent a year and three months at the work: what they used to dig one day would be restored on the next. Two white ravens came to them from the *síd*, and two hounds: Scleth and Samaír.

They went south again to Síd Ban Find. They began digging up the *síd*.

---

10 The puzzling word spelled *deóas* in LU and *déoas* in YBL was left untranslated by Bergin and Best; in a footnote they suggested emending to *doeas* = *dóenacht* 'humanity'. Another possibility might be *deacht* 'divinity', arguably giving better sense in context.

Someone came out to them again, and said to them, 'What is your grievance against us, Eochaid?' he said. 'We have not taken your wife. No wrong has been done to you. Do not presume to say what would be damaging to a king.'

'I will not depart from you,' said Eochaid, 'until you tell me how I can reach my wife.'

'Take blind puppies and blind cats with you, and leave them [there]. That is the work which you must do every day.'

He turned away then; and that thing was done by them, so that it is thus they set about it. While they were digging up the *síd* of Brí Léith they saw Midir coming towards them.

'What is your grievance against me?' said Midir. 'It is injustice [*anfír*] which you are doing me. You put great hardships upon me. You have sold your wife to me. Do not oppress me further.'

'You will not have her,' said Eochaid.

'I will not,' said Midir. 'Go to your house. Your wife will come to you at the hour of terce tomorrow—a test of the same ones and the natives (?),'" said Midir.

'Agreed,' said Eochaid. Midir bound them to this compact, and went from them.

When they were there at the hour of terce next day they saw fifty women, all with the same appearance and clothing as Étaín. The hosts were speechless. There was a gray hag in front of them. She said to Eochaid, 'Choose your wife now, or tell one of the women to stay with you. It is time for us to go home.'

'What will you do,' said Eochaid to the men of Ireland, 'in the dilemma which has come upon you?'

'We have no idea what to do,' said the men of Ireland.

'I have,' said Eochaid. 'My wife is the best at pouring drink in Ireland. I will recognise her by her pouring.'

He arranged twenty-five of the women on the far side of the house, and twenty-five on the near side, and a vessel of liquor was put in the middle of the house. A woman was coming from here, and a woman from there, and still he did not find Étaín. He came to the last two women; one of them poured first. Eochaid said, 'Here is Étaín, yet it is not she.' So thought they all. 'Indeed, it is Étaín,' they said, 'though it is not her pouring.' The other women departed. The men of Ireland were very pleased at the deed which he had done, and the mighty labours which the oxen had performed for them, and the rescuing of the woman from the men of the *síd*.

---

11 This is a literal translation of the enigmatic phrase *Fír na cetnai 7 na n-irradh* in the original. From what follows it seems that *fír* is to be taken here in its sense 'test, ordeal': Eochaid is to distinguish between identical women (*na cétnai*), and find the one who is a native (*aurrae*) not of the *síd* but of the mortal realm.

One beautiful day Eochaid arose, and he and his queen were conversing in the midst of the enclosure when they saw Midir approaching them. 'Well, Eochaid,' said Midir.

'Well,' said Eochaid.

'You have not dealt honestly with me,' he said, 'heaping great labours upon me, and their being behind you (?), and all that you demanded of me. There was nothing which you did not expect of me.'

'I did not sell you my wife,' said Eochaid.

'Tell me: do you look to your conscience with regard to me?' said Midir.

'Until you hit upon something else for us to stake one another,' said Eochaid, 'I will not.'

'Tell me, is your mind content?' said Midir.

'It is,' said Eochaid.

'So is mine,' said Midir. 'Your wife was pregnant when she was taken from you,' said Midir, 'and bore a daughter; and she is the one in your company. Your wife, however, is with me, and it has happened to you that you have relinquished her again.' Then he departed.

Eochaid did not then dare to dig up Midir's *síd* again, for there was a compact upon him. It weighed upon Eochaid that his wife was gone and his daughter had slept with him; and she was pregnant by him, and bore him a daughter.

'By the gods,' said Eochaid, 'I and my daughter's daughter will not look upon one another.' Two of his followers went to put her with wild beasts in a pit. They visited the house of Findlám the cowherd of Tara, which was in Sliab Fuait in the midst of the wilderness. There was no one in the house. They ate food there. They threw the girl to a bitch with puppies, which was in the house in a pen; then they left again. The cowherd and his wife came into the house, and saw the fair child in the pen. That amazed them. They took her from the pen. They raised her, though they did not know from where she came; and she grew well, as she was the daughter of a king and a queen. She was more skilful at needlework than any [other] woman. Her eyes saw nothing which her hands could not stitch. In this way she was brought up by Findlám and his wife, until one day the household of Eterscél saw her, and told the king, and she was taken away by Eterscél by force, and was with him as his wife. And so she was the mother of Conaire son of Eterscél.

Eochaid Airem was in Frémann Tethbai after losing Étaín, and his spirits were weary. Sigmall the Thin came, Midir's grandson (that is, the son of Midir's daughter, whose name was Óicnia), and he burnt Dún Frémainn over Eochaid, and Eochaid fell by him, and his head was taken by Sigmall to Síd Nenta in revenge for the honour of his grandfather Midir. (But that is not true, for Sigmall and Fuamnach Midir's wife were killed by Manannán in Brí Léith long before then, in the reign of the Tuatha Dé Danann; of this the poet said:

> The foolish Fuamnach, who was Midir's wife,
> [and] Sigmall, a hill with trees,
> in Brí Léith, an ample scheme,
> were burned by Manannán.)

This is how the death of Eochaid Airem came about, as the historians relate:

Eochaid Airem was in Frémann Tethbai as we have said, where his chief residence and dwelling were at last. For that reason the tribute of labour imposed on the people of that region and territory grew to be burdensome and excessive, because the king was usually there; and that is why Tethba is called 'a seventh of Ireland', because a seventh part of the tributes and food-rents of the king devolved upon them. At that time it was the Fir Chúl, of the Luaigni of Tara, who lived in Tethba, and it was upon them that that tribute was levied. Mórmael was king of the Fir Chúl at that time, and he was the steward in Frémann. His uterine brother was Sigmall son of Breistine son of Midir, king of Bentraige. They conspired among themselves, and decided to kill Eochaid.

Then both of them went—the Bentraige following Sigmall, and the Fir Chúl following Mórmael—and they seized Dún Frémainn when Eochaid was within, and they burnt the stronghold upon him, and they killed Eochaid there. Then they went into Connacht with their plunder, and took Eochaid's head with them to Síd Nenta iar nUisciu. So to commemorate these deeds the historian recited the following:

> Eochaid Airem, noble, fair, and slender,
> splendid high king of Ireland,
> extended his firm stern tribute:
> it reached throughout Banba of the red cloaks.
>
> The tribes of Tethba, of the mighty deeds,
> endured the tribute to the king of Ireland:
> the lawgiving king who imposed it assigned
> the seventh part of it to them alone.
>
> The host grew greatly weary
> of the unwieldy, unjust law.
> Anger was kindled among them because of it,
> so that Eochaid Airem was killed.

The tribes of Tethba, who were powerful then,
killed Eochaid of Frémann.
It was not might without right in their case,
opposing the unwieldy, unjust law.

Mórmael was the name of the king
by whom the mighty deed was done;
Fir Chúl was the name of the men of Tethba in the east
when Dún Frémainn was overcome.

Although it is said that Sigmall of the spears
killed Eochaid Airem,
his death came sooner in the sequence of leaders
than that of Eochaid of Frémann.

Sigmall of the spears of battle died
encountering smooth bright Manannán,
in the east, without weakness, a very long time
before Eochaid got his death.

The two Sigmalls of Síd Nenta,
firm their stride, mighty their strength (?):
Sigmall son of Cairpre of the battles,
Sigmall who was at Eochaid's death.

Sigmall son of enduring Breistine,
king of Bentraige, with great virtue,
and great Mórmael from the plain
it is by them that Eochaid died.

◆ ◆ ◆ ◆ ◆ ◆ ◆ ◆ ◆ ◆ ◆

§90. *Togail Bruidne Dá Derga*
The Destruction of Dá Derga's Hostel
(abridged) [12]

HERE BEGINS THE DESTRUCTION OF DÁ DERGA'S HOSTEL.

¶ 1.

There was a famous and noble king over Ireland; Eochaid Feidleach was his name. Once he came across the assembly ground of Brí Léith, and he saw at the edge of a well a woman with a bright comb of silver adorned with gold, washing in a silver basin with four golden birds and little, bright gems of purple carbuncle in the rims of the basin. She had a mantle, curly and purple, a beautiful cloak, and in the mantle silvery fringes arranged, and a brooch of fairest gold. She wore a blouse, long, hooded, hard-smooth, of green silk, with red embroidery of gold. Marvellous clasps of gold and silver in the blouse on her breasts and her shoulders and her upper arms on every side. The sun kept shining upon her, so that the glistening of the gold against the sun from the green silk was visible to men. On her head were two golden-yellow tresses, in each of which was a plait of four locks, with a bead at the point of each lock. The hue of that hair seemed to them like the flower of the iris in summer or like burnished red gold.

¶ 2. There she was, undoing her hair to wash it, with her arms out through the sleeve-holes of her smock. White as the snow of one night were the two hands, soft and even, and red as foxglove were the two clear beautiful cheeks. Dark as the back of a stag-beetle the two eyebrows. Like a shower of pearls were the teeth in her head. Blue as a hyacinth were the eyes. Red as rowan berries the lips. Very high, smooth and soft-white the shoulders. Clear white and lengthy the fingers. Long were the hands. White as the foam of a wave was the flank, slender, long, tender, smooth, soft as wool. Polished and warm, sleek and white [were] the two thighs. Round and small, hard and white the two knees. Short and white and rule-straight the two shins. Justly straight, . . . beautiful the two heels. If a measure were put on the feet it would hardly have found them unequal, unless the flesh of the coverings should grow upon them. The bright radiance of the moon was in her noble face: the loftiness of pride in her smooth eyebrows: the light of wooing in each of her regal eyes.

---

12 Based on the translation of Whitley Stokes with extensive modernisations and clarifications of language by the editor. In numerous passages, the sense of the translation has been altered on the basis of the edited text of Eleanor Knott (Dublin, 1936).

   Some leading characters of this story appear elsewhere in this collection. For Étaín, see §89. For King Eterscél(e), see §68. Conall Cernach is a major hero in the Ulster Cycle tales.

A dimple of delight in each of her cheeks, with an alternation[?] in them [at one time] of purple spots with redness of a calf's blood, and at another with the bright lustre of snow. Soft womanly dignity in her voice; she had a steady and slow step: a queenly gait was hers. Indeed, of the world's women it was she who was the dearest and loveliest and most just that the eyes of men had ever beheld. It seemed to them [king Eochaid and his followers] that she was from the *síd*-mounds [dwelling places of the supernatural Tuatha Dé]. It was said of her: Shapely are all till [compared with] Étaín; dear are all till [compared with] Étaín.

¶ 3. A lust for her immediately seized the king; so he sent forward a man of his people to detain her. The king asked tidings of her and said, while announcing himself: 'Shall I have an hour of lying together with you?' 'It is for that we have come this way under your safeguard,' she said. 'I have a question—where are you from and how have you come?' asked Eochaid. 'Easy to say,' she said. 'I am Étaín, daughter of Etar, king of the horsetroop from the *síd*-mounds. I have been here for twenty years since I was born in a *síd*. The men of the *síd*, both kings and nobles, have been wooing me; but nothing was got from me, because ever since I was able to speak, I have loved you and given you a child's love for the great tales about you and your splendour. And though I had never seen you, I knew you at once from your description: it is you, then, I have reached.' 'Coming to find a bad friend far away will not be your fate,' Eochaid said. 'You will have welcome, and for you every [other] woman will be left [by me], and with you alone will I live so long as you have honour.' 'My proper bride-price to me,' she said, 'and afterwards my desire.' 'Yes, you shall have [both],' Eochaid said. Seven *cumals* [the value of seven slave women] were given to her.

¶ 4. Then the king, Eochaid Feidleach, died (having one daughter named, like her mother, Étaín, and wedded to Cormac, king of Ulaid). After the end of a time Cormac, king of Ulaid, [known as] 'the man of the three gifts', forsakes Eochaid's daughter, because she was barren except for one daughter that she had borne to Cormac after the making of the soup which her mother—the woman from the *síd*-mounds—gave her. Then she said to her mother: 'Bad is what you have given me: it will be a daughter that I shall bear.' 'That will not matter,' said her mother. 'She will be pursued by kings.'

¶ 5. Then Cormac weds again his wife, namely Étaín, and this was his desire, that the daughter of the woman who had before been abandoned [i. e. his own daughter] should be killed. So Cormac could not leave the girl to her mother to be nursed. Then his two slaves took her to a pit, and she smiles a laughing smile at them as they were putting her into it. Then their [kindly] nature came to them. They carried her into the calf shed of the cowherds of Eterscél, descendant of Iar, king of Tara, and they fostered her till she became a good embroideress; and there was not a king's daughter dearer than she was in Ireland.

¶ 6. A fenced house of wickerwork was made by them [the slaves] for her without any door, but only a window and a skylight. King Eterscél's tribesfolk saw that house and supposed that it was food that the cowherds kept there. But one of them went and looked through the skylight, and he saw in the house the dearest, most beautiful maiden. This is told to the king and immediately he sends his people to break the house and carry her off without asking the cowherds. For the king was childless, and it had been prophesied to him [by his druids] that a woman of unknown race would bear him a son.

Then the king said: 'This is the woman that has been prophesied to me!'

¶ 7. Now while she was there next morning she saw a bird on the skylight coming to her, and he leaves his bird skin on the floor of the house, and went to her and captured her and said: 'They are coming to you from the king to wreck your house and to bring you to him by force. And you will be pregnant by me, and bear a son—and that son must not kill birds. And "Conaire, son of Mess Buachalla" will be his name' (for her name was *Mess Buachalla* 'the Cowherds' foster child').

¶ 8. And then she was brought to the king, and with her went her fosterers, and she was betrothed to the king, and he gave her seven *cumals*, and to her fosterers seven other *cumals*. And afterwards they were made chieftains so that they all became legitimate; from this there are the two people called Fedlimthi Rechtaidi. And then she bore a son to the king, namely Conaire son of Mess Buachalla, and these were her three urgent prayers to the king: the nursing of her son among three households (that is, the fosterers who had nurtured her and the [two] Honey-worded Maines, and she herself is [the third]]; and she said that any of the men of Ireland as should wish [to do] anything for this boy should give to those three households for the boy's maintenance.

¶ 9. So in that way he was reared and the men of Ireland immediately knew this boy on the day he was born. And other boys were fostered with him, namely Fer Le and Fer Gar and Fer Rogain, three descendants of Donn Désa the champion, an army-man of the army from Muc-Lesi.

¶ 10. Now Conaire possessed three gifts, namely the gift of hearing and the gift of eyesight and the gift of judgement; and of those three gifts he taught one to each of his three foster brothers. And whatever meal was prepared for him, the four of them would go to it. Even though three meals were prepared for him each of them would go to his meal. The four had the same clothing and armour and colour of horses.

¶ 11. Then the king, namely Eterscél(e), died. A bull-feast was convened by the men of Ireland (in order to determine their future king), that is, a bull used to be killed by them and one man would eat his fill of it and drink its broth and a spell of truth was chanted over him in his bed. Whoever he would see in his sleep would be king and the sleeper would perish if he uttered a falsehood.

¶ 12. Four men in chariots were on [the Plain of the River] Liffey hunting their game; [they were] Conaire himself and his three foster brothers. Then his fosterers went to him that he might proceed to the bull-feast. The bull feaster then in his sleep at the end of the night beheld a man stark naked passing along the road of Tara, with a stone in his sling.

'I will go in the morning after you', he said.

¶ 13. He left his foster brothers at their game, and turned his chariot and his charioteer until he was in Dublin. There he saw great white-speckled birds, of unusual size and colour and beauty. He pursues them until his horses were tired. The birds would go [the distance of] a spear-cast before him, and would not go any further. He gets out, and takes his sling for them out of the chariot. He goes after them until he was at the sea. The birds bring themselves onto the wave. He went to them and overcame them. The birds shed their bird skins and turn upon him with spears and swords. One of them protects him and addressed him, saying: 'I am Némglan, king of your father's birds; and you have been forbidden to cast at birds, for here there is no one that should not be dear to you because of his father or mother.' 'Till today,' Conaire said, 'I did not know this.' 'Go to Tara tonight,' Némglan said; 'it is most fitting for you. A bull-feast is there, and through it you shall be king. A man stark-naked, who will go at the end of the night along one of the roads of Tara, having a stone and a sling—it is he who will be king.'

¶ 14. So in this way Conaire proceeded; and on each of the four roads by which men go to Tara there were three kings awaiting him, and they had clothing for him since it had been foretold that he would come stark-naked. Then he was seen from the road on which his fosterers were, and they put royal raiment on him, and placed him in a chariot, and he bound his pledges [taking hostages from subjects submitting to him].

¶ 15. The tribes-folk of Tara said to him: 'It seems to us that our bull-feast and our spell of truth are a failure, if it is only a young beardless lad that we envisioned in it.' 'That is of no moment,' he said. 'For a young, generous king like me to be in the kingship is no disgrace, since the binding of Tara's pledges is mine by right of father and grandfather.' 'Excellent! Excellent!' the host said. They set the kingship of Ireland upon him. And he said: 'I will enquire of wise men that I myself may be wise.'

¶ 16. [Then] he uttered all this as he had been taught by the man of the wave who said this to him: 'Your reign will be subject to a restriction, but the bird-reign will be noble, and this will be your restriction, i. e. your *geis* ['sworn tabu']. You shall not go righthandwise round Tara and lefthandwise round Brega. You must not hunt the evil-beasts of Cerna. And you must not go out every ninth night beyond Tara. You must not sleep in a house from which firelight is visible outside after sunset and in which [light] is visible from outside. And three Reds shall not go before you into a Red's house. And no raiding shall be done in your reign. And after sunset a company of one woman or one man shall not enter the house in which you are. And you shall not settle the quarrel of your two slaves.'

¶ 17. Now there were in his reign great bounties namely, seven ships in every June of every year arriving at Inber Colptha, and acorns up to the knees every autumn, and plenty [of fish] in [the rivers] Bush and Boyne in the June of each year, and such abundance of good will that no one slew any other in Ireland during his reign. And to everyone in Ireland his fellow's voice seemed as sweet as the strings of harps. From mid-spring to mid-autumn no wind disturbed a cow's tail. His reign was neither thunderous nor stormy.

¶ 18. Now, his foster brothers murmured at the taking from them of their father's and their grandfather's occupations, namely theft and treachery and killing of men and raiding. They thieved the three thefts from the same man, namely, a swine and an ox and a cow every year that they might see what punishment for that the king would inflict on them, and what damage the theft in his reign might do the king.

¶ 19. Now, every year the farmer would come to the king to complain, and the king would say to him, 'Go and address Donn Désa's three descendants for it is they that have taken the beasts.' Whenever [the farmer] went to speak to them [Donn Désa's descendants], they would almost kill him and he would not return to the king in order that Conaire might attend to his injury.

¶ 20. Since then, pride and wilfulness possessed [the descendants of Donn Désa]. They took to marauding surrounded by the sons of the lords of the men of Ireland. They had three times fifty as pupils when they were were-wolfing in the province of Connacht, until Maine Milscothach's swineherd saw them. And he had never seen that before. He went in flight. When they heard him they pursued him. The swineherd shouted, and the people of the two Maines came to him and the three times fifty men were arrested, along with their auxiliaries and taken to Tara. They consulted the king concerning the matter and he said: 'Let each [father] slay his son, but let my foster kindred be spared.'

¶ 21. 'Leave, leave!' everyone said: 'it shall be done for you.' 'No indeed,' he said; 'the judgement I have given is no life-sparing pardon by lottery. The men shall not be hung; but let veterans go with them that they may inflict their ravaging on the men of Britain.'

¶ 22. This they did. From there they put to sea and met the son of the king of Britain, namely Ingcél Cáech ['the One-eyed'] grandson of Conmac: three times fifty men and their veterans they met on the sea. They make an alliance and go with Ingcél and performed raiding with him.

¶ 23. This is the destruction which [Ingcél's] own impulse gave him. That was the night that his mother and his father and his seven brothers had been invited to the house of the king of his district. Ingcél murdered all of them in a single night. Then they [the Irish pirates] put out to sea to Ireland's land to seek a massacre [as payment] for that to which Ingcél had been entitled from them.

¶ 24. In Conaire's reign there was perfect peace in Ireland, except that in Northern Munster there was a joining between the two Carbres. Two foster brothers of his were they. And until Conaire came it was impossible to make peace between them. It was a *geis* ['sworn tabu'] of his to go to separate them before they had approached him. He went, however, although [to do so] was one of his tabus, and he made peace between them. He remained five nights with each of the two. That also was a *geis* of his.

¶ 25. After settling the two quarrels, he was travelling to Tara. This is the way they took to Tara, past Uisnech [reckoned as the ceremonial centre of Ireland] of Meath; and they saw the raiding from east and west, and from south and north, and they saw the war-bands and the hosts, and the men stark-naked [because they were going to battle]; and the land of the [southern] Uí Néill was a cloud of fire around him.

¶ 26. 'What is this?' asked Conaire. 'Not hard to answer,' his people answer. 'Not hard to know that the king's law has broken down in it since the country has begun to burn.' 'To what place should we take ourselves?' Conaire asked. 'To the North-east,' say his people. So then they went righthandwise round Tara, and lefthandwise around Brega and the cláenmíl ['evil beasts'] of Cerna were pursued by him. But he did not see it till the chase had ended. The men who made the world that smoky mist of magic were phantoms [and they did so] because Conaire's *gessi* ['sworn tabus'] had been violated.

¶ 27. Great fear then fell on Conaire because they had no way to go except on the Road of Midluachair and the Road of Cualu. So they took their way by the coast of Ireland southward. Then Conaire on the Road of Cualu: 'where shall we go tonight?' 'May I succeed in telling you, my foster kinsman Conaire,' said Mac Cécht, son of Snade Teiched, the champion of Conaire son of Eterscél. 'Oftener have the men of Ireland been contending for you every night than you have been wandering about for a guesthouse.'

¶ 28. 'Judgement goes with good times,' Conaire said. 'I had a friend in this country, if only we knew the way to his house.' 'What is his name,' Mac Cécht asked. 'Dá Derga of the Leinstermen,' Conaire answered. 'He came to me to seek a gift from me, and he did not come away with a refusal. I gave him a hundred cows from the herd. I gave him a hundred mantles made of close-woven cloth. I gave him a hundred fatted swine. I gave him a hundred blue-coloured weapons of battle. I gave him ten red, gilded brooches. I gave him ten vats. . . good and brown. I gave him ten slaves. I gave him ten querns.

I gave him three times nine hounds all white in their silver chains. I gave him a hundred racehorses, swifter than the herds of deer . . . There would be nothing held against him if he were to come again. He should reciprocate. It is strange if he is surly to me tonight when I arrive at his dwelling place.'

¶ 29. 'I know his house,' Mac Cécht said, 'the road on which you are going towards him was the boundary of his habitation. It continues till it enters his house, for through the house passes the road. There are seven doorways into the house, and seven bedrooms between every two doorways; but there is only one door on it, and that door is turned to whatever doorway at which the wind blows.' 'With all [the people] that you have here,' [Conaire said], 'you will go in with your great multitude until you arrive in the middle the house. 'If so,' [answers Mac Cécht], 'that you go [in there], I shall go [on] that I may light a fire there ahead of you.'

¶ 30. When Conaire, after this, was journeying along the Road of Cualu, he noticed before him three horsemen riding towards the house. Three red tunics had they, and three red mantles. They carried three red shields, and three red spears were in their hands. They rode three red steeds, and three red heads of hair were on them. They were all red, both body and hair and clothing, both horses and men.

¶ 31. 'Who is it that goes before us?' asked Conaire. 'It was a *geis* of mine for those three to go before me—the three Reds to the house of Red. Who will follow them and tell them to come behind me?' 'I will follow them,' said Lé Fer Flaith, Conaire's son.

¶ 32. He goes after them, lashing his horse, but he did not overtake them. There was the length of a spear-cast between them, but they did not gain upon him and he did not gain upon him. He told them not to go before the king. He did not overtake them, but one of the three men sang a lay to him over his shoulder:

'Listen here, son, great news, news from a hostel.
. . . Listen here, son!'

They went away from him then. He could not detain them.

¶ 33. The boy waited for the company of his father. He told his father what was said to him. Conaire did not like it. 'Go after them!' Conaire said, 'and offer them three oxen and three bacon-pigs, and so long as they shall be in my household, no one will be among them from fire to wall.'

¶ 34. So the lad went after them, and offered them that, and he did not overtake them. But one of the three men sang a lay to him over his shoulder:

'Listen here, son, great news! A generous king's great ardour whets you, burns you. Through ancient men's enchantments a company of nine yields. Listen here, my son!'

The boy turned back and repeated the lay to Conaire.

¶ 35. 'Go after them,' said Conaire, 'and offer them six oxen and six bacon-pigs, and my leavings, and gifts tomorrow, and so long as they shall be in my household, no one will be among them from fire to wall.' The lad then went after them, and did not overtake them. But one of the three men answered and said:

> 'Listen here, son, great news, weary are the steeds we ride. We ride the steeds of Donn Desscorach from the *síd*-mounds [dwelling place of the supernatural Tuatha Dé]. Though we are alive we are dead. Great are the signs: destruction of life, sating of ravens, feeding of crows, strife of slaughter, wetting of sword-edge, shields with broken bosses in hours after sundown. Listen here, my son!'

Then they went from him.

¶ 36. 'I see that you have not detained the men,' said Conaire. 'Indeed it is not because I failed to try,' said Le Fer Flaith. He recited the last answer that they gave him. Conaire and his retainers were not pleased at that; and afterwards evil forebodings of terror were on them. 'All my *gessi* have seized me tonight,' said Conaire, 'since those Three Reds were banished men.'

¶ 37. The Three Reds went forward to the house and took their seats in it, and fastened their red steeds to the door of the house.

¶ 38. This is the way Conaire went with his army towards Dublin. It is then that a man with black, cropped hair, with one hand and one eye and one foot, overtook them. Rough-cropped hair was on him. If a sackful of wild apples were flung on his crown, not an apple would fall to the ground, but each of them would stick on a hair. Though his snout were flung on a branch they would remain together. Long and thick as an outer yoke was each of his two shins. Each of his buttocks was the size of a cheese on its stick. A forked pole of iron, black-pointed, was in his hand. A swine, black-bristled, singed, was on his back, squealing continually, and a woman, big-mouthed, huge, dark, ugly, hideous, was behind him. Though her snout were flung on a branch, the branch would support it. Her lower lip would reach her knee.

¶ 39. He starts forward to meet Conaire, and made him welcome: 'Welcome to you, dear friend Conaire! Long has your coming here been known.' 'Who gives the welcome?' Conaire asks. 'Fer Caille ['Man of the Woods'] is here, with his black swine for you to consume that you may not be fasting tonight, for it is you who are the best king that has come into the world!' 'What is your wife's name?' Conaire said. 'Cichuil,' he answers. 'Any other night,' Conaire said, 'that pleases you, I will come to you, but leave us alone tonight.' 'No,' said the churl, 'for we will go to you in the place in which you will be tonight, dear pretty little friend, Conaire!'

¶ 40. So [the black man] went towards the house, with his great, big-mouthed wife behind him, and his swine short-bristled, black, singed, squealing continually, on his back. That was one of Conaire's *gessi* and that plunder should be taken in Ireland during his reign was another *geis* of his.

¶ 41. Now plunder was taken by the sons of Donn Désa, and five hundred there were in the body of their marauders, besides what underlings were with them. This, too, was a *geis* of Conaire's. There was a good warrior in the North Country: *Fén tar Crínach* 'Waggon Over Withered Sticks,' this was his name. Why he was called this was because he used to go over his opponent as a waggon would go over withered sticks. Now plunder was taken by him, and there were five hundred in that body of marauders alone, besides underlings.

¶ 42. There was besides a troop of still haughtier heroes, namely, the seven sons of Ailill and Medb of Connacht, each of whom was called 'Maine.' And each Maine had a byname, namely, Maine Fatherlike and Maine Motherlike, and Maine Gentle-pious, Maine Very Pious, Maine Unslow, and Maine Honeywords, Maine Grasp Them-all, and Maine the Talkative. Ravaging was wrought by them. As to Maine Motherlike and Maine Unslow, there were fourteen score in the body of their marauders. Maine Fatherlike had three hundred and fifty. Maine Honeywords had five hundred. Maine Grasp-them-all had seven hundred. Maine the Talkative had seven hundred. Each of the others had five hundred in the body of his marauders.

¶ 43. There was a valiant trio of the men of Cualu of Leinster, namely, the three Red Hounds of Cualu, called Cethach and Clothach and Conall. Now ravaging was wrought by them, and twelve score were in the body of their marauders, and they had a troop of madmen. In Conaire's reign a third of the men of Ireland were marauders. He was of sufficient strength and power to drive them out of the land of Ireland so as to transfer their marauding to Britain, but after this transfer they returned to their country.

¶ 44. When they had reached the shoulder of the sea, they meet Ingcél the One-eyed and Éiccel and Tulchinne, three descendants of Conmac of Britain, on the raging of the sea. A man ungentle, huge, fearful, uncouth was Ingcél. A single eye in his forehead, as broad as an ox hide, as black as a black beetle, with three pupils in it. Thirteen hundred were in the body of his marauders. The marauders of the men of Ireland were more numerous than they.

¶ 45. [The marauders] proceed to a sea-encounter on the water. 'You should not do this,' Ingcél said. 'Do not violate the [sworn] truthfulness of men with us, for you are more in number than I [have].' 'Nothing but a combat on equal terms shall befall you,' said the raiders of Ireland. 'It is somewhat better for you,' said Ingcél; 'let us make peace since you have been cast out of the land of Ireland, and we have been cast out of the land of North and South Britain. Let us make an agreement between us. Come and inflict your

ravaging in my country, and I will go with you and inflict my ravaging in
your country.'

¶ 46. They followed this counsel, and they gave pledges for it on the one side
and the other. These are the sureties that were given to Ingcél by the men of
Ireland, namely Gér and Gabur and Fer Rogain, for the destruction that
Ingcél should choose to cause in Ireland and for the destruction that the sons
of Donn Désa should choose to cause in North and South Britain.

¶ 47. A lot was cast upon them to see with which of them should go first. It
fell that they should go with Ingcél to his country. So they made for South
Britain, and there his father and mother and his seven brothers were slain, as
we have said before. After that they made for North Britain, and there they
made destruction, and then they returned to Ireland.

¶ 48. It was just then that Conaire went towards the Hostel [of Dá Derga]
along the Road of Cualu. It is then that the raiders came till they were on
the sea off the coast of Brega over against Howth. Then said the raiders:
'Strike the sails, and make one band of you on the sea that you may not be
sighted from land; and let some lightfoot be found from among you to go on
shore to see if we could save our honour with Ingcél; that is, murderous
devastation in exchange for the murderous devastation he has given us.'

¶ 49. 'Question: who will go on shore to look? Let someone go,' Ingcél said,
'who possesses in him the three gifts, namely, gift of hearing, gift of far sight,
and gift of judgement.' 'I,' Maine Honeywords said, 'have the gift of hearing.'
'And I,' Maine Unslow said, 'have the gift of far sight and of judgement.' 'It is
well for you to go this way,' the raiders said: 'that strategy is good.'

¶ 50. Then nine men went till they were on the Hill of Howth, to find out
what they might hear and see. 'Be still a while!' said Maine Honeywords. 'What
is that?' asked Maine Unslow. 'The sound of a good king's horse troop I hear.'
'By the gift of far sight, I see,' said his comrade. 'What do you see there?' 'I see
there,' he said, 'horse troops, lofty, beautiful, warlike, somewhat slender, wary,
active, keen, whetted, vehement, a good course that shakes a great covering of
land. They go to many heights, with wondrous waters and estuaries.'

¶ 51. 'What are the waters and heights and estuaries that they traverse?' 'Not
hard to answer: Indein, Cult, Cuilten, Mafat, Ammat, Iarmafat, Finne, Goiste,
Guistine. Grey spears over chariots, ivory-hilted swords on thighs, silvery
shields above their elbows. Half-wheels and half horses. Garments of every
colour about them. After that I see before them special horses, three times
fifty dark-grey steeds. Small-headed are they, red-nosed, pointed, broad-
hoofed, big-nosed, red-chested, fat, easily-stopped, easily-yoked, battle-nimble,
keen, whetted, vehement, with their three times fifty bridles of red enamel
upon them.'

¶ 52. 'I swear by what my tribe swears,' said the man of the long sight, 'these

are the steeds of some good lord. This is my judgement concerning that: it is
Conaire son of Eterscél, with multitudes of the men of Ireland around him,
who is travelling the road.' Back then they went that they might tell the
raiders. 'This,' they said, 'is what we have heard and seen.'

¶ 53. Of this host, then, there was a multitude, both on this side and on that,
namely, three times fifty boats, with five thousand in them, and ten hundred
in every thousand. Then they hoisted the sails on the boats, and steered them
from there to shore, till they landed on the Strand of Fuirbthe.

¶ 54. When the boats reached land, Mac Cécht was striking fire in Dá Derga's
Hostel. At the sound of the spark the three times fifty boats were hurled out,
so that they were on the shoulders of the sea. 'Be silent a while!' said Ingcél.
'What do you reckon that it is, Fer Rogain?' 'I don't know,' Fer Rogain
answered, 'unless it is Luchdonn the satirist in Emain Macha, who makes this
hand-smiting when his food is taken from him forcibly, or the scream of
Luchdonn in Tara Luachra, or Mac Cécht's striking a spark, when he kindles a
fire before a king of Ireland where he sleeps. Every spark and every shower
which his fire would let fall on the floor would broil a hundred calves and two
half-pigs.' 'May God not bring [Conaire] there tonight!' said Donn Désa's sons,
Conaire's foster brothers. 'Sad that he is subject to injury by foes!' 'It seems to
me,' said Ingcél, 'it should be no sadder for me than the murderous devastation
I gave you. It is a feast for me that [Conaire] should chance to come there.'

¶ 55. Their fleet was steered to land. The noise that the three times fifty vessels made in running ashore shook Dá Derga's Hostel so that no spear nor
shield remained on its rack in it, but the weapons uttered a cry and fell all on
the floor of the house.

¶ 56. 'What do you reckon that is, Conaire?' everyone asked; 'what is this
noise?' 'I know nothing like it unless it be the earth that has broken, or the
Leviathan that surrounds the globe and strikes with its tail to overturn the
world, or the ships of the sons of Donn Désa that have reached the shore.
Alas, that it should not be they who are here! Beloved foster brothers of our
own were they! Dear were the champions. We should not have feared them
tonight.' Then came Conaire out upon the green of the Hostel.

¶ 57. When Mac Cécht heard the tumultuous noise, it seemed to him that
warriors had attacked his people. At that he leapt into his armour to help
them. Vast as the thunder-feat of three hundred did they deem his act in
leaping to his weapons. Out of that there was no profit.

¶ 58. Now in the bow of the ship in which Donn Désa's sons were was the
champion, greatly accoutred, wrathful, the lion hard and awful, Ingcél the
One-eyed, descendant of Conmac. Wide as an ox hide was the single eye
protruding from his forehead, with seven pupils in it, which were black as a
black beetle. Each of his knees as big as a cauldron for a heifer; each of his

two fists was the size of a reaping-basket; his buttocks as big as a cheese on its stick; each of his shins as long as an outer yoke. So after that, the three times fifty boats, and those five thousands—with ten hundred in every thousand—landed on the Strand of Fuirbthe.

¶ 59. Then Conaire with his people entered the Hostel, and each took his seat within, both *geis* ['tabu'] and *nemgeis* ['non-tabu']. And the three Reds took their seats, and Fer Caille, with his swine, took his seat.

¶ 60. After that Dá Derga came to them, with three times fifty warriors, each of them having a long head of hair to the hollow of the back of his head, and a short cloak to their buttocks. Speckled-green drawers they wore, and in their hands were three times fifty great clubs with bands of iron. 'Welcome, dear friend Conaire!' he said. 'Though the bulk of the men of Ireland were to come with you, they themselves would have a welcome.'

¶ 61. When they were there they saw a lone woman coming to the door of the Hostel, after sunset, and seeking to be let in. As long as a weaver's beam was each of her two shins, and they were as dark as the back of a stag beetle. A greyish, woolly mantle she wore. Her lower hair reached as far as her knee. Her lips were on one side of her head.

¶ 62. She came and put one of her shoulders against the doorpost of the house, casting the evil eye on the king and the youths who surrounded him in the Hostel. He himself addressed her from within. 'Well, she-phantom,' said Conaire, 'if you are seer, what fortune do you see for us?' 'Truly I see for you,' she answered, 'that neither nail [?] nor flesh of yours shall escape from the place into which you have come, except what birds will carry away in their talons.' 'It was not your omen we were foretold, woman,' he said: 'it is not you that always augurs for us. What is your name, woman?' 'Cailb,' she answered. 'That is not much of a name,' Conaire said. 'Let it be known, many are my names besides.' 'What are they?' Conaire asked. 'Not hard to answer,' she said. 'Samain, Sinand, Seiscleand, Sodb, Saiglend, Samlocht, Caill, Coll, Díchoem, Díchuil, Díchim, Díchuimne, Díchuinne, Dairne, Dáirine, Der Uaine, Égem, Agam, Ethamne, Gním, Cluichi, Cethardam, Nith, Nemain [name of the war-goddess], Noenden, Bodb [another name of the war-goddess], Blosc, Bloar, Huaet, Mede, Mod.' On one foot, and holding up one hand, and breathing one breath she sang all that to them from the door of the house.

¶ 63. 'What do you desire?' Conaire asked. 'That which you, too, desire,' she answered. 'It is a *geis* of mine,' said Conaire, 'to admit the company of one woman after sunset.' 'Though it is a *geis*,' she replied, 'I will not go until my guesting come at once this very night.' 'You tell her,' said Conaire, 'that an ox and a bacon-pig shall be taken out to her, and my leavings, provided that she stays tonight in some other place.' 'If indeed,' she said, 'it has befallen that the king has not room in his house for the meal and bed of a lone woman, they will be got from someone else possessing generosity—if the hospitality of the prince in the hostel has departed.' 'Savage is that answer!' said Conaire; 'let her in though it is a *geis* of mine.' Great loathing they felt after that from the woman's conversation and ill-foreboding; but they did not know the cause of it.

¶ 64. The raiders landed afterwards, and went on till they were at Lecca Cinn Slébe, on the way to Dá Derga's Hostel. Ever open was the Hostel . . .

¶ 65. Great was the fire which was kindled by Conaire every night; that is, [enough to cook?] a *torc caille* ['Boar of the Wood']. Seven outlets it had. When a log was taken out of its side every flame that used to come forth at each outlet was as big as the blaze of an oratory. There were seventeen of Conaire's chariots at every door of the house, and by the raiders from the vessels, who were looking on, that great light was clearly seen through the wheels of the chariots.

¶ 66. 'Can you say, Fer Rogain,' said Ingcél, 'what that great light yonder resembles?' 'I cannot liken it to anything,' Fer Rogain answered, 'unless it is the fire of a king. May God not bring that man here tonight! It is a pity to destroy him!' 'What then is your opinion,' said Ingcél, 'of that man's reign in Ireland's land?' 'Good is his reign,' Fer Rogain answered. 'Since he assumed the kingship, no cloud has veiled the sun for the space of a day from the middle of spring to the middle of autumn. And not a dewdrop has fallen from grass till midday, and wind would not touch a cow's tail until noon. And in his reign, from year's end to year's end, no wolf has attacked anything except one bull calf of each byre; and to maintain this rule there are seven wolves in hostageship at the side wall in his house, and behind this a further security, that is, Macc Locc, and it is he that pleads for them at Conaire's house. In Conaire's reign are the three crowns on Ireland, namely, a crown of corn ears, and a crown of flowers, and a crown of acorns. In his reign, too, each man perceives the other's voice as melodious as the strings of harps, because of the excellence of the law and the peace and the good will prevailing throughout Ireland. May God not bring that man there tonight! It is sad to destroy him. It is a branch through its blossom. It is swine that falls before acorns. It is an infant in age. Sad is the shortness of his life!' 'It was my good luck,' said Ingcél, 'that he should be there, and there should be one murderous devastation for another. His killing is not more grievous to me than my father and my mother and my seven brothers, and the king of my country, whom I gave up to you before coming on the exchange of the ravaging.' 'It is true, it is true!' said the evildoers who were along with the British marauders.

¶ 67. The raiders started off from the Strand of Fuirbthe, and brought a stone for each man to make a cairn; for this was the distinction, which at first the *fian* ['extratribal war-band'] made between a 'massacre' and a 'raid.' A pillar-stone they used to plant when there would be a raid. A cairn, however, they used to make when there would be a massacre. At this time, then, they made a cairn, for it was a massacre. Far from the house was this, that they might not be heard or seen from it.

¶ 68. For two causes they built their cairn: first, since this was a custom in marauding; and, secondly, that they might find out their losses at the Hostel. Every one that would come safe from it would take his stone from the cairn: thus the stones of those that were slain would be left, and by that they would know their losses. And this is what men skilled in story recount, that for every stone in Carn Lecca there was one of the raiders killed at the Hostel. From that Carn Lecca in O'Kelly's country is named.

¶ 69. A *torc tened* ['boar of a fire'] was kindled by the sons of Donn Désa to give warning to Conaire. So that was the first warning-beacon that was made in Ireland, and from it to this day every warning-beacon is kindled. This is what others recount: that it was on the eve of *Samain* [31 October/1 November] the destruction of the Hostel was done, and that from that beacon the [customary] beacon of *Samain* followed, and stones are placed in the *Samain*-fire.

¶ 70. Then the raiders held a council at the place where they had put the cairn. 'Well, then,' said Ingcél to the guides, 'what is nearest to us here?' 'Easy to answer: the Hostel of Dá Derga, chief-hospitaller of Ireland.' 'Good men indeed,' Ingcél said, 'were likely to seek their fellows at that Hostel tonight.' This, then, was the counsel of the raiders, to send one of them to see how things were there. 'Who will go there to reconnoitre the house?' asked everyone. 'Who should go,' said Ingcél, 'but I, for it is I that am entitled to dues.'

¶ 71. Ingcél went to reconnoitre the Hostel with one of the seven pupils of the single eye which stood out of his forehead, to fit his eye into the house in order to destroy the king and the warriors who were around him in it. And Ingcél saw them through the wheels of the chariots. Then Ingcél was perceived from the house. He started off away from it after being seen.

¶ 72. He went till he reached the raiders in the place they were. Each circle of them was set around another to hear the tidings, the chiefs of the raiders being in the very centre of the circles. There were Fer Ger and Fer Gel and Fer Rogel and Fer Rogain and Lomna the Buffoon, and Ingcél the One-eyed. There were six of them in the centre of the circles. And Fer Rogain questioned Ingcél.

¶ 73. 'How is it, Ingcél?' Fer Rogain asked. 'However it is,' answered Ingcél, 'royal is the behaviour, of many hosts is the tumult: kingly is the noise of it. Whether a king is there or not, I shall take the house for what I have a right to. From it will come my return for your depredations.' 'We have left it in your hand, Ingcél!' said Conaire's foster brothers. 'But we should not inflict the murderous devastation till we know who is present in the Hostel.' ' Question: have you examined the house well, Ingcél?' asked Fer Rogain. 'My eye cast a rapid glance around it, and I will accept it for my dues as it stands.'

¶ 74. 'You may well accept it, Ingcél,' said Fer Rogain: 'the foster father of us all is there, Ireland's over-king, Conaire son of Eterscél. Question: what did you see in the champion's high seat of the house, facing the king, on the opposite side?'[13]

• • • • • • • • • • •

¶ 141. 'Rise up, then, you champions!' said Ingcél, 'and get yourselves to the Hostel!' With that the marauders marched to the Hostel, and made a murmur about it. 'Silence a while!' said Conaire, 'what is that?' ' Champions at the house,' said Conall Cernach of Ulster. 'There are warriors for them here,' answered Conaire. 'They will be needed tonight,' rejoined Conall Cernach.

¶ 142. Then Lomna *Drúth* ['the Jester'] went before the host of raiders into the Hostel. The doorkeepers struck off his head. Then the head was flung three times into the Hostel, and three times was thrown out of it, as he himself had foretold.

¶ 143. Then Conaire himself charged out of the Hostel together with some of his people, and they fought a combat with the host [of raiders], and six hundred fell by Conaire before he could get to his arms. Then the Hostel was three times set on fire, and three times put out from inside: and it was proved that the murderous devastation would never have been made had not the use of his weapons been taken from Conaire. After that Conaire went to seek his arms, and he put on his battle dress, and went down to wielding his weapons at the marauders, he together with the band that he had. Then, after getting his arms, six hundred fell by him in his first encounter.

¶ 144. After this the raiders were routed. 'I have told you,' said Fer Rogain son of Donn Désa, 'that if the champions of the men of Ireland and Britain attack Conaire at the house, the murderous devastation will not be made unless Conaire's fury and prowess are quelled.' 'His time will be short,' said the druids accompanying the raiders. This was the quelling [that the druids] brought: a great yearning for drink seized him.

¶ 145. After that, Conaire entered the house, and asked for a drink. 'A drink to me, dear friend Mac Cécht!' Conaire said. Mac Cécht said: 'This is not an order that I have fulfilled for you, to give you a drink. There are waiters and cupbearers who bring drink to you. The command I have previously had from

---

13 What follows in ¶¶75–140 is a prolonged series of descriptions of the rooms of Dá Derga's Hostel in which Ingcél relates the details of each room and its occupants and then Fer Rogain identifies the persons described. This literary pattern, sometimes called 'the watchman device' is similar to what we have in unabridged form in *Mesca Ulad* §82 ¶¶34–47 above. It serves the same purpose here, providing a picture of one side before the battle begins.

you is to protect you when the warriors of the men of Ireland and Britain may be attacking you all around the Hostel. You will go safely from them, and no spear will enter your body. Ask a drink of your waiters and your cupbearers.'

¶ 146. Then Conaire asked a drink of his waiters and his cupbearers who were in the house. 'In the first place there is none,' they said; 'all the liquids that had been in the house have been poured on the fires.' The cupbearers found no drink for him in the [River] Dodder, and the Dodder had flowed through the house.

¶ 147. Then Conaire again asked for a drink. 'A drink to me, fosterer, Mac Cécht! It does not matter to me what death I go to; for I shall perish anyhow.' hen Mac Cécht gave a choice to the champions of prowess of the men of Ireland who were in the house, whether they cared to protect the king or to seek a drink for him. Conall Cernach answered this in the house—and he considered this a cruel point of contention, and ever afterwards he kept up a feud with Mac Cécht, 'Leave the defence of the king to us,' Conall said, 'and go you to seek the drink, for it is you he asked.'

¶ 148. So then Mac Cécht went forth to seek the drink, and he took Conaire's son, Lé Fer Flaith, under his armpit, and Conaire's golden cup, in which an ox with a bacon-pig would be boiled; and he bore his shield and his two spears and his sword, and he carried the cauldron-spit, a spit of iron. He burst forth upon the raiders, and in front of the Hostel he dealt nine blows with the iron spit, and at every blow nine raiders fell. Then he made a feat of leaning the shield and an edge-feat of the sword about his head, and he delivered a hostile attack on them. Six hundred fell in his first encounter, and after cutting down hundreds he went through the band outside.

• • • • • • • • • • •

¶ 152. . . . the people of the Hostel came forward in order, and fought their combats with the raiders, and fell by them, as Fer Rogain and Lomna Drúth [the Jester] had said to Ingcél, that is, that every room would charge forth in its turn and engage in combat, and after that [they would] escape, so that none were left in the Hostel in Conaire's company except Conall [Cernach] and Sencha and Ailill.

¶ 153. Now from the vehement ardour and the greatness of the contest which Conaire had fought, his great parching thirst attacked him, and he perished of a consuming fever, for he did not get his drink. So when the king died [Conall Cernach and Sencha and Dubthach] charged out of the Hostel, and delivered a cunning deed of combat on the marauders, and journeyed on from the Hostel, wounded, broken, and maimed.

¶ 154. Concerning Mac Cécht, however, he went his way till he reached the

Well of Casair [the source of the River Dodder], which was near him in the territory of Cualu; but he could not find enough water in it to fill his cup, that is, Conaire's golden cup which he had brought in his hand. Before morning he had gone round the chief rivers of Ireland; namely, Bush, Boyne, Bann, Barrow, Neim, Luae, Láigdae, Shannon, Suir, Sligo, Sámair, Find, Ruirthech, Slaney, and in them he did not find enough water to fill his cup.

¶ 155–156. [Mac Cécht] went his way till he reached Húarán Garad on Mag Aí. Previously, before morning, he had travelled to the chief Loughs of Ireland; namely, Loch Derg, Loch Luimnig, Loch Foyle, Loch Mask, Loch Corrib, Loch Laig, Loch Cuan, Loch Neagh, Mórloch, and he did not find in them enough water to fill his cup. [The water of Húarán Garad on Mag Aí] could not hide itself from him. He brought his cupful out of it, and the boy fell under his covering [?]. After this he went on and reached Dá Derga's Hostel before morning.

¶ 157. When Mac Cécht went across the third ridge towards the house, there were two men striking off Conaire's head. Then Mac Cécht struck off the head of one of the two men who had beheaded Conaire. The other man then was fleeing with the king's head. A pillar-stone happened to be under Mac Cécht's feet on the floor of the Hostel. He hurled it at the man who had Conaire's head and drove it through his spine, so that his back broke. After this Mac Cécht beheaded him. Mac Cécht then poured the cup of water into Conaire's gullet and neck. Then Conaire's head said (after the water had been put into his neck and gullet):

> A good man Mac Cécht!
>> an excellent man Mac Cécht!
> He gives a drink to a king,
>> he does a deed.

After this Mac Cécht followed the routed foe.

¶ 158. It is this that some books relate: that only a very few fell around Conaire, specifically, nine only. And hardly a fugitive [of those few remaining] escaped to tell the story to the heroes who had been at the house.

¶ 159. [As to the raiders] where there had been five thousand—and in every thousand ten hundred—only one set of five escaped, namely Ingcél and his two brothers Echell and Tulchinne, [called] 'the Yearling of the Raiders' ([those were] the three descendants of Conmac), and the two Reds of Róiriu who had been the first to wound Conaire.

¶ 160. Afterwards Ingcél went to Britain, and received the kingship after his father, since he had taken home spoils of the king of another country.

¶ 161. This, however, is the recension in other books, and it is more probably true. Of the people of the Hostel, forty or fifty fell, and of the raiders three fourths, and there escaped of them only one third [as many as died] from the murderous devastation.

¶ 162. Now when Mac Cécht was lying wounded on the battlefield, at the end of the third day, he saw a woman passing by. 'Come here, woman!' Mac Cécht said. 'I dare not go that way,' the woman said, 'for horror and fear of you.' 'There was a time, woman, when people had horror and fear of me; but now you should fear nothing. I accept you on the truth of my honour and [grant] my safeguard.' Then the woman went to him. 'I do not know,' he said, 'whether it is a fly, or a gnat, or an ant that nips me in the wound.' It really was a hairy wolf that was there, as far in as its two shoulders in the wound! The woman seized it by the tail, dragged it out of the wound, and it took what it held in its jaws out of him. 'Truly,' the woman said, 'this is an ant of an ancient land.' Mac Cécht said, 'I swear what my tribe swears, it seemed to me no bigger than a fly, or a gnat, or an ant.' And Mac Cécht took the wolf by the throat, and struck it a blow on the forehead, and killed it with a single blow.

¶ 163. Then Lé Fer Flaith son of Conaire died under Mac Cécht's armpit, for the warrior's heat and sweat had dissolved him.

¶ 164. After that Mac Cécht, having cleansed the slaughter, at the end of the third day, set forth, and he dragged Conaire with him on his back, and buried him at Tara, as some say. Then Mac Cécht departed into Connacht, to his own country, that he might undergo his cure in Mag Brengair. From that, the name stuck to the plain from Mac Cécht's misery, that is, Mag Brengair.

¶ 165. Now Conall Cernach escaped from the Hostel, and three times fifty spears had gone through the arm, which upheld his shield. He went forth till he reached his father's house, with half his shield in his hand, and his sword, and the fragments of his two spears. Then he found his father before the enclosure surrounding his stronghold in Tailltiu.

¶ 166. 'Swift are the wolves that have hunted you, my son,' said his father. 'This is what we have had of conflict against warriors, you old hero,' Conall Cernach replied. 'Have you any news of Dá Derga's Hostel then?' asked [his father] Amairgen; 'is your lord alive? ' 'He is not alive,' Conall said. 'I swear by the gods by whom the great tribes of Ulster swear, it is cowardly for a man to have gone out of there alive, having left his lord with his foes in death,' said Conall Cernach's father. 'My wounds are not white, you old hero,' Conall said.

¶ 167. He showed him his shield-arm, on which there were three times fifty wounds, which had been inflicted on it. The shield that guarded it is what saved it. But the right arm had been worked over, as far as two thirds of it, since the shield had not been guarding it. That arm was mangled and maimed and wounded and pierced, except that the sinews kept it to the body without separation. 'That arm fought tonight, my son,' Amairgen said. 'True is that, you old hero,' Conall Cernach said. 'There are many that it gave drinks of death to tonight in front of the Hostel.'

¶ 168. Now as to the raiders, every one of them that escaped from the Hostel went to the cairn which they had built on the night before the preceding night, and they brought out of it a stone for each man not mortally wounded. So this is what they lost by death at the Hostel, a man for every stone that is [now] in Carn Lecca.

FINIT.

• • • • • • • • • • •

§91. *Echtra Chorbmaic Uí Chuinn*

The Adventure of Cormac [son of Art and] Grandson of Conn[14]

TRANS. JOHN CAREY

ONCE CORMAC THE GRANDSON OF CONN WAS IN LIATHDRUIM [a.k.a. Tara]. He saw a lone warrior, sober and grey-haired, approaching him across the green of the stronghold. It is thus that he was: a peaceful branch [or 'branch of the *síd*'[15]: *cráeb sídamail*] in his hand, with three apples of red gold upon it, and it was not known what wood it was. And when it was shaken, the sound of the apples was sweeter than all the music in the world; and the men of the world would sleep at that music, and there would be no sorrow or care on anyone who heard that music.

Then Cormac felt a great, unbearable love for the branch, and said that he would give him the three best gifts in Ireland in exchange for it. And the warrior gave him the branch, and bound him to yield those three gifts up to him whenever he should come to ask for them. Then Cormac shook the branch in Druim Caín so that all the people of Ireland, men, children, and women, fell into a single slumber of sleep.

At the end of a year after that the warrior came; and the first gift for

---

14 The most familiar version of this tale is that included in the composite Middle Irish work *Scél na Fír Flatha*, edited and translated by Whitley Stokes as 'The Irish Ordeals, Cormac's Adventure in the Land of Promise, and the Decision as to Cormac's Sword', *Irische Texte* 3.1 (1891) 183-229. The version translated below, edited by Vernam Hull as 'Echtra Cormaic maic Airt, "The Adventure of Cormac mac Airt"', *PMLA* 64 (1949) 871-83, survives in the Book of Fermoy: it seems to belong to the same approximate period as the *Scél na Fír Flatha* version.

15 **cráeb sídamail.** Old and Middle Irish *síd* can mean either 'peace' or the supernatural.

which he asked in exchange for the branch was Ailbe Gruaidbrecc, Cormac's daughter. And she was given to him; and the women of all Ireland made a great wailing and a mighty outcry lamenting the girl, until the branch was shaken at them and their care and sorrow left them at once—for women in labour and wounded men would sleep at the music of the branch.

Then the same warrior came at the end of a year to ask for the second gift, and this is the gift for which he asked: he took Cairpre Lifechair the son of Cormac away with him. And although the outcry of the women because of Ailbe was great, greater was the outcry of the mercenaries and warriors because of Cairpre Lifechair king of Mairge. And then the same branch was shaken at them, so that it took their care and their sorrow from the men and women of Ireland. And the warrior came for a third time to ask for the price of his branch, and this is the gift that he asked: he took Cormac's queen Eithne away with him. Then a pang of jealousy went into Cormac's head, and he went after his wife to take her from the warrior. A cloud of mist was brought between them, so that Cormac did not know where the warrior and the queen had gone.

Then Cormac found himself in the midst of a great plain. There was a great stronghold in the midst of the plain, and a silver rampart around it, and a house half of gold in the midst of the stronghold half-thatched with the wings of birds, and a troop of horsemen of the *síd* gathering the wings of many-coloured birds for the house. And they put those wings upon the house without a splinter [to fasten them], and they were falling off. . .; and thus that troop of horsemen did from the beginning of the world until its end. . . .

After Cormac had gone on he saw a warrior kindling a fire. He would fetch a great tree-trunk, root, and crown, and would put the trunk on the fire and go to fetch another; and nothing of the first tree-trunk would be left when he returned. And this was the business and labour of that man from the beginning of the world until its end.

[Then he saw a bright well within the enclosure, and five streams flowing from it, and multitudes taking turns drinking the water of the streams. Nine everlasting hazels stood above the well. The purple hazels drop their nuts into the well, and the five salmon which are in the well crack them open, and their bubbles (?) are set upon the streams. The sound of the falling of those streams was sweeter than any music.][16]

Then Cormac came to the stronghold, with a rampart of pure silver

---

16 I have supplied the preceding paragraph from the *Scél na Fír Flatha* version. Since both that version and the evidently independent Early Modern Irish version (edition and translation by S. H. O'Grady, 'Faghail Craoibhe Chormaic mhic Airt', *Transactions of the Ossianic Society* 3 (1857) 212-29) speak of magic wells at this point, something similar almost certainly stood in the exemplar of the Fermoy recension.]

around it, and four houses within, and one great house between them. A fair, handsome couple were in the midst of the house. Then the king's feet were washed. After that a man came in with a pig on his back, and a staff in one hand and a hatchet in the other; and he saluted Cormac by name and wished him welcome. Then he slew the pig with the hatchet, and cut it up and put it in the cauldron, and chopped up the staff and put it beneath the cauldron. The man said: 'This pig will not be cooked until we four each tell a true tale.'

Then the lord of the house said: 'Tell yourself, fellow, a tale about your pig.'

'I will,' he said. 'When the pair yonder first took up housekeeping, their property consisted of six cows and an ox and myself as a servant. And with our ox we ploughed a single field of wheat. We had a farmer living next to us who owned many cattle and much property. I came upon his cows in the wheat field, and impounded them until he gave me the pig and hatchet and staff to let them go. And he told me: "Kill the pig with the hatchet, and chop up the staff with the same hatchet; and the staff will provide enough wood to cook the pig, and the pig will sate the hunger of a great company, and your pig and your staff will endure for you every day." I kill that pig and burn that staff every night, and feed the great company thus; and both of them endure for me.'

A quarter of the pig was cooked then.

Then the lord of the house told a tale, and said: 'On that one day every year when we plough, I sowed (?) for a single hour without a horse or man to help me, and it was ripe in that same hour. When I wished to go and harvest it the next day, it was [already] in three great stacks in the midst of the field. When I wished to fetch it home, I found it stacked up in the midst of my stronghold. It remains without decaying; and though a multitude are around the pig, none of them is without wheat.'[17]

Half of the pig was cooked then.

['Now it is my turn to tell a story,' said the woman. 'I have seven cows and seven sheep,' she said. 'The milk of the seven cows is enough for everyone in the Land of Promise. Clothes for all of them come from the wool of the seven sheep.'][18]

All of the pig was cooked except for one quarter. This is the story which Cormac told: his own adventures from the beginning until that time.

---

17 The rendering of the end of this sentence is conjectural, as the manuscript is partly illegible here; the same is the case at the point where I have tentatively supplied 'sowed' above.

18 Only fragments of this passage are legible in the Book of Fermoy; I have supplied the version in Scél na Fír Flatha.

'That is true,' said the man of the house. 'The world from which you have come is the present world. The horsemen you saw thatching the house are the skilled professionals [*aes dáno*] of the world. . .; and everything which they bring home after going on a circuit melts away and decomposes into nothing while they are on the next circuit, without profit or prosperity [remaining]. As for the man kindling a fire, he is the victuallers and young noblemen of the world: it is (?) they themselves who consume everything which they labour to produce. . ., and whatever they consume this year, often they pay for it the next year. This chief stronghold, however, is the chief stronghold of the Land of Promise; and it is I who fetched you the branch and who asked for gifts in exchange for it.'

Then the whole pig was cooked, and his own portion was set before Cormac; but he said that he would not eat his portion until there were fifty in his company. Manannán sang a song to Cormac, and he slept, and when he awoke from his sleep there were fifty in his company, and Eithne and Ailbe and Cairpre Lifechair together with them. The king of Ireland rejoiced then to see his family.

Then a cup was fetched to him, the body of which was of refined red gold.

'That,' said Cormac, 'is the one treasure which I covet most in the world, save only that it is easy to break.'

Manannán gave the cup a blow, so that he made three fragments of it.

'That is a great shame,' said Cormac, 'that the cup should be broken.'

'I give my word,' said Manannán, 'in the presence of the King of Heaven, that your wife and daughter have not been defiled from the time when they went from you until this hour. If that declaration is true, the cup will be intact in its first shape.'

Then the cup was intact in that shape, and Cormac was glad at that. After that Manannán gave his cup and his *fidchell*-board and his branch to Cormac; and Cormac arose next morning in Tara, though it was not there that he had gone to sleep.

◆ ◆ ◆ ◆ ◆ ◆ ◆ ◆ ◆ ◆ ◆

Wisdom Literature

§92. *Audacht Morainn*
The Testament of Morann

TRANS. J. T. KOCH based on the editions of Fergus Kelly, Dublin: Dublin Institute for Advanced Studies (1976), and Anders Ahlqvist, *Études Celtiques* xxi (1984) 151–170.

¶ 1

HERE BEGINS THE TESTAMENT OF MORANN SON OF MÓEN TO FERADACH FIND FECHTNACH SON OF CRAUMTHANN NIA NÁR. This man was the son of the daughter of Lóth son of Delerath of the Pictish folk. His mother took him away in her womb after the destruction by the subject tribes of [all] Ireland's lords, with the exception of Feradach in his mother's womb. He came across afterwards with war-bands, and Morann sent this testament to them. *Id est* :

¶ 2.   Rise up, go forth,
O my Neire well used to declaring.
You are made known by the benefits in the declaration.
Dutiful is the journey you embark upon.
Proclaim, raise up the truth.
Manifest [and] enduring
are my words before my death.
Bring him the profit of uprightness,
which every sovereign lord is entitled to
([as] if you were to go before every king).
I take measure of [my words] for the security of my kindred.

¶ 3.   If you go to royalty,
run to Feradach
Find Fechtnach.
Good and full of life
is the man whose sovereignty will last long
at the establishment of [his] complete sovereignty.
He will repel many tribes
northwards as far as the sea.
He will enlarge his legacy,
fulfilling [it] with heroic ardour.

¶ 4. He should keep my directive which follows here.

¶ 5. Tell him every word.
Bring to him in every word this long-lasting commandment.

¶ 6. He should preserve truthfulness, it will preserve him.

¶ 7. He should raise up truthfulness, it will raise him up.

¶ 8. He should lift up mercy, it will lift him up.

¶ 9. He should be considerate of his tribes, they will be considerate of him.

¶ 10. He should give deliverance to his tribes, they will deliver him.

¶ 11. He should calm his tribes, they will calm him.

¶ 12. Tell him—it is through the sovereign's truth that the death toll of a mighty war-band [and] great lightning bursts are kept away from people.

¶ 13. It is through the sovereign's truth that he judges great tribes [and] great treasures.

¶ 14 It is through the sovereign's truth that he fulfils peace, tranquillity, the well-being of sages, [and] comfort.

¶ 15. It is through the sovereign's truth that he dispatches (great) war parties to the frontiers of [his tribe's] mutual enemies.

¶ 16. It is through the sovereign's truth that every heir plants his house-post in his cherished legacy.

¶ 17. It is through the sovereign's truth that the mouth may taste the abundant fruit of the great forest.

¶ 18. It is through the sovereign's truth that milk-yields of numerous cattle may be traded.

¶ 19. It is through the sovereign's truth that there may be plenty of every high, tall grain.

¶ 20. It is through the sovereign's truth that an abundance of the water's fish swim up streams.

¶ 21. It is through the sovereign's truth that fair offspring, borne of young women, are well begotten.

¶ 22. Tell him of himself   he is young, his sovereignty young.
He should watch the driver of an old chariot,
because the charioteer of an old tyre [= chariot] does not sleep sweetly: he looks before him, he looks back; forward and to the right and to the left.
He looks, he fights back, he protects, in order that it would not be with negligence or abuse that the tyres run under him.

¶ 23. Tell him   he should not promote any judge who does not know the true legal precedents.

¶ 24. It is through the sovereign's truth that every great artisan achieves the diadem of learning. It is after that that [the artisan] will sit to give instructive chanting of the beneficial discipline to which he has submitted himself.

¶ 25. It is through the sovereign's truth that the borders of every sovereign of truth stretch out so that a cow can attain the extent of its [needed] pasturage.

¶ 26. It is through the sovereign's truth that every article of clothing is got for viewing of eyes.

¶ 27. It is through the sovereign's truth that enclosed fields for the protection of cattle [and] of every produce extend for every sovereign realm of truthfulness.

¶ 28. It is through the sovereign's truth that the three legal exemptions from violence at every tribal assembly [óenach] protect every lord and chieftain by the controls which relate to competitive sports [as contained] in the course of the esteemed law.

Racing of horses at tribal assemblies is the first exemption.

Closing in of fortifications is the second exemption.

The benefit of the ale-house is the third exemption—[joining together] with cherished things and with the great bounties of the mead circuit, where [both] fools and sages, familiars and strangers become drunk.

¶ 29. Tell him   not much should he redden fore-courts, because carnage is a vain pouring away of every sovereignty and of the sheltering of the sovereign by the kindred.

¶ 30. Tell him to grant any reciprocal giving to which he is obligated, to enforce any bond he should bind, to nullify the [shameful] blushing of his cheeks with blades on battlefields facing foreign boundaries, against [the offending party's war-]cry, against all their defensive actions.

¶ 31. Tell him—neither fine gifts nor great treasures nor profits should blind him to the weak ones [and their] miseries.

¶ 32. Tell him—he should determine the value of creations of the creator who made them according to how they were made; whatever he will not reckon according to its worth as a luxury will not give them its full fruit.

¶ 33. He should determine the value of the earth according to its fruits.

¶ 34. He should determine the value of the yew wood according to its valuable manufactured goods.

¶ 35. He should determine the value of cattle according to their [abundance during] the overlord's winter itinerary [literally 'circuit of fame'].

¶ 36. He should determine the value of milk according to its abundant porridge.

¶ 37. He should determine the value of grain according to its height.

¶ 38. He should determine the value of streams according to [their] cleansing washing.

¶ 39. He should determine the value of iron according to tribes' qualities . . .

¶ 40. He should determine the value of bronze by its firmness [and] soundness [and] dense artefacts.

¶ 41. He should determine the value of silver according to its worldly worth in bright artefacts.

¶ 42. He should determine the value of gold according to its foreign wonderful ornaments.

¶ 43. He should determine the value of the soil according to its usefulness for tribes seeking fruit.

¶ 44. He should determine the value of sheep according to their coat [of wool] which is chosen for the clothes of the tribes.

¶ 45. He should determine the value pigs according to the fat flank, for it is freeing of every face from [?]dishonour.

¶ 46. He should determine the value of warriors who accompany a true sovereign, because every king possesses the rule of his war-band; whatever he will not reckon according to its worth as luxury will not give them its full fruit.

¶ 47. He should determine the value of unfree persons [and] the masses who serve: let them serve, let them supply food, let them measure, let them give in return for the sovereign's true grants of value.

¶ 48. He should determine the value on old men in the places established by their ancestors with the many profits of honour.

¶ 49. He should determine value of fathers and mothers according to the prosperity of guardianship [and] steadfastness of duty.

¶ 50. He should determine the value of payments for every guild of artisan according to tangible well-made artefacts.

¶ 51. He should determine the value of what is right and correct, truth and obligation, contract and regulation of every true sovereign towards all his clients.

¶ 52. He should determine the value of the correct honour-price of every grade of free and unfree persons of privilege [nemed].[19]

---

19 **Nemed** signifies a special status of legal privilege or exemption. Early Irish royalty,

May you lead away those who can make me blush.

¶ 53. Rise up, go forth,
O my Neire well used to declaring,
to Feradach Find Fechtnach.
Announce to him the prominent details of my words.

¶ 54. (a) Darkness gives way to light. (b) Grief gives way to happiness. (c) An oaf gives way to a learned man. (d) A fool gives way to a sage. (e) The unfree give way to the free. (f) The uncouth gives way to the illustrious. (g) Stinginess gives way to generosity. (h) Avarice gives way to openhandedness. (i) Recklessness gives way to steadiness. (j) Disquiet gives way to pacification. (k) An un-sovereign gives way to a true sovereign. (l) Conflict gives way to peace. (m) Falsehood gives way to truth.

¶ 55. Tell him—: (a) he should be merciful; (b) he should be righteous; (c) he should be equitable; (d) he should be conscientious; (e) he should be steady; (f) he should be generous; (g) he should be hospitable; (h) he should be modest; (i) he should be securely settled; (j) he should be beneficial; (k) he should be capable; (l) he should be genuine; (m) he should be eloquent; (n) he should be constant; (o) he should be true-judging.

¶ 56. For there are ten things which overwhelm the falsehood of every sovereign. Beware that you do not do it; beware of everything, O all sovereigns! Announce [as received] from me the ten: sovereignty and worth, fame and victory, children and kindred, peace and life, destiny and tribes.

¶ 57. Tell him—: he may die, he will die; he may leave, he will leave; how he was, how he will be; it is these that will be declared. He is not a sovereign unless he controls these actions.

¶ 58. Tell him—: there are four sovereigns: the true sovereign and the sovereign by his wits, the sovereign who takes possession with warbands and the bull sovereign.

¶ 59. First the true sovereign—that one is stirred towards everything good. He smiles on the truth when he hears it. He raises it up when he sees it. For he is no true sovereign whom living men do not glorify with blessings.

¶ 60. The sovereign by his wits—that one protects frontiers and tribes who yield their treasures and entitlements to him.

¶ 61. The sovereign who takes possession with war-bands from abroad—that

---

nobility, and the higher grades of crafts were accorded *nemed* status. In the Old Irish legal texts we find these privileged classes subdivided into *soer-nemed* and *doer-nemed* or free- and base-*nemed* persons. The cognate Old Celtic word *nemeton* is common in place-names on the European mainland and in Britain, where the form signifies sacred groves of pagan ritual significance. The Old Welsh form *nïuet* occurs in *Y Gododdin* [B².29 = A.68], where it means, roughly, 'rightful nobility, privilege'.

one's war-bands turn inwards. They withhold his requirements, for a well destined man does not turn outside.

¶ 62. The bull sovereign—that one strikes, is struck; defends, is defended against; digs up, is dug up; attacks, is attacked; pursues, is pursued. It is because of him that there is perpetual clamour with horns.

¶ 63. Rise up, go forth,
    O my Neire well used to declaring,
    to Feradach Find Fechtnach,
    a noble, illustrious sovereign,
    for every sovereign who holds sway with the truth.
    He should adhere to my words.
    They will bring him to victory.
    I take measure of them for the security of my kindred.
    (Urgent compulsion seizes me.)

FINIT.

• • • • • • • • • •

§§93–96. Selections from the Finn Cycle
TRANS. JOHN CAREY

§93. The Boyhood Deeds of Finn[20]

THERE WAS A CONTENTIOUS ASSEMBLY and a hostile struggle concerning the *fianaigecht* and the chief-stewardship of Ireland between Cumall son of Trénmór and Uirgrenn son of Lugaid Corr of the Luaigni. Cumall belonged to the Corcu Óche of Cúl Contuinn; for from them derived his tribe, the Uí Thairrsig. Torba daughter of Eochaman of the Érainn was Cumall's wife until he married Muirne Muinchaem.

After that the battle of Cnucha was waged between them, that is, between Cumall and Uirgrenn. Dáire Derg son of Eochu Find son of Cairpre Galach son of Muiredach, and his son Aed, were fighting in the battle on Uirgrenn's side. Another name of Dáire's was Morna Muinchamm. Then that battle was fought. Luichet and Aed son of Morna met in the battle. Luichet wounded Aed so that he put out one of his eyes, so that is why the name Goll ['one-eyed'] stuck to him ever after. Luichet was slain by Goll. Then the man who kept the *corrbolg* [literally 'crane-bag'] in which were his [i.e. Cumall's] own treasures wounded Cumall in the battle. Goll son of Morna slew Cumall in the battle, and carried off his spoils and his head; so that that was the origin of the enmity between Finn and the sons of Morna.

Concerning this the historian sang:

> Goll son of Dáire Derg, with fame,
> son of Eochu Find, bright his valour,
> son of Cairpre Galach, with courage,
> son of Muiredach from Findmag.

> Goll slew Luichet of the hundreds
> in the battle of Cnucha, it is no lie:
> Luichet Find, of the bright weapons,
> fell at the hand of Morna's son.
> At his hand fell the great Cumall

---

20 This important text is a composite work, which attempts to provide a unified account of Finn's youth by stitching together a number of disparate traditions. For some of this material see the stanzas devoted to Finn in Gilla in Choimded's poem 'A Rí ríchid, réidig dam', translated by Kuno Meyer, *Fianaigecht* (Dublin: Dublin Institute for Advanced Studies, rpt. 1993) 46-51.

in the battle of Cnucha of the armies.
The harsh battle was waged
concerning the *fianaigecht* of Ireland.

The clans of Morna were in the battle,
and the Luaigni of Tara;
for theirs was the *fian*-ship of the men of Ireland
at the hand of every king, with boasting.

Victorious Cumall had a son:
bloody Finn of the hard blade.
Finn and Goll, great their fame:
mightily they waged war.

Afterwards they made peace,
Finn and Goll of the hundred deeds,
until Banb Sinna was slain
because of the pig in Temair Luachra.

Aed was the name of Dáire's son
until Luichet smote him, with splendour:
since the savage spear had struck him,
that is why he used to be called Goll.

Cumall left his wife Muirne pregnant; and she bore a son, and the name Deimne was given to him. Fiacail son of Conchenn and Bodbmall the druidess and the Grey One of Luachair came in search of Muirne, and took the boy away with them, for his mother did not dare to be together with him. Afterwards Muirne slept with Gleór Lámderg, king of the Lámraige, which is how it came to be said that Finn was the son of Gleór. Then Bodbmall and the Grey One went with the boy into the woodlands of Sliab Bladma. The boy was reared there in secret. That was fitting; for there were many stubborn violent youths, and venomous hostile warriors, and wrathful irritable *féinnidi* ['warriors living apart from the tribe'] of the war-band of the Luaigni and of the sons of Morna, on the track of that boy and of Tulcha son of Cumall. Those two *banfhéinnidi* [female *féinnidi*] reared him for a long time in that way.

At the end of six years his mother came to get tidings of her son; for she had been told that he was in that place, and she feared for him because of the sons of Morna. At all events, she went from one wilderness into another until she came into the woodlands of Sliab Bladma. She found the *fian*-hut, and the boy sleeping in it. And she lifted the boy to her bosom then and embraced him; and she was pregnant then. So that that is when she uttered these quatrains, out of love for her son:

'Sleep a sweet sleep', &c.

Then the young woman wished the *banfhéinnidi* farewell, and told them that they should watch over the boy until he should be fit to be a *féinnid*. And the boy grew after that until he was ready to begin hunting.

One day the boy went out alone and saw ducks on the lake. He made a cast at them and sheared the feathers and wings from one of them and cast it into a stupor; and then he took it and brought it with him to the *fian*-hut. So that was Finn's first hunt.

After that he went fleeing from the sons of Morna with some craftsmen, so that he was with them in the Crotta. These were their names: Futh and Ruth and Regna Madfeda and Temle and Oilpe and Rogein. *Imbuile* [*imm-maíle* 'great baldness'?] came upon him then, so that it made him mangy; that is why he was called Deimne the Bald. There was a brigand in Leinster at that time, Fiacail son of Codna. Fiacail came upon the craftsmen in [the wood called] Fid Gaible, and killed them all except for Deimne alone. After that he stayed with Fiacail son of Codna in his house in Seiscenn Uairbéoil. The two *banfhéinnidi* came southward to Fiacail son of Codna's house in search of Deimne, and he was handed over to them; and they took him northward, back to where he had been at first.

He went out alone one day until he came to Mag Life and a stronghold that was there, and he saw a troop of young boys playing hurley on the green in front of the stronghold. He went to run and to hurl against them. He came the next day, and they brought a quarter [of their number] against him. Next time they brought a third against him. In the end they all arose against him, and he was able to play against them all.

'What is your name?' they said. 'Deimne,' he said. The boys told that to the man whose stronghold it was. 'Let him be slain—if you can do it, if he is so powerful (?),' he said. 'We would be able to do nothing against him,' they said. 'Did he tell you his name?' he said. 'He said,' they said, 'that his name was Deimne.' 'What did he look like?' he said. 'A lad handsome and fair-haired (*finn*)' they said. 'His name is Deimne Finn, then,' he said. So therefore the boys used to call him 'Finn'.

Next day he came to them and began playing with them. They threw their hurley sticks at him all at once. He turned them back upon them, and knocked down seven of them; then he went away from them into the woodlands of Sliab Bladma.

At the end of a week he came back to the same place. The boys were swimming in a lake nearby. They challenged him to come so that they could try to drown each other. At that he sprang into the lake and drowned nine of them beneath the lake, and himself went off towards Sliab Bladma afterward. 'Who drowned the boys?' said everyone. 'Finn,' they said. That is how the name 'Finn' stuck to him.

Once he went out across Sliab Bladma, and the two *banfhéinnidi* together with him, and they saw a fierce herd of wild stags on the ridge of the mountain. 'Alas!' said the two old women, 'that we cannot manage to catch one of them yonder.' 'I can' [he replied]; and he rushed at them and caught two of the stags and brought them with him to their *fian*-hut. He hunted for them regularly after that. 'Go from us now, lad,' said the *banfhéinnidi* to him, 'for the sons of Morna are seeking to slay you.'

He departed from them and went by himself until he came to Loch Léin above Luachair, and there he took service as a warrior under the king of Bentraige. He did not give his name there; but nevertheless there was not at that time any hunter to equal him. And so the king said to him, 'If Cumall had left a son,' he said, 'I would think that you were he. But we have not heard that he left any son apart from Tulcha son of Cumall, and he is in military service with the king of Britain.'

After that he wished the king farewell and went away from them to Cairbrige, which is called Ciarraige now, and took service as a warrior under the king. One day the king came to play *fidchell*. He was giving him advice, and he won seven games in succession. 'Who are you?' said the king. 'The son of a tenant farmer of the Luaigni of Tara,' he said. 'No,' said the king. 'You are the son whom Muirne bore to Cumall. Do not stay here any longer, lest you be slain while under my protection.'

Then he went to Cuillenn Ua Cuanach, to the house of Lóchán the royal smith. He had a beautiful daughter named Cruithne. She gave her love to the lad. 'I will give you my daughter,' said the smith, 'although I do not know who you are.' The girl slept with the lad after that. 'Make spears for me,' said the lad to the smith. So Lóchán made two spears for him. Then he wished Lóchán farewell and went off. 'Boy,' said Lóchán, 'do not take the road on which is the sow named the Beó ['living one'].' It was she who had laid waste the heart of Munster; and it so befell that the lad took the road on which the sow was. Then the sow rushed upon him. He made a cast of his spear at her, so that it went through her and left her lifeless. Then he bore the sow's head to the smith as a bride-price for his daughter. From that Sliab Muicce ['sow's mountain'] in Munster is named.

Then the lad went on into Connacht in search of Crimall son of Trénmór. As he was on his way he heard the wailing of a lone woman. He went towards her, and found the woman by turns weeping tears of blood and vomiting blood, so that her mouth was red. 'You are red-mouthed, woman,' he said. 'No wonder,' she said; 'my only son has been slain by a great, terrible lone warrior who came upon me.' 'What was your son's name?' he asked. 'Glonna,' she said. From that are [named] Áth nGlonna and Tóchar nGlonna on Moenmag; and from that mouth-redness (*bél-deirge*) Áth mBéldeirge has been named ever since. Then Finn went after the warrior and they fought a combat and he fell at his hand. And he had with him the *corrbolg* of the treasures, i.e. the treasures of Cumall: he who had fallen there was the Gray One of Luachair, who had first wounded Cumall in the battle of Cnucha.

After that he went into Connacht and found Crimall, an old man in a desolate forest; and a company of the old *fian* were there with him, and it is they who hunted for him. Then he showed him the *corrbolg*, and told him from beginning to end the tale of how he had slain the keeper of the treasures. Finn said farewell to Crimall and went on to study poetry with Finnéces who dwelt beside the Boyne. He did not dare to live in Ireland until he had learnt poetry, for fear of Uirgrenn's son and of the sons of Morna.

Finnéces had spent seven years beside the Boyne waiting for the salmon of Linn Féic; for it had been prophesied to him that he would consume the salmon of Féic, and that after that there would be nothing which he did not know. The salmon was caught, and was entrusted to Deimne to cook; and the poet told him not to eat any of it. The lad brought the salmon to him after he had cooked it. 'Did you eat any of the salmon, lad?' said the poet. 'No,' said the lad; 'but I burnt my thumb and put it in my mouth after that.' 'What is your name, lad?' he said. 'Deimne,' said the lad. 'Finn is your name, lad,' he said, 'and it is you who were destined to eat the salmon; truly you are the fair one (*in finn*).' The lad ate the salmon after that. That is what gave the knowledge to Finn: whenever he put his thumb in his mouth and chanted through *teinm laíde* [a technique of divination involving chewing flesh], what he did not know would be revealed to him.

He learned the three things which qualify a poet: *teinm laíde*, and *imbas forosnai* ['the light of illumination'], and *díchetal di chennaib* ['incantation over heads']. It is then that Finn composed this poem, giving proof of his poetic knowledge:

'May Day, fair the time,' &c.[21]

Then Finn went to Cethern son of Fintan to study poetry with him as well. There was at that time a beautiful girl in Brí Éile—that is, in the *síd* of Brí Éile—who was named Éile. The men of Ireland were contending for the girl; each in turn would go to woo her. The wooing used to be undertaken

---

21 For a translation of this poem see James Carney, 'Three Old Irish accentual poems', *Ériu* 22 (1971) 23–80: 45–6.

every year at Samain: for the *síde* of Ireland were always open at Samain, for at Samain no concealment could be upon the *síde*. This is what used to happen to every man who went to woo her: one of his followers would be slain. This was done to put the expedition to the test; and it was never found out who did it.

Cethern the poet went to woo the girl like everyone else. Finn did not think it good that Cethern should go on that errand. And at that time his name was Finn Éces ['Finn the poet'] son of Cumall. They divided themselves into three bands as they went to the wooing, with nine men in each band. When they came to the *síd* one of the company was slain in their midst, and it was not known who had slain him. Oircbél Éces was the name of the man who was slain there, from which [it is called] Fert Oircbéil in Cluain Fota. They dispersed after that, and Finn went away from them and would not come with them (?). Finn was grieved at what had happened, and felt great shame at it.

He went to the house of the *féinnid* Fiacail son of Conchenn on Sliab Mairge; that is where he dwelt at that time. Finn complained to him of what was troubling him, and told him how the man had been slain in their midst at the *síd*. Fiacail told him to go and sit on the two Paps of Anu west of Luachair. He went then, and sat between the two strongholds which are between the Paps of Anu.

While Finn was there on the night of Samain he saw the two *síde*—that is, the two strongholds—laid bare around him after their concealing enchantment (*fé fiada*) had dissolved. He saw a great fire in each of the two strongholds, and heard a voice from one of them saying, 'Is your *suabais* good?'[22]

'Good indeed,' said the voice in the other *síd*. 'Shall something be carried from us to you?' 'If it is given to us, something will be fetched over to you after that.' As Finn sat there he saw a man come out of the *síd*. There was a kneading-trough in his hand with a pig of *slainsi* (?) on it, and a cooked calf, and a bunch of wild garlic on that day of Samain.[23]

The man went past Finn towards the other *síd*. Finn made a cast with the spear of Fiacail son of Conchenn; he hurled it northward from him towards Sliab Mairge. Then Finn said, 'If the spear should reach any one of us, may

---

22 **suabais.** This word is usually an adjective meaning 'soft, pleasant'; Kuno Meyer translated it 'sweet food'. That it was some specific kind of food is suggested by the poem 'Atberim frib, líth saine', which lists the special foods of Beltaine (May Day) as ale, root vegetables, curds, and *suabais* (Kuno Meyer, *Hibernica Minora*, Oxford 1894, 49): see the next note for a further reference to Otherworld people eating springtime foods at Samain.

23 The point of this statement is presumably the fact that wild garlic (*crem*) grows not in November but in May; cf. the preceding note. *Crem* plays a similar role in 'The Adventure of Nera': in both cases the unseasonable plant is a sign of the discrepancy between Otherworldly and mortal time.

he survive it! But I think that I have avenged my comrade.'

The man fled; and all at once he heard lamentation and a great keening:

> 'With a pointed spear, beside the Berba,
> Aed son of Fidga has been slain.
> With the spear of Fiacail son of Codna
> Finn has slain him after many [failed].'

After that Fiacail came to Finn, so that he was at the Paps of Anu. Fiacail asked him whom he had killed. 'I do not know,' said Finn. 'Although he has obtained no benefit from the cast which you have made, it is likely,' said Fiacail, 'that you have managed to wound someone. And I think,' said Fiacail, 'that if you have not done it tonight, you cannot until the end of a year from now.' Then Finn said that he had made a cast, and that he thought it likely that he had hit someone; and they heard a great keening within the *síd*, with the words

> 'Poison is this spear,
> and poison he whose spear it is,
> and poison he who cast it:
> poison for the one to whom it should be given.'

Finn seized a woman outside the *síd* of Cruachu of Brí Éile in pledge for the return of his spear. The woman promised that the spear would be sent out in exchange for herself. Finn let the woman go into the *síd*. It is then that the woman said, as she went into the *síd*:

> 'Poison is the spear,
> and poison the hand which cast it.
> If it is not put out of the *síd*
> rabies will seize the land because of it.'

The spear was put out of the *síd* then, and Finn took it with him to the place where Fiacail was. 'Good,' said Fiacail. 'Let the spear with which you did the wondrous deed belong to you.' Then Fiacail said that it had been a heroic adventure on which the man was slain who had slain Finn's own comrade. 'The man who slew him here,' he said, 'is the same who used to slay every man who went to woo the girl, for he loved the girl himself.'

Then Finn and Fiacail journeyed onward. Fiacail was to meet the *fían* in Inber Colptha. He said to Finn that each of them (?) should go home, since their errand was accomplished. Finn said, 'Let me come with you.' 'I do not want you to come with me,' said Fiacail, 'for decay of strength might come upon you.' 'I will find out,' said Finn. Then they set out. Fiacail had twelve balls of lead around his neck to restrain his vigour, such was his swiftness. He was throwing away each ball in turn, and Finn brought them with him; and even so Fiacail ran no more swiftly than Finn.

They came to Inber Colptha. Then Finn gave him his twelve lead balls, and he was pleased at that. They slept there that night. It was entrusted to Finn to watch that night; and he told him that he should wake the *féinnid* if he heard any [sound of] violence. As Finn was there that night he heard a cry from the north, and he did not wake the *féinnid*. He went alone towards the cry, to Sliab Slánga. When he arrived there at midnight, in the territory of the Ulaid, he saw before him three women with the beauty of women of the *síde*, on a green mound. As they keened on the mound, they all placed their hands upon it. The women fled from Finn into the *síd*. Finn caught up with one of the women as she was going into the *síd* of Slánga, and snatched her brooch from her mantle. The woman came back for it, and asked Finn to give her the brooch from her mantle, and said that it was not fitting for her to enter the *síd* with a blemish; and she offered a reward. . . .[24]

• • • • • [

§§94–96. Severed Heads at Feasts from the Finn Cycle

§94. From *Bruiden Átha Í*, ed. K. Meyer, *Revue Celtique* xiv (1893) 24

. . . THAT CUIRRECH was a son of Fothad Canainne's mother. He was lying in wait for Finn, until at last they made a pact with one another, and Finn prepared a feast for Fothad, and he was invited to come. But it was a *geis* ['sworn tabu'] for Fothad Canainne to drink ale without dead heads in his presence. This was not easy at that time, for the peace of [King] Cormac [son of Art, son of Conn] was in Ireland for the space of seven years, that no one should be killed in connection with Finn. 'There are, however, places where killing a man carries no penalty,' said Finn: 'the road of Midluachair, and Áth Fir Diad, Áth Cliath, Belach nGabráin, Áth Noa, Cnámchaill, - Conachlad, and the two Paps of Anu on Luachair Dedad.'

---

24 Here the text breaks off.

§95. From 'The death of Finn mac Cumaill',

ed. K. Meyer, *Zeitschrift für celtische Philologie* i (1897) 464–5.

THEY BORE [FINN'S] HEAD with them into an empty house; and they cooked their fish and divided it in two. His head was before the fire. 'Give it a morsel,' said a dark mischievous man, 'since Aiclech no longer lives.' Three times the fish was divided in two, and each time there were three portions. 'What is this?' said one of them. It is then that the head said, from (where it was) before the fire: 'It is this which causes the third portion (to be) among you, without any flattery: because you do not give me my portion of the meal . . . .'

§96. From *Sanas Cormaic* (the glossary of Bishop and King Cormac mac Cuilennáin,

died 908), s.v. *orc tréith*; text in K. Meyer, *Fianaigecht*, pp. xix–xx.

THEN THEY FETCHED THE DOGS, and loosed them on the track of the warriors; and he found them in an empty house cooking fish on a griddle, and Lomnae's head was on a stake beside the fire. Cairpre divided the first portion which was set on the griddle among the three companies of nine, but not a morsel was placed in the mouth of the head. That was a *geis* [tabu] for Finn. Then the head said to them: '*Oirc brec broindfind brúchtas di magar fo muirib*', in other words, 'A salmon from spawn, that is its substance'. The second portion which he set upon the fire or upon the griddle Cairpre divided in the same way, and the head said: [cryptic utterance]. 'Put the head outside, it is an evil word for us', said Cairpre. Then the head was heard outside, saying: [cryptic utterance]. Then Finn came in and slew him.

• • • • • • • • • •

---

§97. A Dynastic Foundation Legend

Echtra Mac nEchach
The Adventures of the Sons of Eochaid Mugmedón
TRANS. JOHN CAREY

THERE WAS A WONDROUS NOBLE KING OVER IRELAND, EOCHAID MUGMEDÓN. He had five sons: Brian, Ailill, Fiachra, Fergus, Niall. Mongfhind daughter of Fidach was the mother of Brian and Fiachra and Fergus and Ailill. Cairenn Casdub, daughter of Saxall Balb king of the Saxons, was the mother of Niall. The queen had a hatred of Niall, for it was in infidelity to her that the king had begotten him upon Cairenn; and so the queen put great hardship upon Cairenn. This is how great the hardship was: she alone had to carry the water of Tara, and every slave woman was left to her own will apart from her. And she was forced to do all this when she was pregnant with Niall, so that the infant might perish in her womb.

She reached her time of giving birth, and for all that she did not cease from her toil. Then she bore a son upon the green of Tara, lying beside her bucket. And she did not dare to take the boy up from the ground but left him in that place exposed to the birds; and none of the men of Ireland dared to take him away for fear of Mongfhind, for everyone stood in great fear of her.

After that Torna the poet came into the midst of the green and saw the baby all alone, and the birds attacking him. Torna took the boy into his bosom, and revealed to him everything which would happen after that, so that he said:

'Welcome, little guest:
he will be Niall Noígiallach.
Armies will tremble in his day,
plains will be enlarged
hostages will be carried off,
battles will be waged.
Long-sided one of Tara,
commander of the armies of Mag Femen,
keeper of Moenmag,
famous, great in slaughter,
veteran of the Liffey,

white-knee of Codal,
for twenty-seven years
ruler of Ireland.
And from him there will be a portion forever,
for good was the beginning and the end,
rough-haired witness,
until he perished on a Thursday afternoon above Muir nIcht after he was
    wounded by Eochaid son of Énna Cennselach.'

After that Torna took the boy with him and reared him; and neither Torna
nor his fosterson came to Tara after that until the boy was fit for kingship.
After that he and Niall came to Tara, and came upon Cairenn fetching water
to Tara. Then Niall said to her, 'Leave the work alone.' 'I do not dare,' she
said, 'because of the queen.' 'My mother will not be toiling,' he said, 'and I
the son of the king of Ireland.' Then he brought her to Tara, and put a
purple garment upon her.

The queen was angry, and thought ill of that. The men of Ireland were
saying then that Niall would be king after his father. Mongfhind said to
Eochaid: 'Judge between your sons,' said she, 'which of them will get your
inheritance.' 'I will not,' he said, 'but Sithchenn the druid will judge.'

Then Sithchenn was sent for, the blacksmith who was in Tara; and he was
a marvellous prophet. After that the blacksmith set the smithy on fire when
they were within.

Niall came out bringing with him the anvil with its block. 'Niall with
mastery,' said the druid, 'and he will be a firm anvil forever.'

Brian came, and brought the hammers with him. 'Brian for your
battlefields,' said the druid.

Fiachra came, a bucket of ale and the bellows with him. 'Your beauty and
your skill with Fiachra,' said the druid.

Ailill came, and the box in which were weapons. 'Ailill to avenge you,' said
the druid.

Fergus came with a bundle of withered sticks, and a yew tree in it.
'Withered Fergus,' said the druid. That was true, for the progeny of Fergus
was of no worth except for one, Cairech Dergán of Cluain Bairenn—so that
is the reason for the yew stick in the withered bundle.

To bear witness to this the historian recited:

'Eochaid's five sons: Niall an anvil,
great Brian a hammer for true smiting,
Ailill a box of spears against kindred,

Fiachra bellows, Fergus withered wood.

'With Fiachra the drinking of ale;
with Ailill the murderous spear;
with Brian, entry into battle;
with Niall the reward.'

That was hard for Mongfhind to bear, and she said to her sons, 'Do you four boys fight [among yourselves] until Niall comes to separate you, and kill him.' They fought then. 'I would like to separate them,' said Niall. 'Do not,' said Torna; 'the sons of Mongfhind will be peaceful.' So that is the source of the proverb.

Mongfhind said that she would not accept that judgement. The same Sithchenn was sent for, to ask for weapons from him. Then they came to the smith and he made weapons for them; and the most splendid of those weapons he put into the hand of Niall, and he gave the other weapons to the other sons. 'Now go to hunt, and test your weapons,' said the smith.

Then the boys went and hunted. They went far astray after that, after it closed up around them on every side.[25]

When they rested from their wandering they built a fire and cooked some of what they had killed in the hunt, and ate until they were full. After that they were parched with a great thirst from the cooking.

'Let someone go to find us water,' they said.

'I will go,' said Fergus. The lad went to find water until he came upon a well; and he found an old woman guarding the well. This is how the hag was: every joint and limb of her from top to toe as black as coal. The gray bristly hair growing through the top of her head was like the tail of a wild horse. She could cut off the green branch of an acorn-bearing oak with the sickle of green teeth that was in her head, reaching to her ear. Her eyes were black and smoky; her nose crooked and wide-nostrilled; her belly sinewy, speckled, fluxy, diseased; her shins crooked, twisted, knotty, broad as shovels; and she had big knees and gray nails. Fearsome was the appearance of the hag.

'Well, then,' said the lad.

'Well, then, indeed,' said she.

'Are you guarding the well?' said the lad.

'I am,' said she.

---

25 This rather obscure expression seems to be an early allusion to the *fód seachráin* or 'stray sod' of Irish folk belief: a fairy enchantment which renders one's way home magically inaccessible.

'Will you permit me to take some of the water with me?' he said.

'I will,' she said, 'if I get a kiss on the cheek from you.'

'No,' he said.

'No water will be obtained from me,' she said.

'I give my word,' he said, 'that I would sooner die of thirst than give you a kiss.' After that the lad went to where his brothers were, and told them that he had not found water.

Ailill went in search of water, and came upon the same well, and refused to kiss the hag; and he turned back without water and did not admit that he had found the well.

Brian, the eldest of the sons, went in search of water and came upon the same well; and he refused to kiss the hag and turned back without water.

Fiachra went and found the well and the hag and asked for water. 'I will give it,' she said; 'and give me a kiss for it.' He gave her a peck [literally, 'the tip of a kiss']. 'You will visit Tara,' she said. That came true: two kings of his race obtained the kingship of Ireland, Dathí and Ailill Molt; and none obtained it from the race of the other sons, Brian, Ailill, and Fergus. Then he turned back without water.

Niall went in search of water and came upon the same well. 'Give me water, woman,' he said.

'I will,' said she; 'and give me a kiss.'

'Besides giving a kiss, I will lie beside [you].'

Then he sank down upon her and gave her a kiss. But when he looked upon her after that, there was no girl in the world whose manner or appearance were lovelier than hers. Every joint of her from top to toe was like new-fallen snow in hollows. She had plump queenly forearms, long slender fingers, straight rosy calves, with two sandals of white metal on her gentle soft white feet and a great mantle of purple fleece upon her clasped with a brooch of white silver. She had bright pearly teeth, and a large sagacious eye, and a mouth red as *partaing*.[26]

'That is a change of shape, woman,' said the lad.

'That is true,' she said.

'Who are you?' said the lad.

'I am the sovereignty [*in flaithes*],' she said. And she said this:

---

26 **partaing**. A term repeatedly used in comparisons to evoke a vivid red; Whitley Stokes suggested a derivation from *Parthica pellis* 'Parthian leather'.

'King of Tara, I am the sovereignty;
I will tell you its great benefit.
  [It will belong] to your descendants forever, above every kindred;
  that is the true reason for which I speak.

  With your hospitality, and your harsh advance in battle,
  men will not be able to withstand you.
  You will be strong and skilful. . .;
  you will be a bloodstained victorious leader.

  Brilliant sturdy Tara will be yours,
  and supremacy over the men of Ireland;
  your progeny will not be deprived of its fief
  save [by] two from the lineage of Fiachra.

  Although the men of Munster are fierce in battle
  the sovereignty of Tara will be parted from them:
  . . . .
  only one king of them takes Ireland.'

'Go now to your brothers,' she said, 'and take water with you. And you and your descendants will have the kingship forever except for two from the race of Fiachra—Dathí and Ailill Molt—and one king from Munster—Brian Bóroma. All of those kings will be without opposition. And as you have seen me at first fearsome, wolfish, terrifying, and at last beautiful, thus is the sovereignty: for it is not obtained without battle and conflicts; but at last it is fair and gracious to anyone. But do not give the water to your brothers until they give you gifts: until they cede their seniority to you, and you hang up your weapon a hand's breadth above theirs.'

'It will be done thus,' said the lad.

After that the lad said goodbye to her, and took the water to his brothers; and he did not give it to them until they granted every condition which he asked of them as the girl had instructed him. Then he bound them not to go against him or his descendants forever.

After that they went to Tara. They hung up their weapons, and Niall hung his up the breadth of a warrior's hand above theirs. They sat down, and Niall in the midst of them. Then the king asked their tidings. Niall answered, and told their adventures, and how they went in search of water and came upon the well and the woman, and how she had prophesied to them.

'Why does not the eldest, Brian, tell the tidings?' said Mongfhind.

'We ceded our seniority to Niall, and our first term of kingship, in exchange for the water,' they said.

'You have ceded it forever,' said Sithchenn, 'for the supremacy and kingship of Ireland will belong to him and his descendants forever, from this hour forth.'

That came true. For no one else took the kingship of Ireland from Niall's time onward except for his children or descendants until the time of the mighty smiter of Uisnech, Mael Sechlainn mac Domnaill, unless it were taken with opposition; for Fiachra took it from the Uí Néill in the south or in the north, i.e., there were ten kings descended from Conall and sixteen from Eógan; as it is said:

> I know the company which took
> Ireland after Niall of lofty combats:
> from the prince Lóegaire, happy is he,
> until the mighty smiter of Uisnech.
>
> Lóegaire and his son, I will not conceal it,
> Diarmait and mighty Tuathal,
> the nine of wholesome Aed Sláine,
> and the seven of the family of Colmán.
>
> Sixteen kings from lofty Eógan,
> ten from hard savage Conall.
> Niall obtained, with propitious swiftness,
> kingship forever for his race.

◆ ◆ ◆ ◆ ◆ ◆ ◆ ◆ ◆

§§98–99. Patrician Texts from the Book of Armagh

(Excerpts) TRANS. J. T. KOCH based on the edited Latin text of Ludwig
Bieler, *Patrician Texts in the Book of Armagh* Dublin: Dublin Institute
for Advanced Studies (1979).

§98. From the **Life of Patrick** by **Muirchú Moccu Macthéni** (*c.* 690).

¶ 10 (9) (1)

IN THOSE DAYS when these events took place there was in those regions a
certain great king, a ferocious pagan, an emperor of barbarians, who was
ruling in Tara [Temoria], which was then the capital of the kingdom of
the Irish. His name was Lóegaire son of Níall, a descendant of the kindred
that held the kingship of almost the whole island. (2) In his company, he had
with him wise men and druids [*magi*], prophets and enchanters, and the
inventors of every evil art, who were able to know and to foresee everything
before it happened through the practices of paganism and idolatry. (3) There
were two of these whom he favoured over the others, whose names are these:
Lothroch, who was also known as Lochru, and Lucet Máel, who was also
known as Ronal; (4) and these two, by their magical art, often used to
foretell that a foreign lifestyle was to come to them, a kingdom of sorts, with
an unknown and oppressive doctrine, brought from far across the seas, related
by few, accepted by many, to be honoured by all. It would subvert kingdoms,
kill the kings who resisted, seduce the crowds, destroy all of their gods, throw
out all the works of their art, and would rule the world for ever. (5) They
also identified and predicted the man who was about to bring and urge this
lifestyle upon them in the following words, which were in the form of a sort
of verse which was often repeated by them, especially during the two or three
years prior to Patrick's arrival. (6) These then are the words of the verse; the
meaning is obscure, due to the unusual idiom of the language:

> Adze-head will come,
> with his staff bent in the head,
> from his house with a hole in its head
> he will chant blasphemy
> from his table; in the front part of his house,
> all his household will answer, 'May it be so, may it be so.'

(7) This can be made more intelligible in other words: 'When all this happens,
our kingdom, which is pagan, will not stand.' So it happened afterwards. When
Patrick arrived the worship of idols was stamped out, and the catholic Christian
faith filled all parts of our country. Enough said of this matter . . .

§99. From **Tírechán's Account of St. Patrick's Churches** (*c.* 670).

¶ 26. (I)

THEN SAINT PATRICK came to the spring called Clébach, on the hill sides of Cróchu [i.e. Cruachu, Cruachan] eastward, before sunrise, and they sat beside the spring. (2) And here came the two daughters of King Lóegaire, Ethne the Fair-haired and Fedelm the Red-haired, to the spring, as it is women's habit to wash in the morning. And they found the synod of holy bishops with Patrick by the spring. (3) And they did not know from what place these men had come or what form [of men they were] or of what people or from what realm, but thought they were men of the *síd* ['Otherworld'] or gods of the earth or a phantasm; (4) and the daughters asked them: 'Where are you from, and what place have you come from?' And Patrick said to them: 'You would be better to acknowledge our true God than to inquire concerning our race.' (5) The first daughter asked: 'Who is God and where is God and whose God is he and where is the place he resides? Does your God have sons and daughters, gold and silver? Does he live forever, is he beautiful, is his son fostered by many, are his daughters beloved and beautiful to the people of the world? (6) Is he in the sky or in the earth, or in the water, in the rivers, in the mountains, in the valleys? (7) Tell us your description of him; how might he be seen, how is he loved, how is he found? Is it in youth or in old age that he is found?' (8) Then in response, Saint Patrick, being filled with the Holy Spirit, said: 'Our God is the God of all people, the God of heaven and earth, of the seas and the rivers, God of the sun and the moon and all the stars, the God of the lofty mountains and the deep valleys; (9) God above heaven and in heaven and under heaven, He resides in heaven and earth and sea and in everything that is in them; he breathes in all things, gives life to all things, is greater than all things, maintains all things. (10) He lights up the sun's light, he separates the light of the night with the stars, he has made springs in the arid land and dry islands in the sea and placed the stars in attendance to the great lights. (11) He has a Son, who is eternal like him, he is like him. The Son is not younger than the Father nor is the Father older than the Son, and the Holy Spirit blows [breath] into them. The Father and the Son and the Holy Spirit are not separate. (12) Truly I desire to marry you to heaven's king because you are daughters of an earthly king, if [only] you will believe.' (13) And the daughters said together in one voice and of one heart: 'Teach us most diligently how we can believe in heaven's king, so that we may see him face to face. Tell us, and what you say we shall do.' (14) And Patrick said: 'Do you believe that through baptism you throw off your father's and mother's sin?' They answered: 'Yes, we believe.' 'Do you believe in penance after sin?' 'Yes, we believe.' 'Do you believe in life after death? Do you believe in resurrection on judgement day?' 'Yes, we believe.' 'Do you believe in the unity of the

Church?' 'Yes, we believe.' (15) And they were baptised and a white garment was put over their heads. And they asked fervently to see Christ's face, and Saint [Patrick] said to them: 'Unless you taste death you cannot see Christ's face, and unless you receive the sacrament.' (16) And they answered: 'Give us the sacrament so that we can see the Son, our bridegroom', and they accepted God's eucharist and fell asleep in death, and their friends placed them onto a single funeral bed and completely covered them with garments, and made a wailing and great keening. (17) And the druid [*magus*] Caplit, who had fostered one of them, came and cried, and Patrick preached to him and [Caplit] believed, and the hair of his head was shaved off. (18) And his brother Máel came and said: 'My brother has believed Patrick; but not me, I shall turn him back to paganism', and he spoke hard words to Mathon and Patrick. (19) And Patrick preached the faith to him and converted him to God's penance, and the hair of his head was shaved off, in other words, [it had been] the druidic style [of hair] seen on his head [previously], the *airbacc giunnæ*, as it is called. It is from this incident that the very well-known Irish proverb comes: 'Máel is like Caplit', because they [both] believed in God. (20) And the days of mourning for the king's daughters were finished, and they entombed them by the spring of Clébach, and they made a round ditch similar to a *ferta*, because this is what the pagan Irish people used to do then. We, however, call it a *relic*, in other words, the 'remains' of the maidens. (21) And the *ferta* with the bones of the holy women was dedicated to Patrick, and to his successors after him forever, and he made a church of earth in that place.

◆ ◆ ◆ ◆ ◆ ◆ ◆ ◆ ◆ ◆

¶ 40. (1) AND SAINT PATRICK came through the plains in the lands of Macc Erce in Dichuil and Aurchuil. (2) And in Dichuil Patrick came to a tumulus of of great size, of wondrous width and excessive length, which his followers had found. And they were marvelling, with great awe, that it stretched 120 feet, and they said: 'We do not believe that there could ever have been any man so long.' (3) Patrick answered: 'If you wish to, you will see him', and they said: 'Yes, we wish to', and he struck his staff on the side of the stone at [the grave's] head. He blessed the tumulus with the sign of the cross, and he said: 'Open, O Lord, the tumulus', and it opened. (4) And a man whose body was great and intact rose up and said: 'Thank you, O holy man, for raising me from my sufferings even if it might be for only a single hour', (5) and then this man was seen to weep miserably, and he asked: 'May I walk with you?' They answered: 'No, we cannot let you walk with us, because people cannot look upon your face for fear of you. (6) But believe in the heaven's God and accept the baptism of the Lord, and you will not go back to the place where you were. And tell us to whom you are related.' (7) 'I am the son of Mac Cass son of Glas; I was the pig keeper of Lugar king of Hirota. The *fían* ['extratribal war-band'] of the sons of Macc Con killed me during the kingship of Coirpre Nie Fer a hundred years before today.' (8) And he was baptized, and he made God's confession, and became silent, and was put back into his tumulus.

• • • • • • • • • •

§§100–101. The Death of Diarmait Mac Cerbaill[27]

TRANS. JOHN CAREY

§ 100.

ONCE DIARMAIT MAC CERBAILL'S panegyrists were praising the king and his peace and his good conduct. Áed Dub son of Araide was standing before Becc mac Dé. Now Diarmait had killed Araide of the Ulaid and had fostered his son, Áed Dub. Becc said:

> 'I see the wolfish hound
> who will wreck the wondrous peace.'

'Becc,' said Áed Dub, 'who is that hound?'

'Perhaps it is yourself,' said Becc.

'What is this?' said Diarmait.

'Not hard to answer,' said Becc. 'It is this hand of Áed Dub's which will set the drink of death to your lips in the house of Banbán and Bainbsech. And you will be wearing a shirt of a single flax seed and a mantle of a single sheep, and ale of a single grain will be in your horn, and the bacon of a pig which was never born will be upon your plate.'

---

27 These two closely related stories are found at the ends of two longer sagas printed by S. H. O'Grady, *Silva Gadelica* (London, 1892), 66–82. §100 is found in the Book of Lismore, §101 in London, B.L. Egerton MS 1782.

'He will not be in Ireland,' said Diarmait, 'as long as I am alive.' 'Kill him,' said everyone. 'No,' said Diarmait; 'but let him be banished from Ireland.' After that Áed Dub was banished into the territory of Alba [(North) Britain].

One day Diarmait saw a warrior in his house.

'From where have you come?' said Diarmait.

'Not from far,' he said. 'Come with me, so that you may consume a night's hospitality with me.'

'Good,' said Diarmait; 'tell Mugain.'

'I will not go,' she said, 'upon an invitation for as long as I live.'

Nevertheless they went with Banbán to Ráith Bicc. When they were seated they saw a fair shapely young woman in fine clothing going past them through the midst of the house.

'Where is the woman from?' asked Diarmait.

'She is my daughter,' said Banbán. 'So then, woman,' said Banbán to his daughter, 'have you a garment with you for Diarmait?'

'I have indeed,' said the woman. She gave him a shirt from her basket, and a mantle, and he put them on. 'The shirt is good,' said everyone.

'Good,' said Banbán, 'is the shirt of a single flax seed. Our daughter yonder is a fanciful girl: it is she who caused a single flax seed to be planted so that she made a sheaf of it, so that at length it was a furrow.'

'The mantle is good,' said everyone.

'Good,' said Banbán, 'is the mantle; it was made of the wool of a single sheep.'

After that food and drink were brought to them. 'The bacon is good,' said everyone.

'It is good,' said Banbán, 'for the bacon of a pig which was never born.'

'How is that?' they said.

'Not hard to answer,' he said: 'certain pigs were with young (?): knives were taken to them, so that their piglets were taken out of them alive, and they were fed.'

'The ale is good,' said everyone.

'It is good,' said Banbán, 'for the ale of a single grain. One day when I went out to look at the ploughland, I killed a wood pigeon. A grain was found in its craw, it was not known of what kind. It was planted at the end of a furrow, so that at last a sickle's portion came from it. So that is its grain, and this is the ale from it.'

Then Diarmait looked up. 'The lower part of the house is new,' he said, 'but the upper part is not new.'

'Once,' said Banbán, 'we went in currachs to catch fish, and saw the ridgepole of a house floating towards us on the sea. I had a house made beneath that ridgepole.'

'It is true,' said Diarmait: 'that is the ridgepole of my own house, cast by me into the sea. And the saints of Ireland promised me that I would never die until all of these certain tokens [appeared] to me; and that it would be under the ridgepole of my own house that I would meet my death. And it is therefore that I cast that ridgepole into the sea.'

And with the glance which Diarmait cast beyond the ridgepole he saw a little flock of white [cows?] with red heads grazing; and that was a *geis* [tabu] of his.

'Come out before us,' said Diarmait. 'No,' said Áed Dub son of Suibne— who had returned from the exile in Alba into which Diarmait had sent him, and who had caused him dishonour at the assembly of Tailtiu.

The house was seized upon Diarmait, and burnt upon him; and he repented fervently and died. And he went to heaven after enduring that torment here below, as Brendan promised to him. As Flann Mainistrech said:[28]

> Áed Dub son of Suibne of the ranks
> was illustrious king of the Ulaid.
> It is he, without dark concealment,
> who killed Diarmait mac Cerbaill.

§ 101.

. . . Then his druids were brought to Diarmait, and he asked them by what death he would die.

'Killing,' said the first druid; 'and a shirt of a single flax seed and a mantle of the wool of a single sheep will be upon you on the day of your death.'

'That is easy to avoid,' said Diarmait.

'Drowning,' said the second druid; 'and you will have ale from a single grain on that night.'

'Burning,' said the third druid; 'and the bacon of a pig which was not born will be on your platter.'

---

28 This translation reflects a slight rearrangement of the original wording, which reads *amal ro gheall Brenuinn do Fhlann Mainisdrech ut dixit*—literally, 'as Brendan promised to Flann Mainistrech; as he said'. Since Brendan was a saint of the sixth century, and Flann a poet of the eleventh, some emendation seems called for.

'That is not likely,' said Diarmait.

After that Diarmait went on his royal circuit sunwise around Ireland. For this is how the king of Tara used to go through Ireland: from Tara into Leinster, from there into Munster, from there into Connacht, and finally into Ulster; so that he would return to Tara at the end of a year's time, at Samain, to spend Samain with the men of Ireland [celebrating] the *feis Temro* ['Feast of Tara', associated with the confirmation of the king].

One day when Diarmait was on that circuit he saw a warrior coming towards him in the house. 'From where do you come?' said Diarmait.

'Not from far,' said the warrior. 'Come with me to my house, so that you may be my guest tonight.'

'Good,' said Diarmait; 'tell Mugain.'

'No,' said Mugain. 'I will not go on an invitation for as long as I live. And if you go it is in defiance of me; for it is ill fame [*drochscél*] for you to go on an invitation.'

Diarmait went with Banbán to Ráith Bicc. When they were seated in the house they saw a fair young woman come in, wearing fine garments. 'Where is the woman from?' said Diarmait. 'She is my daughter,' said Banbán; 'and she will sleep with you tonight to spite Mugain, since she did not come with you.' 'That pleases me,' said Diarmait. A bed was made for them until the time when the food was served.

'Well, woman,' said Banbán, 'do you have clothing with you for the king?'

'I have,' said the girl. She brought forth a shirt and a mantle from the basket, and the king put them on.

'The shirt is good,' said everyone.

'It suits you,' said Banbán: 'the shirt of a single flax seed. It is a fanciful daughter that I have, that girl yonder. It is she who caused the single seed to be sowed so that she produced a sheaf from it; that was the full of a furrow.'

'The mantle is good,' said everyone.

'It is good,' said Banbán: 'it was made from the wool of a single sheep.'

After that food and drink were brought for them. 'Good is the bacon of the pig which was not born,' said Banbán.

'How is that?' said Diarmait.

'There were pigs with young (?); knives were taken to them, so that their piglets were taken out of them alive, and fed.'

'The ale is good,' said everyone.

'It is good,' said Banbán: 'it is the ale of a single grain. One day I went out to look at my ploughland, and I killed a wood pigeon. A grain was found in its craw, it was not known of what kind. It was planted at the end of a furrow, until a sickle's portion was gathered from it. Then it was planted; so that this is its grain, and its ale.'

After that Diarmait looked upward. 'The bottom of the house is new,' he said, 'and its top not new.'

'Once,' said Banbán, 'we went in currachs to catch fish. We saw the ridgepole of a house [floating] towards us on the sea. Because of its strangeness, I made a house using it.'

'It is truly,' said Diarmait; 'that the prophecies of Becc and the druids were made concerning my death. . . This is my house,' said Diarmait; 'let us get out, men!' He himself sprang up to leave.

'No; this is your way [out],' said Áed Dub, standing in the door of the house and thrusting his spear into his breast until it broke his back. He turned back into the house after that. The Ulaid outside seized the house, and burnt it over those who were within. Diarmait went into the ale vat until the ridgepole of the house fell upon his head and killed him.

The king's body was hacked and burnt apart from his head. After that his head and his corpse were taken to Clonmacnoise, so that he was buried in the Crooked Mound or in the assembly place. For that is where he himself chose his burial spot, when he fasted in the Little Church when he was healed of his headache after performing a fast against the saints of Ireland, and after failing to find a remedy before that. Concerning this death this was recited:

> In mortal shelter (?), in Ráith Bicc,
> was the slaying of Diarmait. . .:
> the killing of a king of many battles;
> woe to the one who will bring about his betrayal!

So that is the death of Diarmait mac Cerbaill. Cerball, i.e. *Cerr-bél*, i.e. 'Crooked-mouth' [*bél cerr*].

FINIT.

• ◆ ◆ ◆ ◆ ◆ ◆ ◆ •

§§102–105. Tales of Mongán

§102. *Compert Mongáin*   The Birth of Mongán

¶ 1.

FIACHNA LURGA, MONGÁN'S FATHER, WAS SOLE KING OF THE province [of Ulster]. He had a friend in North Britain, i.e. Áedán son of Gabrán [ruler of Scottish Dál Ríata AD 574–606]. A message went from [Fiachna] to Áedán. A message went from Áedán to [Fiachna] that he should come to his aid. He was at war with the Anglo-Saxons. A frightful soldier had been brought by them for the death of Áedán in the battle. Then Fiachna went across. He left his queen at home.

¶ 2. While the hosts were fighting in North Britain, a distinguished man came to his wife in his stronghold of Ráith Mór in Mag Line. There were not many in the stronghold when he came. He told the woman [to find] a place where they could meet alone. The woman said that there were not in the world possessions or treasures for which she would do anything that would disgrace her spouse's honour. He asked her whether she would do it to save her husband's life. She said that if he were, when in danger, to encounter any difficulty, she would help him with whatever might be in her power. He said that she should do it, 'because your spouse is in great peril. A frightful hero has been brought against him who cannot be slain [?]. And [your husband] will die by him. If you and I engage in love making, you will bear a son from it. That son will be remarkable. Moreover, he will be Fiachna's. I shall go to the battle that will be fought tomorrow at the third hour after sunrise in order to save him. And I shall fight the [enemy] soldier in front of the men of North Britain. And I [shall] tell to your spouse what we have done and that it is yourself who have sent me to aid him.'

¶ 3. So it was done. When the hosts advanced towards each other, the armies saw something: a distinguished man at the front of the host of Áedán and Fiachna. He came right to Fiachna in particular. And he told him that he had spoken to his wife the day before and that he had pledged to come to his aid at this time.

¶ 4. After that, he advanced against the host, towards the opponent. And he fought the soldier. And Áedán and Fiachna won the battle. And Fiachna went back to his territory. And the woman [i.e. his wife] was pregnant, and she bore a son, i.e. Mongán son of Fiachna. And he thanked his spouse for what she did for him, and she admitted all that had happened to her. Thus, a son to Manannán son of Ler is this Mongán, even though it is Mongán son of

Fiachna that he is called. For, [the stranger] left behind a quatrain with [Mongán's] mother, when he went from her in the morning, which said:

> I go freely.
> The pure-white morning approaches.
> Manannán son of Ler is
> the name of the man who came to you.[29]

* * * * * * * * *

§103. Scél asa mBerar Combad hé Find Mac Cumaill Mongán 7 aní día fil Aided Fothaid Airgdig a Scél so sís

A Story from which it is Inferred that Mongán was Find mac Cumaill and Concerning the Cause of the Death of Fothad Airgdech

TRANS. ANNE LEA from Lebor na hUidre 133^{a25}–133^{b17}

ONGÁN HELD THE KINGSHIP IN RÁITH MÓR IN MAG LINE. Forgoll the poet came to him. There were many couples with him on his visit. The poet used to tell a story to Mongán every night. He had so many that they were thus from Samain to Beltaine—the poet receiving as his due wealth and food from Mongán in return. One day, Mongán asked his poet how Fothad Airgdech had died. Forgoll said he was slain in Dubthair in Laigin [Leinster]. Mongán said that was false. The poet said he would satirize him for contradicting him and that he would satirise his father and his mother and his grandfather and that he would recite a satire upon their waters so that fish would not be taken in their river-mouths. He would recite it upon their trees so that they would not give fruit, on their plains so that they would be barren always of all produce. Mongán offered him whatever property he wished up to seven *cumals* ['slave women' or the equivalent value] or fourteen *cumals* or twenty-one *cumals*. At length he offered one-third, or half of his land, or his entire land at last, except for his freedom alone and that of his wife Breothigirnd, unless he was released before the end of three days. The poet refused all unless the woman were included. Mongán agreed for the sake of his honour.

The woman was full of sorrow then. She would not wipe a tear from her cheek. Mongán told her not to be sorrowful: perhaps help would come to

---

29 **Manannán mac Lir** is a well known supernatural figure in early Irish literature, possessing the attributes of a sea-god.

them. It came up to the third day. The poet set about exacting his bond. Mongán told him to wait till evening. Mongán and his wife were in their upper room. The woman weeps when the time of her handing over was near and she saw no help. Mongán told his wife not to be sad. 'The man who comes to help us now washes his feet in the Labrinne River.'

They wait then. The woman wept again. 'Don't cry, woman; the man who comes to help us now washes his feet in the Máin.' They were waiting in this way between every two hours in the day: she kept weeping and he kept saying to her—'Don't cry, woman; the man who comes to help us now washes his feet in Lemain, in Loch Léin, in the Samaír between the Uí Fhidgente and the Araid, in the Siuir upon Femen in Munster, in the Echar, in the Berba, in the Ruirthech, in the Bóand [Boyne], in the Tuairthesc, in Snám Aignech, in the Nid, in the Rig, in the Ollarba [Larne] before Ráith Mór.'

When night came, Mongán was on his couch in his king's house and his wife on his right hand and she was sad. The poet was demanding their pledges and their bonds. While they were there, a man was announced approaching the rampart of the fortress from the south. A cloak in folds was around him and a spear-shaft that was not very small was in his hand. He leaps with that spear-shaft over the three ramparts so that he was in the midst of the enclosure, from there [he leaps] so that he was in the midst of the king's house, from that [he leaps] so that he was between Mongán and the inside wall, next to the pillow. The poet was in the west of the house, facing Mongán from the west.

The problem is discussed in the house before the warrior who had come. 'What is the difficulty?', the warrior asked. 'I have made a wager with the poet over there,' said Mongán, 'about the death of Fothad Airgdech. He has said it was in Dubthor in Laigin. I have said that that is false.'

The warrior said to the poet that the poet was wrong. 'It is [some] veteran from a church who is contradicting me,'[30] said Forgoll. 'That is not true,' the warrior said. 'It will be proven. We were with you, with Finn,' the warrior said.

'Stay quiet! That is not good,' Mongán said. 'We were with Finn then,' he said. 'We came from Britain. We encountered Fothad Airgdech here on the Ollarba river. We fought a battle there. I threw a cast at him so that it went through him from the opposite side into the earth and left the iron head in the earth. This is the spear-shaft that was in that spear. The bare stone from which I made that cast will be found and its iron head will be found in the

---

30 Veteran from a church: an *athlaech* 'ex-warrior' was a fighter who left his earlier life to embrace religion. Often, presumably, he did so simply to find support in his declining years; Forgoll appears to be saying that Caílte is nothing but a broken-down has-been of this type.

earth and the tomb of Fothad Airdech will be found a little to the east. There is a stone coffin around him there in the earth. There are his two silver rings and his two arm-bands and his silver neck-torc on his casket, and there is a standing stone by his tomb, and there is an ogam inscription in the end which is in the earth by the tomb. It is this that is there: "This is Eochaid Airgdech. Caílte slew him fighting against Finn.'"

They went with the warrior. Everything was found to be so. It was Caílte, Finn's fosterson, who had come. And so Mongán was Finn, but he would not allow it to be told.

§104. *Tucait Baile Mongán inso*
The Occasion of the Recital of 'Mongán's Frenzy'
TRANS. ANNE LEA from *Lebor na hUidre* 134[b9-35]

MONGÁN'S WIFE, FINDTIGERND, entreated Mongán to give her a true account of his adventures. He requested from her a period [of delay] of seven years. So it was done. Then that time came for him. There was [then] a great assembly of the men of Ireland in Uisnech in Meath in the year of the death of Ciarán son of the Carpenter and the slaying of Tuathal Máel Garb and the taking of the kingship by Diarmait. The hosts were upon [the mound of] Uisnech. A great hail-shower assailed them there. Its magnitude was such that one shower left twelve major streams in Ireland until Judgement Day. Mongán rose with his seven men and went aside from the mound together with his queen and his reciter of lore, Cairthide son of Marcán. They saw an excellent dwelling rimmed by trees. They go to it. They went into the rampart. They went into the wonderful chamber there. There was glittering bronze on the house. There were delightful open balconies upon its windows. There were seven distinguished persons there. They were providing wonderful things in the house, featherbeds and coverlets and remarkable jewels. Seven vats of wine were there. Welcome is given to Mongán in the house. He remained there. He took intoxicating drink. It was then that Mongán sang the 'Supernatural Utterance' to his wife there since he had promised he would tell her something of his journey. It seems to them it was not very long they were in the house. It was not the extent of but one night to them. They were there about a year in the house. When they awoke they saw it was Rath Mór in Mag Léna in which they were.

• • • • • • • • •

§105. The Conversation of Colum Cille[31] and the Youth at Carn Eolairg (Some say that he was Mongán mac Fiachna.)

TRANS. JOHN CAREY

COLUM CILLE SAID TO HIM—:

'From where do you come, youth?' said Colum Cille.

Respondit iuuenis: 'I come,' said the youth, 'from lands of strange things, from lands of familiar things, so that I may learn from you the spot on which died, and the spot on which were born, knowledge and ignorance.'

Respondit Colum Cille: 'A question,' said Colum Cille. 'Whose was it formerly, this lough which we see?'

Respondit iuuenis: 'I know that. It was yellow, it was flowery, it was green, it was hilly; it was rich in liquor, and strewn rushes, and silver, and chariots. I have grazed it when I was a stag; I have swum it when I was a salmon, when I was a seal; I have run upon it when I was a wolf; I have gone around it when I was a human. I have landed there under three sails: the yellow sail which bears, the green sail which drowns, the red sail under which bodies were conceived (?). Women have cried out because of me, although father and mother do not know what they bear, with labour for living folk, with a covering for the dead.'

Colum Cille said again to the youth: 'And this sea to the east of us, what is under it?'

'Not hard to answer,' said the youth: 'there are long-haired men with broad territories beneath it; there are fearsome greatly-pregnant cows beneath it, whose lowing is musical; there are bovine oxen; there are equine horses; there are two-heads; there are three-heads—in Europe, in Asia, in lands of strange things, in a green land, above its many borders, as far as its river-mouth (?).'

'That is enough,' said Colum Cille. Colum Cille arose as his followers watched, and went aside to speak with him and to ask him about the heavenly and earthly mysteries. While they were together thus for half the day, or from one hour to the next, Colum Cille's followers watched them from a distance.

---

31 Saint Columba or Colum Cille was a member of the Cenél Conaill sub-branch of the northern division of the Uí Néill dynasty (the descendants of Niall Noígiallach; see §97 for their foundation legend). Colum Cille was a native of the region that is now in Co. Donegal. He and his kinsman-successors founded numerous important monasteries, including Iona off the western coast of Scotland, Durrow, Derry, and Kells in Ireland, and Lindisfarne in Northumbria (now northern England). He died in 597. Folklore about Colum Cille has continued strongly to the present century in parts of Donegal. Together with Patrick and Brigit, he may be considered one of the three principal native saints of Irish tradition.

When they separated, they saw that the youth was suddenly hidden from them. They did not know where he went nor from where he came. When Colum Cille's followers were asking him to reveal to them something of what had passed between them, Colum Cille told them that he could not tell them even a single word of anything that he had been told (?); and he said that it was better for mortals not to know it.

FINIT.

• • • • • • • • •

§106. The First Utterance Of Aí Son Of Ollam[32]
TRANS. JOHN CAREY

ONCE WHEN FIACHNA SON OF DELBAETH, KING OF IRELAND, went on a royal circuit with his brother Ollam son of Delbaeth, and they were eating a meal in Inis Tige in the west of Ireland, a gust of wind came as they were consuming the feast.

'What does this gust of wind foretell?' Fiachna asked his druid.

'A child to be born to your brother,' said the druid, 'and his rank will be the same as your own.'

Then, at once, the boy was born in that house. 'Kill him!' said the king. 'Lift me up,' said the boy. He is lifted up then. 'Give me something for your honour's sake, Fiachna,' he said. 'What shall I give you?' asked Fiachna.

It is then that he said: 'My territory, my couple, a cauldron of provisions with a vat; let division of gifts (?) be granted by the king of Mugna; a vessel, a cup, a chariot, an ivory–hilted sword, thirty cows, a quern of the war–bands of Fiachna.'

'Hence the boy will be called Aí,' said Fiachna; i.e. *aí* means recitation, from Aí son of Ollam son of Delbaeth. That is the first utterance of Aí son of Ollam.

---

32 Translated from the text as edited by Rudolf Thurneysen, 'Die drei Kinder, die gleich nach ihrer Geburt Sprachen,' *ZCP* 20 (1936) 192–200: 193–4. Note that *aí* is an old word meaning 'poetry, poetic art', cognate with Welsh *awen*; the original sense of their shared root seems to be 'breath, wind; blows', a circumstance perhaps reflected in the wind which foretells Aí's imminent birth. *Ollam* means 'master' (and may indeed be modelled on Latin *magister*): it can be applied to one who has reached the highest rank in any of the skilled professions (Modern Irish *ollamh* means 'professor'), but is most often used to mean specifically 'master poet'. *Fiachna*, unlike the other names in the story, was quite commonly borne by real people; its use here though probably involves a punning association with *fiach* 'debt, payment'.

§107. *Scél Tuáin meic Chairill* The Story of Tuán Son of Cairell
TRANS. JOHN CAREY

AFTER FINNIA[33] had come with the Gospel into the land of Ireland, into the territory of the Ulaid, he went to the house of a wealthy layman (*laech*) there. He would not let them into his house. They fasted against him all Sunday. The layman's faith was not good. Finnia said to his followers: 'A good man will come to you. You will find solace; and he will tell you the history of Ireland since its first settlement.'

Next morning a venerable cleric came to them and wished them welcome. 'Come with me to my hermitage,' he said. 'It is more fitting for you.' They went with him. They performed the offices of Sunday: psalmody, preaching, eucharist. Finnia asked him his lineage. He told them 'I am of the Ulaid who dwell here; my name is Tuán son of Cairell. I have succeeded to my father's inheritance, from Mag nÍtha as far as this hermitage, to Benna Bairrche.'

Finnia besought him to reveal what had happened in Ireland since the time of Partholón son of Agnoman; he said that they would not accept any food until [he told them]. Tuán said to Finnia, 'Do not confine me to that subject; I would rather meditate on what you may have to tell me concerning the word of God.' 'Nevertheless,' said Finnia, 'it is granted to you to tell us about your own adventures, and events in Ireland.'

'Ireland, then,' [said Tuán], 'has been settled five times up until now. It was not settled before the Flood; and it was not settled after the Flood until 1002 years had passed since the Flood went from the dry land. Then the son of Agnoman son of Starn landed, of the race of the Greeks. They came in a company of twenty-four couples, for great was their sharpness (?) to each other. They settled Ireland until their descendants numbered a thousand; [then] a plague came upon them between two Sundays so that they all died except for one man. For it is not usual for there to be a destruction without a fugitive (*scéola*) escaping to tell the tale (*scél*) after that. I am that man.

'After that I fled from hilltop to hilltop and from cliff to cliff, protecting myself from wolves. Ireland was a wilderness for thirty-two years. At last I became decrepit, and could no longer travel: I dwelt in cliffs and waste places, and certain caves were special to me.

---

33 It is likely that Finnia here is to be identified with the mid 6th-century Brittonic missionary remembered in Breton sources as Uinniau. The opening of the story seems to recollect his foreign origin. In the endnote mentioned below, he is identified with St Finnian of Mag Bili in the territory of the Ulaid (now Moville, Co. Down), who is possibly the same individual as Uinniau.

'Agnoman's son landed, my father's brother. I used to see them as I hid from them on the cliffs: my hair and nails had grown long, and I was shrivelled, naked, wretched, miserable. One night as I slept I saw myself pass into the shape of a stag. I was in it after that. I was young and in good spirits; I was the leader of a herd, and used to make the circuit of Ireland in the midst of a great herd of stags. I passed that time—the time of Nemed, and of his children's settlement. For when Nemed came to Ireland it was with a company of thirty-four ships, and thirty in each ship. The sea drove them about for a year and a half. They were drowned, and died of hunger, except for three couples including Nemed. Their lineage spread over Ireland until there were 34,000 couples there; then they all died.

'Decrepitude came upon me at last, and I was fleeing from men and wolves. One night I was in the door of a cave. I remembered, and knew how to pass into another shape. I went into the shape of a wild boar. That was opportune for me: I was in good spirits, and was the leader of a herd of boars, and used to make a circuit of Ireland. And there was still a dwelling for me to visit in this territory of the Ulaid in the time of my old age and wretchedness; for it is in one place that I used to change all these shapes.

'Sémión son of Stairai settled this island. From him are the Fir Domnann and the Fir Bolg. Decrepitude came upon me and my spirits were oppressed, and I could no longer keep up with the boars and the herds but dwelt alone in caves and cliffs. Always I returned to my dwelling. I remembered every shape in which I had been. I fasted for three days. I had no strength. I went into the shape of a hawk (that is, a great cormorant). It was well with me then; my spirits were mighty. I was satisfied, eager. I used to fly across Ireland, learning all things.

'Beothecht son of Iordanen conquered this island from the peoples who were in it. From him are the Gaileóin, and the *Tuatha Dé ocus Andé* ['tribes of gods and un-gods'], whose origin the learned do not know; but they think it likely that they belong to the exiles who came from heaven.

'I was in the shape of the hawk for a long time, until I had outlived all these peoples who had settled the land of Ireland. The sons of Míl conquered this island from the Tuatha Dé by force. I went, in the hawk's shape in which I was, so that I was in the hollow of a tree above a stream. My spirits were oppressed. I could not fly, and I feared other birds. I fasted for a ninefold interval then, and went into the shape of a river salmon. God put me in the river. That was wonderful for me then: I was contented, vigorous, supreme in swimming. I used to escape from every peril: from the hands of those who spread nets, and from the claws of hawks, and from the spears of fishermen, so that their scars are upon me.

'At last, when it seemed to God that it was time to help me, and water-monsters were attacking me, and every fisherman knew me in every pool, I was caught in a net and fetched to the wife of Cairell, the king of this country. I remember then how the man took me and cooked me, and the woman alone ate me so that I was in her womb. I remember then the time when I was in her womb. . . and what people were saying to each other in the house, and what was done in Ireland during that time. I remember then how speech came to me, as to every baby; and I was learning everything that used to be done in Ireland. And I was a prophet, and a name was given to me: Tuán son of Cairell. After that Patrick came with the Faith. I was very old then; I was baptised, and I alone believed in the King of all things, with His creation.'

After that they sang the office, and went into the refectory: Finnia with his followers, and Tuán. They were well fed. They remained there conversing for a week; every history and genealogy in Ireland derives from Tuán son of Cairell. Patrick had spoken with him before that, and he had told [these things] to him; and Colum Cille had spoken with him. And Finnia spoke with him in the presence of the people of the region, and entreated him to dwell with him; but he did not obtain that. 'Illustrious will be your place,' said Tuán.

¶Note. In the manuscript that best preserves the text's original form there is a concluding passage in mixed Latin and Irish: 'Tuán was in Ireland after Fintan for 100 years in the shape of a man, 20 years in the shape of a pig, 80 years in the shape of a stag, 100 years in the shape of an eagle, 30 years beneath a pool in the shape of a fish; then in the shape of a man again until he grew old, until the time of Finnia of the Dál Fiatach. The end.'

♦ ♦ ♦ ♦ ♦ ♦ ♦ ♦ ♦ ♦

§108. The Book of Invasions (First Recension)
Lebor Gabála Érenn   TRANS. JOHN CAREY

¶ 1.

IN PRINCIPIO FECIT DEUS CAELUM ET TERRAM; i.e., God made heaven and earth at first, and he himself has no beginning or end. First he made unformed matter and the light of the angels, on the first Sunday. He made the firmament on Monday. He made the earth and seas on Tuesday. He made the sun and moon and stars of heaven on Wednesday. He made the birds of the air and the reptiles of the sea on Thursday. He made the beasts of the earth besides, and Adam to rule over them, on Friday. Then on Saturday God rested after completing the new creation; and it is not from ruling (that he rested).

¶ 2. Then he granted the stewardship of heaven to Lucifer, together with the nine orders of the angels of heaven. He gave the stewardship of the earth to Adam and Eve, together with their children. After that Lucifer transgressed, so that he became leader of a third of the angelic host. The King imprisoned him in Hell, together with a third of the host of the angels. Then God said to the household of heaven: 'This Lucifer is too proud. *Venite ut vidiamus et confundamus consilium eius.*'

¶ 3. Lucifer was jealous of Adam; he was certain that he would be set in heaven in his place. That is why Iofar Niger went in a serpent's form, and tempted Adam and Eve to sin by eating the apple from the forbidden tree. That is why Adam was driven from paradise into the common earth. The Lord went to them after that and said to Adam: '*Terra es et in terram ibis*' (that is, 'You were made of earth and will go into the earth'). '*In sudore vultus tui comedes panem tuum*' (that is, 'You will not get food without toil'). Then he said to the woman: '*Cum dolore et gemitu paries filios tuos et filias tuas*' (that is, 'With groaning and sickness you will bear your offspring and your sons').

¶ 4. . . .greed and envy. That is why God brought the Flood over the whole world.

¶ 5. Seth son of Adam, however, was the pre-eminent third son that Adam had. From him descend the men of the whole world, i.e. Noah son of Lamech son of Methuselah son of Enoch son of Jared son of Mahalaleel son of Cainan son of Enos son of Seth son of Adam. For Noah is the second Adam, back to whom the men of the whole world are traced. For the Flood drowned all of Adam's descendants except for Noah with his three sons, i.e. Shem, Ham, and Japhet; and their four wives, i.e. Coba and Olla and Oliva and Olivana. When

God brought the Flood over the whole world, none of the world's people escaped from the Flood except the company of the Ark, i.e. Noah with his three sons, and Noah's wife and his sons' wives. *Unde poeta cecinit* ['of which the poet sang']:

¶ 6.   A troop which a false omen did not mislead:
Noah, who was not backward in valour—
it was a tale which was made plain terribly—
Shem, Ham, and Japhet.

Fair-complexioned women of great worth
[who sailed] above the Flood without fatalities:
Coba—the white swan was vigorous—
Olla, Oliva, Olivana.

¶ 7.   Shem settled in Asia, Ham in Africa, Japhet in Europe:
Shem settled in pleasant Asia,
Ham with his children in Africa;
it is noble Japhet and his sons
who settled in Europe.

¶ 8. Shem had thirty sons, including Arphaxad, Asshur, and Persius. Ham had thirty sons, including Cush and Canaan. But Japhet had fifteen, including Madai, Grecus, Hispanius, and Gomerus. Or else Shem had twenty-seven sons:

¶ 9.   Thirty gentle sons, a splendid undertaking,
descended from Ham son of Noah;
twenty-seven are from Shem,
fifteen from Japhet.

¶ 10. It is from Japhet son of Noah that the northern part of Asia derives: Asia Minor, Armenia, Media, and the men of Scythia; and from him are the people of all Europe. From Grecus son of Japhet are Great Greece and Little Greece and the Greece of Alexandria. From Hispanius son of Japhet is Hispania. Gomerus son of Japhet had two sons: Emoth and Ibath.

¶ 11. From Emoth descend the people of the north of the world. Ibath had two sons, Bodb and Baath. Bodb's son was Dói. Elanius son of Dói had three sons: Armen, Negua, Isicón. Armenon had five sons: Gotus, Cibidus, Viligotus, Burgandus, and Longbardus. Negua had three sons: Saxus, Boarus, Vandalus. Isicón, however, the third son of Elanius, had four sons: Romanus, Francus, Britus, Albanus. It is Albanus who took Alba [(North) Britain] first, and it is named Alba after him; then he was driven across Muir nIcht by his brother Britus, so that Albania on the Continent is derived from him *hodie* ['today'].

¶ 12. From Magog son of Japhet are descended the peoples who came to Ireland before the Gaels, i.e. Partholón son of Sera son of Srú son of Esrú

son of Braimin son of Faithecht son of Magog son of Japhet; and Nemed
son of Agnoman son of Paimp son of Tait son of Sera son of Srú; and
Nemed's descendants, i.e. the Gaileóin and Fir Domnann and Fir Bolg and
Tuatha Dé Donann. As the poet said:

¶ 13. Magog, Japhet's splendid son,
whose descendants are well known:
among them was Partholón of Banba,
whose feat was seemly.
Among them was valiant Nemed,
only son of Agnoman;
among them were Gann and Genann,
Sengann and noble Sláine.

The numerous descendants of Elatha:
among them was Bres, without falsehood,
son of Elatha skilled in combat,
son of Delbaeth, son of Nét,

son of Innuí, son of Allduí.
Allduí was the son of Tait,
son of Tabarn, son of Eno,
son of Baath, son of pleasant Ebath,

son of Bethach, son of Iardan,
son of Nemed, grandson of Paimp.
Paimp was the son of Tait, son of Sera,
son of Srú, son of fair Braimin.

Braimin was the son of Faithecht,
son of Magog, great the renown;
it is in their time that I was
revealing myself at large [?].

¶ 14. Baath was the second son of Ibath son of Gomer son of Japhet, and
from him descend the Gaels and the men of Scythia. His son was the wonderful pre-eminent man named Fénius Farsaid. He was one of the seventy-two
leaders who went to build the tower of Nimrod, when the languages were
divided. Fénius however had two sons: Noenual, whom he left behind in
Scythia; and Nél, who was born at the Tower, and was an expert in the many
languages. That is why Pharaoh sent for him, so as to learn the many languages from him. Fénius, however, came from Asia to Scythia, whence he had
gone to build the Tower. At the end of forty years as ruler of Scythia he died,
and gave the leadership to his son Noenual.

¶ 15. Forty-two years after the building of the Tower, Ninus son of Belus became king of the world. For no one except him alone had tried to bring the

government of the tribes and the many peoples under a single tribute and tax and law. There had indeed been leaders before then: whoever was noblest and most generous in the tribe was the chief councillor for everyone, who used to punish every injustice and reward every justice—but he would not seek to attack or dominate another people.

¶ 16. That is the time when Gáedel Glas, from whom descend the Gaels, was born to Scotta, daughter of Pharaoh. It is after her that the Gaels are named 'Scots', *ut dictum est* ['so it is said']:

> The Féni were named after Fénius,
> vigour without restraint;
> the Gaels from generous Gáedel Glas,
> the Scots from Scotta.

¶ 17. It is Gáedel Glas who fashioned Gaelic from the seventy-two languages. These are their names: *Bethin, Scithin, Scill, Scartin*, Goths, Greeks, Germans, Gauls, *Poimp*, Phrygia, Caspia, Dardania, Pamphylia, Morini, Ligurians, *Oatri*, Crete, Corsica, Sicily, Rhaetia, Sardinia, Macedonia, Thessaly, Armenia, Dalmatia, Romans, *Rugind*, Moesia, Narbonne, Spain, *Gairit, Humind*, Saracens, *Broes*, British, Norica, Burgundy, Belgae, *Mucaig*, Boeotia, India, Parthia, Chaldaea, Syria, Galatians, Achaea, Athens, Albania, Saxon, Hebrew, *Ardáin*, Moesia, Thrace, Edessa, *Uesogum*, Tripoli, Zeugis, Numidia, Mauretania, *Hicail*, Gaelic, Media, *Foirni, Grinni*, Franks, Frisians, Lombards, Lacedaemonia, Trojans, Colchis, Caspia, Egypt, Ethiopia. *Unde poeta cecinit*:

¶ 18. Consider the languages of the world:

> *Bethin, Scithin, Scill, Scartin*,
> Goths, Greeks, Germans, Gauls with terror,
> *Poimp*, Phrygia, Dalmatia, Dardania,
>
> Pamphylia, Morini, numerous Ligurians,
> *Oatri*, Crete, Corsica, Cyprus,
> Thessaly, Caspia, splendid Armenia,
> Rhaetia, Sicily, Saracens, Sardinia,
>
> Belgae, Boeotia, British, melodious *Brais*,
> Spain, Romans, *Rugind*,
> *Humind*, India, Arabia rich in gold
> *Mucaig*, Moesia, Macedonia,
>
> Parthia, Chaldaea, Syria, Saxon,
> Athens, Achaea, Albanian,
> Hebrew, *Ardáin*, pure Galatians,
> Troy, Thessaly, Colchis,
>
> Moesia, Media, *Fairni*, Franks,

Grinni, Lacedaemonia, Lombards,
Thrace, Numidia, Edessa of waters,
lofty *Icail*, Ethiopia, Egypt.

From those languages, without corruption,
Gáedel extracted Gaelic.
Familiar to him, thanks to his learning,
were the families of the many languages.

¶ 19. It is Srú son of Esrú son of Gáedel who led the Gaels out of Egypt, after Pharaoh had been drowned in the Red Sea pursuing the sons of Israel; that happened four hundred and seventy years after the Flood. Srú departed from Egypt with four ships; and there were twenty-four couples and three mercenaries in each ship. Srú and his son, Éber Scot, were the leaders of that fleet.

¶ 20. At that time Noenual descendant of Fénius died, i.e. the ruler of Scythia; and immediately after coming to Scythia Srú died also. Éber Scot took the kingship of Scythia by force from the children of Noenual, until he was killed by Noenual's son Noenius. There was strife between Noenius and Boamain son of Éber Scot. Boamain took the kingship until he was killed by Noenius. Noenius took the sovereignty until he was killed by Ogamain son of Boamain, in vengeance for his father. Ogamain took the kingship until his death. Refill son of Noenius took the kingship until he was killed by Tait son of Ogamain. After that Tait fell by the hand of Reflóir son of Refill. There was strife concerning the sovereignty then, between Reflóir son of Noenius [*sic*] and Agnoman son of Tait, until Reflóir was killed by Agnoman. That is why the descendants of Gáedel, i.e. Agnoman and his son Lámfhind, were driven into exile upon the sea, so that for seven years they were voyaging around the world to the north. They suffered more hardships than can be counted.

¶ 21. This is why Agnoman's son was called Lámfhind ['White-hand']: because the light of candles was not brighter than his hands rowing. They had three ships, and a chain between them so that none of them might be parted from each other. They had three leaders after Agnoman's death on the expanse of the great Caspian Sea: Lámfhind and Alloith and Caicher the druid.

¶ 22. It is Caicher who gave them a remedy when the mermaid was beguiling them—that is, sleep was overpowering them because of the music. This is the remedy that Caicher found for them: pouring wax into their ears. It is Caicher who addressed them when the wind drove them out into the ocean, so that they suffered greatly there from hunger and thirst.

¶ 23. At the end of a week they came to the great promontory which extends northward from the Rhipaean Mountains. On the promontory they found a well with the taste of wine, and drank from it, so that they were sleeping for three days and three nights until Caicher the druid spoke. 'Arise!' he said. 'We will not rest until we reach Ireland.' 'Where is Ireland?' said Lámfhind son of

Agnoman. 'Farther than Scythia,' said Caicher; 'and it is not we who will reach it but our children, three hundred years from today.'

¶ 24. Thereafter they settled in the Maeotic Marshes. And it is there that a son was born to Lámfhind: Éber Glúnfhind ['White-knee'], i.e., there were white marks on his knees. He was the leader after his father. His grandson was Febri Glas, whose grandson was Nuadu. Bráth was son of Deáith son of Ercaid son of Alloith son of Nuadu son of Noenual son of Febri Glas son of Agni Find son of Éber Glúnfhind son of Lámfhind son of Agnoman son of Tait son of Ogamain son of Boamain son of Éber Scot son of Srú son of Esrú son of Gáedel Glas son of Nél son of Fénius Farsaid.

¶ 25. It is Bráth who left the Marshes, going across the Mediterranean to Crete and Sicily; and they reached Spain after that. They took Spain by force.

¶ 26. (Agnoman son of Tait is the Gael-leader who came from Scythia. He had two sons: Lámfhind and Alloith. Lámfhind had one son: Éber Glúnfhind. Alloith had a son Éber Dub, [born] at the same time in the Marshes. Two descendants of theirs shared the sovereignty: Toíthecht son of Tetrech son of Éber Dub, and Noenual son of Febri son of Agni son of Éber Glúnfhind— also Soítecht son of Mantán son of Caicher.)

¶ 27. The Gaels came to Spain in four ships: there were fourteen couples in each ship, and seven mercenaries without wives. Bráth led a ship's company. Occe and Ucce led two ships' companies; they were brothers, the sons of Alloith son of Noenual son of Nemed son of Alloith son of Ogamain. Mantán led a ship's company; he was the son of Caicher son of Ercaid son of Oitecht.

¶ 28. They won three battles after reaching Spain: a battle against the Toeséni, a battle against the Lombards, a battle against the Barchai. Then a plague overtook them so that twenty-four of them perished, including Occe and Ucce. None escaped from the two ships except ten men, including Én son of Occe and Ún son of Ucce.

¶ 29. Bráth had a worthy son: Bregon, by whom were built the tower and the city [Brigantia was the city's name]. It is from Bregon's Tower that Ireland was seen one winter evening. *Unde* Gilla Coemáin *cecinit*:

¶ 30.   Gáedel Glas, from whom are the Gaels,
      was the son of Nél the mightily prosperous;
      strong in the west and in the east
      was Nél son of Fénius Farsaid.

      Fénius had two sons (I speak the truth):
      our father Nél and Noenual.
      Nél was born at the Tower in the east,
      Noenual in shield-pure Scythia.

      Srú son of Esrú son of Gáedel,

our grandfather who rejoiced in armies:
it is he who went northward from his home
across the Red Sea.

He had a host of four ships' companies
crossing the Red Sea:
in each planked dwelling, it is granted,
were twenty-four couples.

The ruler of Scythia, a pure cry,
was the lad named Noenual;
he died in his house yonder
when the Gaels came.

Éber Scot of the champions
seized power boldly from Noenual's children,
until he was killed, without pleasant kindliness,
by Noenius son of Noenual.

Mighty after that was the son of Éber
whose true right name was Beomain:
he was king as far as the shore of the Caspian Sea
until he fell at the hand of Noenius.

Noenius son of powerful Noenual
took shield-speckled Scythia;
the fair and ample ruler was killed
by Ogamain son of Beomain.

Thereafter Ogamain was ruler,
after Noenius good in might,
until he died in his territory, without benefit of
    clergy [?];
Refill was king after him.

Refill fell after that
at the hand of Tait son of Ogamain;
Tait fell—it was no feeble cast—
at the hand of Reflóir son of Refill.

Reflóir and faultless Agnoman
contended for four years
until radiant Reflóir was killed
by Tait's son, by Agnoman.

Noenual and Refill, with harmony,
the two sons of Reflóir son of Refill,
drove Agnoman into exile

across the great grey frenzied sea.

Good were the leaders, it was sufficient,
who came from Scythia:
Agnoman, Éber without reproach,
the two sons of Tait son of Ogamain.

Elloth, Lámfhind, and zealous Lámglas
were the three sons of brilliant Agnoman;
Caicher and Cing, fame with victory,
were Éber Echruad's two fine sons.

Three was the number of their ships
crossing the heavy waves:
three score in each ship, clear the telling,
and women [making up] each third score.

Agnoman died, it was no disgrace,
in the islands of the great Caspian Sea—
a place where they were for a year,
and discovered a great secret.

They came to the broad Libyan Sea,
a sailing voyage of six full summer days;
Glas son of Agnoman—he was not feeble—
died there in *Caronis*.

They found a fair island there,
in the Libyan Sea of the warriors' swords;
for a year and a season, with renown,
they dwelt in that island.

They sail upon the sea, illustrious effort,
by night and day;
the radiance of the hands of bright Lámfhind
was like fair candles.

They had four leaders, it was not feeble,
after crossing the Libyan Sea:
Elloth, Lámfhind swift across the deep,
Cing and his brother Caicher.
Caicher found a remedy for them
against the mermaid's beguiling;
this is the remedy which fair Caicher found:
pouring wax into their ears.

It is Caicher, an illustrious union,

who prophesied to them
at the Rhipaean Mountains, with harmony:
'There is no rest for us until [we reach] Ireland.'

'Where is lofty Ireland?'
said Lámfhind the savage warrior.
'Far away,' said Caicher:
'not we but our fair children will reach it.'

They set their course [?] venomously, in their company,
southward past the Rhipaean headlands;
the descendants of Gáedel, with purity,
conquered the Marshes.

An illustrious child was born there
to Lámfhind son of Agnoman:
Éber Glúnfhind, the pure gryphon,
curly-haired grandfather of Febri.

The kindred of bright nimble Gáedel
were in that land for three hundred years;
they dwelt there from then
until the coming of victorious Bráth.

Bráth, fair son of dear Deáith,
came to Crete, to Sicily;
a company of fair ships, on a safe voyage
sunwise around Europe to Spain.

Occe and Ucce, without reproach,
were the two sons of Elloth son of Noenual;
Mantán son of Caicher, Bráth the good—
those were their four leaders.

Fourteen men, with their wives,
was the crew of each warrior-laden ship,
together with six splendid mercenaries;
they won three battles in Spain.

Lofty was the first battle, I will not conceal it,
which they won against the armies of the Toeséni;
a battle against the Barchai, it was savagery,
and a battle against the Lombards.

After the sinister battle
a single day's plague visited them:
the crew of the ships of Elloth's son, without fault,
all died except for ten men.

Ún and Én escaped from that,
the two fine sons of the mighty warriors;
after that Bregon was born,
Bile's strong and furious father.

He won many contests and battles
against the many-coloured host of Spain.
Bregon of illustrious valour, of combats:
by him Brigantia was built.

It is Bile son of Bregon, fair and fortunate,
whose son was Míl;
Míl had seven sons (goodly their company)
including Éber and Éremón.

Bregon's ten sons, without weakness:
Brego, Fuat, and Muirthemne,
Cuailnge, Cualu, Blad—whoever he be—
Ebléo, Nár, Íth, and Bile.

Íth son of Bregon, with melodious fame,
came first to Ireland;
he is the first man who settled it
of the famous race of the mighty Gaels.

¶ 31. Now let us cease from stories of the Gaels, so that we may tell of the seven peoples who took Ireland before them. Cesair daughter of Bith son of Noah, then, settled forty days before the Flood. Partholón son of Sera, three hundred years after the Flood. Nemed son of Agnoman of the Greeks of Scythia, at the end of thirty years after Partholón. Fir Bolg after that. Fir Domnann after that. Gaileóin after that. Tuatha Dé Donann after that. *Unde* Fintan *cecinit* ['of which Fintan sang']:

¶ 32. Ireland: whatever is asked of me,
    I know precisely
    every taking which took it
    since the beginning of the harmonious world.

Cesair came from the east—
the woman was Bith's daughter—
with her fifty maidens,
with her fifty men.

The Flood overtook Bith
on his mountain [*sliab*], without secret;
Ladru in Ard Ladrann,

Cesair in her hollow [cúil].

I was beneath the Flood for a year
in rugged Tul Tuinne;
I did not find in my lifetime
any sleep that was better.

I was here in Ireland
(my journey was unending)
until Partholón reached it
from the east, from the land of the Greeks.

I was in Ireland still,
and Ireland empty,
until the son of Agnoman came:
Nemed, whose ways were magnificent.

The Fir Bolg and Fir Gaileóin
came, a long journey;
the Fir Domnann came
and took Irrus in the west.

Thereafter the Tuath Dé came
in their masses of distant [sic] smoke,
so that my time passed with them,
though it was a lengthy period.

Thereafter the sons of Míl came
from Spain in the south,
so that my time passed with them,
though theirs was a great while.

A long life came
to me, I will not conceal it;
until the Faith reached me,
from the King of the heaven of clouds.

I am white Fintan
son of Bóchra, I will not conceal it;
from the Flood until now
I have been a lofty noble sage.

¶ 33. A query, then: who first took Ireland after the creation of the earth? Not difficult: Cesair daughter of Bith son of Noah, forty days before the Flood. This is the reason for her coming: to escape the Flood. For Noah said to them 'Arise, [and go] to the western edge of the world. Perhaps the Flood will not reach it.' They came in three ships to Dún na mBárc in the territory of

Corcu Duibne. Two of the ships sank. Cesair and the crew of her ship escaped, i.e. fifty maidens and three men. [The men were] Bith son of Noah, after whom Sliab Betha is named (he was buried there, in the great cairn on Sliab Betha); and Ladru the steersman, from whom Ard Ladrann is named (he is the first dead man to be buried in Ireland); and Fintan son of Bóchra, from whom is named Fert Fintain above Tul Tuinne. Cesair with her fifty maidens died in Cúil Cesra, in Connacht. These are their names, *ut* Fintan *cecinit* ['so that Fintan sang']:

¶ 34. We made a fair division between us,
    myself and Bith and fierce Ladru;
    it was made for the sake of peace and reason
    with regard to the fifty great maidens.

    I got seventeen wives, including Cesair:
    Lot and Luam and Mael and Barr,
    Froecar, Femair, Faible, Foroll,
    Ciper, Torrian, Tamall, Tamm,
    Abba, Ulla, Raichne, Sille—
    that is the number that we were.

    Bith got seventeen including Bairind:
    Sella, Della, Dúib, Addeós,
    Fota, Traige, Nera, Buana,
    Tamall, Tuama, Nathra, Leós,
    Fodarg, Rodarg, Dos, Clos, it is heard—
    they too were [of] our company.

    Sixteen for Ladru after that:
    Alba, Bona, Albor, Aíl,
    Gothiam, Germán, Aithne, Inne,
    Rodarg, Rinne, Iachor, Aín,
    Irrand, Espa, Sine, Sommall—
    that was our fair compact.

¶ 35. No one else of Adam's race took Ireland before the Flood.

¶ 36. After that Ireland was uninhabited for three hundred years—or three hundred and twelve, *quod verius est*—until Partholón son of Sera son of Srú came there. It was he who first took Ireland after the Flood, on a Tuesday, on the fourteenth of the month, in Inber Scéne. (For Ireland was taken three times from Inber Scéne.) Partholón was descended from Magog son of Japhet. *Anno autem sexagesimo aetatis* of Abraham *tenuit* Partholón *Hiberniam*, i.e., in the sixtieth year of Abraham's life Partholón took Ireland.

¶ 37. Partholón came as one of four lords: himself; and his son Láiglinne, after whom Loch Láiglinne in Uí Mac Uais Breg is named; and his two other sons, Slánga and Rudraige, from whom are named Sliab Slánga and Loch Rudraige. It was when Rudraige's grave was dug that the lake burst forth upon the land.

¶ 38. Partholón had been in Ireland for seven years when the first of his followers died: Fea, from whom is named Mag Fea. For that is where he was buried, in Mag Fea. In the third year after that, Partholón won the first battle fought in Ireland in Slemna Maige Ítha, against Cichol Gricenchos of the Fomoiri; and it is men with single arms and single legs who fought against him.

¶ 39. There were seven lake-bursts in Ireland in Partholón's time: Loch Láiglinne among the Uí Mac Uais Breg; Loch Cuan and Loch Rudraige among the Ulaid; Loch nDechet and Loch Mesc and Loch Con among the Connachta; Loch nEchtra among the Airgialla. For Partholón found only three lakes and nine rivers before him in Ireland: Loch Fordremain in Sliab Mis, Loch Luimnig upon the land, Findloch in Irrus; and the river of Liffe and Luí and Muad and Slicech and Samaír (on which is Ess Ruaid) and Find and Modorn and Buas and Banna (between Lé and Elle). Four years before Partholón's death was the bursting of Brénnae across the land.

¶ 40. Four plains were cleared by Partholón in Ireland: Mag nÍtha among the Laigin, Mag Tuired among the Connachta, Mag Lí among the Uí Mac Uais, Mag Láthrann among the Dál nAraide. For Partholón found before them in Ireland only one plain: Senmag nÉtair. This is why it was called Senmag ['Old Plain']: no root nor shoot of a tree had ever grown there.

¶ 41. And it is there that Partholón died, along with five thousand men and four thousand women, of a week's plague on the calends of May. The plague came upon them on a Monday, and killed them all except for one man: Tuán son of Starn son of Sera, Partholón's brother's son. And God transformed him into many shapes; and that lone man lived on from the time of Partholón until the time of Finnian and Colum Cille. And so he related to them the takings of Ireland, from the time of Cesair who first took Ireland until that time; and he is the same as Tuán son of Cairell son of Muiredach Muinderg. It is concerning all that that the sage of history recited this poem which follows:

¶ 42. Lords of the plain of fair bright Conn,
    of the land of the men of Fál, as I declare:
    what band was it, after the creation of the earth,
    which was placed in Ireland first?

    Ireland, before the bright-hued Flood,
    as I reckon its history,
    obtained a shining-white, clever troop
    along with Cesair daughter of Bith.

Bith son of Noah of the many peoples. . .

. . . .

died in Sliab Betha (it is grim);
Ladru died in Ard Ladrann.

Fintan went upon a journey of weakness:
his grave was found (it was a wild leap).
He was not in a church enclosure at once,
but in a barrow above Tul Tuinne.

To Dún Bárc, to a feast with its furnishings,
an unbounded limitless journey bore them;
at her cairn, by the noble sea,
Cesair died in Cúil Cesra.

Forty full, long days
before the roar of the Flood
the delicate, slender company came in their ship:
they settled the territory of the land of Ireland.

There arose, upon a mission of truth-telling,
through the power of the King whom he used to worship,
Fintan, who was a man with tales
for the mighty champions of the earth.

For three hundred years, I boast,
I speak, I reckon by rules,
fair Ireland, I say, I proclaim,
was empty after the Flood.

Partholón came first—
a royal course across the much-rowed sea—
as one of four dear, noble warriors:
among them was the lordly being Slánga.

Slánga, sword-wielding Láiglinne—
noble and sturdy was their planked currach—
three celebrated lords
along with the very manly Rudraige.

Plains were hewn from the great forest
by him, out of love for his dear offspring:
Mag nÍtha in the south, Brí Buadchind,
Mag Lí of swift spears, Mag Láthrainn.

Seven lake-bursts, whatever you may reckon;
illustrious their names, whatever you may demonstrate—
they filled islanded Ireland

in his time, under a fetter of valleys.

Loch Láiglind, firm Loch Cuan,
red Rudraige without restraint,
Loch nDechet, intoxicating Loch Mesc,
Loch Con, Loch nEchtra of swans.
Over Ireland, beauty of colour,
as I relate every matter,
he found, on the world's surface,
only three lakes [there] before him.

Three great hostile lakes
and nine rivers of wisdom:
Loch Fordremain, Loch Luimnig,
Findloch above the borders of Irrus.
The river of Liffe, Luí—let us relate [it]—
which every swift slender druid. . . .;
the history of the ancient rivers of Ireland
is a witness of the fair portent of the Flood.

Muad, Slicech, Samaír, mention [them];
Buas, a torrent, famed radiance of a peak.
Modorn, Find with . . . . appearance,
Banna between Lé and Elle.

Partholón of the numerous band
died after vaunting, along with [his] heroes.
They were struck down, with their property and treasures,
upon Senmag nElta nÉtair.

This is the reason why it is the prosperous Senmag ['Old Plain']—
pure-formed God brought it about—:
throughout its expanse, which an inlet of the sea divides,
no root nor shoot of a tree was found.

His grave is there, according to true accounts,
though he was not mighty among the saints.
Under plagues his sleep was silent;
it is no pious lament for our lords.
Three hundred years, whatever you may say,
on secret, prosperous lands,
the bright, harmonious, enduring troop
[ruled] over ancient noble Ireland.

Man, woman, boy and girl
on the calends of May, a great hindrance;
not healthy was the summer's collective distribution,

the pestilence of Partholón in Bregmag.

For thirty desolate years
[Ireland] was empty, throughout savage seasons,
after the death of their host in a week
in their flocks upon Mag nElta.

Let us adore the King of creation,
the fair summit, shelter of our people;
his is every company, his every race,
his every head, his every beauty.

I am Flann's grandson, who apportions truths;
I have chosen a portion among kings.
May whatever I say be an utterance of grace,
in accordance with sanctity, lords!

¶ 43. Ireland was empty then for a space of thirty years after Partholón, until Nemed son of Agnoman of the Greeks of Scythia took it with his four lords—they were the four sons of Nemed. He had forty-four ships on the Caspian Sea for a year and a half, but only his own ship reached Ireland. These were the four lords: Starn and Iarbonél Fáith and Ainnind and Fergus Lethderg, the four sons of Nemed.

¶ 44. There were four lake-bursts in Ireland in Nemed's time: Loch Cál among the Uí Nialláin, Loch Munremair among the Luigne, Loch nDairbrech, and Loch nAinnind in Mide. When the mound and grave of Ainnind son of Nemed were dug, it is then that the lake burst across the land.

¶ 45. It is Nemed who won the battle of Ros Froecháin against Gann and Sengann, the kings of the Fomoiri; and both of them were killed there. Two royal forts were dug by Nemed in Ireland: Ráith Chimbaíth in Seimne, and Ráith Chinn Eich among the Uí Nialláin. It is the four sons of Matán Muinremar of the Fomoiri who dug Ráith Chinn Eich in a single day: Boc and Roboc, Ruibne and Rotan. Nemed killed them in Daire Lige before morning, before they could finish the digging.

¶ 46. Twelve plains were cleared by Nemed in Ireland: Mag Cera, Mag nEba, Mag Cúile Tolad, and Mag Luirg in Connacht; Mag Seired in Tethba; Mag Tóchair in Tír Éogain; Mag Seimne in Íraide; Mag Macha among the Airgialla; Mag Muirthemne in Brega; Mag mBernsa among the Laigin; Lecmag and Mag Moda in Munster.

¶ 47. He won three battles against the Fomoiri, i.e., the sea-rovers: the battle of Bodbgna in Connacht, the battle of Cnámros among the Laigin, the battle of Murbolg in Dál Riata. After that Nemed died of pestilence in Ailén Arda Nemid, in the territory of the Uí Liatháin.

¶ 48. Nemed's descendants experienced great hardship after he was gone, from

Morc son of Dela and from Conann son of Febor, after whom is named Conann's Tower (i.e., Torinis Cheitne today). The great fleet of the Fomoiri was inside it. Two thirds of the children and grain and milk of the men of Ireland were brought to them in Mag Ceitne every Samain night.

¶ 49. The men of Ireland became angry and disgusted at the harshness of the tribute, and they all went to fight with the Fomoiri. There were three champions among them: Semul son of Iarbonél Fáith son of Nemed, Érglan son of Beoán son of Starn son of Nemed, and Fergus Lethderg son of Nemed. Thirty thousand of them went by sea, and thirty thousand by land. They sacked the tower, and Conann and his family were killed. After the sack Morc son of Dela came upon them, with a fleet of sixty ships. They died in mutual slaughter, and the sea covered the men of Ireland; none escaped from the other, what with the fierceness of the fighting, and none survived except a single ship in which were thirty warriors. They departed, dispersing out of Ireland in flight from the plague and the tribute—for Bethach died in Ireland of plague. His ten wives survived him by twenty-three years.

¶ 50. Matach and Érglan and Iartach, the three sons of Beoán, went to Domon and Erdomon in the north of Britain.

¶ 51. Sémión went into the lands of the Greeks. His progeny multiplied there until they numbered in the thousands. The Greeks imposed servitude upon them: hauling soil onto rough mountains so that they became flowering plains. Five thousand of them escaped; and they made ships for themselves from their bags, and came back to Ireland, to their old homeland, two hundred and thirty years after Nemed. These were their leaders: Gann and Genann, Rudraige and Sengann and Sláne.

¶ 52. As for Fergus Lethderg and his son, i.e. Britán Mael from whom descend the Britons of the world: they took Maind Conáin, and filled the great island (i.e., *Britannia insula*) with their descendants. Then came Hengist and Horsa, sons of Wihtgils king of the Old Saxons, and they overcame them and drove the Britons to the edges of the island. Those are the adventures of Nemed's descendants after the sack of Conann's Tower. *Unde* the sage of history *cecinit*:

¶ 53. Great Ireland, which the Gaels govern:
    I tell of the multitude of their companies.
    Many sturdy princes have taken it,
    of the haughty race of Adam.

    From fierce, truly harmonious Adam
    until the Flood—[its] fame was ordained—
    no one warmed its fierce, vigorous habitation
    save for Cesair, one of fifty maidens.

    Save for Bith and Ladru, let us mention [them],
    [and] Fintan, with regard to . . . of [the] land,

no famous, keen, slender man found
Ireland before the Flood.

Three hundred years, whatever you say,
after the Flood—secret journeys—
Partholón son of Sera brought
a pure crown to acts of valour.

The people of sinful Partholón
were without any fair canon of psalms;
the entire number of their company perished
on their 'Old Plain' in a week.

For six score years, without increase,
without protection—it was a sickly gloom—
every region was empty as far as the sounding sea:
none took it except for Nemed.

Nemed, with the wrath of all
because of abundance of fetters and fury;
his was the land of battle, or war-bands,
after the destruction of the other kindreds.

He used to secure triumph without hazards—
Nemed son of Agnoman,
with pride and shrewdness—against the haughty;
although . . . , he was fortunate.

Starn, who was killed by Febor's son;
Iarbonél Fáith, who was steadfast;
Ainnind, with leather fetters:
Nemed's three venomous lords.

Nemed, who ordained the distribution of gifts [?],
was a plague of fire upon doomed men.
In his time, graces responding to a mighty summons,
there was the bursting of four lakes.

Loch Muinremair of the pleasant shore,
wild, strong-ridged, mighty;
Loch nDairbrech, across the rampart altogether [?];
Loch Cál and Loch nAinnind.

Two strongholds were swiftly dug
to serve as secure fortresses against armies:
Ráith Chinn Eich, in a muster of weapons,
and Ráith Chimbáith in Seimne.

There were cleared by him, it was a prosperous course,
twelve plains, ruddiness of flame:
Mag Cera in Connacht of gifts,
Mag Moda and Mag nEba.

Mighty Mag Tóchair was cleared,
Lecmag from the great plain of Munster,
Mag mBernsa, . . . against a secret,
Mag Cúile Tolad, Mag Lugad.

Mag Sered, vigour of a stream;
Mag Seimne, radiance of colour;
Mag Luirg, dark obscurity of shores [?];
Mag Muirthemne, Mag Macha.

He won the victories of the Modarn,
he overthrew [?] the host of the Fomoiri:
the mighty youth's battle of great Murbolg,
the battles of Bodbgna and Cnámros.

In the territory of the Uí Liatháin, in Munster,
he died of a pestilence of dark death of princes
together with [his] savage, knowledgeable followers
in Ailén Arda Nemid.

The race which Nemed founded
was not secure against the burden
[imposed] by hard-bodied Conann
and by Morc son of Dela.

Two thirds of their shapely offspring—
it was not proper in times of weakness [?]—
a tribute enduring through the ages,
two thirds of their grain and milk.

To harsh Mag Ceitne of [the] weapons,
beyond Ess Ruaid, wondrous knowledge,
it was fetched as sustenance, as provisions,
to them every Samain night.

Semul son of joyful Iardan;
. . . Fergus, a proud onset;
Érglan son of boastful Beoán:
the three heroes of their hosts.

The army of Ireland, with its company,
went—it was a stride of strength—
a war-band drenched in blood

westward to sack Conann's Tower.

Conann's Tower, with abundance of slaughter,
a crime which combined a hundred ravagings,
a fortress of revelry, of skill,
of the wrath of the Fomoiri of the sea.

The men of Ireland, after the sack,
with [their] great bravery in marching forward:
there did not escape, clamour of battle,
any except thirty of Nemed's descendants.

The warriors with sorrowful, mighty valour,
were not at peace in their inheritance;
of the thirty splendid champions
each chieftain went his own way.

Into the land of the Greeks, the remnants of the massacre,
went Sémión—it was a journey skilfully accomplished—
with distinction, [prevailing] over a splendid region,
Fergus went into Maind Conáin.

Britán Mael was the prince's son,
noble was [his] posterity, [ruling] over armies;
son of the Red-side [*Lethderg*] from Lecmag,
from whom are the Britons of the world.

Bethach, tidings of fame [?] in accordance with dignity,
died in Ireland, in safety [?];
his ten wives survived him
by twenty-three years.

Good was Sémión, who fathered hundreds:
[his progeny] was as numerous as a legion among the Greeks.
They were not accepted by the champions,
but were enslaved by the Greeks.

This was the task of the lords:
dragging bags—it was not illustrious—
of soil onto a stony craggy mountain
so that it was a plain with flowers and herds.

They set out, with no treacherous alliance,
upon the dark furious sea,
fleeing their harsh, public [?] slavery
with ships and with bags.

These were the proud names

of the lean, meagre kings, with fame:
Gann, Genann—with abundance of fair portions—
Rudraige, Sengann, Sláine.

Sémión's race, spear-division of a host,
by force and bright desire, radiance of violent deeds:
the Gaileóin, men of scant inheritances,
Fir Bolg and Fir Domnann.

Their wholeness and their division endure:
they divided Ireland into five, without diminution,
without mishap to their slender-sided dwelling,
from delightful Uisnech.

Let us worship Christ—it is fitting—
who overwhelmed the mighty beneath a flood;
His is the world with its inhabitants,
His is every land, His is Ireland.

¶54. The sacking of Conann's Tower, with valour,
upon Conann son of Febor:
the men of Ireland went thither
with three noble leaders.

Érglan son of Beoán son of Starn,
Semul son of harsh Iardan;
in front of the fleet went the warrior of the battlefields:
Nemed's son, Fergus Lethderg.

Three score thousand, a glorious undertaking,
by land and by sea:
that is the number of Nemed's race
who went from their homes to the sack.

Torinis, island of the tower,
stronghold of Conann son of Febor:
Conann son of Febor fell
at the hand of Fergus, who waged battle.

Morc son of Dela came there
to help Conann.
Conann had already fallen:
it was the cause of great sorrow to Morc.

Morc son of Dela came
across the sea with three score ships;
he overtook the race of Nemed
with overwhelming force, before they could return to the land.

All the men of Ireland were in the battle
after the coming of the Fomoiri:
the sea drowned them all
except for three score men.

Érglan, Matach, splendid Iartacht,
the three sons of Beoán son of star-white Starn;
Bethach, Britán, after the battle,
renowned Baath and Ebath.

Bechad, Betach, Bronal, Pal,
Gorthigern, German, Glasan,
Ceram, Gobran, pure Gothiam,
Gam, Dam, Ding and Deal.

Sémión, Fortecht, bright Gosten,
Griman, clever Gulliuc,
Taman, Turruc, and Glas,
Feb and curly-haired Foran.

There were three score men in the harmonious voyage
who departed from Ireland then;
they divided their portion in three
after the sack of Conann's Tower in the west.

The third of victorious Bethach [sonorous renown]
was from Torinis to the Boyne;
he died in Inis Fáil
two years after Britán.

The third of Sémión son of splendid Érglan
[extended] to Belach Con Glais, with horror;
Britán's third (Flann's grandson said it)
thence to Conann's Tower.

The race of Israel set forth
from Egypt at that time;
and the race of Gáedel Glas
[came] in exile to Scythia.

Fair Christ, with beauty of aspect,
King of the paternoster, of the haven of Paradise:
our refuge is in your glorious heaven;
may you choose me, King of the earth!

¶ 55. As for the Fir Bolg, they brought five leaders with them, *ut diximus*: Gann and Genann, Rudraige and Sengann and Sláne. They were the five sons of

Dela. Their five wives after that: Anust, Liber, Cnucha, Fuat, Etar; *unde dicitur*:

¶ 56.   Fuat wife of Sláne, you are not in error;
Etar wife of Gann, with valour;
Anust wife of Sengann of the spears;
Cnucha was the wife of pure Genann.

Liber, wife of Rudraige of the [spear-]cast—
a fragrant company, it is not cramped [?].
Rudraige, overlord of the feats:
I think it likelier that his wife was Fuat.

¶ 57. These men, then, were the offspring of Dela, i.e. the Fir Bolg. The five kings of the Fir Bolg were Dela's five sons: Gann, Genann, Rudraige, Sengann, Sláne. Sláne was the eldest, son of Dela son of Loth son of Oirthet son of Tribuat son of Gothorb son of Goiscen son of Fortech son of Sémión son of Érglan son of Beoán son of Starn son of Nemed son of Agnoman.

¶ 58. Nine of their kings took Ireland. Sláne ruled for one year: he died in Duma Sláne, the first of the Fir Bolg to die in Ireland. Rudraige ruled for two years until he died in the *Brug* ['Dwelling place'] of red cloaks. Gann and Genann ruled for four years until they died of plague in Frémainn. Sengann ruled for five years until he died at the hand of Fiachu Cendfhinnán, son of Starn son of Rudraige son of Dela. Fiachu ruled for five years—all the cows of Ireland were white-headed [*cendfhinna*] in his time—until he fell at the hand of Rinnal son of Genann son of Dela. Rinnal ruled for six years until he fell at the hand of Odbgen son of Sengann son of Dela in Eba Coirpri. Odbgen ruled for four years until he fell in Mag Muirthemne at the hand of Eochu son of Erc son of Rinnal son of Genann son of Dela.

¶ 59. Eochu son of Erc ruled for ten years. There was no rain, but only dew during that time; there was no year without mast. Spears were banished from Ireland in his time. It is by him that law was first enacted in Ireland. Eochu son of Erc fell at the hand of the three sons of Nemed son of Badruí. He is the first king who was slain with a spear in Ireland; *unde* Colum Cille *cecinit*:

¶ 60.   Answer my questions, lad,
and tell me tales:
it is long since every evil was spread abroad
after the body of Eochu son of Erc was pierced.

Eochu son of Erc: such was his virtue
that he was better than any king except holy Christ.
He is the first king who was wounded
with a spear in white Inis Fáil.

The three sons of the warrior Nemed killed [him]:

the youths were reckoned to be Nemed's children.
They thrust woeful spear-shafts through him,
so that they trampled Odba underfoot [?].

There was no peace nor ease in it—
a frenzy of grief was on the multitude—
from peaceful noble Eochu
until the time of great Míl's sons.

Great was the fleet at the hour or terce
(the death of Erc's son was the reason it was not difficult):
men in bags, great their might,
divided Art's pure noble island.

The plain of Ireland: Sláne's portion
was southward from Níth Némannach
to the Meeting, a cunning tale [?],
of the Three Waters, the three cataracts.

Gann, without violence or weakness,
ruled as far as Belach Con Glais.
Sengann ruled from Belach in Chon:
his border extended to Luimnech.

Genann, mindful of secrets, secured
[the land] from Luimnech to Ess Ruaid;
the arm of splendid Rudraige extended
from there to enduring Tráig Baile.

Harsh is the company which afflicted them:
the Tuatha Dé Donann from afar.
They landed, a splendid savage troop,
on stern Sliab Conmaicne Réin.

They slew the enduring Fir Bolg;
from that there were grave-mounds of nobles
[reared] there—it was a rush like fury—
by tall Nuadu Argatlám.

Eithliu's warlike son chastened them;
ample Lug was an honourable, handsome man.
He had the victory—he was a bloody wolf
in the battle of Mag Tuired in the west.

The chieftains came to Ireland,
the sons of noble Míl,
into a warm, abundant land
which had been seen from the Tower of boastful Bregon.

The first man of the lineage of sweet-voiced Bregon
who died in great Ireland:
Donn son of Míl (leaving Ír aside),
after whom is named populous Tech Duinn.

The first man who was buried, without a grey spear-point,
in Ireland (his attempt was seemly):
Ladru, of rough meagre vigour,
from whom is Ard Ladrann in the south.

The first man drowned, insofar as it was attained [?],
of the race of Míl's sons, a multitude of ships:
Íth son of Bregon, it was a great deed;
the wave seized him upon the shore.

The first woman who went into the cold earth
of the company from the Tower of fair Bregon:
Tea of Brega, wife of the king,
from whom is named 'true Tara of Fál'.

The daughter of Magmór, it is not a deceitful assembly,
the wife of Eochu son of Dui Garb:
Tailtiu, bosom of a splendid assembly,
foster mother of Lug son of Scál Balb.

There is done in enduring Bréfne
a deed which will cause much sorrow—
the oak-land is sorrowful once more—
the killing of the pilgrim from Rome.

Nertach son of Domnall wreaks
the holy one's destruction—may his house-post be crooked!
There will not be in Ireland, without blame,
woman nor farm nor fire nor smoke.

¶ 61. Those are the kings of the Fir Bolg and their deaths. *Unde poeta cecinit*:

The Fir Bolg were here for a while,
in the great island of the sons of Míl.
They brought five leaders hither with them:
I know their names.

A year to Sláne, this is true,
until he died in his fair Duma:
he was the first of the Fir Bolg of the peaks
who died in the island of Ireland.

Red Rudraige two years

until he died in the *Brug* ['Dwelling place'] of red cloaks;
Gann and Genann four
until plague slew them in Frémainn.

Five years to Sengann, it was pleasant,
until Fiachu son of Starn slew him;
for five more, with conflict,
Fiachu Cendfhinnán was king.

Fiachu Cendfhinnán before everyone;
his name will endure until Doom.
All the cows of Ireland, without reproach,
were white-headed [*cendfhinna*] in his time.

Until he fell at the hand of red Rinnal,
he got six [years] as a noble reign;
therefore Dela's grandson fell
by Odbgen's hand in Eba.

Four to splendid Odbgen
until the battle of Muirthemne of the princes:
Odbgen fell, without reproach,
at the hand of Erc's son, lofty Eochu.

Ten years to Eochu son of Erc—
he did not obtain a feeble border—
until the three sons of Nemed son of Badruí
slew him upon the battlefield.

Until Rinnal flourished they did not have
a point upon a weapon in Ireland,
upon harsh spears, without fair concealment—
they were like stalks of grain.

The fair Tuath Dé Donann brought
spears with them in their hands:
it is with those that Eochu was killed
by the offspring of strong-judging Nemed.

The names of the three sons of Nemed:
Cessarb, Luam, and Luachra.
It is they who slew the first man—
Eochu son of Erc—with a spear-point in Ireland.

Thereafter the Tuath Dé fought
against the Fir Bolg, it was a brutal deed;
they took away their wealth
and their lordship from the Fir [Bolg].

¶ 62. Fintan *cecinit* concerning the division of the provinces:

> The five divisions of Ireland,
> both sea and land;
> I see the fair candles
> of every province.

> From swift fierce Drobaís
> is the first noble division,
> as far as the white wide Boyne
> south of fair Bairche.

> From the fair foaming melodious Boyne,
> with hundreds of companies,
> to the populous [?] Meeting
> of the Three cold Waters.

> From that same Meeting,
> with winding course [?],
> to the Pass of the fierce Hound
> which is called Grey [=*Belach Con Glais*]. . . .

> . . .From Luimnech great in ships,
> broad its expanse,
> to Drobaís pure with the arms of hosts,
> against which the sea breaks.

> Wise is the division
> [whereby?] roads are travelled;
> complete is the arrangement
> . . . . into five.

> The points of those provinces
> converge [?] on Uisnech;
> each of them goes from its own art
> to the stone, so that there are five.

¶ 63. All the Gaileóin and Fir Domnann, then, are descendants of Sémión. Thirty years after Genann and Rudraige the Tuatha Dé Donann came to Ireland.

¶ 64. The descendants of Bethach son of Iarbonél Fáith son of Nemed were in the northern islands of the world, learning magic and knowledge and sorcery and cunning, until they were pre-eminent in the arts of the heathen sages. They are the Tuatha Dé Donann who came to Ireland.

¶ 65. It is thus that they came: in dark clouds. They landed upon the mountains of Conmaicne Réin in Connacht. They put a darkness upon the sun for three days and nights. Battle or kingship they demanded of the Fir Bolg. A battle was fought between them, the first battle of Mag Tuired, in which a hundred thousand of the Fir Bolg fell. After that they took the kingship of Ireland.

¶ 66. It is the Tuatha Dé Donann who brought with them the Great Fál which was in Tara, namely, the stone of knowledge after which Ireland is called Mag Fáil. The one beneath whom it shrieked used to be king of Ireland, until Cú Chulainn split it; for it did not shriek beneath him or his foster son, Lugaid son of the Three White Ones of Emain. And the stone did not shriek from that time onwards, except under Conn only. Its heart sprang out of it, from Tara to Tailtiu, so that that is 'the heart of Fál'. As it happens, it is not that which caused the idols to break without Lugaid taking kingship, but Christ being born at that time.

¶ 67. Nuadu Argatlám, then, was king of the Tuath Dé Donann for seven years before coming to Ireland, until his arm was cut off in the first battle of Mag Tuired. Edleo son of Alldoí was the first of the Tuath Dé Donann to be killed in Ireland, at the hand of Nerchon descendant of Sémión. In the first battle of Mag Tuired there fell Ernmas and Échtach and Etargal and Fiachra.

¶ 68. Bres son of Elatha took the kingship of Ireland after that, until Nuadu's arm was healed at the end of seven years; then Nuadu Argatlám ruled for twenty years. Dian Cécht the physician, helped by Creidne the artisan, put a silver arm on him, with the full vigour of an arm in every finger and in every joint.

¶ 69. Tailtiu, daughter of Magmór king of Spain, was the queen of the Fir Bolg. After the slaughter of the Fir Bolg in the first battle of Mag Tuired she came to Caill Cuan, and the wood was felled by her so that before the end of the year it was a plain flowering with clover. This Tailtiu was the wife of Eochu son of Erc, who was king of Ireland until the Tuatha Dé Donann killed him. Eochu son of Erc fetched her from Spain, from her father Magmór Mall the king of Spain. As for Tailtiu, she dwelt in Tailtiu, and slept with Eochu Garb son of Dui Dall of the Tuatha Dé Donann; and Cian son of Dian Cécht (Scál Balb was his other name) gave her his son Lug in fosterage. Eithne daughter of Balar Balcbéimnech was [Lug's] mother. After that Tailtiu died in Tailtiu, so that it was named after her; and her grave is to the north-east of the assembly-platform of Tailtiu. Her funeral games were held by Lug every year, a fortnight before Lugnasad and a fortnight after Lugnasad. *Lugnasad*, that is, the assembly [*násad*] of Lug son of Eithne, is the name of the games.

¶ 70. Nuadu Argatlám fell in the second battle of Mag Tuired, together with Macha daughter of Ernmas, at the hand of Balar Balcbéimnech. In that battle Ogma son of Elatha son of Nét fell at the hand of Indech son of Dé Domnann king of the Fomoiri. Bruidne and Casmael fell at the hand of

Ochtriallach son of Indech. After the death of Nuadu and these others in that battle, the Tuatha Dé Donann gave the kingship to Lug; and he killed his grandfather, that is Balar, with a stone from his sling. Many were killed in that battle, and Bres was among them. As Indech son of Dé Domnann, the king, said—and he was a man with arts and skills—when Lug asked him how many had fallen in the battle of Mag Tuired: 'Seven men, seven twenties, seven hundreds, seven fifties; fifty, nine hundred, twenty hundred, a hundred and forty, ninety including Nét's grandson' (i.e., including Ogma son of Elatha son of Néit). Then Lug son of Eithne held the kingship of Ireland for forty years after the second battle of Mag Tuired. (There were twenty-seven years between the two battles of Mag Tuired.)

¶ 71. Eochu Ollathair, i.e. the Dagda Mór, son of Elatha, held the kingship of Ireland for eighty years. It is over him that the men of Ireland raised Síd in Broga. His three sons were Oengus and Áed and Cermait Cáem. Dian Cécht had three sons, i.e. Cú and Cethen and Cian—and Miach was the fourth son, although many do not include him—and his daughter Etan the woman poet, and Airmed the woman physician his other daughter, and Cairpre son of Etan the poet. Crichinbél and Bruidne and Casmael the three satirists. Bé Chuille and Dinann the two witches. Cermait son of the Dagda had three sons: Mac Cuill, Mac Cécht, Mac Gréne. Sethor and Tethor and Cethor were their names. Fótla and Banba and Ériu were their three wives. Fea and Nemain were the two wives of Néit, a quo Ailech Néit. Badb and Macha and Anann (from whom are the Cíche Anann in Luachair), the three daughters of Ernmas the witch. Goibniu the smith and Luichne the carpenter and Creidne the artisan and Dian Cécht the physician.

It is to commemorate them that the poet, i.e. Eochaid, recited the poem which follows:

¶ 72. Armies stretched across the ancient plain
of Ireland, with pride and spears.
They were raiders westward as far as the sunset,
its ravaging troops around Tara.

Thirty years after Genann
troops of splendid [?] phantoms overcame
the Tuath Bolg, boasts of fury—
the visitation of the Tuath Dé Donann.

[Their] numbers were sufficient, whatever impelled them;
they alit, with horror, in warlike manner,
in their cloud, evil wars of spectres,
upon the mountains of Conmaicne in Connacht.

Without. . . to skilful Ireland,
without ships, a savage journey;

the truth concerning them was not known beneath the starry heaven—
whether they were of heaven or earth.

If from the demons, it is devils
that composed the troop of. . . famous exiles,
a blaze [?] [drawn up] in ranks and hosts;
if from men, they were Bethach's offspring.

They belong properly among mortals;
the noble enduring origin of the vigorous race
was swift Bethach, an island of war-bands [?],
son of Iarbonél son of Nemed.

They did not spare assembly or privilege
throughout the expanse of Ireland westward;
there were flame and conflict
at last in Mag Tuired.

The Tuatha Dé, an assault of strength,
contended [?] for kingship with the Tuath Bolg;
in their host, with great pride,
a company of a hundred thousand perished.

The sons of Elatha, splendour of weapons,
divisions of wolves against a troop of men [?]:
Bres from the wise-rimmed [?] Bruig of Ireland,
the Dagda, Delbaeth, and Ogma.

Ériu, whatever haven [?] she may reach,
Banba, Fótla, and Fea,
Nemain of the . . . ,
Donann mother of the gods.

Badb and Macha, great wealth;
the Morrígan, foundation of sorcery:
the guides of savage battle,
the splendid daughters of Ernmas.

Goibniu, who was no fool at the smelting,
Luichne the carpenter, Creidne the wright,
Dian Cécht who journeyed the roads [?],
Mac ind Óc, Lug son of Eithne.

Crichinbél, famous Bruidne,
Bé Chuille, fair Dinann,
Casmael, with accurate verse,
Cairpre son of Etan, and Etan.

The Dagda's grandsons, who made the threefold partition,
divided in three Ireland of the drinking horns;
noble dutiful princes, let us heed [it],
the three sons of Cermait of Cualu.

Although Ireland contains [?] many thousands,
they divided their land into three,
the great lords of haughty deeds,
Mac Cécht, Mac Cuill, Mac Gréne.

It is clear that the one who wiped them from their land,
from the royal plain, was the Son of God; I proclaim [it].
Despite the valour of their deeds in their bright division
their race does not remain in Ireland.

It is Eochaid, without fury of enchantments [?],
who arranges their fair divisions;
apart from knowledge of the companies we declare,
though we enumerate them, we do not worship them.

Adore the name of the King who apportioned you,
the distributor of every truth which we relate.
He has arranged every season for which we hope,
He has shaped the beautiful land of Ireland.

¶ 73. After the Dagda, Delbaeth held the kingship of Ireland for ten years until he and his son, namely Ollam, fell at the hand of Caicher son of Náma, the brother of Nechtan. Fiachna son of Delbaeth held the kingship of Ireland after his father for ten more years, until he and the six sons of Ollam fell at the hand of Éogan of Inber Mór. The grandsons of the Dagda, i.e. Mac Cuill, Mac Cécht, and Mac Gréne, held the kingship of Ireland for twenty-nine years. They divided Ireland into three parts between them, and left no sons whatever. It is to them that the Gaels came [when they came] to Ireland, so that they fell at the hand of the sons of Míl Espáine in revenge for Íth and Cuailnge and Fuat, three sons of Bregon. To commemorate them the historian, i.e. Tanaide, recited this poem:

¶ 74. The Tuatha Dé Donann, under concealment,
men who did not observe the faith,
young hounds of the territory which does not decay,
men of the flesh and blood of Adam.

The nobles of the mighty tribe yonder,
the troop of the withered hill [?]:
let us, in the season in which we live,
relate their times and their kingship.

Noble slender Nuadu ruled for seven years
over the fair-haired wolf-pack;
[that was] the eager fair-headed man's reign
before coming into Ireland.

In grievous Mag Tuired, without predestined death,
the yoke of battle fell;
his kingly arm was severed
from the bright champion of the world.

Bres ruled seven years, no bright interval,
because of the beauty of the lord of poems;
he held the kingship of the plain of tender nuts
until the arm of Nuadu was healed.

Thereafter Nuadu, for twenty years,
passed judgement on [the] host,
until Lug the spear-fighter was made king,
the Many-skilled One, without respite.

For forty years Lug—it was laid bare—
was king over the territory of Ireland.
He did not reach the heavenly . . . . :
eighty years to the Dagda.

Ten years to ardent Delbaeth—
until there comes a fore-wind of torment [?]—
[ruling] faultlessly over the land of savage spears;
ten more [years] to Fiachna.

For twenty-nine years, let us consider them,
over every wooded mound [?] in Ireland,
the grandsons of the swift slender Dagda
ruled over great radiant Ireland.

Then came the sons of Míl,
they came to shed their blood:
the offspring of the wild great warrior, it was boasted,
from Spain, without respite.

And so the active Gaels assailed them
with an army, through cunning;
it is not from boasting, not from folly,
that the Tuath's traces are few.

¶ 75. Nuadu Argatlám son of Échtach son of Etarlam son of Ordam son of
Alldui son of Tait son of Tabarn son of Éna son of Baath son of Ebath son
of Bethach son of Iarbonél son of Nemed son of Agnoman son of Paimp

son of Tait son of Sera son of Srú son of Esrú son of Braimind son of Faithecht son of Magog son of Japhet son of Noah.

¶ 76. Néit son of Induí son of Allduí son of Tait.

¶ 77. Midir of Brí Léith son of Induí son of Échtach son of Etarlam.

¶ 78. Dagda and Ogma and Elloth and Bres and Delbaeth, the five sons of Elatha son of Delbaeth son of Néit son of Induí son of Allduí son of Tait son of Tabarn.

¶ 79. Lug son of Cian son of Dian Cécht son of Erarc son of Néit son of Induí son of Allduí.

¶ 80. Fiachu [leg. Fiachna] son of Delbaeth son of Ogma son of Elatha son of Delbaeth son of Néit.

¶ 81. Aí son of Ollam son of Delbaeth son of Ogma son of Elatha son of Delbaeth son of Néit.

¶ 82. Caicher and Nechtan, the two sons of Náma son of Echu Garb son of Dui Temen son of Bres son of Elatha son of Delbaeth son of Néit.

¶ 83. Siugmall son of Cairpre Cromm son of Elcmar son of Delbaeth son of Ogma son of Elatha son of Delbaeth son of Néit.

¶ 84. Oengus in Mac Óc and Áed Cáem and Cermait Milbél: those are the Dagda's three sons.

¶ 85. Cairpre Fili son of Tuara son of Tuirill son of Catt Conatchend son of Ordam son of Allduí son of Tait.

¶ 86. Gaíla son of Oirbsen son of Elloth son of Elatha son of Delbaeth son of Néit.

¶ 87. Oirbsen *proprium nomen* of Manannán, *unde dicitur Stagnum Orbsen apud occasum. Quoniam quando Manannanus sepultus est, stagnum venit per terram per tumulum eius.*

¶ 88. The six sons of Delbaeth son of Ogma son of Elatha son of Delbaeth son of Néit: Fiachna, Ollam, Innuí, Brian, Iuchorba, Iuchair. Donann, daughter of that same Delbaeth, was the mother of the last three of them, i.e. of Brian and Iuchair and Iuchorba. They were the three gods of skill [*trí dee dána*] after whom Sliab na Trí nDé is named; and it is that Delbaeth who is named Tuirill Bicreo.

¶ 89. Tuirill son of Catt, however, was the grandfather of Cairpre Fili; and Etan daughter of Dian Cécht was Tuirill's mother.

¶ 90. As for the three sons of Cermait: Mac Cuill, i.e. Sethor, the hazel [*coll*] was his god. Mac Cécht, i.e. Tethor, the plough [*cécht*] was his god. Mac Gréne, i.e. Cethor, the sun [*grian*] was his god. Fótla was the wife of Mac Cécht, Banba the wife of Mac Cuill, Ériu the wife of Mac Gréne; they were three daughters of Fiachna son of Delbaeth.

¶ 91. Ernmas daughter of Etarlam son of Nuadu Argatlám was the mother of those three women, and the mother of Fiachna and Ollam. Ernmas had three more daughters: Badb and Macha and Morrígu (whose name was Anann). Her three sons were Glonn and Gním and Coscar.

¶ 92. Boind daughter of Delbaeth son of Elatha.

¶ 93. Fea and Nemain, the two wives of Néit son of Induí, were the two daughters of Elcmar of the Bruig.

¶ 94. Uillenn son of Cathaír son of Nuadu Argatlám.

¶ 95. Bodb of Síd ar Fhemun son of Echu Garb son of Dui Temen son of Bres son of Elatha son of Delbaeth son of Néit.

¶ 96. Abcán son of Bec Felmas son of Cú son of Dian Cécht, Lug's poet.

¶ 97. Én son of Bec Én son of Satharn son of Edleo son of Allduí son of Tait son of Tabarn. It is at Tait son of Tabarn that the testimonies concerning the Tuath Dé Donann converge.

¶ 98. So that it is concerning their deaths that Flann Mainistrech recited this poem:

> Listen, scholars without flaw,
> if it please you, so that I may relate
> the deaths (with cunning yonder),
> the testimonies of the Tuath Dé Donann.

> Edleo son of Allduí of the cliffs
> was the first of the Tuath Dé Donann
> who fell in virgin Ireland
> at the hand of Nerchon descendant of Sémión.

> Ernmas, whose courage was lofty,
> Fiachra, Échtach, Etargal,
> Tuirill Bicreo of the region of Brega
> fell in the first battle of Mag Tuired.

> Alloith was slain in strife,
> the great rough father of Manannán,
> and fair generous Donann,
> by Dé Domnann of the Fomoiri.

> Cethen and Cú perished
> of horror in Aircheltra.
> Brian, Iuchorba, and Iuchair
> slew Cian far from his house.

> Great Cairpre son of Etan
> died from a stroke of the pure sun.

Etan died above the pool
of sorrow for fair-haired Cairpre.

In Mag Tuired, in battle,
there fell Nuadu Argatlám
and Macha, after that Samain,
at the hand of Balar Balcbémnech.

Although he was not feeble, Ogma fell
at the hand of Indech son of Dé Domnann.
Casmael and noble Bruidne fell
at the hand of Ochtriallach son of Indech.

Dian Cécht and Goibniu the smith
died of sudden plague [?].
Luichne the carpenter died
from a potent fiery arrow.

Creidne the skilful craftsman was drowned
on the tumultuous sea
bringing gold ore
to Ireland from Spain.

Bres perished in Carn Uí Néit
because of Lug's trickery, without falsehood;
it was a matter for dispute,
drinking bog-water disguised as milk.

Bé Chuille and fair Dinann,
the two witches, died
at last one evening by magic,
from brown aerial demons.

There fell on the eastern shore,
on the slope of Ráith Ailig,
great Induí son of fair Delbaeth
at the hand of Gann son of white-fisted Dána.

Fea, whose fame was enduring, died
a month after he was killed,
at the same fort—we remember it—
from grief for fair-haired Induí.

Boind died from her arrogance [?]
at the well of the son of noble Náma.
Áine daughter of the Dagda died
because of the love which she gave to Ireland.

Cairpre fell—remember it!—
at the hand of Nechtan son of Náma.
Nechtan was killed by poison
by Siugmall grandson of noble Midir.

Abcán son of cold Bec Felmas,
poet of Lug, with full ability,
fell at the hand of Oengus, without blame,
for satirising Midir of noble deeds.

Midir, son of the other Induí,
fell at the hand of Elcmar.
Elcmar of the battle fell
at the hand of flawless Oengus.

Brian, Iuchorba, and Iuchair,
the three gods of the Tuatha Dé Donann,
died on Man, above the Irish Sea,
at the hand of Lug son of Eithliu.

Noble Cermait Milbél fell
at the hand of fierce Lug son of Eithliu
because of jealousy concerning his wife, a great matter,
when the druid seduced her on his behalf.

At the hand of Mac Cécht, without fault,
fell Én the harper.
Lug fell above the wave
at the hand of Mac Cuill son of Cermait.

Áed son of the Dagda fell
at the hand of fair valiant Corcenn,
without falsehood—it was a sure justification—
after he eloped with his wife.

Corcenn from Cruach,
the fierce swift warrior, died
from the rock which he erected on the shore
over the grave of noble Áed.

Crooked perverse Crichinbél,
the chief satirist of the Tuath Dé Donann, died
from the gold which was found in the wild [Banna],
at the hand of the Dagda, grandson of Delbaeth.

As the son of the ruddy-visaged Dagda
was coming from chilly Alba,
here in the estuary of the Boyne—

it is there that Oengus was drowned.

The only son of spirited Manannán,
the first love of the sad-faced maiden,
the tender youth fell in the plain
at the hand of wild Bennán from Bregmag.

Néit son of Induí and his two wives,
Badb and Nemain, without falsehood,
were killed in Ailech, without fault,
by Neptúir Derg of the Fomoiri.

Foolish Fuamnach, who was Midir's wife,
Siugmall and Brí, with injuries,
were burned by Manannán
in Brí Léith, it was a great deed.

Alloith's son fell fighting,
the wealthy diadem Manannán,
in the battle in harsh Cuillenn
at the hand of red-browed Uillenn.

Uillenn fell, with pride,
at the hand of Mac Gréne with pure virtue.
The wife of the brown-haired Dagda died
of plague on the slope in Liathdruim.

The Dagda died from a haemorrhage
in the Bruig, it is no lie,
from a wound given him by the woman Cethnenn
in the great battle of Mag Tuired.

Delbaeth and his son fell
at the hand of Caicher, noble son of Náma.
Caicher fell beside the turbulent Boyne
at the hand of Fiachna son of Delbaeth.

Fiachna and splendid Aí fell
at the hand of flawless Éogan Inbir.
Éogan of the cold Estuary [Inber] fell
at the hand of Cermait, fair of form.

Ériu and Fótla, with pride,
Mac Gréne and Banba, with virtue,
Mac Cuill, Mac Cécht with purity,
[fell] in the battle of Tara of pure soil.

Mac Cécht by splendid Éremón,

Mac Cuill by flawless Éber,
Ériu by Suirge after that,
Mac Gréne by Amairgen.

Fótla by Etan, with pride,
Banba by Caicher, with virtue;
wherever they sleep, those
are the deaths of the champions—listen!

Those are the tidings of the Tuath Dé Donann.

¶ 99. As for the Gaels, we have brought their adventures from Japhet son of Noah and from Nimrod's Tower down to this point: how they came from Egypt and from Scythia to the Maeotic Marshes, and along the Mediterranean to Crete and Sicily; and we have related how they conquered Spain, and we left them in Spain at Bregon's Tower. Now we will speak of them in detail.

¶ 100. It was Íth son of Bregon who first saw Ireland, on a winter evening, from the top of Bregon's Tower. For a man's vision is best on a clear winter evening. Íth came to Ireland with a hundred and fifty warriors, and they landed at Bréntrácht in Irrus Corco Duibne when they arrived. There was, however, an assembly of the men of Ireland at Ailech Néit, following the killing of Néit son of Induí Ailig by the Fomoiri. The three kings were dividing the cattle and treasures of Ailech.

¶ 101. Then Íth son of Bregon came from Corcu Duibne into Ciarraige Luachra and Luachair Dedad, into Machaire na Muman, into Mag Cliach, from there northward into Éle, into the territory of the Fir Chell, across the Mide, into the region of the Luigni, across Sliab nGuaire, across the woods of Fernmag, into the expanse of the plain of Fernmag, across the height of Sliab Bethach, into Sliab Toad, into the bog of Sírlam's land, into the region of Modorn, into Mag nÍtha, across the end of Loch Febail, into the territory of Néit, to Ailech Néit.

¶ 102. It is there that the three kings were: Mac Cuill, Mac Cécht, and Mac Gréne. They welcomed him, that is, Íth son of Bregon. Íth surpassed the judges of Ireland in cleverness and pleading, and he righted every complaint and contention that there was among them, and he said: 'Enact rightful law, for you dwell in a good land. Abundant are its mast and honey and wheat and fish. Balanced are its heat and cold.' Then they plotted to kill Íth, and they banished him from Ireland; and he departed from them in Ailech and came into Mag nÍtha. Emissaries followed him, and slew him there in Mag nÍtha, *unde* Mag nÍtha ['Plain of Íth'] *nominatur*. And so it was to avenge Íth that the sons of Míl (that is, the Gaels) came; for Íth's corpse had been fetched to Spain.

¶ 103. The learned say that thirty-six lords and noblemen of the Gaels came, and each of them had a ship (that is, thirty ships [*sic*]); and that they had twenty-four slaves, and each of them had a ship; and that there were twenty-four slaves with each of those slaves in each of those ships besides that.

¶ 104. These are the thirty-six chieftains who came to Ireland, as Fintan son of Bóchra wrote, who was born seven years before the Flood and [lived] until the seventh year of the reign of Diarmait son of Cerball; that was his age when he was at the knee of Finnén of Mag Bile and Colum Cille. And it is thus that Tuán son of Cairell wrote, in the presence of the men of Ireland and of Finnén of Mag Bile; and thus that his pupils related it, i.e. Laidcend son of Bairchid, and Colmán son of Comgellán, and Cenn Fáelad son of Ailill, and Senchán son of Colmán, and Cú Alad from Cruachna, and Bran of Bairenn, &c.

¶ 105. Those are the pupils of Finnén and Tuán; and what they have related is that the Gaels came to Ireland with these thirty-six leaders: The ten sons of Bregon, and Íth was the tenth: Brego, Bile, Blad, Cualu, Cuailnge, Fuat, Muir-themen, Ebléo, Nár, Íth. Bile's one son: Míl Espáine. The seven sons of Míl: Donn, Colptha, Amairgen, Éber, Ír, Éremón, Érech Febria—and Érennán, the youngest of the children. The three sons of Éremón: Muimne, Luigne, Laigne. The four sons of Éber Find: Ér, Orba, Ferón, Fergna. The ten battle-warriors, moreover: Caicher, Fulmán, Mantán, Setga, Suirge, Sobairche, Én son of Occe, Ún son of Ucce, Etan, Gosten. Twenty-four slaves: Aidne, Aí, Asal, Mede, Morba, Mide, Cuib, Cliu, Cera, Ser, Slán, Life, Line, Ligen, Traig, Dul, Adal, Aire, Dése, Dela, Fea, Femen, Fera.

¶ 106. And Lugaid son of Íth came, the harsh violent mighty warrior with the strength of a hundred, to avenge his father together with the rest. Míl's eighth son, that is, the youngest, Érennán, climbed the mast to look upon Ireland, and fell from the mast into the sea. His grave is in Inber Scéne, and the grave of Amairgen's wife Scéne is on the other side [of the estuary]. She died when they were at sea, so that Amairgen said: 'The port where we land will be named Scéne.'

¶ 107. The sons of Míl had a rowing competition as they approached Ireland, [starting] from the place where they had sighted it. Ír son of Míl drew a *muirchrech* [?'sea charge'] ahead of the other ships. Then Éber Donn son of Míl, the eldest of the children, was jealous, so that he said, 'Not good is the omen, that Ír leaps past Íth' (that is, past Lugaid son of Íth). Then the oar which was in Ír's hand broke, so that he fell over backward; and he died the following night, and his body was taken to Sceillec, west of Irrus Deiscirt Chorco Duibne. Éber Find and Éremón and Amairgen were grieved at the death of their brother, and they said that it would be fitting if Éber Donn did not enjoy the land concerning which he had envied his brother, i.e. Ír. Next day Scéne and Érennán were buried at Inber Scéne; and they were both buried, and their two mounds and their two graves are side by side there still.

¶ 108. As he set his right foot upon Ireland, Amairgen Glúngel son of Míl recited this poem:

> I am a wind in the sea (for depth).
> I am a sea-wave upon the land (for heaviness).
> I am the sound of the sea (for fearsomeness).
> I am a stag of seven combats (for strength).
> I am a hawk on a cliff (for agility).
> I am a tear-drop of the sun (for purity).
> I am fair (i.e. there is no plant fairer than I).
> I am a boar for valour (for harshness).
> I am a salmon in a pool (for swiftness).
> I am a lake in a plain (for size).
> I am the excellence of arts (for beauty).
> I am a spear that wages
> battle with plunder.
> I am a god who forms
> subjects for a ruler.
> Who explains
> the stones of the mountain?
> Who invokes
> the ages of the moon?
> Where lies
> the setting of the sun?
> Who bears cattle
> from the house of Tethra?
> Who are the cattle
> of Tethra who laugh?
> What man, what god
> forms weapons?
> Indeed, then;
> I invoked a satirist. . .
> a satirist of wind.

¶ 109. *Item* Amairgen *cecinit*:

> Sea full of fish,
> an awesome land,
> bursting forth of fish,
> full of fish there under wave,
> with flights of birds,
> broad [sea] of beasts,
> . . . . ,
> bursting forth of fish,
> sea full of fish.

¶ 110. Three days and three nights after that the sons of Míl defeated the demons, i.e. the Tuath Dé Donann, in the battle of Sliab Mis. It is there that Fás the wife of Ún son of Ucce fell, after whom is named Fert Fáise between Sliab Mis and the sea. Sliab Mis, that is, the worst mountain [*sliab as messu*] that they found after coming to Ireland; for it is there that they fought their first battle in Ireland.

¶ 111. Lugaid son of Íth washed himself in Loch Luigdech. Lugaid's wife Fial, however, washed herself in the river, which flows from the lake. Her husband went to her naked, so that she saw his private parts and died of shame. *Unde* Loch Luigdech and Fial and Inber Féile *nominantur.*

¶ 112. The sons of Míl and Banba conversed on Sliab Mis. She said to them: 'May your journey not be lucky, if you have come to conquer Ireland.' 'Indeed,' said Amairgen Glúngel the poet, 'that is why we have come.' 'I have a request of you,' said she. 'What request?' they said. 'That my name be upon this island,' said she. 'It will be this island's name,' said Amairgen.

¶ 113. They spoke with Fótla in Ébliu. She said the same to them, and asked that her name be upon the island. Amairgen said that the island would be called Fótla.

¶ 114. They spoke with Ériu on Uisnech. 'Warriors,' she said, 'you are welcome. Long ago prophets foretold your coming. This island will be yours forever, and as far as the east of the world there will be no island that is better. No race will be more perfect than your race.' 'That is good,' said Amairgen. 'The prophecy is good.' 'We will not thank her for it,' said Donn the eldest of the sons of Míl, 'but our own gods and powers.' 'It doesn't matter where you're concerned,' said Ériu. 'You will have no profit from this island, nor will your descendants. I have a request, sons of Míl and offspring of Bregon,' she said: 'that my name be upon this island.' 'It will be its chief name,' said Amairgen.

¶ 115. The sons of Míl and the sons of Bregon advanced until they were in Druim Caín, i.e. Tara. The three kings of Ireland were there: Mac Cuill, Mac Cécht, Mac Gréne. They appealed to the sons of Míl, that the island should be left to them until the end of three days, to grant or give hostages, or to muster an army. They thought it likely that they would not return, for their druids would make spells against them so that they would not attempt to come back. 'We will submit,' said Mac Cuill son of Cermait, 'to what Amairgen, your own judge, will tell you. For if he gives a false judgement we will slay him.' 'Pronounce the judgement, Amairgen,' said Éber Donn. 'I shall pronounce it,' said Amairgen: 'let this island be left to them.' 'Where shall we go?' said Éber. 'Only across nine waves,' said Amairgen; and that was the first judgement given in Ireland:

¶ 116.　　The lawful manner of occupying land
　　　　　is across nine blue-backed waves of the sea.
　　　　　Do not seize it without gods, without powers.

> Let counsel be taken swiftly;
> we adjudge the possession of fertile lands.
> If you wish, submit to law;
> if you do not wish, do not submit.
> It is not I who speaks to you.

¶ 117. They went southward from Tara until they reached Inber Féile and Inber Scéne, for their ships were there. Then they went out across nine waves. The druids and poets of Ireland recited incantations against them so that they were borne far from Ireland, and became weary [wandering] across the sea. 'This is a druid wind,' said Donn. 'Look to see whether the wind is above the mast;' and it was not. 'Wait until Amairgen comes,' said Érech son of Míl, the steersman of Donn's ship. [Érech was Amairgen's foster son.] They all gathered in one place. Donn, the eldest, said, 'This is a disgrace upon the people of skill.' 'It will not be a disgrace, however,' said Amairgen; and he recited the following:

¶ 118. I invoke the land of Ireland:
> surging is the mighty sea,
> mighty is the upland full of meadows,
> full of meadows is the rainy wood,
> rainy is the river full of waterfalls,
> full of waterfalls is the spreading lake,
> spreading is the spring of multitudes,
> a spring of peoples is the assembly,
> the assembly of the king of Tara.
> Tara is a tower of tribes,
> the tribes of the sons of Míl,
> warriors of ships, of vessels.
> Ireland is a mighty vessel,
> flourishing is Éber Donn,
> a very wise incantation
> of the very wise wives of Bres,
> outcry of the wives of Buaigne.
> Ireland is a vast woman:
> Éremón smote her,
> Ír, Éber entreated her.

¶ 119. At once the wind grew calm for them. Donn said, 'Now I will bring under the edge of spear and sword all that there is in Ireland.' The wind separated from them the ship in which were Donn and Érech, two sons of Míl, and the ship in which were Bres and Buas and Buaigne, so that they were drowned on the sand-bars [dumacha] of Tech Duinn; each man's grave-mound [duma] is there. And that is where Díl wife of Donn was drowned, *ut alii dicunt.* She was a daughter of Míl; and Éremón himself placed a sod upon her. 'This is a sod upon Díl [*fót for Díl*],' he said; *unde* Fótla, *ut alii aiunt.*

¶ 120. Odba daughter of Míl, however, was the mother of the three sons of Éremón: Muimne, Luigne, Laigne. It is she whom Éremón left in Spain, and he took Tea in her despite. But Odba came from the south, in a lone ship with her sons; and they looked after her until she died in Odba—*unde* Odba. It is Tea, however, daughter of Lugaid son of Íth, whom Éremón married after Odba; and the bride-price on which she decided was whatever hill in Ireland she might choose. Druim Caín was that hill, i.e. Tara, 'Tea-rampart' [*Tea-múr*], the rampart of Tea daughter of Lugaid son of Íth. Lugaid, i.e. 'little Íth' [*Lug- Íth*], i.e. an Íth who was less than his father.

¶ 121. Éremón sailed with thirty ships righthandwise around Ireland north-eastward. These were their leaders: Brego, Muirthemne, Fuat, Cuailnge, Éremón, Éber son of Ír, Amairgen, Colptha, Muimne, Luigne, Laigne, Gosten, Setga, Suirge, Sobairche. These, moreover, were the slaves: Aidne, Aí, Asal, Mide, Cuib, Cera, Sér, Slán, Ligen, Dul, Line, Traig, Adal. They landed at Inber Colptha ['Colptha's estuary'], i.e. Colptha son of Míl. It is he who landed first, so that his name was given to the landing place, i.e. Inber Colptha.

¶ 122. As for the sons of Bregon, they did not leave descendants, but their names remain on the high places of Ireland. The descendants of the warriors—Setga and Gosten and Sobairche and Suirge—are not reckoned.

¶ 123. From Amairgen are the Corcu Achrach among the Éli and Orbraige, the Corcu Artbind and the Corcu Artbi.

¶ 124. From Éber son of Ír are descended the offspring of Ollam Fótla, i.e. the race of Rudraige. All the Ulaid descend from him. From him descend the Con-maicne and Ciarraige and Corco Mruad and Corco Duibne, the Dál Moga Ruith [i.e. Fir Maige Féne], the Laígse Laigen, the Araid Chliach, and the seven Sogain.

¶ 125. As for Éremón, leader of the fleet, he is the ancestor of Leth Cuinn, i.e. the four families of Tara, i.e. Conall, Éogan, Colmán, Áed Sláine. From him descend the three Connachts and the Airgialla, the Laigin and the Osairge, the Déisi Muman and the Érnai Muman, from whom are the Clanna Dedad, of which was Conaire Már with his descendants, i.e. the men of Alba and the Dál Riata and the Múscraige and the Corco Baiscinn; and to the Érnai belong the Dál Fiatach, i.e. the royal dynasty of the Ulaid. All of those are descended from Éremón. Together with them are the Fotharta, to whom belong Brigit and Fintan of Cluain Eidnech and the Uí Ailella and the Uí Chaecháin; all those belong to the Fotharta.

¶ 126. Éber remained in the south with thirty ships. These were their leaders: Bile, Míl, Cualu, Blad, Ebléo, Nár, Éber Donn, Éber Finn, Érech, Érennán, Lugaid, Aer, Orba, Ferón, Fergna, Én, Ún, Etan, Caicher, Mantán, Fulmán.

These were the slaves, and each of them had a ship: Adar, Aire, Déise, Dela, Cliu, Morba, Fea, Life, Femen, Fera.

¶ 127. From Bile and Míl all the Gaels are descended. Cualu and Blad and Ebléo did not leave descendants, but their names are upon the principal mountains. Nár son of Bile *a quo* [from whom (is)] Ros Náir. The descendants of the warriors—Én, Etan, Caicher, Fulmán, Mantán—are not reckoned. Neither Éber Donn nor Érech left children, for they were drowned *ut diximus.* Érennán *non habuit prolem quoniam mersus est statim in palude Scéne.*

¶ 128. *Quattuor autem filii Ébir non habuerunt prolem; id est, Aer, Orba, Ferón, Fergna. Quoniam hi non regnaverunt nisi per spatium unius annis* [sic], *quando Íriél occidit eos in causam fratrum suorum, ut. . . .*

¶ 129. Five kindreds descend from Lugaid son of Íth, i.e. the race of Dáire Doimthech, i.e. the five Lugaids. Lugaid Cál, *a quo* Cálraige Connacht. Lugaid Corr, *a quo* Corpraige. Lugaid Corp, *a quo* Dál Coirpri Cliach, *ut alii dicunt.* Lugaid Oircthe, *a quo* Corco Oircthe. Lugaid Loígde, *a quo* Corco Loígde, to whom belonged Lugaid son of Dáirine, i.e. Lugaid Mac Con ['Son of a Hound']: i.e., it is Ailill Áulomm who fostered him, and he could not be made to sleep except with Elóir, Ailill's hound.

¶ 130. As for Éber, from him are descended the Dál Cais, and the Dál Céin, and the Delbna, and the Déisi Tuaiscirt, and the Dál Mes Corp *ut alii aiunt*, and the Dál Máthra, and the Uí Derduib, and the Cathraige, and the Éli, and Tuath Tuirbe, and Éoganacht Caisil, and Éoganacht Áine, and Éoganacht Locha Léin, Éoganacht Raithlind, and Éoganacht Glennamnach, and Éoganacht Árann, and Éoganacht Ruis Argit. All those are of the race of Éber.

¶ 131. There was a dispute concerning the kingship between the sons of Míl, that is, between Éber and Éremón; and Amairgen was summoned to judge between them. Amairgen said: 'The inheritance of the first [i.e. Donn] to the second, to Éremón; and his inheritance to Éber after him.' But Éber did not accept that, but [demanded] the partition of Ireland. For these were the first three judgements delivered in Ireland among the sons of Míl: the judgement which Amairgen gave in Tara; and this judgement, in Sliab Mis; and the judgement which Amairgen gave in Cenn Sáile in Munster concerning deer and game and herds. *Ut poeta dixit*:

¶ 132. It is here that Amairgen gave the judgement—
        his neighbours do not conceal it—
        at Áth Málann, honour without decay,
        between the hosts of the sons of Míl.

        He adjudged his proper share to each
        when they were hunting.
        Each took that to which he was entitled
        through the justice of lofty Amairgen.

The [?] *closach* to whoever gives the first wound (it was known),
whether it be man or hound which tears the skin.
The haunch to the stag hound [?], though I conceal it not;
the belly to the territory where it is overtaken.

The flanks to the flayer, if he succeeds;
the short neck to the weapon;
the feet of the deer to the tracking dog:
he did not reckon whatever else there might be.

The guts to the man who comes last,
whether it please him or not.
It is certain that [his share] is not made
greater than that
in the distribution of the general allotment.

A common apportioning to everyone
besides that (it is not a deceitful practice),
without excess on one side or the other—
that is the judgement that Amairgen gave here.

¶ 133. In the end, then, there were six chieftains in the south and six in the north; and kingship belongs to Éber in the south and to Éremón in the north. The six in the south: Éber himself, Lugaid son of Íth, Etan son of Occe, Ún son of Ucce, Caicher, Fulmán. The six in the north: Éremón, Éber son of Ír, Amairgen, Gosten, Setga, Sobairche, and Suirge *septimus dux*.

¶ 134. It is concerning that that Raigne the poet, son of Ugaine, spoke to Mál son of Ugaine, to his brother, when Mál demanded: 'Recite your narrative.' *Unde dixit* Raigne:

¶ 135.   O splendid son of Ugaine,
what do you seek concerning the lore of Ireland?
'Let us leave Scythia'
[said] Fénius Farsaid of the wagons.
Nél journeyed to Egypt.
They spent a fitting interval
with Pharaoh, by seasons.
Scotta was betrothed to Nél—
it is her conception of our father Gáedel
which instituted 'Scot' as an additional name—
the fair daughter of Pharaoh.
—Until the people of the good God had departed,
until the great host was destroyed,
when Cenchres perished:
the Red Sea drowned them.

They rowed around the promontory,
they conquered Scythia;
Éber Scot slew them,
they slew Reflóir.
Agnoman [and] Lámfhind
sailed past the Caspian,
they went around Libya,
they made for the Mediterranean,
they continued past Africa,
they reached Spain
where were begotten Éremón
[and] Éber by Míl.
Bile sets out swiftly
to avenge Íth.
They distributed [themselves] in their ships,
sixty their number.
They turned truth into wrath [?]:
they divided Ireland
between twice six champions.
It is lore of the past that sustains a man:
at the end his inquiry is keen.

¶ 136. Or perhaps these are the two sixes who were mentioned: the six sons of Míl and the six sons of Bregon, i.e. Éremón, Éber, Lugaid, Amairgen, Colptha, Ír, Brego, Bile, Fuat, Blad, Cualu, Cuailnge. Thus, then, did the Gaels take Ireland.

¶ 137. F I N I T to the takings thus far.

◆ ◆ ◆ ◆ ◆ ◆ ◆ ◆ ◆ ◆

§109. From Giraldus Cambrensis's
Topographia Hibernie

TRANS. PHILIP FREEMAN

¶ 67.

VARIOUS MIRACLES IN KILDARE: THE FIRE WHICH NEVER DIES AND WHOSE ASHES DO NOT INCREASE, IN KILDARE IN LEINSTER, WHICH THE GLORIOUS BRIGID HAS MADE FAMOUS. There are many miraculous wonders worth noting. The first of these is the fire of Brigid, which is said to be inextinguishable. Strictly speaking, it can be extinguished, but the nuns and holy women have long nourished and fed the flame with such great care and diligence that since the time of the virgin saint herself it has never gone out. Moreover, in all this time the ashes of the fire have not increased.

¶ 68. BRIGID TENDS THE FIRE ON HER OWN NIGHT. In the time of Brigid, there were twenty nuns serving the Lord, with Brigid herself being the twentieth. But since the time of her death there have been only nineteen with the number never increasing. Each takes her turn for a single night tending the fire, but when the twentieth night comes, the nineteenth nun places a log near the fire and says, 'Brigid, tend your fire. This is your night.' In the morning, the wood has been burnt as usual and the fire still blazes.

¶ 69. THE HEDGE AROUND THE FIRE WHICH NO MAN MAY CROSS. Brigid's fire is surrounded by a circular hedge that no man may cross. And if by chance some presumptuous male does enter, as certain foolish ones have attempted, he does not escape unpunished. Only women are allowed to blow on the fire, and not with their mouths but with bellows or winnowing fans. Also, because of a curse by the virgin saint, goats never bear their young in that place. There are beautiful plains in the area, called 'Brigid's Pastures', but no one dares to plough them. It is said to be a miracle that although the animals of the whole province graze there, in the morning the grass is as tall as ever. About these pastures one could say: all the day-long grazing of the herds the cool dew of a single night renews.

◆ ◆ ◆ ◆ ◆ ◆ ◆ ◆ ◆

¶ 77. HOW AN ARCHER WHO CROSSED THE HEDGE WENT MAD AND ANOTHER MAN LOST HIS LEG. In Kildare there was a certain archer from the family of Richard who leapt over the hedge and blew on Brigid's fire. He jumped back immediately and went mad. Thereafter he would go around blowing in peoples' faces and saying, 'See! That's how I blew on Brigid's fire.' He went around to all the houses blowing on whatever fire he might find and saying the same words. Eventually he was captured and bound, but asked to be led to the nearest water. When he was brought there his mouth was so dry that he drank excessively, so that his belly ruptured and he died still in their hands. Another man began to cross the hedge but was restrained by his friends while only his lower leg had crossed the boundary. That foot immediately shrivelled up, and for the rest of his life he remained lame and feeble.

◆ ◆ ◆ ◆ ◆ ◆ ◆ ◆ ◆ ◆

¶ 101. PROOF OF WICKEDNESS SHOWN BY THEIR MAKING OF TREATIES. Among the many examples of their deceitful behaviour, there is one that stands out. They come together at some holy place under the pretence of religion and peace with him whom they plan to kill. First they join in a treaty based on their common ancestors, then they circle the church three times in turn. After entering the church, they swear many oaths before the relics of saints placed on the altar. Finally with Mass and words from the priest completed, they swear an indissoluble oath as if it were a promise of marriage. For the confirmation of both their friendship and agreement, they each drink the blood of the other, drawn especially for this purpose. Oh, how often at this very moment has blood been shed or, in a manner unheard of elsewhere, a bloody divorce takes place during the vows themselves.

¶ 102. THE CONFIRMATION OF A KING. There is in the most northern and remote part of Ulster, that is, in Kenelcunill [i.e. Tír Chonaill, now western Co. Donegal], a certain group that customarily inaugurates their king in a totally barbarous and abominable manner. When all the people of that land have been gathered into one place, a white mare is led into the middle of the assembly. The one who is to be raised up—not as a leader but as a beast, not as a king but an outlaw—while having intercourse with the mare like a beast, proclaims that he also is a beast. Immediately after, with the horse having been killed and cooked in water, a bath is prepared for the new king in the same water. He sits in the water surrounded by his people, all eating the meat of the mare which is brought to them. He doesn't use a cup or even his hands to drink the broth, but puts his mouth in the broth all around and swallows. When this abominable rite has been completed, his kingship and dominion are confirmed.

¶ 103. MANY IN THE ISLAND HAVE NOT BEEN BAPTISED NOR HEARD THE TEACHINGS OF THE FAITH even though the faith has been maturing, so to speak, in Ireland all this time, there are still corners of the land where many are not baptised and, through negligence of pastors, the Faith has not reached. I heard from some sailors that one time during Lent they were driven by a storm to the northern and unknown vastness of the sea of Connacht. Finally they found refuge from the wind in the lee of a small island. They had a difficult time maintaining their position even though they let down their anchors and used ropes of triple thickness. The storm subsided after three days and the wind and sea became calm again. They then saw in the distance a land that was unknown to them. Not long afterwards they saw a small boat leaving the land and moving towards them. The boat had a wicker frame and was covered with animal skins. There were two men in the boat who were naked except for a covering of animal hides about their waists. Their hair was long and blond, as is the case with most Irish, and came down over their shoulders to cover most of their bodies. When the men on the ship heard them and realised they were Irish-speakers from some part of Connacht, they took them on their ship. These two men wondered at everything they saw as if it were completely new. They said they had never before seen a large wooden ship nor the elements of civilisation on board. They were offered bread and cheese, but refused, not knowing what this food was. They said that meat, fish, and milk were their only nourishment. They did not normally wear clothes, but occasionally put on animal skins if it were necessary. They asked if the sailors had any meat on board, but were told they did not eat meat during Lent. However, the two men knew nothing of Lent. Neither did they know about the year, month, week, nor the names of the days of the week. When asked if they were Christians and baptised, they responded that they had neither heard nor knew anything about Christ. The two then returned home, taking a loaf of bread and some cheese with them.

◆ ◆ ◆ ◆ ◆ ◆ ◆ ◆ ◆ ◆

PART III

Brittonic & Brittonic Latin Sources

MOSTLY WELSH

---

§110. Excerpts from the Welsh Latin

History of the Britons
Historia Brittonum

TRANS. PAMELA S. M. HOPKINS & J. T. KOCH

¶ 7.

THE ISLAND BRITAIN is so called for the Roman consul Brutus. It stretches from the south-west to the north, lying in the west. Its size is 800 miles in length and 200 in width. In it there are twenty-eight *civitates* ['towns' or 'tribes'] and innumerable promontories, also innumerable strongholds built of stone and brick; and four peoples live there Scots [i.e. Gaelic speakers], Picts, [Anglo-]Saxons, and the Britons.[1]

---

1 As it survives, *Historia Brittonum* is a text in Latin compiled by a Welsh writer in ad 829/30. It is apparent, however, that it embodies a number of distinct and earlier strands of tradition, both oral and Welsh and literary and Latin, as well as Old Irish material resembling an early version of *Lebor Gabála Érenn* (§108 above). At least some of these sources once existed as separate texts, some in Wales and others in North Britain and Ireland. See further Kenneth

¶ 8. It has three large islands, one of which verges upon Armorica [Brittany] and that is called *Ïnïs Gueith* [the Isle of Wight]; the second is situated in the very middle of sea between Ireland and Britain, and it is called [in Latin] *Eubonia* [the Isle of Man], i.e. *Manau* [in Welsh]; the other is sited at the extreme edge of Britain's world, beyond the Picts, and is called *Orc* [the Orkneys]. Thus, it is said in the old proverb, when rulers or kings are discussed: 'He ruled Britain with its three islands.'[2]

¶ 9. There are many rivers in it, which flow to all sides, that is to the east, the west, the south, the north; however, two rivers are more important than the various others, *Tamesis* [the Thames] and *Sabrina* [the Severn], as if they were Britain's two arms, over which ships used to carry goods for the sake of trade. Once the Britons occupying it from sea to sea ruled it.

¶ 10. If anyone wishes to know when this island was inhabited after the Flood, I have come upon this two-fold explanation. In the Annals of the Romans it is written that after the Trojan War Aeneas came to Italy with his son Ascanius, defeated Turnus, and married Lavinia, daughter of Latinus, son of Faunus, son of Saturnus. After the death of Latinus, he acquired the kingship of both the Romans and the Latins. Aeneas founded Alba and then took a wife, and she bore him a son named Silvius. Silvius took a wife, and she became pregnant. When it was reported to Aeneas that his daughter-in-law was pregnant, he sent word to his son Ascanius, to send a wizard [*magus*] to examine the woman, and discover what she bore in her womb, whether the child was male or female. The *magus* examined the woman and returned. Because of this prophecy the *magus* was killed by Ascanius, for he told Ascanius that the woman bore a son in her womb who would be a son of death, who would kill his father and his mother and would be hated by all

Jackson, 'On the Northern British Section in Nennius', in *Celt and Saxon: Studies in the Early British Border*, Cambridge: Cambridge University Press, 1963, 20–62; David N. Dumville, '"Nennius" and the *Historia Brittonum*,' *Studia Celtica*, 10/11 (1975–76) 78–95; 'The Historical Value of the *Historia Brittonum*', *Arthurian Literature*, 6 (1986) 1–26.

As it survives, *Historia Brittonum* is a text in Latin compiled by a Welsh writer in ad 829/30. It is apparent, however, that it embodies a number of distinct and earlier strands of tradition, both oral and Welsh and literary and Latin, as well as Old Irish material resembling an early version of *Lebor Gabála Érenn* (§108 above). At least some of these sources once existed as separate texts, some in Wales and others in North Britain and Ireland. See further Kenneth Jackson, 'On the Northern British Section in Nennius', in *Celt and Saxon: Studies in the Early British Border*, Cambridge: Cambridge University Press, 1963, 20–62; David N. Dumville, '"Nennius" and the *Historia Brittonum*,' *Studia Celtica*, 10/11 (1975–76) 78–95; 'The Historical Value of the *Historia Brittonum*', *Arthurian Literature*, 6 (1986) 1–26.

2 Kenneth Jackson ('Rhai Sylwdau ar "Kulhwch ac Olwen"', *Ysgrifau Beirniadol*, 12 (1982) 12-23, at 15-17) explained the original sense of the perplexing Welsh formula *teir Ynys Prydein* 'the Three Islands of Britain' as the southern two thirds of Britain, Britain beyond the Forth, and Ireland.

men. Thus it came to pass: the woman died in child-birth, the boy was reared, and he was named Britto ['the Briton']. After some time, according to the *magus'* prophecy, while he was at play with others, he killed his father with an arrow shot, not purposely, but accidentally. He was exiled from Italy, . . . and came to the islands of the Tyrrhene Sea. He was driven from Greece because of the death of Turnus, whom Aeneas had killed, and he reached Gaul, and there founded the city of Turonus [Tours, now France], which is called Turnis. After that he reached this island, to which he gave his name, that is Britain, and he filled it with his race, and lived there. Britain was inhabited continuously from that day to this.

¶ 11. Aeneas reigned for three years among the Latins. Ascanius reigned thirty-seven years. After him, Silvius, son of Aeneas, reigned twelve years, Postumus for thirty-nine years; from him the kings of the Albani are called the Silvi; his brother was Britto. When Britto was ruling in Britain, Heli the High Priest ruled in Israel, and at that time the Ark of the Covenant was seized by foreigners, and Postumus, his brother, ruled among the Latins.

¶ 12. After an interval of many years, no less than eight hundred, the Picts came and took the islands which are called the Orcades [Orkneys], and later they laid waste to many regions from the islands, and took those islands on the north coast of Britain, and they have remained there from that day to this. They held and hold a third of all Britain to this day.

¶ 13. The Scotti came very recently from parts of Spain to Ireland. First came Partholōn with one thousand people, both men and women, and they increased until they were nearly four thousand strong, and a plague came over them, and in one week all perished and not a single one of them remained. Nïmeth[3], son of Agnoman, was the second to come to Ireland, who, it is said, sailed the sea for a year then made port in Ireland, his ships dashed to pieces, and remained there for many years, then sailed once again with his people, and returned to Spain. After that the three sons of *Miles Hispaniae* ['the Spanish soldier'] came with thirty keels among them and with thirty women in each keel, and they remained there for the space of one year. Later, they spied a glass tower in the middle of the sea, and they spied people upon the tower, and they endeavoured to speak with them, but none would respond. So for one year they hastened to attack the tower with all of their keels and all of their women, except for one keel, which was destroyed by shipwreck, in which were thirty men and an equal number of women. The other ships sailed to attack the tower, and, while all landed on the beach that was around the tower, the sea covered them, and they were overwhelmed, and not a single one of them escaped. From the crew of that ship that was left behind because of shipwreck, all Ireland was populated to this day. And afterwards, little by little, they came from parts of Spain and held very many regions.

---

3 Nïmeth = OIr. *Nemed* in *Lebor Gabála* (§108).

¶ 14. The *Dām-hoctor* ['Company of Eight' in Old Irish] came later and lived there in Britain with all his race until today. Istoreth, the son of Istorinus, held Dāl-Ríata [Gaelic Scotland] then; Builc [eponym of the Fir Bolg] and his people held the island of Eubonia [Isle of Man] and all those islands around it. The sons of Liethan were in possession of Demetia [Dyfed, South-west Wales] and in other regions, that is Guïr Cëtgueli [in South Wales], until they were driven out by Cuneda[g] and his sons from all the regions of Britain.

¶ 15. If anyone wishes to know when Ireland was inhabited and deserted, this is what the Irish scholars have related to me. When the sons of Israel came across the Red Sea, the Egyptians came, they followed and were overcome, as may be read in the Law. There was one nobleman from Scythia among the Egyptians, with a great company, and he was driven from his kingdom, and he was there when the Egyptians were drowned, but he did not press on after the people of God. Those who remained formed a plan to expel him, so that he should not besiege their kingdom and seize it, because their forces had been drowned in the Red Sea; and he was driven out. Meanwhile, he wandered across Africa for forty-two years, and they came to the Altars of the Philistines and across the Salt Lake, and they went between Rusicada and the mountains of Azaria, and they came by the river Malva, and they crossed through Maritania and the Pillars of Hercules, and they sailed the Tyrrhene Sea, and they arrived in Hispania [Spain and Portugal], and lived there for many years, and they thrived and multiplied beyond measure, and their people multiplied greatly. Then they came to Ireland after 1002 years when the Egyptians were drowned in the Red Sea, and to the regions of Dā[l]-Rīeta [Dál-Ríata, Gaelic Scotland], at which time Brutus was ruling among the Romans, who began the Consuls, then the Tribunes of the Plebs and the Dictators. And the Consuls held the State for 447 years, which previously had been oppressed by the rule of kings.

The Britons came in the Third Age of the World; the Irish, however, possessed Ireland in the Fourth Age. The Irish, who were in the west, and the Picts from the north, fought endlessly in unity and common assault against the British, because the Britons did not make use of weapons. After a great deal of time the Romans gained possession of the rulership of the whole world.

¶ 16. From the first year when the Saxons came to Britain, to the fourth year of Mermïn's reign, 429 years are counted. From the birth of the Lord to the coming of Patricius [i.e. St Patrick] to the Irish, there are 405 years. From the death of Patricius to the death of Saint Brigid, 60 years. From the birth of Columba [Colum Cille] to the death of Brigid, 4 years.

The start of the reckoning: 23 cycles of nineteen years from the birth of the Lord to the coming of Patricius to Ireland, and these years make 438, and the coming of Patricius to the cycle of nineteen years in which we are, are 22 years, that is 421, two years in Ogdoad until this year, in which we are.[4]

¶ 17. I have found another explanation concerning this Brutus from an old book of our elders.

After the Flood, Noah's three sons divided the world into three parts. They extended their boundaries: Sem in Asia, Cham in Africa, Jafeth in Europe. The first man to come to Europe of the race of Jafeth was Alanus with his three sons, who were named Hessitio, Armeno[n], and Negue. Hessitio had four sons, they were Francus, Romanus, Britto, and Albanus. Armenon had five sons: Gothus, Valagothus, Gebidus, Burgundus, Langobardus. Negue had three sons: Wandalus, Saxo, Boguarus. Four peoples are descended from Hisitio: Franci [Franks], Latini [Latins], Albani, and Britti [Britons]; from Armenon, five: Gothi [Goths], Walagothi, Gebidi [Gepidae], Burgundi [Burgundians], Langobardi [Lombards]; from Negue, four: Boguari, Vandali [Vandals], Saxones, Turingi. These races are subdivided throughout Europe. Alanus, so they say, was the son of Fetebir, son of Ougomun, son of Thous, son of Boib, son of Simeon, son of Mair, son of Aurthach, son of Oth, son of Abir, son of Rea, son of Ezra, son of Izrau, son of Baath, son of Iobaath, son of Jovan, son of Jafeth, son of Noah, son of Lamech, son of Matusalem, son of Enoch, son of Jareth, son of Malaleel, son of Cainan, son of Enos, son of Seth, son of Adam, son of the Living God. I found this information in the account of the ancients.

¶ 18. The first inhabitants of Britain were the British, descended from Brutus, son of Hisitio, son of Alanus, son of Rea Silvae, daughter of Numa Pampilius, son of Ascanius, son of Aeneas, son of Anchises, son of Trous, son of Dardanus, son of Flisus, son of Juvanus, son of Jafeth. Jafeth had seven sons; the first was Gomer, (from whom the Galli; the second was Magog, from whom the Scythi and Gothi, the third was Madai), from whom the Medi; the fourth was Juvan, from whom the Graeci; the fifth, Tubal, from whom (the Hiberei [Iberians] and) Hispani and Itali; the sixth, Mosoch, from whom are descended the Cappadoces; the seventh, Tiras, from whom the Traces [Thracians]. These are the sons of Jafeth, son of Noah, son of Lamech.

◆ ◆ ◆ ◆ ◆ ◆ ◆ ◆ ◆ ◆

¶ 31. Guorthïgïrn [Vortigern] ruled in Britain, and as he was ruling in Britain,

---

4 This section is based on the *computus* used by the early church for reckoning the date of Easter. Such Easter tables are thought by some scholars to have been the starting point for the annals, or yearly historical records, kept by the early Insular peoples, beginning with brief notes of a year's events jotted down alongside a date in the table. It seems likely from this section that *Historia Brittonum*, in part or in whole, developed as an outgrowth of an Easter table. The Mermïn mentioned in this section is King Merfyn Frych ('M. the Freckled') who founded the second dynasty of the most powerful Welsh kingdom (Gwynedd in North Wales) in A D 825. The writer of *Historia Brittonum* (or this particular section of it, at least) has therefore dated his activities to a d 829/30.

he was constrained by fear of the Picts and Scots and of attack by the Romans, not to mention fear of Ambrosius. Then three 'keels' came, driven in exile from Germania, in which were Horsa and Hengist. They were brothers, sons of Guictgils, son of Guitta, son of Guectha, son of Woden, son of Frealaf, son of Fredulf, son of Finn, son of Fodepald son of Geta, who was, they said, the son of god; but not the God of gods, amen, the God of hosts, but rather one of their idols that they worshipped. Guorthïgïrn made them welcome and handed over to them the island which is called in their language *Tanet* and in Brittonic *Ruhim*.

Gratian reigned for the second time with Equitius when the Saxons were received by Guorthïgïrn, CCCXLVII years after the passion of Christ.

◆ ◆ ◆ ◆ ◆ ◆ ◆ ◆ ◆

¶ 36. And it happened then, after the Saxons were placed in the island mentioned above, the aforementioned king promised to give them food and clothing indefinitely without fail. And they came to terms, and [the Saxons] agreed to fight strongly against [Guorthïgïrn's] enemies. However, these barbarians multiplied in number. The Britons could not feed them. When they demanded food and clothing, as had been promised to them, the Britons said: 'we cannot give you food and clothing, for your number has grown. Rather, you should go back, away from us. We do not need your help.' And so then [the Saxons] held counsel amongst their senior men, and determined there to break the peace.

¶ 37. Hengist however was an intelligent man, shrewd and experienced. Gauging the powerlessness of the king [Guorthïgïrn] and the military weakness of his people, he held council [with the Britons], and he said to Britain's king: 'We are few; if you desire, we will send to our homeland and invite warriors from the warriors of our land, so that greater will be the size of the force that will fight for you and your people.' And [Guorthïgïrn] commanded that they do so, and emissaries were sent across the North Sea. And they returned with sixteen keels. And chosen warriors came in these. And in one keel among these, there came a beautiful and most comely girl, Hengist's daughter. Then, after the keels arrived, Hengist prepared a feast for Guorthïgïrn and his warriors and his interpreter, who was called Ceretic. And he ordered the girl to serve them wine and liquor. And all of [the Britons] became drunk and sated. As they drank, Satan entered Guorthïgïrn's heart so that he fell in love with the girl. And he asked for her from her father through his interpreter and said 'Ask what you will of me, even up to half my kingdom.' And Hengist held counsel with his senior men from the Island of Oghgul [Angeln, now Fyn, Denmark], as to what they would ask of the king. And they all agreed to ask for the region which is called *Canturguoralen* in their language and *Ceint* in ours [modern Kent]. So [Guorthïgïrn] gave it to them, while Guoyrancgon who was ruling Kent did not know that his kingdom was being handed over to the pagans, and that he himself was being given over into their power. And so, the girl was given in marriage, and he slept with her and loved her greatly.

¶ 38. And Hengist said to Guorthïgïrn: 'I am your father, and I will be your father and consultant. And never ignore my counsel, for you need not fear your overthrow by any man or people, for my people are strong. Invite my son with his cousin   they are strong fighters   so that they may fight against the Scotti [Gaels]. And give them lands in the North, next to the wall called *Guaul* [probably Hadrian's Wall].' And so [Hengist] ordered that [Guorthïgïrn] invite them, and he invited Octha and Ebissa with forty keels. So then they sailed around the Pictish country, laid waste the Orkney Islands, and they came and occupied many districts beyond the Frenessic Sea [=? the Humber Estuary] up to the boundary of Pictland. And Hengist continued to invite more keels, until the land they came from became uninhabited. And his people became stronger and more numerous, as they came to the aforementioned tribeland of Kent.

[from LIBER SANCTI GERMANI]

¶ 39. Then, set on top of all his other evil deeds, Guorthïgïrn took his own daughter as his wife, and had a son by her. And when this came to be known by St Germanus, he came to accuse him with all the Britons' clergy. And then a great synod of clerics and laymen was convened in one counsel. This king had previously told his daughter to come to the council and then to put her son in Germanus' arms and to say that he was the son's father. And the woman did as she was instructed. Nonetheless, Germanus sweetly accepted him and turned to him saying: 'I shall be a father to you and shall not put you aside, unless a razor, scissors, and comb are given to me and are given by you to your natural father.' And the boy heard him, and turned towards his grandfather, his natural father Guorthïgïrn, and said to him: 'You are my father, crop my head and cut my head's hair.'[5] And [Guorthïgïrn] became enraged, and rose up, and fled from St Germanus. And was cursed and was condemned by St Germanus and the entire council of the Britons.

¶ 40. Then the king [Guorthïgïrn] summoned *magi* [wizards] to him, so that he might ask them what he should do. To that they replied: 'Go to the outermost reaches of your kingdom, and find a fortified stronghold so that you might defend yourself, for the people whom you have accepted into your kingship envy you, and will strike you down through trickery, and after your death they will take all the regions you loved, as well as all your people.' Then he came to get the stronghold with his *magi*, and they besieged many regions

---

5   The theme of cutting a person's hair as an acknowledgement of relationship recurs repeatedly in the Arthurian prose-tale *Culhwch ac Olwen*.

and provinces without finding it, until they finally reached the area which is called Guïned [modern Gwynedd], and he searched in the mountains of Herëri [Modern Welsh *Eryri* 'Snowdonia'], until at last he reached a place in the mountains suitable for building a stronghold. The *magi* told him: 'Make a stronghold in this place, because it will be eternally secure from barbarian peoples.' He assembled builders, that is stonecutters, and he gathered wood and stones, and when all the material had been collected, it disappeared in a single night. He ordered it to be collected three times, yet it was nowhere to be seen. He sent for the *magi* and interrogated them about what could be the cause of this evil and how this might have happened. They answered him: 'Unless you find a child who is without a father, and he is slain, and the fortress is sprinkled with his blood, it will never be built.'

¶ 41. So he sent ambassadors from the council of *magi* throughout Britain, so that they might discover whether there was a child without a father. And, having searched all the provinces and many regions, they came to Campus Elleti [Plain of Elleti], which is in the area called *Gleguïssing* [in South Wales], and boys were playing ball. Two of them were arguing with each other, and one said to the other: 'You are fatherless, and will come to no good.' They questioned the boys carefully about the boy, and asked the mother if the boy had a father. She denied [it] and said: 'I do not know how he was conceived in my womb, but one [thing] I do know is that I have never known a man.' She swore to them that the child had no father. They took him with them to King Guorthïgïrn and presented him to the king.

¶ 42. The next day a meeting was held, so that the boy might be killed. And the boy said to the king: 'Why have your men brought me to you?' To which the king replied: 'So that you may be killed, and your blood sprinkled around this keep, so that it may be built.' 'Who told you that?' the boy asked. 'My *magi* told me,' the king replied. So the boy said: 'Call them to me.' The *magi* were summoned, and the boy said to them: 'Who revealed to you that this keep should be sprinkled with my blood, since unless it were sprinkled with my blood, it would never be built? Who disclosed this about me so that you might know it?' Again the boy said: 'I will explain everything to you alone, king, and sufficiently in truth; but I will quiz your *magi*: what is in the foundation of this place? I want them to show you what is beneath the foundation.' They said, 'We do not know.' And he said: 'I do know. There is a pool in the middle of the foundation; come and dig, and you will find this.' They came, and dug, and it fell down. And the boy said to the *magi*: 'Reveal to me what is in the pool.' But they were silent and could not reveal it to him. He said to them: 'I will reveal it to you: you will find two vessels.' They came and saw this. The boy said to them: 'What is held in the sealed vessels?' They were silent and could not tell him. He declared: 'In the middle of them is a cloth, divide them and you will find this.' The king ordered them to be parted, and so a rolled cloth was found, just as he had said. Again the boy questioned the *magi*: 'What is in the middle of the cloth? Even now, speak.' But they could not. So he told them: 'In it are two worms, one white, the other red; unroll the cloth.' They unrolled it and found two sleeping worms. The boy said: 'Wait and watch what the worms will do.' The worms began to drive each other out; one would place its shoulders so that it could drive out the other all the way to the other half of the cloth; they did this three times: sometimes the red worm would seem weaker, and then the white would be stronger and would drive the other off the cloth. Then one chased the other across the pool, and the cloth vanished. The boy questioned the *magi*: 'What is the meaning of this wondrous sign which has occurred on the cloth?' And they replied: 'We do not know.' So the boy responded: 'Ha! This mystery is revealed to me, and I will make it clear to you. The cloth is the symbol of your kingdom; the two worms are two dragons; you are the red dragon, and the pool is the symbol of this world. But the white dragon is another people, those who have seized many peoples and regions of Britain, and will extend nearly from sea to sea, but later our people will rise up, and will courageously drive the English [Anglo-Saxons] across the sea. Go from this keep, because you cannot build it, and travel around many provinces, until you find your keep; I will remain here.' The king said to the youth: 'What is your name?' He replied: 'I am called Ambrosius,' that is, he was shown to be Embreis Guletic ['Ambrosius the Sovereign']. The king said: 'From what family are you descended?' He replied: 'My father is one of the consuls of the Roman people.' The king gave him the keep with all of the kingdoms of the western region of Britain, and he went with his *magi* to the northern regions and all the way to the region which is called *Guunessi*, and he built a city there, which is called by his name, *Caïr Guorthïgïrn* ['G.'s Stronghold'].

¶ 43. Meanwhile, Guorthemïr, son of Guorthïgïrn, was fiercely fighting against Hengist and Horsa and with their people, and drove them as far as the island mentioned above which is called Tanet, and confined them there three times and besieged them, striking, crushing, and terrifying them. They sent messengers across the sea as far as Germania to call on keels with a great number of warriors. And thereafter, they used to fight against the kings of our people, sometimes they would be victorious and would broaden their borders, other times they would be conquered and driven out.

¶ 44. Guorthemïr fought four great battles against them. The first battle on the river Derguentïd; the second at the ford which is called in their language *Episford*, in our language *Rïth-ër-gabail* ['Ford of the Conquest'] and there Horsa fell along with Guorthïgïrn's son, whose name was Catëgïrn. The third battle took place in the field by the Inscribed Stone, which is on the shore of the Gallic Sea, and the barbarians were defeated and he was the victor, and they fled to their keels and drowned as they boarded them like women. But he [Guorthemïr] died soon after, but before his death he told his people to place his tomb on the coast in the port from which they [the barbarians] had withdrawn, saying 'I leave you this: Although they may hold a British port in another area or may have dwelled there, nonetheless they will never remain in this land.' They disregarded his command and did not bury him where he had commanded them.

¶ 45. But the barbarians returned eagerly since Guorthïgïrn was their friend, and because of his wife, and no one was strong enough to boldly drive them out, because they did not occupy Britain by their own strength, but by God's will. Who can resist God's will, even if he tries? But the Lord did as He wished, and He rules and governs all people.

It happened that after the death of Guorthemïr, son of King Guorthïgïrn, and after the return of Hengist and his troops, they incited a deceitful plan, to snare Guorthïgïrn with his troops. Meanwhile, they sent messengers to make peace and to bring about a lasting alliance between them. But Guorthëgïrn took counsel with his elders to consider what they should do. At length, they were of one mind, to make peace, and their messengers were sent back. Later, they convened an assembly where each side, British and Saxon, would meet together without arms, to seal the alliance.

¶ 46. But Hengist ordered all his troops to put their knives beneath their feet between their shoes: 'And when I call to you and say "Saxons, draw!", draw your knives from your shoes, and attack them, and stand firmly against them. But do not kill the king; but hold him on account of my daughter, whom I gave to him in marriage, because it is better for us that he be ransomed from our hands.' So they convened the assembly, and came together, and the Saxons, meanwhile, friendly in speech, but wolfish in mind and manner, arrived and sat, man by man, in a spirit of fellowship. Hengist, as he had said, cried out, and all the three hundred elders of King Guorthïgïrn were slain, and he alone was captured and chained, and in exchange for his life gave them many regions, that is *Est Saxum* [Essex], *Sutsaxum* [Sussex], . . .

¶ 47. Saint Germanus admonished Guorthïgïrn so that he would convert to his Lord, and so that he would separate himself from his illicit marriage. But he desperately fled as far as the region that took his name, Guorthïgïrniaun, and hid there with his wives. So Saint Germanus pursued him with all the British clergy, and remained there for forty days and forty nights, standing upon a rock, and pleading day and night. Again Guorthïgïrn withdrew in dishonour as far as Guorthïgïrn's Stronghold, which is in the region of the Demeti [Dyfed, South-west Wales], beside the River Teibi [modern Teifi]. So Saint Germanus pursued him, as was his way, and fasted there with all the clergy for three days and as many nights to achieve his goal, and on the fourth night, about midnight, the whole keep suddenly fell by fire sent from heaven, and the fire of heaven glowed. Guorthïgïrn and all who were with him and his wives died. This is the end of Guorthïgïrn, which I discovered in the Book of the Blessed Germanus. Others have related other versions.

¶ 48. Afterwards all of his own people hated him, because of his crime, both the strong and the weak, the unfree and free, monk and layman, the poor and great. He wandered from place to place for a time, until at last his heart cracked, and he died without honour. Others say that the earth opened and swallowed him on the night in which the stronghold burst into flame around him, because no remains were found of those who were burned with him in the keep.

He had three sons, who were named Guorthemïr, who fought against the barbarians, as we said above, the second, Catëgïrn, the third Pascent, who reigned in two regions, Büelt and Guorthïgïrniaun, after the death of their father, by the generosity of Ambrosius, who was a king among all the kings of the British people. Faustus was a fourth son, who was his child by his daughter, and Saint Germanus baptized him, and raised him, and educated him, and he founded the great center upon the bank of the river called Renis [in southern Gaul], and it remains to this day. And he had one daughter, who was the mother of Saint Faustus.

¶ 49. This is his genealogy, which goes back to the beginning. Fernmaïl son of Teudubïr, who reigns now in the two regions of Büelt and Guorthïgïrniaun Teudubïr son of Pascent, son of Guoïdcant, son of Moriüd, son of Eldat, son of Edoc, son of Paul, son of Mepurit, son of Briacat, son of Pascent, son of Guorthïgïrn Guortheneü ['Guorthïgïrn the Excessively Thin'], son of Guitaul, son of Guitolin, son of Gloïu, is himself king of the region of Büelt. Bonus, Paul, Mauron, Guotolin are four brothers who were the sons of Gloïu, who built the great city upon the bank of the River Sabrina [Severn], which is called *Caïr Gloïu* in the British language, but *Gloecester* [mod. *Gloucester*] in Saxon. Enough has been said concerning Guorthïgïrn and his family.

◆　◆　◆　◆　◆　◆　◆　◆　◆

¶ 56. [The Arthurian battle-list]

At that time, the English increased in number and grew in Britain. On Hengist's death, his son Octha came down from the north of Britain to the Kentishmen's kingdom, and from him are descended the kings of the Kentishmen. Then Arthur fought against them in those days, together with the kings of the Britons, but he was their battle leader [*dux bellorum*].

The first battle was at the mouth of a river called Glein [*ostium Glein*]. The second, the third, the fourth and the fifth were on another river, called Dubglas, which is in the country of Lindsey [*Linnûïs*]. The sixth battle was on a river called Bassas. The seventh battle was in the Caledonian Forest, that is, the Battle of the Caledonian Forest [*Cat Coït Celïdon*]. The eighth battle was in Guinnion castle, and in it Arthur carried the image of the Holy Mary, ever-

Virgin, on his [shield (MSS say *humeros* 'shoulders'),] and the heathen were routed on that day, and there was a great slaughter of them, through the intercession of Our Lord Jesus Christ and the power of the holy Virgin Mary, his mother. The ninth battle was fought in the city of the Legion. The tenth battle was fought on the bank of the river called Tribruit. The eleventh was on the hill called Agned [a.k.a. *Bregomion*]. The twelfth battle was on Badon's Heights and in it nine hundred and sixty men fell in one day, from a single charge of Arthur's, and no one killed them but he alone; and he was victorious in all his battles.[6]

[¶¶ 57–65. 'THE NORTHERN HISTORY'[7]]

¶ 57. (a) Aelfret [= Æthelfrith of Bernicia 595–616 and all Northumbria 605–616] i.e. Aedlferd *Flesaur* ['The Twister' < Lat. *Flexārius*].

(b) Echgfrïd [= Ecgfrith of Northumbria, ruled 671–685] made war against his cousin, who was the king of the Picts, namely Bïrdei [otherwise known as Bridei son of Bili], and he [Ecgfrith] fell with the full strength of his army, and the Picts and their king were victorious, and never again did the rapacious Anglo-Saxons grow strong enough to take tribute from the Picts. That battle is called *Gueith Lïnn Garan* [Pictish/Old Welsh 'Battle of Crane-Lake' = Nechtanesmere, 20 May 685].

(c) Osguïd [= Oswiu of Northumbria 642–671] moreover had two wives, of whom the one was called Rie[in]melth, the daughter of Royth, the son of Rün [the son of Urbgen], and the other was called Eanfled, daughter of Eadguïn [= Edwin of Northumbria 617–633] son of Ælle.

---

6   It is now generally accepted that this chapter, the oldest historical tract about 'King' Arthur, is a translation of a Welsh battle-listing poem, like the following several items. We can even reconstruct the rhyme-scheme of the lost original: . . . *Bassas* | . . . *Dubglas* | . . . *Cat Coït Celidon* | . . . *Castell Guïnnion* | . . . *Caïr Legion* | . . . *Tribruït abon* [*abon* = 'river'] | . . . *Bregomion* | . . . [*mïnïd*] *Badon* | ; see further Thomas Jones, 'The Early Evolution of the Legend of Arthur,' *Nottingham Mediaeval Studies* vii (1963) 3–21. The metre appears to have been long monorhyming stanzas, for which the Welsh term is *awdl*. Incidentally, the fact that Badon rhymes indicates that this important battle (which we know from other sources was historical, a major turning point in the Anglo-Saxon conquest of Britain) was ascribed to Arthur in the poem and not merely tacked on for good measure by the 9th-century writer. his is an important point for historians.

7   This section, which is probably derived from an originally separate history compiled by the Britons of Cumbria, takes the form of notices of Brittonic interest interspersed into the body of Anglian [Northern and Midland English] royal genealogies. In the following, the purely English material is omitted. The extreme partisanship in the 'Northern History' shown for Uryen of Reget [Old Welsh *Urbgen*] and his descendants strongly implies that this material was compiled in a kingdom or a monastery that regarded Uryen (or a member of his family) to be its founder.

¶ 61. (a) Osfird and Eadfird were two sons of Edgu[in] [= Edwin of Northumbria], and with him they fell in the battle of Meicen[8] and the kingship was never revived from their lineage, for none from their line escaped from that battle, but rather they all were killed with him by the army of Catguollaun [Cadwallon], the king of the realm of Guenedota [= Gwynedd].

(b) Ecgfird [= Ecgfrith of Northumbria] i.e. Ecgfird *Ail-guin* ['White-Eye-brow'].

(c) Aeta, i.e. Eata *Glin-maur* ['Big-Knee'].

(d) Ida son of Eobba [king of Bernicia 547–59] held territories in the northern part of Britain, i.e. of the Humber Sea, and he joined Din–Guaïroï [Bamburgh] to Berneich [Bernicia = Northern Northumbria].

¶ 62. (a) Then [Ö]utïgïrn in that time fought bravely against the English folk. Then Talhaern Tat--Aguen ['Iron-brow Father of Inspiration'] acheived renown in poetry; and Neirin, and Taliessin, and Bluchbard, and Cian, who is called *Gue*[*ni*]*th Guaut* ['Wheat of Inspired Verse'], were at the same time [*c.* 547 × 559] famous in Brittonic poetry.

(b) Maïlcun [*c.* 534 × 549] the great king was reigning amongst the Britons, that is in the realm of Guenedota [Gwynedd], for his ancestor, i.e. Cunedag, with his sons, whose number was eight, had come from the northern region, from the country called Manau Guotodin, 146 years before Maïlcun reigned, and they expelled the Irish from these regions with enormous slaughter, so that they never returned to inhabit them.

¶ 63. (a) Four kings fought against him (Urbgen, Rïderch the Old, Guallauc, and Morcant). Theodoric fought strongly against Urbgen and his sons. At that time, sometimes the enemy and then the countrymen used to gain victory, and [Urbgen] penned them up for three days and three nights in the island of Medcaut [Lindisfarne], but, during this expedition, he was killed out of envy at the instigation of Morcant, because his military skill and leadership surpassed that of all the other kings.

(b) Eadfered [Æthelfrith] 'The Twister' ruled twelve years in Berneich [Bernicia] and another twelve in Deur [Deira, Southern Northumbria]; 24 years he ruled between the two realms, and he gave his wife Din-Guoïroï, who is called Bebbab, and from his wife's name it was named, i.e. Bebbanburh [Bamburgh].

(c) Edguïn son of Ælle ruled 17 years. And he occupied Elmet [in present-

---

8 Though a place Meigen is known in Wales, in Powys, near the English border, English sources give the place of Edwin's death as the battle of Haethfelth, on 12 October 633. That was probably in the Hatfield region in what is now the English counties of South Yorkshire and Nottinghamshire.

day South Yorkshire] and expelled Certic, the king of that region. Eanfled, his daughter, was baptised the twelfth day after Whitsun together with all of his people, both men and women, with her. Eadguïn himself was baptised the following Easter, and 12,000 people were baptised with him. If anyone wishes to know who baptised them, Rün son of Urbgen baptised them, and for forty days he did not cease in baptising the whole rapacious race and through his teaching many believed in Christ.

¶ 64. (a) Oswald son of Eadferd [Æthelfrith] ruled nine years [634/5 –642]. He is Oswald *Lamn-Guïn* ['White-Blade']. He slew Catgublaun [Cadwallon], king of the country of Guenedota [Gwynedd], in the battle of Cantscaul [= Denisesburna, 634], with a great slaughter of his army.

(b) Osguïd [Oswiu] son of Eadlfrïd [Æthelfrith] ruled 28 years and 6 months [5 August 642–670]. During his reign a great plague came. Catgualatr [Cadwaladr] ruled amongst the Britons following his father, and he perished in [the plague]. And [Osguïd] slew Pantha [Penda, the pagan English king of Mercia] in the field of Gai [= Winwæd, 15 November 655], and now that was the slaughter of the field of Gai, and the kings of the Britons were slain, who went out with king Pantha in the campaign as far as the stronghold which is called Iüdeu [Stirling, Scotland].

¶ 65. (a) Then Osguïd gave all the riches which were in that stronghold into the possession of Penda, and Penda distributed them to the kings of the Britons, that is *Atbret Iüdeu* ['The Restitution of Stirling']. But the only one to escape was Catgabaïl, king of the realm of Guenedota, with his army, rising by night, for which he is called *Catgabail Catguommed* ['Battle-Seizer Battle-Shirker'].

(b) Ecgfrïd son of Osbïu [Oswiu] ruled nine years [actually 671–685]. In his time St Cudbert [Cuthbert] the bishop died in the island of Medcaut [Lindisfarne; actually in 687]. It is he who made war against the Picts and was killed therein.

(c) Penda son of Pybba ruled ten years. He was the first to separate the kingdom of the Mercians from the kingdom of the Northerners [Northumbrians]. He treacherously killed Onnan, king of the East Angles, and St Oswald, king of the Northerners. He fought the battle of Cocboy, in which his brother, Eobba son of Pybba, and Oswald, king of the Northerners, fell. And [Penda] was victorious through diabolical arts; for he was unbaptised and never believed in God.

¶ 66a. THE CITIES OF BRITAIN, whose number is XXVIII—:

1. Caïr Guorthïgïrn
2. Caïr Guïnntguic [Winchester]
3. Caïr Mïncïp [Verulamium, nr. St Albans]
4. Caïr Lïguälïd [Carlisle]
5. Caïr Meguaïd
6. Caïr Colün [Lincoln or Colchester]
7. Caïr Ebrauc [York]
8. Caïr Cüst<o>eint ['Constantius' Stronghold']

9. Caïr Caratauc
10. Caïr Grau[n]th [Cambridge]
11. Caïr Maunguïd
12. Caïr Lündein [London]
13. Caïr Ceint [Canterbury]
14. Caïr Guïragon [Wroxeter]
15. Caïr Peris
16. Caïr Daun [Doncaster]
17. Caïr Legion [Chester]
18. Caïr Guricon [Wroxeter]
19. Caïr Segeint [nr. Caernarfon]
20. Caïr Legion guar Uïsc [Caerllion-ar-Wysg]
21. Caïr Guent [Caerwent]
22. Caïr Brïthon
23. Caïr Lerion
24. Caïr Draïtöü
25. Caïr Pensa vel Coyt
26. Caïr Urnarc
27. Caïr Celemion
28. Caïr Luït Coyt [Wall nr. Lichfield]

◆ ◆ ◆ ◆ ◆ ◆

[MIRABILIA BRITANNIAE, THE WONDERS OF BRITAIN]

¶ 69. Another wonder is Oper Lïnn Liuan. The estuary of that river flows into the Sabrina [Severn], and when the Sabrina is overflowing to the Sissa, and the sea, likewise, floods the estuary of the above-said river and is carried back into the estuary's pool like a whirl-pool, and the sea does not rush upwards. And there is a shore beside the river, and as long as the Sabrina is overflowing to the Sissa, this shore is not concealed, and when the sea recedes from the Sabrina, then Stagnum Liuan vomits all that it devoured from the sea, and the shore is concealed like a mountain, and vomits and bursts forth in one wave. And if the troops of the whole region in which it is located were to be there, and were to form a line against the wave, then the strength of the wave drags the troops down, their clothing filled with water, and horses, likewise, are dragged down. If however, the army puts its back against it, the wave does not harm them, and when the sea recedes, then the whole shore that the wave covered is again exposed, and the sea recedes from it.

◆ ◆ ◆ ◆ ◆ ◆ ◆

¶ 73. There is another wonder in the region that is called Büelt. There is a pile of stones there, and one stone, set on top of the pile, has a dog's footprint on it. When Cabal, who was the dog of the warrior Arthur, hunted the boar Troynt [read Troït], he made the footprint in the stone, and later Arthur gathered the pile of stones beneath the stone in which his dog's footprint was, and it is called Carn Cabal. So men come and take the stone in their hands for a day and night, and on the next day it is found upon its pile.

There is another wonder in the region that is called Ercïng. There is a grave by a fountain, which is called Lïcat Amr [the 'Eye' or 'Spring of Amr'], the name of the man who is buried in the tomb, is Amr. He was the son of the warrior Arthur, and he killed him in that place, and buried him. Men come to measure the tomb; sometimes it is six feet in length, sometimes nine, some times twelve, sometimes fifteen. In whatever measurement you may measure it on that occasion, later you will not find it in the same measure, and I myself have tried it.

◆   ◆   ◆   ◆   ◆   ◆   ◆

§§111–136. Early Welsh Heroic Poetry
TRANS. J. T. KOCH

§111. *Marwnad Cunedda* The Elegy of Cunedag[9] [? *fl. c.* AD 380 × 450]
BOOK OF TALIESIN 69.9–70.15

i   [*I am ardent Taliesin.*
ii   *I endow the world with inspired song,*
iii   *as one who relates the course of the world's wonders.*]

---

9   The text is edited and annotated in Modern Welsh by J. E. Caerwyn Williams in *Astudiaethau ar yr Hengerdd: Studies in Old Welsh Poetry*, ed. R. Bromwich, R. B. Jones (Cardiff: University of Wales Press, 1978) 208–233.

It is a typical elegy of the traditional type and may be taken as illustrative of the relationship of poet and patron and stressing the chieftainly virtues that public praise was supposed to call forth. The leader must be bold and effective in battle, defending his people and causing immeasurable destruction to their foes, in this case the fortified towns of late Roman Britain. The leader is illustrious in his ancestry and belongs to the rightful dynasty, in this case, the descendants of the patriarch Coel. The leader is superlative in his generosity. The poet conventionally represents the death of the leader as the loss of defense and security for the chief's followers (including the poet himself), loss of sustenance, and loss of peace of mind. The whole world is represented as being thrown out of joint by the downfall of a figure whose rôle is viewed as so colossal as to be the linchpin of the universal order.

In the transmission of the poem, the tenses have become confused, so that some lines speak as though the subject were still alive.

Cuneda is relevant to the *Gododdin* because he came from that tribe. *Bryneich* is the less-Christianised province of Gododdin between the Tweed and Hadrian's Wall, after the later sixth century the northern province of Anglo-Saxon Northumbria, i.e. Bernicia.

The opening lines are probably a later addition.

ƁETWEEN THE SALTY SEA and the steep rock [*Allt*, of the Clyde] and
    the fresh-water lakes [*echwyδ*, ?of Cumbria],

2   [the land] will shake for Cunedag, the relentless raider.

3   In Caer Weir [the fortified town on the River Uedra] and Caer Lliwelyδ [the
    fortified town of Luguualium],

4   combat will shake the *ciuitates* [*kyuatawt*, the Romano-British tribal cantons]—

5   an all-enveloping wave of fire, a wave

6   that crosses seas. Chieftain will force chieftain to submit,

7   for the high station [Cunedag] seized over this world (in Albion),

8   like the sigh of the wind against the ash wood.

9   His hounds [i.e. war-band] will keep vigil on his frontier.

10   They will constrain the Coeling in a truce of peace.

11   They will invest the rightfully qualified bards who sing

12   of the death of Cunedag for which I lament as you lament.

13   There is lamentation for the thick defensive door at the wide breach,

14   merciless, peerless, none so profound,

15   deeply based (?Dumn, tribal ancestor of the Dumnonii), deeply dug (?as
    Dumn), deeply founded.

16   The words he uttered were hard and plain.

17   He was harder than bone against the enemy.

18   Cunedag's upward onrush: before [going to his] sleeping place of earth,

19   his honour was maintained.

20   A hundred times (in a hundred battles) before the fall of our protective gate's
    upright,

21   the men of Bryneich [Bernicia] were assembled and conveyed into the grey lead
    [of battle].

22   There was singing in the face of [battle's] fear and terror

23   [advancing on] the cold march. Before an allotment of earth was his bed,

24   there used to be a swarm like an encircling hedge of men and horses.

25   He knew that cowardice was worse than death.

26   It is for this death that I grieve in horror —

27   for Cunedag of many courts and many raids.

28   For the abundant salmon of the brine, for the vital bounty of
    the sea, for the spoils of the oven I shall perish.

29   It is the inspired verse with which poets [?] sought favour with which I [?] seek
    favour,

30   and what others counted, I shall count:

31   the account of our warfare will be taken — 'a gift of a hundred
    steeds before [the claiming of] Cunedag's share;

32   he used to grant me milch cows in the summer;

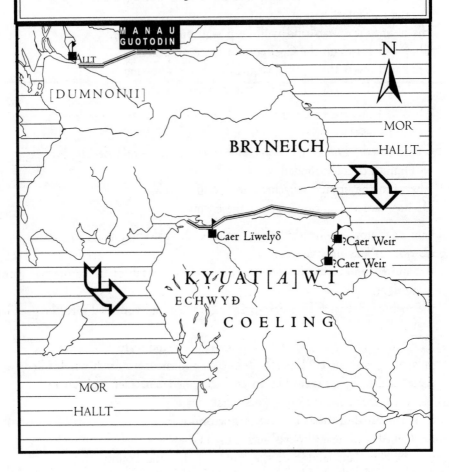

The Elegy of
C U N E D A G
SON of ÆTERN

MANAU
GUOTODIN

ALLT

[DUMNONII]

BRYNEICH

N

MOR
HALLT

Caer Lïwelyδ

?Caer Weir

?Caer Weir

KYUAT[A]WT
ECHWYÐ

COELING

MOR

HALLT

33   He used to grant me horses in the winter;

34   he used to grant me bright wine and oil;

35   he used to grant me a band of slaves for a homestead.'

36   He was the fierce and destructive raider,

37   the watchman (*speculator*), the chief with a lion's visage.

38   The borderland was always in ashes before the son of Æternus, before the
      eternal sorrow.

39   He was vigilant, merciless, unyielding,

40   a gushing flood of limitless death.

41   He used to carry his shield in the post at the vanguard. Valorous men were his
      lords.

42   I am awakened by the dirge, the stop to the wine of Cunedag; sleep has been
      destroyed by the Coeling [and so has the unique man].

◆ ◆ ◆ ◆ ◆ ◆ ◆

§§112–115. Poems Mentioning Arthur

¶NOTE. There is inadequate sound historical documentation to confirm beyond doubt that
Arthur existed. In legendary history, his career is placed in the late fifth to earlier sixth
century. What is known of this period at least confirms that it was a time when the Celtic
Britons were relatively successful in resisting the advance of the Anglo-Saxons. There are
various other traces of the activities of an 'Arthur-like' figure or figures at this time. The
office of a post-Roman Brittonic high kingship can be discerned in the careers of leaders
known as Guorthïgïrn [a.k.a. Vortigern], Guorthemïr, and Riothamus, whose names or titles
mean respectively 'Over-Lord', 'Summit-King', and 'Superlative-King'. It is possible that
Arthur continued this office or aspired to do so.

Arthur is mentioned in two places in *Historia Brittonum* ¶¶56, 73 above, and in *Vita Sancti
Uuohednouii*, below. The *Annales Cambriae* ('Welsh Annals') contains the two following
Arthurian notices.

518   The Battle of Badon in which Arthur carried the cross of our Lord Jesus Christ
       for three days and three nights on his shoulders and the Britons were vic-
       torious.

539   Gueith Camlann ['the Battle of Camlann'] in which Arthur and Medraut fell,
       and there was a great mortality [plague] in Britain and Ireland.

In the high mediaeval Arthurian romances, Old Welsh *Medraut* figures as Arthur's incestuously
begotten son and nemesis *Mordred*.

§112. *Gereint fil. Erbin* The Elegy of Gereint son of Erbin[10] (fl. 6th century)
BLACK BOOK OF CARMARTHEN 71.12–73.10

¶ 1.

BEFORE GEREINT, the enemy's bane,
I saw white stallions mangled and bloody,
and after the battle cry, rude burial.

¶ 2. Before Gereint, the expeller of the enemy,
I saw stallions mangled and bloodied by warfare,
and after the battle cry, grim contemplation.

¶ 3. Before Gereint, the enemy's calamity,
I saw stallions whose hides were white,
and after the battle cry, a crude shelter.

¶ 4. In Llongborth I saw wrath
and biers burdened beyond capacity
and men reddened by Gereint's onrush.

¶ 5. In Llongborth I saw hacking down,
men in tumult and blood about crowns of heads,
before Gereint, his father's great son.

¶ 6. In Llongborth I saw spurs,
and men who did not flee before lances,
and the drinking of wine from a bright glass.

¶ 7. In Llongborth I saw weapons
of men and gore pouring out,
and after the battle cry, a disorderly retreat.

¶ 8. In Llongborth I saw Arthur
bold men who used to hew down with steel
the emperor [*ameraudur* < Latin *imperātor*], director of labour.

¶ 9. In Llongborth Gereint was slain.
Bold men from the region of Dyfneint [=Domnonia, Devon nd
Cornwall]):
and before they were slain, they slew.

---

10 The chieftain lamented here lived in the sixth century and came from southwest Britain,
the same area traditionally connected with King Arthur. Arthur is mentioned in this poem
and called emperor. The place-name *Llongborth* means 'Port of Ships', so it is likely that
there was an amphibious dimension to the engagement. Portsmouth and Langport,
Somerset, have been suggested as the site.

¶ 10. They were swift steeds that advanced under Gereint's thigh,
long-legged, grain-fed,
blood-spattered, swooping like speckled eagles.

¶ 11. They were swift steeds that advanced under Gereint's thigh,
long-legged, they had grain,
blood-spattered, swooping like black eagles.

¶ 12. They were swift steeds that advanced under Gereint's thigh,
long-legged, grain-depleting,
blood-spattered, swooping like red eagles.

¶ 13. They were swift steeds that advanced under Gereint's thigh,
long-legged, grain-scattering,
blood-spattered, swooping like white eagles.

¶ 14. They were swift steeds that advanced under Gereint's thigh,
long-legged, like stags,
tumult of conflagration on the mountain wasteland.

¶ 15. They were swift steeds that advanced under Gereint's thigh,
long-legged, desiring grain,
a bright blaze of silver at the tips of their manes.

¶ 16. They were swift steeds that advanced under Gereint's thigh,
long-legged, deserving grain,
blood-spattered, swooping like dark gray eagles.

¶ 17. They were swift steeds that advanced under Gereint's thigh,
long-legged, whose food was grain,
blood-spattered, swooping like gray eagles.

¶ 18. When Gereint was born, heaven's gates stood open;
Christ gave what was prayed for
a magnificent aspect, the glory of Britain (*Prydein*).

◆　◆　◆　◆　◆　◆　◆

§113. *Preiðeu Annwvyn* The Spoils of the Unworld
BOOK OF TALIESIN 54.16–56.13

[I EXALT THE SOVEREIGN LORD, PRINCE, KING OF THE REALM
who has extended his dominion over the *tractus mundi*.]

GWEIR'S PRISON was prepared in the *sídh* stronghold [MW *sidi* < OIr. *síd*
'fairy mound'].
According to the tale of Pwyll and Pryderi,

None before him went into it.   5
The heavy blue chain held the faithful youth.
And for the spoils of the Unworld he sang shrilly.
And until Judgement he will persist as an imploring bard.
Three fullnesses of Prydwen we went into it.[11]
Except seven, none rose from Caer Sidi, the *Sídh* fort.   10

I am renowned: resplendent is my song that was heard.
In the four-cornered fort, four-sided,
my poetry was uttered from the cauldron.
By the breath of nine maidens it was kindled.
It was the cauldron of the Chief of the Unworld that was sought
a ridge of pearls around its brim.   16
It does not boil a coward's food; it was not destined (to do so).
A sword of lightning slaughter was raised to it
and was left in the hand of Lleminawc.
And before the door of hell's gate, lanterns burned.   20
And, when we went with Arthur   a brilliant labour
except seven, none returned from the Fort of Intoxication.

I am renowned, resplendent is my song that they hear.
In the Four-cornered Fort, Island of the Strong Door,
running water and jet are mixed   25
bright wine was the liquor for their host.
Three fullnesses of Prydwen, we went on sea.
Except seven, none returned from the Frigid Fort.

I set no value on the director's wretched scribes.
Through the Glass Fort they did not see Arthur's courage.   30
Six thousand men were standing on its wall.
Conversing with their sentinel was difficult.
Three fullnesses of Prydwen went with Arthur.
Except seven, none returned from the Concealed Fort.

I set no value on weak men, limp-shielded.   35
They know not what was created on what day,
what hour of the day it was born (and) where,

---

11 The speaker here is Taliesin. 'Prydwen' is the name of Arthur's ship. This is a mysterious,
allusive poem about an otherworldly expedition led by Arthur to gain supernatural spoils,
including the *Peir Penn Annwvyn* 'Cauldron of the Chief of the Unworld'. There are several
direct and oblique references to episodes in the Mabinogi. The poem probably dates back
to the 8th or 9th century, which makes it one of the earliest pieces of Arthurian literature.
    See further R. S. Loomis, *Wales and the Arthurian Legend* (Cardiff: University of Wales
Press, 1956); Marged Haycock, ' "Preiddeu Annwn" and the Figure of Taliesin', *Studia
Celtica*, 18/19 (1983–84), 52–78.

. . .

They know not the speckled ox with its massive headring,
one hundred and forty facets to its collar.   40
And when we went with Arthur   an appalling tribulation,
except seven, none returned from Caer-Vanðwy [?the Fort of the Divine
    Place].

I set no value on weak men of deficient ferocity.
They know not on what day the chieftain was appointed,
what hour in the day the lord of the land was born,   45
what beast they keep with a silver head.
When we went with Arthur   a woeful conflict,
except seven, none returned from the Caer-Ochren [?the Enclosed Fort].

Monks cluster in a pack like a troop of dogs,
[shrinking] from encounter with the lords who know   50
whether it is the path of the wind or that of sea water
or that of the sparks of an unquenchable uproar of fire.

Monks cluster in a pack like wolves,
[shrinking] from encounter with the lords who shall find them out.
They know not when dawn and darkness divide.   55
They know not which course, which onset,
which place is wasted, which land strikes

. . . .

[I EXALT THE SOVEREIGN, great prince.
[Christ provide for me, so that I may not be sorrowful.]]

◆ ◆ ◆ ◆ ◆ ◆ ◆

§114. *Pa Gur yv y Porthaur?* Who is the Gate-keeper?

BLACK BOOK OF CARMARTHEN 94.1–96.16

[Arthur:]   WHO IS THE GATE-KEEPER?'
[Glewlwyd:]   'Glewlwyd Mighty-grasp.

                 Who is asking?'
[Arthur:]   'Arthur and Fair Kei.'

[Glewlwyd:]   'Who goes with you?'   5
[Arthur:]   'The best heroes in the world.'

[Glewlwyd:]   'Into my house you will not go
                 unless you can make a way for them [by proving them
                    worthy].'

[Arthur:]   'I can make a way for them,
and you will see it   10
          . . . ,
and all three of them sages,

Mabon son of Modron,
the man of Uthïr Pendragon,
Kysteint son of Banon,   15
and Guïn Godybrion.
My servants were violent
fighting for their laws.

The counsel of Manawïdan son of Llŷr
was profound.   20
Manaûïd bore back
a broken shield from Trywrûïd;

and Mabon son of Melld [Lightning]
used to splatter blood on the grass;

and Anguas the Winged   25
and Lluch Windy-Hand
kept defence
at Eidïn [Edinburgh] on the borderland.

A lord would give them refuge
wherever he would avenge them.   30
Kei would entreat them
as he slew every third one.
When Kelli was lost,
there was fury.
Kei would be entreating them   35
as he continued to hew them down.
Though Arthur laughed,
the blood flowed.

In Awarnach's hall,
he fought with a hag,   40
he slew Pen-Palach
in the settlements of Dissethach.
In the Mount of Eidïn [Edinburgh]
he fought with dog-heads.   44
Every group of a hundred would fall.
There fell every group of a hundred.

Before four-sinewed Beduïr [Bedwyr]
on the shores of Trywrûïd

in the struggle with Rough-Grey,
he was fierce in affliction   50
with sword and shield.

A host was useless
against Kei in battle.
He used to grip a sword
Hostage-exchange was rejected from his hand.
He was constant in seniority   56
over the army to the realm's benefit.

Beduïr and Brïdlav,
nine hundred listening,
six hundred scattering,   60
was the cost of their incitement.

I had men in service.
It was better while they lived.

Before the kings of Emreis [Ambrosius]
I saw Kei hasten,   65
leading plundered livestock,
a hero long-standing in opposition.

His revenge was heavy.
His vengeance was pain.
When he drank from the ox horn,   70
he drank them by fours.

When he went to battle,
he would slay them by hundreds.
Unless it were God who worked it,
Kei's death could not be achieved.   75

Fair Kei and Llachev,
they made battles
preceding the suffering of blue lances.
On the summit of Ysta-Wïngun,
Fair Kei slew nine witches.   80
Fair Kei went to Anglesey
to destroy lions.

His shield was polished
against Cath Paluc [a monster cat].
When people ask   85
who slew Cath Paluc

(180 bright hounds
would fall for its food;
    180 centurions . . .)[12]

]. . . .

§115. *Marwnat Vthyr Pen* The Death-Song of Uthyr Ben ['the Awesome Head/Chief'] BOOK OF TALIESIN 71.7–72.8

I AM THE ONE mighty in hosts in furore.
    I would not yield between war-bands without bloodshed.
I am the one who is called [steely] lustrous blue.
My battle-belt was a [captive's] collar to my enemy.

It is I who am a prince in the gloom,   5
causing my appearance . . .

I am like a second ?*cawyl* in the gloom.
I would not yield without bloodshed whilst amongst the war-band of the court.
It is I whose heroic deed contended,
seeking to annihilate the kinsmen of Casnur.   10
It is I who poured blood for victory.
I am the one whose champion's feats partook in
a ninth part of Arthur's valour.

It is I who broke a hundred fortified towns.
It is I who killed a hundred mayors of strongholds.   15
It is I who gave out a hundred cloaks.
It is I who cut off a hundred heads.
It is I who gave the ancient leader
enormous sword strokes in protection.
It is I who have made the [?]thundering   20
of the [?]fiery iron door of the mountaintop.

◆ ◆ ◆ ◆ ◆ ◆ ◆

I am a bard, my talent praiseworthy.
Let it be by means of crows and eagles and the rage of battle,
[as when] perfect darkness descended so broadly,
when the four men plied weapons between two hosts.

Climbing to heaven was my desire,
against eagles and fear of injury.

---

12 The manuscript breaks off here.

I am a bard, and I am a harpist.

I am a piper, and I am a player of the lyre [*crwth*],

140 musicians . . . protection . . .

◆   ◆   ◆   ◆   ◆   ◆   ◆

[with] my tongue to sing my death-song . . .

◆   ◆   ◆   ◆   ◆   ◆   ◆

§116. *Trawsganu Kynan Garwyn*
The Panegyric of Kynan Garwyn [son of Brochvael] [13]
BOOK OF TALIESIN 45

1–2	KYNAN BATTLE-DEFENDER
3–4	gave me tribute;
5–6	for there is no deceit in delighting in these things
7–8	before the hunting hounds of the household [i.e. the war-band]:
9–10	one hundred steeds who run together, equally swift
11–12	with silver trappings,
13–14	one hundred purple mantles
15–16	each the same in length,
17–18	a hundred arm-rings in my lap,
19–20	and fifty ?cats,
21–22	a sword with a stone[?-encrusted] sheath
23–24	bright hilted, better than any.
25–26	In Kynan one has
27–28	the dearest friend,
29–30	of the lineage of Cadell,
31–32	unshakable in battle.
33–34	Battle was waged on the River Wye;
35–36	[there were] innumerable spears;
37–38	men of Gwent were slain
39–40	with a gory blade;
41–42	battle in Anglesey, so fair,
43–44	renowned, and praised —
47–48	a steed and vast herd

---

13 This is a battle-listing poem like that which is believed to be the source of *Historia Brittonum* §110 ¶56 ['The Arthurian Battle-List'] above.

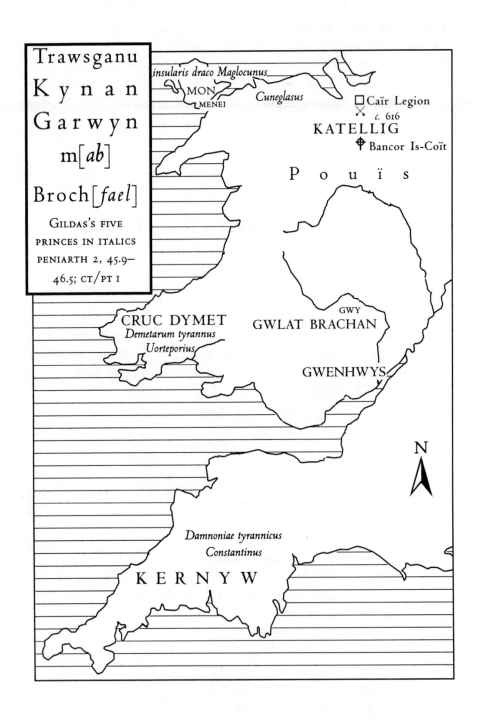

Trawsganu
Kynan
Garwyn
m[*ab*]
Broch[*fael*]

GILDAS'S FIVE
PRINCES IN ITALICS
PENIARTH 2, 45.9–
46.5; CT/PT I

insularis draco Maglocunus
MON
MENEI
Cuneglasus
□ Caïr Legion
✕ *c.* 616
KATELLIG
✝ Bancor Is-Coït

P o u ï s

CRUC DYMET
Demetarum tyrannus
Uorteporius

GWY
GWLAT BRACHAN

GWENHWYS

N

Damnoniae tyrannicus
Constantinus

KERNYW

45–46	driving across the Menai Straits.
49–50	Battle on the Ridge of Dyfed:
51–52	Aergol['s dynasty and household] mustered for action,
53–54	a lord whose cattle
55–56	had never been driven before anyone.
57–58	Frontier-extending son of Brochfael,
59–60	desirous of property,
61–62	Cornwall was entreated.
63–64	([Though] their fate is not an object of praise.)
65–66	He brought hardship to them
67–68	until there was supplication.
69–70	My support is from Cynan,
71–72	foremost in battles
73–74	with his vast radiance
75–76	used to raising conflagration;
77–78	battle in the land of Brachan [i.e. Brycheiniog] —
79–80	a battle enclosure under thunder.
81–82	Doomed chieftains,
83–84	you quake before Cynan,
85–86	breastplate in combat,
87–88	?a dragon-like by nature,
89–90	of like nature to Cyngen,
91–92	mighty one of the broad land.
93–94	I have heard conversation:
95–96	everyone saying,
97–98	over the circuit of the world under the sun:
99–100	'They are slaves to Cynan.'

◆ ◆ ◆ ◆ ◆ ◆ ◆

§117. Y Gododdin
The Gododdin Elegies

¶NOTE. The collection of heroic death-songs called *Y Gododdin* (Middle Welsh *Godo6in*) is of interest from three viewpoints: its testimony concerning the post-Roman Dark Age, the relentless portrayal of the heroic ethos, and the possibility of recovering a substantial specimen of the Archaic Neo-Brittonic language once spoken over most of Britain. The most recent scholarship basing itself closely on the text of the manuscript (the 13th-century 'Book of Aneirin') and its contents supports the proposition that a written text of *Y Gododdin* had its beginnings in the 7th century in the northern Brittonic kingdom of Strathclyde, either in or near Glasgow in present-day Scotland. Though we have only this one pre-modern manuscript, and this is incomplete owing to mutilation in the Middle Ages, it is now clear that it contains portions of three different versions of the text which had undergone lengthy and very different evolutions, both in copying by scribes and the creative activities of poet-performers. By comparing the three texts contained in the Book of Aneirin [BA], a clearer idea of their original starting point, the Dark Age North British text, can be gained. In short these three components can be distinguished as (1) the portion of BA written in the hand of the first scribe [A] and largely in 13th-century Middle Welsh orthography, (2) the first half of the work of the second scribe [B] which is in a somewhat more conservative and erratic form of Middle Welsh spelling, and (3) the latter half of B's work which was mostly left in the Old Welsh spelling of the centuries-old exemplar from which he copied. Significantly, these three texts in BA are distinct in the contents as well as their language and handwriting. The following is a brief synopsis of some the more important differences and what the editor has inferred about their separate text histories.

Text A, reflecting the Third (post *c.* 655) and Fourth (post *c.* 825) Recensions [= stanzas A.1-A.88]: annihilation of forces from the kingdom of Gododdin at the Battle of Catraeth (on which see further below in this headnote); the enemy are Deira and Bernicia (i.e. Northern and Southern Northumbria under the leadership of Oswy6); the Gododdin host includes Picts; primarily serves political interests of the Kynwydyon dynasty of Strathclyde; interest in the Welsh kingdom of Gwynedd; interest in the Coeling (dynasties descended from Coel Hen) of the Pennine region; interest in Taliesin, Myrddin (Merlin), Llywarch Hen, and other characters popular in Welsh literature in the earlier Middle Ages; the poet Aneirin is treated as a saga character in his own right; Christianity; Early Middle Welsh spelling with a relatively infrequent Old Welsh and Archaic Welsh throwbacks; this version influenced other pieces of mediaeval Welsh literature, echoes stanza openings of two other early poems which mention the battle of Catraeth.

Text B[I], reflecting common intermediary AB[I], i.e. the Second Recension (*c.* 643) [= stanzas B.1-B.23]: annihilation of Gododdin forces at Catraeth; the enemy is Deira; the Gododdin host includes Picts; primarily serves interests of the Kyn ydyon dynasty of Strathclyde; one mention of the kingdom of Gwynedd; no interest in the Coeling of the Pennine region; no interest in Taliesin, Myrddin (Merlin), or Llywarch Hen; the poet

Aneirin is assigned composition of the elegies in a semi-external prologue; Christianity; more eccentric Early Middle Welsh spelling with more frequent Old Welsh and Archaic Welsh throwbacks; this version did not influence other pieces of mediaeval Welsh literature, and does not echo other early poems which mention Catraeth.

Text B², reflecting the First Recension, the *Ur*-Text [U] (pre *c.* 638) [= stanzas B.24, B.26–B.42]: Gododdin forces not annihilated at Catraeth, defeat not admitted; the enemy is Deira; more mention of Picts in the Gododdin host; primarily serves interests of the Kynwydyon dynasty of Strathclyde; no mention of the kingdom of Gwynedd; no interest in the Coeling of the Pennine region; no interest in Taliesin, Myrddin (Merlin), or Llywarch Hen, but Arthur is mentioned once in rhyming position; no attribution to Aneirin; no Christianity; mostly Old Welsh spelling with Archaic throwbacks; this version did not influence other pieces of mediaeval Welsh literature, and does not echo other early poems which mention Catraeth.

It follows that B² is our best reflection of the original *Gododdin* of the 6th or 7th century in contents as well as language. The relationship of texts A, B¹, and B² is expressed in the following stemma, in which [O] represents a possible *oral orginal* and U the first written *ur-text.*

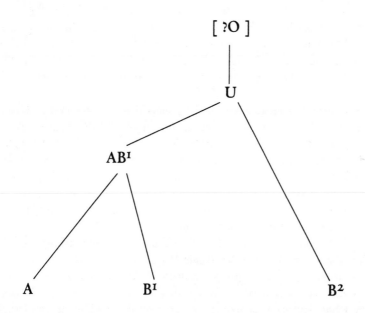

Early Welsh poetry is not as a rule used for narrative, and *Y Gododdin* is no exception. Nonetheless, there are repeated references to a battle fought at a place called *Catraeth*, and this may be regarded as the single most important event commemorated in the original collection. Sufficient details slip through in the elegies to infer some circumstances of the engagement and the events which immediately preceded it.

The name of the battle site is given as *Catraeth* 23 times in BA.² It is now agreed that the place meant is Catterick on the Swale, near Richmond, in the northern end of the Vale of York, east of the Pennine watersh
ed. Most probably it is specifically the Roman fortified town at Catterick, the older name of which had been *Cataractonium* or *Cataracta* (*Caturaxtā* by Celtic popular

etymology) in Roman times, so called for the nearby falls of the Swale.

The home base of the attacking war-band is called *Din-Eidïn* (B¹.19.1158) or *Eidïn Vre* (B².34.1224) 'the Hill-Fort of Eidïn', *Eidyn Ysgor* 'Eidyn's Fold' (A.13.113), *Kynte Eidyn* 'Eidyn's Capital, Chief Seat' (A.17.157), or simply *Eidïn|* (B¹.21.1167), *Eidyn* (B¹.6.490 A.18.183). It is now agreed that this is Edinburgh, most probably a continuation or successor to the Iron Age fortified settlement which has recently come to light on Castle Rock, which would then have been in the northern part of the Brittonic tribal kingdom of Gododdin (MW Godo in).

According to the A text and the less conservative former half of B [B¹], the battle of Catraeth was a disaster for the attackers (the host of Gododdin). On the other hand, the more conservative *awdlau* comprising B² [B.24–42], speak of great carnage, implicitly on both sides, but never tell us of the defeat and explicit annihilation of the Gododdin. B².26, in fact, by referring to Catraeth as better (*guell*) than another of the hero's exploits, implies that it was a victory, or at least an honourable draw. References to great loss of life can be attributed to the *Ur*-Text. The phrase *dial am dâl me* 'retribution in payment for mead' [B².40.786=A.63.788], which refers to the slaughter at Catraeth, could mean either that Gododdin heroes killed to pay for their mead, or were killed, or both. Though B².29 is missing its last line, its close variant A.68 tells that 'but one man of a hundred would return [from battle]'. While it is likely that this is the ultimate source of the references in texts A and B¹ to the Gododdin army's annihilation (with one or a very few survivors), the line in question would more naturally bear the meaning of a less literal impression of horrific ferocity. Therefore, it is doubtful that the *Ur*-Text conceded its heroes' defeat at Catraeth.

It is clear from a number of references within the poems that the attackers at Catraeth were mostly Welsh-speaking Britons and that their enemies included the Anglo-Saxons of Deira. However, there are other references in early Welsh poetry to a battle fought at Catraeth (including §§118, 132 below), which seem to indicate that the Britons of Reget under Uryen (OW *Urbgen*; see above §110 ¶¶57–63) and his kin were defending Catraeth from northern attackers in a battle at about the same period. The politics of the time were probably more complex than we can now easily appreciate and often involved ethnically mixed war-bands and unstable short-term coalitions. Where there is direct historical evidence, as there comes to be for the 7th century, such inter-ethnic coalitions are commonplace, the alliance of the Mercian Angle Penda and Cadwallon of Gwynedd would be one important example. The group loyalties of the period were more often small-scale, dynastic, tribal, and even personal. If we view Celtic/Anglo-Saxon relations as invariably motivated by ethnic and national feelings, we are probably looking anachronistically through the spectacles of modern ideology. The Anglicisation of lowland Britain is perhaps better comprehended as a prolonged ethnolinguistic imbalance against a background of near-continuous low-level tribal and dynastic warfare. It took more than three centuries after the end of Roman rule in Britain (*c.* AD 410) before most of what was to become England was solidly English speaking. In retrospect, this may look like the result of a great war of invading Anglo-Saxons against indigenous Celts. The actual process was probably more complex and piecemeal.

Ideas about the date of the battle of Catraeth vary from *c.* AD 540–*c.* 600. The editor believes that it was *c.* 570 and was a victory, as least a strategic victory, for Uryen of Reget and his Deiran English allies.

The text is not given here following its order in BA, but rather the most conservative Text B² first and the most innovative Text A last. Where variant versions of a single verse appear in more than one text, the translation is provided for the reconstructed common original *awdl* ('stanza') and the equivalence is noted at the position of both variants. In the conviction that history would never forgive me (and that few would follow me) if I were to introduce yet another system of verse and line numeration for *Y Gododdin*, the following hybrid was adopted. Lines are quoted according to Sir Ifor Williams' lineation in his landmark 1938 edition *Canu Aneirin* [CA]. The stanzas have codes beginning with the letter A, B¹, or B² (designating the manuscript's two scribes and the more and less archaic portions of the B-scribe's copy) followed by a one- or two-digit number indicating the position of the stanza in the work of each scribe:[1] thus, e.g., line A.1.1 ('with the nature of hero, though the age of youth') = line 1 of CA, which belongs to the first stanza in hand A. Where variants of a stanza recur in BA, the line numbers and stanza numbers of all variants are given. The elegies do not have titles in BA. Here, each stanza is headed with a list of the names mentioned in it in order. Names are given in modernised Welsh spelling in the English translation.

There are a considerable number of lines that appear to be secondary additions to an older verse. These are indicated with brackets and indentation.

THE MOST ARCHAIC TEXT B²

[B².24 = B¹.3 = A.48]
[Introductory Verse Attributed to Aneirin in B¹]
GODODDIN, DIN DYWYD, GRUGYN

588|575|597	The rock of Lleu's tribe,
	the folk of Lleu's mountain stronghold
589|576|598	at Gododdin's frontier; the frontier was held.
590|577	Counsel was taken,
580|601	storm gathering;
591|602	the vessel from over the Firth
	of the war-band from over the Firth.
593|603	[A man] who nurtures war-bands
595|584|606	came to us
594|583|605	out of Din Dywyd [or Dywydd]
582|604	to be an obstruction to a king's war-band.
596|587|607	The shield of Grugyn before the bull of battle
	had a broken boss.

[B².25 = B².35 = A.42]
CYNHAFAL, A GODODDIN TRIBESMAN

508|497|519	The hero used to attack
509|498|520	against the wall of a fortified town brilliantly.
510|499|521	Gory and [?]unconquered was the fighter in slaughter.
511|500|522|523	A [?]Saxon dirk

512|524|501   was made to do benefit to the birds.
513|525|502   The [?]wielder of the [?]border country considered it beautiful.
[AB¹   514|503   No one alive tells | of the feats of the leader
        515|504   about . . .]
526|506|517   A Gododdin man does not tell that on the day of battle
527|507|517   Cynhafal was not a supporter.

[B².26] HEINI SON OF NEITHON, CATRAETH

1186   I receive [?]embroidery
1187   from the hand of Heini,

1188   one who excels in protecting us,
1189   possessing most distinguished reputation.

1190   He slew a great host
1191   to earn renown.

1192   The son of Neithon slew
1193   gold-torqued men,

1194   a hundred chieftains,
1195   so that it might be considered.

1196   It was better still when he went
1197   with the men to Catraeth.

1198   He was a fosterling, a wine-fed hero
1199   of extensive courage.

1200   Heini was a fierce hero.
1201   He was a scatterer of mail coats.

1202   He was hard; he was impetuous
1203   on the back of his horse.

1204   No soldier girded his flanks in grey —
1205   who performed skilful feats with his spear and shield,

1206   and his sword and dagger —
1207   who would be a better man
(1208   *gloss:* than Hei[ni] son of Neithon).

[B².27]
MERIN IDDEW (THE FIRTH OF FORTH), BUFON

1209   Over the Firth of Forth, most valiant in battle,
1210   three times worse than the ferocity of the vigorous lion,

1211   Bufon wrought great fury.

[B².28]
GODODDIN, YRFAI SON OF WOLSTAN, LORD OF EIDYN

1212   It was usual for him to be mounted upon a high-spirited horse

1213   defending Gododdin

1214   at the forefront of

1214   the men eager for fighting.

1215   It was usual for him to be fleet like a deer.

1216   It was usual for him to attack Deira's retinue.

1217   It was usual for Wolstan's son—though his father was no
        sovereign lord—

1218   that what he said was heeded

1219   It was usual for the sake of the mountain court that shields be broken through

1220   [and] reddened before Yrfai Lord of Eidyn.

[B².29 = A. 68] A GODODDIN TRIBESMAN, MADAWG

843|831   The chief men maintained the praise of rightful privilege,

845|832   like a bright fire that has been well kindled.

846|833   On Tuesday they put on their dark covering.

847|834   On Wednesday their common purpose was bitter.

848|835   On Thursday envoys were pledged.

849|836   On Friday corpses were counted.

850|837   On Saturday their joint action was swift.

851|838   On Sunday their red blades were redistributed.

852|839   On Monday a stream of blood as high as the thigh was seen.

853|840   A Gododdin man tells that when they would come back

854|841   before Madawg's tent after [battle's] exhaustion,

    |842   but one man of a hundred used to return.

[B².30]
EITHINYN SON OF BODDWADAF

434   He attacked in force for the herd(s) of the East.

435   The man that I admire was [?]like that in [?]combat:

436   [?]violence at the borders was payment for the mead
       by the man of greatest valour

437   and a fine man of destiny, the splendid elder,

438   celebrated Eithinyn son of Boddwadaf.

[B².31] EITHINYN, THE FEAST OF THE MOUNTAIN(S)

439 Proud men went from among us.
440 They had been nurtured on wine and mead.
441 Because of the feast at the mountain court,
442 I grow sorrowful
443 for the loss of the harsh man of battle.
444 Like the thunder bolts of heaven,
446 against the charge of Eithinyn,
445 shields used to burst through.

[B².32 = A.70] THE LORD OF DUMBARTON

880|869 He rose early in the morning,
881 when the centurions hasten in the mustering of the army
882|871 following from one advanced position to another.
883|872 At the front of the hundred men he was first to kill.
884|875 As great was his craving for corpses
885|874 as for drinking mead or wine.
886|877 It was with utter hatred
888 that the lord of Dumbarton, the laughing fighter,
887|878 used to kill the enemy.

[B².33 = A.69] ?GWANAR

861|855 He rose early in the morning
862|856 to contend with the [?]Parisī (*or* a ruler) before the border.
  [B² 863 He was an invitation to bitterness
    864 in the front rank of a host,
    865 a beloved foster-brother
    866 in [the land] the land where he [?]loved.]
  [A 857 He was a gap; he was a fiery breach.
    858 Like a wild boar he led the [men of] the hill-fort.]
867|859 He was luxury, courtesy, he was a place to rest,
868|860 [and] he was a chief to the errant warriors [*lit*. beasts of prey] in dark blue [armour].

[B².34] THE HILL-FORT OF EIDYN, YDAR

1221 His blades were seen in the war-band
1222 in the struggle with the hard foe.
1223 Before the rumble of his shield there was flight:
1224 innumerable men fled before Eidyn's hill-fort.
1225 As much as his hand could grip

1226 there did not return of it;

1227 there was wax on it, and it was painted white—

1228 the contentious pierced lime-washed shield.

1229 He pushed, he was pushed.

1231¹ The man that he had struck,

1230 did not strike back,

1231² [but] he had been slain.

1232¹ Frequent were

1233/2 his gifts to the foe following the feast.

1234 It was [in fact] poison that was received.

1235 And before he was buried under clods of earth,

1236 Ydar had deserved his drink of mead.

[B².36] TUDFWLCH

762 With red-sided blades

763 concealing the ground,

764 the reddened manslayer in fury;

765 the laureate hero would slay men.

767 The warrior in his station, the wolf of the company,

766 used to be joyful.

768 The herb garden of the host,

769 a laureate hero striking;

770 before his blinding [in death], he was not weak.

771|759 Most truly are you called for your righteous acts—

772|760 the governor, helmsman, rampart of the tribeland's every boundary,

773|761 Tudfwlch violent in slaughter, a fortified citadel.

[B².37 = A.74] LLYFRDDELW

936|925 The black slayer of the plundering host

935|924 confronted violence.

937|926 He was neither inconspicuous nor aloof.

938|927 He was not a bittersweet drinking companion.

939|928 Pale steeds moved at his will.

940|929 It was no benefit to the land of Pobddelw.

[B² 941 The bull of battle did not retreat the width of a single acre:

942 Llyfrddelw's purpose was opposition.]

[A 930 He is called great and first man in combat

931 in the breaking through of spears, spears of equal measure,

932 the feats of whetted iron of a champion in a war-chariot,

933 a dart in turmoil, in tumult,
934 a virile hero, flaming steel against the foe.]

[B².38] ARTHUR, GORDDUR

1237 More than three hundred of the finest were slain.
1238 He struck down at both the middle and the extremities.
1239 The most generous man was splendid before the host.
1240 From the herd, he used to distribute horses in winter.

1241 [Gorddur] used to bring black crows down in front of the wall
1242 of the fortified town—though he was not Arthur—
1243 amongst men mighty in feats
1244 in the front of the barrier of alder wood—Gorddur.

[B².39 = A.65]
CYNON, AERON, CATRAETH, GODODDIN BRITONS

808 | 800   A most fitting song for Cynon of the rightful privileges:
809 | 801   he was slain; and before the defensive barrier of Aeron was laid waste,
810 | 802   he reckoned [the deeds of] his gauntlet, measuring in   grey eagles;
811 | 803   [for] in urgency, he made food for scavengers.
812 | 805   For the sake of the subject mounted warriors from the mountain country,
813   he put his side in front of the spear(s) of enemies.
814 | 804   Before Catraeth there were swift gold-torqued men;
[A   815   they slew; they cut down those who would stand.
        816   The whelps of violence were [far] away from their [home] regions.]
817 | 806   A great rarity in battle on the side
818 | 807   of the Gododdin Britons was any [?]cavalryman superior to Cynon.

[B².40 = A.63] CATRAETH, ?GWYDDNO

782 | 774   We have most deserved poetry for a host.
783 | 775   Our warriors made embroilment around Catraeth.
784 | 776   Fallen multicoloured cloth and gore were trampled.
785 | 777   The trees of battle were trampled —
786 | 778   vengeance in payment for mead.
787 | 779   It was corpses that were met.
788 | 780   Gwyddno does not tell of it after the uproar of battle:
789 | 781   [for] though he was entitled to a [victor's] share, [?death] overtakes him.

[B².41] GWYDDNO SON OF GWYNGAD

1245   The hand fed birds.
1246   I esteem the man who used to slaughter,
1247   who tore at the furthest limits.

1250	The man who used to slaughter in wolfish rage
1248	wore gold
1249	at the forefront of battle.
1251	The man with the fair brow, ruddy in battle,
1252	one of the violent three,
1253	pursued combat.
1254	The terrifying bear fought in opposition.
1256	The army was long to hear
1255	of the heroic champion of the royal retinue:
1257	Gwyddno son of Gwyngad was splendid.

[B².42]
CYNDDYLIG OF AERON, THE NOVANTIAN MEN

825|819	A most fitting song for an élite host.
826|820	He had no desire for a happy little place in the world.
821	This he sought: the acclamation of bards across the world's circuit,
822	and gold, and great horses, and mead's intoxication;
82	but whenever he came from battle [he sought this]—the glorification
824	of Cynddylig of Aeron by the Novantian men.[14]

♦ ♦ ♦ ♦ ♦ ♦

THE LESS ARCHAIC TEXT B¹

[B¹.1 = A.78]
KINTYRE, THE GRANDSON OF NEITHON,
DOMNALL BRECC 'The Srath Caruin *Awdl*'[15]

972|966	I saw an array that came from Kintyre,
973|967	who brought themselves as a sacrifice to a holocaust.
974|968	I saw a second [array] who had come down from their settlement,
975|969	who had been roused by the grandson of Neithon.
976|970	I saw mighty men who came with dawn.
977|971	And it was Domnall Brecc's head that the ravens gnawed.[16]

---

14 Novantian men, manuscript Nouant. The *Novantae* appear in Ptolemy's World Geography (2nd century ad) as a tribe in what is now South-west Scotland, nr. Ayrshire, i.e. *Y Gododdin*'s Aeron.

15 *Awdl* is the Welsh term for a long monorhyming stanza and poems comprising of one or more such stanzas.

16 We are particularly fortunate in knowing more-or-less fully, from independent sources, the historical background of this verse. The honorand is called *ẹ‹i›»r Nwython* in text B¹ and

[B¹.2 = A.52]

GODODDIN TRIBESMAN, ANEIRIN SON OF DWYWAI, THE GODODDIN TRIBE 'The Reciter's Prologue'

649|640	Gododdin man, I desire to entertain you—
650|642	here in the war-band's presence, exuberantly in the court—
651|643	with the transmitted poetry from Dwywai's son, a man of high valour.
652|641	Let it be made known; and thereby, it will prevail!

653|647	Since the refined one, the bull of battle, was slain,
654	since earth was pushed over Aneirin,
655|648	song and the Gododdin tribe are now separated.

[B¹.3 = B².24 = A.48]

[B¹.4 = A.86]

RHUFONIAWG, THE RIVER ALED, GORTHYN SON YRFAI, LORD OF THE VENEDOTIANS, CILYDD

1078|1055	Destructive in every lowland,
1070|1056	his slave-chain was filled to capacity.
1080|1057	His shield [?< wheeled car] would be broken fronted,
1081|1058	a warlike man of enduring ferocity,

⟨g⟩ŵyr Nwythyon in A, pointing to an original *ẽr Ne(i)thon 'the grandson of Neithon'. In the Annals of Ulster for 641 (= 642), the event is noted: *Domnall Brecc in bello Sraith Cairuin in fine anni in Decembri interfectus est ab Höan rege Britonum; annis .xu. regnauit* 'Domnall Brecc was slain in the battle of Strathcarron at the end of the year in December by Öan king of the Britons; he ruled fifteen years.' The 'grandson of Neithon' and *Höan rex Britonum* are the same person. In the Old Welsh genealogy of Strathclyde (London Manuscript Harley 3859), he is *Eügein map Beli map Neithon*, and Eügein is the great great great grandson of Cïnŵit, the eponym of the Kynŵydyon dynasty of Strathclyde. Domnall Brecc was the erratically aggressive king of Dál Ríata in Britain. As a member of the Cenél nGabráin sept, Domnall Brecc's ancestral lands in Kintyre, Cowall, and Bute lay closer to Strathclyde and Gododdin than any other part of Dál Ríata. The editor believes that the appearance of this verse in this position (immediately before the courtly public recitation introducing the *Gododdin* elegies) is best explained by assuming that a reciter performed *Y Gododdin* (as a collection of traditional material from the extinct neighbouring court of Din Eidïn) in about 643 for Eügein of Strathclyde on the occasion of the celebration of the victory at Srath Caruin, after which Eügein was the leading regional power and in position to annex lands that had not long before belonged to the Brittonic kingdom of Gododdin. This poet of *c.* 643 addresses his patron Eügein as 'Gododdin man' to enhance his claim to the Edinburgh region.

1082 | 1059	the defender of Rhufoniawg [in north-east Wales].
1083 | 1060	In a second battle his war horses and bloody armour
1084 | 1061	were seen about the river Aled.
1085 | 1062	The host was unshaken.
1087 | 1064	When the fierce men
1088 | 1065	had been enraged
1086 | 1063	they would be great in battle.
1089 | 1066	In force in combat he used to slay with blades.
1090 | 1067	He would bear back a bitter warning from battle.
1091 | 1068	He would make preparation for a hundred at New Year's.
1092 | 1069	The son of Yrfai could be approached,
1093 | 1070	the arrogant boar could be approached,
1094 | 1071	by any queen and a maiden and a nobleman,
1095 | 1072	because he was the son of a rightful hereditary king,
1096 | 1073	lord of the Gwynedd folk, of the blood of Cilydd the Deliverer [*or* the Caledonian Deliverer].
1097 | 1074	Before the setting down of earth on the cheek,
1098 | 1075	he was generous and wise,
1099 | 1076	his tribute and praising were assured. It is sad
1100 | 1077	that there is a grave for tall Gorthyn of Rhufoniawg's highland.

[B¹.5, A.40, B¹.6, A.41]
MORIEN, HEATHEN TRIBES OF SCOTS AND PICTS, GWENABWY SON OF GWEN

470 | 459 | 486 | 478	. . . ,
471 | 460 | 487	around the bright and precipitous landscape,
461 | ?480 | 488	for the [?]sword stroke falling about the chieftain,
472 | 468 | 489 | 485 | [494]	[there were] three heroes ready for violence following [?]sunrise:
473 | 463 | [465] | [475] | 491	with his gauntleted hand, Morien vanquished
(474 | 480	aggressively . . .)
475 | 492	against heathen tribes of both Scots and Picts.
493 | 482	A man who would shake a wolf's neck without a wooden shaft in his hand
494 | 483	must possess a superb inborn fury under his mantle:
477 | 469 | 496	Gwenabwy son of Gwen of skillful deeds.

[B¹.7 = A.51] ADDONWY, BRADWEN, THE ANGLO-SAXONS

634 \| 627 A good outcome, O Addonwy, finely you had promised me:

635 \| 628 what Bradwen would do, you would do—you would kill, you would burn.

636|630   [In fact] you defended neither the extremity nor the vanguard.
637|631   With your bold eyes unencumbered by headgear,
638|632   you did not see the great mêlée of the mounted warriors:
639|633   they [?]fought; they gave no mercy to the Saxons.

[B¹.8] THREE HUNDRED GOLD-TORQUED MEN

1126 Three hundred gold-torqued men charged forth
1127 fighting for the variegated and ruddy [land]: there was slaughter.
1128 Before they were slain, they slew.
1129 And till the end of the world, they will be esteemed.
1130 Of all of us who went as fellow kinsmen,
1131 alas! only one man escaped.

[B¹.9] THREE HUNDRED GOLD-TORQUED MEN

1132 Three hundred gold-torqued men,
1133 combat-loving, provoking;
1134 three hundred haughty men,
1135 unified and armed alike;

1136 three hundred spirited horses
1137 that charged with them;

1138 the thirty and the three hundred,
1139 alas! they did not return.

[B¹.10] BLEIDDIG SON OF BELI

1140 Vigilant in battle, reaping in contention;
1141 in encounter, it was not peace that he used to make.
1142 On the day of fighting, it was not battle that he would avoid.
1143 Bleiddig son of Beli was a boar [< wolf] of fury.
1144 He drank wine from full glass vessels,
1145 and in the day of feats, it was a feat that he would do
1146 from upon the back of a very white steed. Before he perished,
1147 it was reddened corpses that he used to leave behind him.

[B¹.11; cf. A.23] THE SON OF BLEIDDGI

268   Before the ford he had borne the burden among hosts.
269   The array of the [?] battle leader's host
270   used to attack brilliantly mindful of the [?] objective.
271   A fortunate leap,
272   his . . . he has [or I have] heard poetry.
273|264   He used to make men prostrate
274|265   and wives widows before his death.
275|266   As a special privilege, Bleiddgi's son

276|267   had been used to causing bloodshed with spears.

[B¹.12 = A.20] BREICHIAWL

227+000   Fine conduct in battle was what you used to accomplish.

228   Before its spear points, you contended against it.

[A 221   He drank [> you drank] wine and mead in the great hall.

222   Because you drank, you attacked the border region—a sorrowful destiny!]

229|224   When everyone was in retreat, you used to attack.

[B¹ 230   If the blood of the men you used to slay were wine,

231   you would receive enough for three years and four,

232   mightily would you decrease it for your steward.]

233|225   May heaven's land be yours, because you would not flee,

234|226   O world-renowned Breichiawl the tenacious!

[B¹.13; cf. A.22] BANNAWG, THE YOUNG SON OF CIAN

250   When he attacked the realm's frontier, his fame was exquisite.

251   The gold-torqued man used to deserve his wine.

252   The splendid man used to present a sheer, bright array.

254   A foreign horseman of most refined nature,

253   the noble hero used to lead a hundred men,

255   Cian's only young son from beyond Bannawg.

256|248   After the battle a Gododdin tribesman does not tell

257|249   that anyone had been keener than Llif ('the Saw').

[(B¹.14=) B¹.15 = A.62 ; cf. B².36] MERIN SON OF MADIAN

733|717   The anchor, the driver of the Deirans,

734|718   the serpent with the hideous barb,

735|770   before the army.

[755|721   Before the summit of provision,

756|722   ferocity [forcing] through affliction,

757   may it pay back

758|723   the oppression of spears.]

730|736|737   Most truly are you called for your righteous deeds:

731|738   the governor, the helmsman, rampart of the people's every frontier.

732|739   You were born auspiciously, o Merin son of [?]Madian.

[B¹.16]

GARTH MERIN ?'THE ENCLOSURE BY THE FIRTH [OF FORTH]'

740   [Amid] the bright flood, [like] a gray wolf—the dreadful following water —

741   the anchor, driver of the Deirans,

742 [was as] an unshaken rock
743 before the host;
744 blood-stained multitudes
745 of both horses and men
746 before Gododdin tribesmen;
747 swift dogs baying,
748 mustering of the region,
749 an all-encompassing vapour
750 in front of the enclosure by the Firth.

[B¹.17]
1148 With his shield suffering violence, he would submit to no one.
1149 It was love of honour that sustained him.
1150 He returned from horses' [?]flanks in the front rank of battle's uproar.
1151 Heroic men scattered gory holly spears.
1152 When my foster brother was slain, he slew others.
1153 It was not with dishonour that he conducted himself.
1154 Vigilant in keeping the ford; he used to take delight
1155 as he bore off the portion of fame in the great hall.

[B¹.18 = A.26] MARCHLEU
312|300   Most truly have the songs told
313|301   that no one's horses could catch Marchleu (the steed of [the god] Lleu).
314|304   Because he was nurtured, he performed feats around a fort's portal.
315|305   Before he was slain, mighty was the sword stroke
316|306   of the hero who had once scattered his ash wood [spears] from the four clefts
317|307   of his hand while he was mounted upon a bright slender steaming [steed].

[B¹.19] DYN EIDYN, LLOEGR, GWAEDDNERTH
1156 Protective guidance to heaven, dwelling place in the longed-for land!
1157 Woe to us for the grief and constant sorrow!
1158 When the noblemen came from Din Eidyn's [?]grazing-meadow,
1159 the chosen men of every enlightened domain,
1160 in contention with Lloegr's mixed hosts,
1161 180 around each mailed warrior,
1162 masses of horses and armour and silken clothes,
1163 Gwaeddnerth used to safeguard what was his due from the battle.

[B¹.20 = A.60] THE FEAST OF THE MOUNTAIN(S), CATRAETH
703   From the retinue of the mountain court
704|697 a bright array charged forth, who had taken sustenance together around

the bowl.

705|699 For the feast in the mountain stronghold they were to perish.

706|700 Too many have I lost of my true kinsmen.

707|701 Of the three hundred gold-torqued men who attacked Catraeth,

708|702 alas! only one escaped.

[B¹.21]

THE RETINUE OF GODODDIN, EIDYN, THE COUNSEL OF
THE MOUNTAIN COURT

1164 The retinue of Gododdin from [their mounts] on rough hair

1165 of horses the colour of swans with harness [?]drawn tightly,

1166 and in the first rank of the host that attacked the multitude,

1167 fighting for the groves and mead of Eidyn;

1168 due to the taking of counsel in the mountain court,

1169 shields had gone over,

1170 blades had fallen

1171 on white cheeks.

1172 They loved [?] killing . . . in the attack.

1173 The men who would not flee bore no shame.

[B¹.22] CATRAETH, MADAWG OF ELMET

1174 He drank mead in his mobilisation for hosting.

1175 He was wine nourished for Catraeth in that same provision.

1176 When he slew with his blades, he was unshaken

1177 in battle. He was not weak wherever he was to be seen.

1179 The vengeful shield-bearer Madawg of Elmet

1178 was not inept, he was a [battle-]sprite providing deliverance.

[B¹.23] CYNON, THE AVENGER OF AERON, THE BRITONS

1180 When he used to go to confrontation,

1181 he did not conduct himself as one who would escape alive.

1182 The avenger of Aeron

1183 used to plunder gold ornaments

1184 (from the Britons' opponent)

1185 and spirited horses—Cynon.

◆ ◆ ◆ ◆ ◆ ◆

THE MOST INNOVATIVE TEXT A

[RUBRIC: This is *Y Gododdin* that Aneirin sang.]

[A.1] YWAIN THE ONLY SON OF MARRO

1 With the instinct of a hero, [though] immature in years,
2 [with] boisterous valour,
3 [and] with a swift, thick-necked horse
4 under the thigh of the splendid youth,
5 [with] a broad light shield
6 on the crupper of his slender swift [horse],
7 [with] bright blue swords
8 of painstaking gold wirework.
9 It will not be . . .
10 hate between me and you.
11 I shall do better with you,
12 praising you in inspired song.
13 His blood flowed to the ground
14 before his wedding rite.
15 His flesh went to crows
16 rather than to thy burial rite.
17 Dear foster brother Ywain,
18 it is sorrowful that he is under stones.
19 I wonder in what land
20 was slain Marro's only son.

[A.2] MADAWG, GODODDIN

21 Wearing an ornament of rank and in the front line's array wherever he went;
22 the man who paid for his mead would be breathless before a maiden.
23 His [?] round shield [< wheeled car] used to be broken-fronted wherever he heard [battle's] uproar.
24 He would give no mercy to those he pursued.
25 He would not return from feats till the blood flowed.
26 As if they were rushes he used to hew down the men who did not flee.
27|853|840   On the floor of the great hall a Gododdin tribesman tells
28|854|841   that when he returned to the front of Madawg's tent
29| |842   but one man of a hundred used to come back.

[A.3]

GODODDIN, THE VARIEGATED AND RUDDY [LAND] OF MANAWYD, CADFANNAN

30 A fighter with an ornament of rank, snare of the realm's frontier,

31 with the rush of an eagle when taking prey in a river mouth,

32 his compact was a pledge that was kept.

33 His martial purpose was excellently conceived: there was no retreat.

34 There was flight before the army of Gododdin,

35 a mighty compulsion against the variegated and ruddy [land] of Manawyd.

36 Neither a [?] Scot's targe nor shield protected the . . .

37 No one can—unless well nourished—

38 hold against Cadfannan's blow.

[A.4]

GWEFRFAWR SON OF YSGYRRAN, GWYNEDD, THE NORTH

39 [Regularly] wearing an ornament of rank, in the front line's array, wolfish in fury,

40 the man in the torque won amber jewellery for sharing out.

41 Gwefr[f]awr was of great value in exchange for a wine draft.

42 He pushed back the heat [of the attack] with blood running down his cheek.

43 Though Gwynedd-men and Northerners used to come to his unit,

44-45for the counsel of Ysgyrran's son: [there were] shattered shields.

[A.5; cf. A.1]

[DEIRA AND BERNICIA,] BRÂN[, HYFAIDD]

46 Wearing an ornament of rank, in the front line's array, armed in battle's uproar,

47 before the day [of his fatal battle] he was a hero in deeds,

48 a centurion counter-thrusting against armies.

49 Five fifties would fall before his blades

⟨50 there fell of men of Deira and Bernicia ⟩

51 twenty hundred laid waste at one time.

52 Rather than to a wedding rite, his flesh went to wolves,

53 rather than to the altar, his victory spoils to the crow,

54 rather than a proper funeral, his blood flowed to the ground,

55 [all] in exchange for mead in the pre-eminent seat with the assembled hosts.

56 For as long as there are singers, Hyfaidd will be praised.

[A.6] THE GODODDIN TRIBE, THE SON OF BODDWGAD

57 The men despatched to the Gododdin tribe, provoked to laughter,

58 —bitter in combat with spears gathered in formation—

59 during the short year in peace, they were in a loyal retinue [in their lord's court].

60 (The deed of) the hand of the son of Boddwgad did vengeance

63|73 to impale them in the inexorable confrontation with death.

[A.7] THE MEN WHO WENT TO GODODDIN, RHEITHFYW

64 The men who went to Gododdin, laughing noblemen,

65 attackers in a host, merciless in combat,

66 they // he slew with blades without great clamour. [17]

67 The pillar of battle, Rheithfyw, used to give delight.

[A.8] THE MEN WHO WENT TO CATRAETH

68 Ready was the host of the men who went to Catraeth.

69 Blue mead was their feast, and it was poison —

70 three hundred preparing for battle according to plan,

71 and after rejoicing, there was silence.

72 Though they would go to churches to do penance //[18]

73 to impale them in the inexorable confrontation with death.

[A.9]
THE MAN DESPATCHED TO CATRAETH, THE RETINUE OF BERNICIA, THE YOUNG SON OF CIAN, THE STONE OF THEVENICONES [MAENGWYNGWN]

74 The man despatched to Catraeth, mead-nurtured ruler,

75 mighty, virile—it would be wrong if I were not to call him to mind.

[76 Around reddened blades, enormous and dark-socketed,

77 the hounds of slaughter fought severe and undaunted.

78 For Bernicia's host they deemed it a burden.

79 Not a man [of them] left the Deluge alive.]

80 It was a foster-brother that I have lost; I was unswerving.

81 Brutally I am parted from the man adept in hand-to-hand combat.

82 The heroic man did not seek a father-in-law's dowry —

83 the young son of Cian from the Stone of the Venicones.

[A.10]
THE MEN DESPATCHED TO CATRAETH, THE RETINUE OF THE LUXURIOUS MOUNTAIN COURT

84 The fears of the men despatched to Catraeth with dawn

85 shifted their dwelling place.

---

17 This *awdl* shifts from a plural to singular honorand in a confused way in line 66. It is likely that a later poet-transmitter has modified an earlier verse.

18 There is a break in sense between lines 72 and 73, probably the result of the substitution of new lines and/or omission of old during the transmission process.

86 A hundred thousand opposed to three hundred men throwing
   weapons at each other
87 splattered spears with blood.
88 They stood most valorously in the mighty action
89 for the retinue of the luxurious mountain court.

[A.11]
THE MEN DESPATCHED TO CATRAETH, THE RETINUE OF
THE LUXURIOUS MOUNTAIN COURT

90 The nature of the men who were despatched to Catraeth with the dawn
91 shortened their lives.
92 They drank yellow sweet filtered mead.
93 For a year many musicians were happy.
94 Their swords are red, and their spears
95 will not be cleansed. There were whitewashed shields and four-clefted [spear-]heads
96 before the retinue from the luxurious mountain court.

[A.12]
THE MEN DESPATCHED TO CATRAETH, GODODDIN'S
HOST, NEIRTHIAD

97 The men who were despatched to Catraeth with the day //
98 He made disgrace of armies.
99 // made biers a certainty
100 fully armed, adversity across the world.
101 Rather than exchanging hostages for a truce, this man made
102 a bloodbath and death for his opponent.
103 When he [?]would be before Gododdin's host,
104 Neirthiad the fighter conceived a bold intent.

[A.13]
CATRAETH, EIDYN, ?OSWIU, SAXONS
TUDFWLCH SON OF CILYDD

105 The man despatched to Catraeth with the day
106 drank a mead feast at midnight.
107 The lamentation of the assembled hosts was sorrowful
108 for the mission compelled upon the fiery hero who died.
109 None attacked Catraeth
111 whose preparing for battle [while carousing] over mead drinking
110 had been so mighty.
112 None so completely

114   drove off [?]Oswiu[19]

113   from the stronghold of Eidyn.

115   Tudfwlch, [while he remained] for a long time away from his land and its
       settlements,

116   used to slay Saxons each seventh day.

117   His manliness will endure as a legacy

118   through the memory of him amongst his splendid comrades.

119   Wherever Tudfwlch— the strength of the tribesmen—arrived,

120   the place of spear shafts would be a bloody enclosure—Cilydd's son.

                                        [? or son of the Caledonian]

[A.14] [THE MEN DESPACTHED TO CATRAETH,] ERTHGI

       [121   The men despatched to Catraeth with the dawn . . .]

122   In his war-band—a defensive stronghold of shields—

       [123   . . . were wont to attack in bloodshed, were wont to collect booty.]

124   in the [?]din—the sound of the boards [of shields] like thunder—,

       [125   a hero]

       126   was wont to rend and pierce with points [of weapons].

       127   Above the bloodshed, he used to slay with blades

128   in the affliction of hardened iron against the front of heads.

129   In the great hall, he bowed low before [?]worthies.

130   Before Erthgi, war-bands howled.

[A.15]
CATRAETH'S VARIEGATED AND RUDDY [LAND],
THE DESCENDANTS OF [COEL HEN] GODEBAWG,
TUDFWLCH, CYFWLCH

131   It is concerning Catraeth's variegated and ruddy [land] that it is told—

132   the followers fell; long were the lamentations for them,

133   the immortalised men; [but] it was not as immortals that they
       fought for territory

134   against the descendants of Godebawg, the rightful faction:

135   long biers bore off blood-stained bodies.

136   It was the fate of the condemned—certain doom—

137   that was destined to Tudfwlch and tall Cyfwlch.

138   Though we drank bright mead by the light of tapers,

---

19 Oswiu, corresponding to Old Welsh Osgüïd (see *Historia Brittonum* §110 ¶¶57, 64–65
    above) and Middle Welsh Oswy was the name of the king of Northumbria who ruled
    between 642–670. It is likely that the same Anglo-Saxon prince was present at the siege of
    Din Eidyn (*obsesio Etin*) noted in the Annals of Ulster for 638.

139   [and] though its taste was good, its revulsion was long-lasting.

[A.16]

THE FORTIFIED SETTLEMENT OF EIDYN, THE MEN OF THE FORTH

140   Foremost from the fortified settlement of Eidyn, he used to fight brilliantly;
141   the noble men of the Forth used to follow him.
142   On his feather cushion, foremost would he dispense
143   the aurochs horn in his luxurious palace.
144   Foremost were liquor and malt drink to be brought to him.
145   Foremost he was in taking delight in gold and purple [clothing].
146   Foremost it was that well-fed horses were accustomed to running under him
147   directed by his harsh cry. His spirit merited these.
148   Foremost he would raise the piercing shout of victory.
149   Like a bear, he was always slow [i.e. not foremost] to retreat.

[A.17]

THE ISLAND OF BRITAIN, EIDYN'S CHIEF SEAT, GWRFELLING (? GWRFELYN)

150   The place of honour in the first rank
151   at the sun's rising.
152   Lord, where can one find
153   the Island of Britain's champion?   [MS 'heaven']

154   [At] the rough ford facing the violence,
155   [with] a shield like a cattle-fold;
156   the aurochs horn was lustrous
157   in Eidyn's royal centre,

158   his ostentatious regal manner,
159   his intoxicating mead.
160   He used to drink wine's strong liquor.

161   He was a reaper in sword play.
162   He used to drink bright wine.
163   Daring slaughter in armed action,
164   a reaper of the leeks of battle,

165   the brilliant wing of battle —
166   they used to sing a song of battle —

167   armed in battle,
168   the winged one of battle.

169   His shield was not usually whole

170   owing to the spears of combat.

171   Men of the same generation would fall

172   in battle's combat.

173   His [?]vigorous cry,

174   he avenged them without disgrace.

175   His wildness was transformed

176   before there was a green covering

177   on the grave of mighty [?] Gwrfelling.

[A.18]
THE NOVANTAE, EIDYN, THE BRITONS, CYNRI, CYNON, ?CYNRAIN, AERON, DEIRA

179   The three cudgels of the Novantae

178   esteem rightful privilege —

181   [of the host] of the thirty and the three hundred,   [180 *gloss:* [of the
                                   host] of the fifty and the five hundred]

182   the three directors of the cavalry brigades

183   of Eidyn of the gold smiths;

184   three of the mail-clad host;

185   the three gold-torqued chieftains;

186   the three vigilant horsemen;

187   three battle peers;

188   three fierce lords who rushed forward in unison

189   harshly routed the enemy.

190   Three in combat under heavy pressure

191   slew with ease with lead[-tipped weapons].

192   Heroes in an arrayed host,

193   the three chieftains of the loyal followers

194   who came from the Brython:

195   Cynri and Cynon
        ?[and . . .],

196   the centurions of Aeron.

197   Heathen tribes

198   of Deiran brigands used to ask

199   whether there came from the Brython

200   a man better than Cynon,

201   the serpent in the enemy's path.

[A.19]

CADWAL SON OF SYWNO, ATHRWYS, AFFRAI, THE GWYNEDD MEN

202   He drank wine and mead in the great hall.

203   Great was his spears' extent

204   in the confrontation of men.

205   It was food for eagles that used to delight him.

206   When Cadwal attacked, he used to raise up

207   the battle cry with the green dawn. He used to set together

208   the planks [of shields]; it was shattered splinters he would leave behind.

209   (With) rough lances he used to tear.

210   He would hew down in battle.

211   In front of the war-band, he used to destroy.

212   It was the son of Sywno—as the seers saw—

213   who exchanged his life's breath

214   for his honour to be considered.

215   With a whetted blade he used to slay.

216   He slew both Athrwys and Affrai.

217   To fulfil his contract he took arms.

218   He used to exult in the corpses

219   of fierce men of combat.

220   In front of the Gwynedd men, he used to stab.

[A.20; see B^{I}.12]

[A.21]

THE MEN WHO WENT/WERE SENT TO CATRAETH, AERON, CYNON

235   The men who went to Catraeth were famous.

236   Wine and mead from gold was their liquor,

237   for a year according to the custom of the [?]tribal leaders,

238   three men and sixty and three hundred wearing golden torques.

239   Of all those that hastened from around the over-abundant mead,

240   but three escaped by the valour of combat:

241   the two battle hounds of Aeron and Cynon ran back,

242   and myself spilling my blood in exchange for my inspired poetry.

[A.22] GODODDIN, LLIFIAU

243   My comrade, my true and noble friend did not distress us,

244   if only it were not for the feast of the severe chieftain.

245   He was not denied the fellowship of the mead drinking in the tribal capital.

246   Against destruction he wrought destruction in armed struggle.

247   He was unfallen in the host, unfallen in the unit.
248   After combat, a Gododdin tribesman does not tell
249   that anyone would be keener than Llifiau.

[A.23; cf. Gorchan Tudfwlch, B¹.ıı]
THE TRIBELAND OF THE LOWLANDERS, ‹GREID› SON OF BLEIDDGI

258   [With] armament disarrayed
259   [and] ranks broken, he was unshaken.
260   [With] great destruction
261   he rocked the ground of the Lowlanders' tribeland.
262   He scattered javelins
263   in the front rank of shields in the spear fighting.
264   He used to make men prostrate
265   and wives widows before his death.
266   Greid son of Bleiddgi
267   would cause bloodshed with spears.

[A.24]
BRÂN, ELEIRCH FRE 'THE HILL OF SWANS', BUDDWAN SON OF BLEIDDWAN

277   The hero with the protective shield under its polychrome boss,
278   (with movement like a colt)
279   was tumult on slaughter's high ground, was fire.
280   His spears were readied, they were [like] the sun.
281   He was food for ravens [brein, sg. brân]. He was spoils for Brân (the Raven).

[282   And before the eagle of the graceful swoop was left at the fords
  283   with the dew
  284   and with the wave's spray against the hillside,
  285   the bards of the world judge the men of heart.]

286   His counsel deprived him of his entitlement.
287   His centurions' hundred-man units [cannwyr] perished.
288   And before he was buried under Eleirch
289   Fre [the Hill of Swans], there was valour in his breast.
290-91 The blood of courageous Buddwan son of Bleiddwan washed over his
        cuirass.

[A.25] ‹BRITAIN›, GWENABWY MAB GWEN, CATRAETH
292   It would be wrong to leave unremembered the hero of far-reaching feats.
293   He would not leave the breach [in the ranks] for cowardice.

294 The benefits for aristocratic praise poetry did not depart from his court
295 on the first day of January; as he mobilised for warfare,
296 his land was not ploughed, though it lay waste—
297 the man fierce in battle, the wide-ranging chieftain,
298 a chieftain in bloodshed after being nurtured on wine
299 [was] Gwenabwy son of Gwen in the contention of Catraeth.

[A.26 = B¹.18]

[A.27]
ISAG MAB GWYDDNO, THE SOUTHERN REGION

318 Most courteous Isag from the southern region,
319 his manners were like the inrush of the sea
320 for grace and generosity
321 and fine mead drinking.
322–3 Wherever his weapon(s) struck, the point was made.
324 He was not harsh and then moderate, false and then genuine.
325 His sword resounded in the heads of mothers.
326 A wall of fury was the praised son of Gwyddno.

[A.28] CEREDIG

327 Ceredig whose fame was beloved [to him]
328 used to seize and to guard repute.
329 The wild one is now silent. Before
330 his [death] day came, his manners were splendid.
331 May the beloved of song receive acceptance
332 in heaven's land, residence of recognition.

[A.29] CEREDIG

333 Ceredig, the beloved centurion,
334 the champion in the raging battle,
335 gold filigreed shield of the battle enclosure,
336 [amid] splinters of broken spears,
337 the careful powerful sword-stroke;
338 like a hero he was wont to hold the place of shafts.
339 Before handing him over to the earth, before the grief,
340 he purposefully defended his forward position.
341 May he receive inclusion in the company
342 with the Trinity in perfect unity.

[A.30]
CARADAWG, YWAIN SON OF ?EULAD, ?GWRIEN, GWYN, GWRIAD, CATRAETH, BRYN HYDDWN

343 When Caradawg hastened to battle,
344 like a wild boar he was wont to cut down thirty [men],

345 the bull of the host slew in combat.
346 Wolves took prey from his hand.

[347 My witness is Ywain son of Eulad
[348 and Gwrien and Gwyn and Gwriad
[349 concerning Catraeth, concerning the slaughter,
[350 of Bryn Hyddwn before it was taken.
[351 After bright mead in hand,
[352 no man [of them] saw his father [again].

[A.31]
THE RETINUE OF THE MOUNTAIN COUNTRY, CARADAWG, MADAWG, PYLL, IEUAN, GWGAWN, GWIAWN, GWYN, CYNWAN, PEREDUR, GORDDUR, AEDDAN

353 The men who charged lunged forth in unison,
354 short-lived men intoxicated over mead-filled [?]*situlae*,
355 the retinue of the mountain domain, famed in urgency [of battle].
356 The price of their feast of mead was their lives:
357 Caradawg and Madawg, Pyll and Ieuan,
358 Gwgawn and Gwiawn, Gwyn and Cynwan,
359 Peredur of the steel armament, Gorddur and Aeddan,
360 a conqueror (or conquerors) in the uproar of battle with shields disarrayed,
361 and though they were slain, they slew.
362 None returned to their districts.

[A.32]
GWLYGAWD THE GODODDIN TRIBESMAN, THE FEAST OF THE MOUNTAIN COUNTRY, THE VARIEGATED AND RUDDY [LAND] OF CATRAETH

363 The heroes who attacked were nurtured together
364 for a year over mead; their purpose was great.
365 How sad their story! Ravenous longing!
366 Their resting place was horrific. No son that mother nurtured
367 was grieved or yearned after for so long after his passing
368 as were the brilliant heroes of the wine-fed province.
369 For the swift ones, Gwlygawd the Gododdin tribesman
370 devised the wine feast of the renowned mountain citadel,
371 and this [was to be] the ransom for the purchase of Catraeth's variegated and ruddy [land].

[A.33]
THE MEN WHO WENT / WERE SENT TO CATRAETH, RHUFAWN

372 Men went to Catraeth fighting and raising the battle cry.
373 A force of stallions and dark armour and shields,

374 upturned javelins and sharp lances
375 gleaming mail coats and swords,
376 was accustomed to forcing breaches through hosts.
377 Five times fifty used to fall before their blades.
378 Rhufawn [< Latin *Rōmānus*] used to give much gold to the altar
379 and gifts and fine offerings to the singer.

[A.34] MORIEN, CYNON, GWID SON OF [N]EITHAN

380 Never was there built a hall more exquisite—
381 so huge, so overly huge its disaster!
382 You deserved your mead drinking, ardent Morien.
383 The singular armoured spearman of extensive renown
384 who would never have said that Cynon would make no corpse.
385 His sword resounded at the peak of the enclosure.
386 No more than a stone of vast girth is moved
387 was Gwid son of *Neithan* shaken.

[A.35] MORIEN, CARADAWG, FFERAWG, GODODDIN

388 There was never built a hall more exquisite. . .//
389 Except for Morien—like a second Caradawg
390 no bold one bolder than the son of Fferawg escaped from
391 the dire oppression of battle in the unimpeachable manner of an aristocrat.
392 His fierce hand would kindle the flight of mounted warriors—
393 the battle lord, a fortress to the frightened army.
394 For the sake of Gododdin's host, fragments of his shield were scattered far.
395 He withstood fierce pressure.
396 On the day of fighting, he was ready. His death was cruel.
397 The man nurtured at the mountain stronghold deserved his horns of mead.

[A.36] CYNON

398 There was never built a hall more durable.
399 [. . .] Cynon—a sovereign whose bejewelled breast was generous—,
400 it was he who used to sit at the head of the couch.
401 Whoever he struck would not be struck again.
402 His lances were very sharp.
403 With his lime-white shield pierced, he used to pierce armies.
404 His stallions were very swift descending into battle.
405 On the day of wrath, his blades were ferocious,
406 when Cynon attacked with the green dawn.

[A.37] ELFFIN, EITHINYN

418 He attacked in force at the forefront.
420 The lance of battle, the laughing warlord,
419 drove the oppressor to flight, established the frontier,
421 valour in attack like that of Elffin,

422   praised Eithinyn, wall of fury, bull of combat.

[A.38; cf. A.53, B².30]   GODODDIN, EITHINYN

423   He attacked in force at the forefront
424   in exchange for mead in the tribe's chief residence and strong wine.
426   For Gododdin, the illustrious horseman
425   scattered his blades between the two armies
427   praised Eithinyn, wall of fury, bull of combat.

[A.39]   BELI, CADFANNAN

447   He attacked in force for the herds of the Eastland,
448   inciting a host with trailing shields.
449   A broken shield for the sake of the cattle of Beli of the great shout,
450   the lord above the carnage hastening to the front.
451   The grey wolf was kept at the front ranks
452   on the spirited steed whose rough image was that of a gold-torqued ox.
453   The boar set conditions at the line of the boundary,
454   deserving legal entitlements, an opponent in the outcry of battle.
455   He who calls us to heaven, let Him be . . .
456   In battle, his fighting spears were brandished.
457   Cadfannan . . . of great fame
458   there was never fighting in which there was not a war-band for the laureate
champion.

[A.40 = B¹.5/B¹.6]

[A.41 = B¹.5/B¹.6]

[A.42 = B².25 = B².35]

[A.43]   GWYNFYD

528   When you were a famed warrior
529   fighting for the summit of the uplands,
530   deservedly we were called resplendent, noteworthy men.
531   There was an unyielding door, an unyielding battle piercer.
532   There was courtesy to those who sought largess;
533   There was a fortress to the army who believed.
534   Wherever he was called upon, Gwynfyd would be there.

[A.44]   CYNY

535   Though there would be a hundred men in a single house,
536   I realise the anxieties of Cyny,
537   a leader of men who deserves the end of the bench.[20]

---

20 The verse is actually an *englyn* (three-line stanza, not the metre of *Y Gododdin*) from the

[A.45] CATRAETH, ANEIRIN, TALIESIN, *Y GODODDIN*

538   I am no vexed courtier.
539   I do not avenge what offends me.
540   I laugh no laugh
541   under the worms.
542   My knee is outstretched
543   in the earthen house,
544   with an iron chain,
545   around my knees.
546   Because of the mead from the aurochs horn,
547   [and] because of the band of Catraeth,
548   it is I and yet not I, Aneirin.
550   Taliesin of skilful song
549   knows it.
551   I sang *Gododdin*,
552   before the dawn of the following day.

[A.46] CENAU SON OF LLYWARCH

553   A hero wrought the valour of the North,
554   generous-hearted, most liberal in his nature.
555   There treads not the earth, no mother has given birth to,
556   any more comely or steadfast in iron armour.
557   By the might of his sword he fought brilliantly.
558   From the hostile earthen prison he delivered me,
559   from the place of death, from an enemy country
560   dauntless and harsh Cenau son of Llywarch.

[A.47]
THE HIGH MOUND OF SENYLLT, GODODDIN AND BERNICIA, HEILYN

561   The high mound of Senyllt bore no disgrace
562   with its vessels full of mead.
563   He used to administer the sword to the iniquitous.
564   He used to provide feats in war.
565   Biers were loaded by his arm
566   for the sake of the army of Gododdin and Bernicia.
567   Swift horses were known in his hall,
568   carnage and dark armour.
569   A long yellow spear shaft in his hand,
570   and hastening in his wrath . . .
572   unloving and loving in turn.

Llywarch Hen cycle. See below.

573 The men were not seen in retreat.
574 Heilyn would control every border.

[A.48 = B².24 = B¹.3]

[A.49]   TRIN-TRA-CHWARDD, BANCARW, RHYS

608 Enemies quake before his weapon(s),
609 those who will fight against the onslaught of Trin-Tra-Chwardd [the hero who fights while he laughs].
610 His stag antlers are sharp about the crag of Banncarw.
611 The fingers of the freckled one smash head(s).
612 A man of many moods—light-hearted, boisterous;
613 a man of many moods   contemplative, humorous;
614 it is vigorously and swiftly Rhys will turn in his expression;
615 not so the man who fails to achieve his mission.
616 Whatever man he might overthrow and wound cannot escape.

[A.50] CYNWAL

617 Not fortunately was the shield pierced,
618 for Cynwal was buried under stones.
619 Not fortunately did he put his thigh
620 upon the tawny long-legged slender-
621 grey [steed]; his spear shaft was tawny;
622 tawnier was his saddle.
623 Your man is in his cell
624 gnawing the leg
625 of a buck, the spoils of his . . .;
626 may it be unusual for him.

[A.51 = B¹.7]

[A.52 = B¹.2]

[A.53; cf. A.38, A.54]

[A.54] MORIAL

656 There was a mustering of warriors whose status was privileged
657 in the dominion of mighty action. Let their follower be heard!
658 The wave (the bright traveller) crashed down
659 wherever they were at the furthest angle.
660 From the cattle corral you might not see the smallest shaft.
661 The deserving chief does not appease provocation.
662 Morial, following them, bears no disgrace,
663 with his steely blade, ready for a stream of blood.

[A.55]

664   There was a mustering of warriors whose status was privileged
665   in the dominion of mighty action. Let their follower be heard!
666   He slew with a club and lance
667   mounds [of corpses] while fighting men of battle.

[A.56] THE LOWLANDERS = THE ENGLISH

668   Warriors mustered. They met
669   together. With a single intention they attacked.
670   Their lives were short. Their friends' grieving was long.
671   They killed seven times their number of men of England.
672   In combat they made wives widows,
673   many a mother with tears in her eyes.

[A.57] CYNON SON OF CLYDNO

407   Never was there built a hall so faultless,
408   gracious, a nobleman so generous with a lion's fury, most far-ranging,
409   than the generous-hearted Cynon, fairest lord.
410   His ardour was a fortress on the wide frontiers
411   the door, the army's anchor, the supreme plunderer.
412   Of those that I have seen and shall see in battle,
413   plying weapons on the stony ground, his valour was mightiest.
414   He slew the enemy with the keenest of blades.
415   Like rushes they fell before his hand.
416   The son of Clydno, I sing praise to you, O lord,
417   praise without bound, without limit.

[A.58] THE HILL OF THE VICTORY SPOILS, RHEITHUN

[674   Wine-nurtured and mead-nurtured men
[675   dealt death.]

676   A great man of legal status, meriting singular praise
677   used to take joy before the summit,
678   before the hill of the victory spoils,
679   [as] ravens rose, ascending the sky;
680   centurions falling,
681   like a grey swarm on him,
682   without the hero retreating.
683   [?]Perceiving the sensation of movement
684   [?]from the lips of pale [steeds]
685   and at the high point of sword blows.
686   The foremost man in the unsleeping feast
687   is unwaking today
688   great [?]Rheithun, director of power.

[A.59] CATRAETH

689   Of the wine-nurtured and mead-nurtured men they were sent from us.
690   I know grief for the death of the mail-clad warriors.

691   Before they could prevail, they were killed.
692   Their host was ready for Catraeth.
693   Of the host of the mountain court—so grievous!
694   of the three hundred, only one man came back.

[A.60 = B¹.20]

[A.61] GODODDIN, CADFANNAN

709   Thus would he be as the world would muster
710   like a [?]ball . . .
711   Thus would he be until the return.
712   Thus the Gododdin tribesman fought
713   for mead and wine in the fierce fight,
714   in the conflict on the border;
715   and under Cadfannan there was a ruddy herd
716   of horses—a horseman, severe in the morning.

[A.62 = (B¹.14=) B¹.15; cf. B².36]

[A.63 = B².40]

[A.64] GWAEDDNERTH SON OF LLYWRI

790   A fitting song for a renowned company:
791   the din of fire and thunder and flood-tide,
792   the horseman of manifest valour was wont to cause uproar,
793   the red reaper who yearned for war.
794   The man of battle tirelessly reaped
795   in combat, in as many countries as he heard of it.
796   With his shield on his shoulder he would take hold of
797   the spear as if it were bright wine from glass vessels.
798   With silver around his mead, it was gold that he deserved.
799   Gwaeddnerth son of Llywri was mead-nurtured.

[A.65 = B².39]
[A.66 = B².42]

[A.67] THE DAUGHTER OF TALL EUDDAF

827   Deserved poetry for brilliant high hosts,
828   for the purpose of the courtly subjects of the mountain realm

829   and the daughter of Tall Euddaf, [there came] the violence of border fighting.
830   The breakers of countries were dressed in purple.

[A.68 = B².29]

[A.69 = B².33]

[A.70 = B².32]

[A.71] YWAIN

889   He fell into the depths over his head.
890   The purpose of the rightfully-entitled chief was not held.
891   The learned one of [?]Brigantia was slain on a spear-shaft.
892   The habit of Ywain was to make for the front,
893   lowering his chosen spear-shaft before rushing over.

. . .

896   Dark-blue was his left gauntlet
897   which he carried on his mail-stripping hand;
898   a sovereign dispensing payment [i.e. vengeance]
899   purchasing it with the thrusting of wood.
900   Praise for the frigid, bloody white cheeks:
901   a man of learning when a woman was chief judge,
902   who possessed horses and dark armour and icy shields,
903   a man among his contemporaries in the fighting, rising, falling.

[A.72]

904   A battle leader has led warfare.
905   A sovereign's host loved the powerful reaper.
906   The mighty Forth is blood about a fresh grave.
907   He owned armour over his red [garments].
908   The armoured trampler who used to trample on armour.
909   The likeness of death fell on the exhausted.
910   Spear-shafts in shields at the outset of battle;
911   a path towards the light was the purpose of the spear thrusts.

[A.73]
LOWLANDERS (= ENGLISHMEN), GWYNEDD, THE BATTLE- SEIZER OF GWYNEDD, GODODDIN'S BORDER REGION

912   I sang a poem about the destruction of your chamber
913   and the hall where it was.
914   It merited sweet ensnaring mead.
915   The fury at the court of the battle hero with the dawn,

916   a brilliant tribute to the leader of England's men;

917   it is too dear a penance until they will leave.

918   May the distinction of the man nurtured by Gwynedd be heard!

919   Gwanannon is the grave

920   of Gwynedd's steadfast battle-seizer,

921   he who was bull of the army in the violent combat of chieftains.

922   Rather than a covering of earth, rather than a laying to rest,

923   it is Gododdin's frontier zone that is [his] grave.

[A.74 = B².37]

[A.75] CATRAETH, HEIDDYN

943   He supported battle horses and blood-spattered

944   battle harness, a reddened herd before Catraeth,

945   the army's fortress who feeds the tips of wood.

946   The battle hound fought against the hill-fort.

947   [?]He/we are called renowned, brilliant . . .

948   from the hand of iron-clad Heiddyn.

[A.76] [?MYNAWG,] GODODDIN, EIDYN

949   Of the courteous one of Gododdin they tell,

950   courtly in sharing, he is lamented.

951   For Eidyn, a bold flame, he will not return.

952   He put his whole inherited worth at the front line.

953   He set a thick barrier against the assault.

954   Boldly he attacked ferocious men.

955   Because he drank he bore the awesome burden.

956   Of the retinue from the mountain court escaped

957   but one defensive weapon from the chasm.

[A.77] MORIED

958   Because of the loss of Moried, there were no shields [i.e. protection].

959   They maintained, they extolled the laureate champion.

960   In his gauntlet he had carried blue blades.

961   Heavy spears endangered the chief endangerer,

962   who was mounted on a dapple grey horse with headgear.

963   Combat fell over his blades in sliced layers.

964   When he was overcome in battle, he was not retreating.

965   Moried deserved sweet ensnaring mead.

[A.78 = B¹.1]

[A.79] CYNDDYLIG OF AERON

978 Auspicious and triumphant, sprightly and fair, a [resolute] bone to the cohorts,
979 by means of his bluish [weapon], the sea-journeying enemy were put to flight.
980 Valiant and bold was the mighty hand
981 of the stout-hearted man-slayer. They struck against him.
982 His instinct was to attack
983 against the hosts of nine kings,
984 in the midst of blood and armies,
985 hurling defiance.
986 I love the triumphant one who had the couch under him
987 outstandingly bold Cynddylig of Aeron.

[A.80] CATRAETH, THE SON OF CEIDIAW

988 They desired to attack Catraeth standing foremost
989 in exchange for mead in the centre of assembly and strong wine.
990 They desired . . .
991 Before he was killed . . .
992 They loved the heir of fame who made blood flow.
993 He set his sword into the ferocity.
994 A valiant man will not tell the Gododdin tribesmen
995 that Ceidiaw's son was not a singular man of combat.

[A.81] RHUFAWN, GWGAWN, GWIAWN, GWLYGAWD

996 I am wretched after exhaustion,
997 suffering the agony of death because of the disaster.
998 And a second oppressive sorrow for me is the vision
999 of our men falling head over heels
1000 and the long moaning and grievous mortality
1001 in the wake of the brilliant men from the region of . . .
1002 Rhufawn and Gwgawn, Gwiawn and Gwlyged,
1003 the men withstood most valiantly the hard force.
1004 Afterwards, may the Trinity receive their souls,
1005 inclusion in heaven's realm, bounteous dwelling place.

[A.82]

1006 He threw back the attack across a lake of blood.
1007 As a bold man, he slew the column that did not flee.
1008 Throwing a spear and with a Scottic shield, as he would throw back a
1009 glass of mead in the presence of chieftains, so would he throw armies over.
1010 His counsel was minded where not many
1011 might speak, and had he been ignoble, they would not have listened.
1012 Because of the onslaught of axe-blows and whetted
1013 swords, [?]many have come to speak afterwards.

[A.83] TYNGYR

1014 Haven of the army,
1015 a haven of spears,
1016 and the charge of a host
1017 in the onrush,
1018 in the day of combat,
1019 in contention,
1020 they were splendid.
1021 After the intoxication
1022 and mead drinking,
1023 it was not deliverance
1024 that the laureate hero made
1025 in the day of the virile [men];
1026 so it is related
1027 the host's front was smashed,
1028 both horses and men;
1029 Tyngyr was doomed.

[A.84] GERAINT, THE SOUTH

1028 As there comes to me
1029 much dis-ease, I anxiously contemplate the renowned man,
1030 and with failing breath,
1031 [as with] forceful running, I weep.
1032 I took my living from the dear one,
1033 I had loved the dear one, [? they loved] the famed stag.
1034 With the men of Argoed
1035 woefully it was to be his way to array himself.

1036 Well did he set
1037 pressure against hosts for the benefit of kings,
1038 against the rough (shafts of) wood,
1039 against the deluge of adversity, [in return] for feasts.

1040 Feasting with the host, he brought us before the brilliant fire
1041 and [while seated] on the white pelt, sweet (?wine).

1042 It was Geraint who raised the battle cry against the South.
1043 A white flash, a white hole in the shield

1044 from the javelin of the praiseworthy generous lord.
1045 I know the nature of the great hero of courtesy.
1046 I know Geraint, you who were a generous nobleman.

[A.85] EIDDEF

1047 Unconstrained was his fame and his high renown,

1048 unswayable anchor among the retinue,
1049 indomitable eagle of men in fury.
1050 Eiddef who withstood combat was dazzling.
1051 His very fleet horses ran ahead
1052 in the engagement; [he was] nurtured on wine from a fine vessel.
1053 Before the green grave and before his cheek turned livid,
1054 he was a fellow feaster over fine mead from the cup.

[A.86 = B¹.4]

[A.87]
DINOGAD, GIFF, GAFF, THE FALLS OF DERWENNYDD

1101 Dinogad's bunting is speckled, speckled;
1102 I made it from martens' pelts
1103 whistle, whistle, a whistling,
1104 I would sing to him, the eight slaves would sing to him.

1105 When your father would go hunting,
1106 staff on his shoulder and club in his hand,

1107 he would call his ready hounds,
1108 'Giff, Gaff, catch! catch! fetch! fetch!'
1109 He would kill a fish in his coracle,
1110 as when the brilliant lion slays.

1111 When your father would go to the mountain,
1112 he would bring back a roebuck, a wild sow, a stag,
1113 a speckled grouse from the mountain,
1114 a fish from the Falls of Derwennydd [now Lodore Cascade, Cumbria, England].

1115 Of all that would come against your father and his flesh dart
1116 of wild sows and foxes from the Wood of Llwyfain
1117 none would escape if it were not on wings.

[A.88] GWEIR THE ONLY SON OF FFERFARCH

1118 An unexpected [?]disaster has befallen me
1119 There does not come, there will not come, anything heavier.
1120 No man nurtured in a hall was more gracious [lit. 'lighter']
1121 than he, nor was any steadier in battle,
1122 and at the far verge of the ford, his steeds were in the lead.
1123 With his far-ranging fame, his white-washed shield . . .
1124 And before Gweir's long burial under the turf,
1125 deserving of mead horns was the only son of Fferfarch.

• • • • • • • • •

§§118–128. Poems & Tales Relating to Uryen of Reget & His Dynasty, The Kynverching

(= Old Welsh *Urbgen; fl.* second half of 6th century[21])

§118. *Gweith Gwen Ystrat* The Battle of Gwen Ystrad
BOOK OF TALIESIN 56.14–57.13

1 THE MEN OF CATRAETH ARISE WITH THE DAY

2 around a battle-victorious, cattle-rich sovereign:

3 this man's name is Uryen, the most senior lord.

4 He restrains chieftains and hews them down—

5 the warlike force, most truly the chief leader of Baptism['s forces].

6 The Picts advancing towards combat, on the warpath:

7 [to] Gwen Ystrat [the ?Blessed Valley], where the warrior(s) stood their ground for battle.

8 Neither open plain nor woods gave shelter

9 to your oppressors, o protector of the folk, when they arrived.

10 Their shrill battle cries were like waves across the face of the land.

11 I saw fierce men assembled for war.

12 And after the morning battle: mangled flesh.

13 I saw the throng of the three frontiers laid waste.

14 A fierce and energetic cry was heard.

15 In the fight for Gwen Ystrat,

16 one could see a constricted barrier of laureate champions forced to a standstill.

---

21 Urbgen's career as a battle leader opposing the Bernician English is described in *Historia Brittonum* §110 ¶63 above. The proper names in this group of translations are generally given in the Middle Welsh spellings of the manuscripts. The Modern Welsh spelling of his name is *Urien.*

17 In the entry of the ford, I saw blood-stained men—
18 arms relinquished before the hoary (captive-taking) ruler.
19 They wanted peace because they had fought to exhaustion—
20 hands in the sign of the cross ?shivering on the gravel bank of the white cranes.
21 Their centurions were ?counted up according to ?seniority.
22 Waves washed the manes of their horses.

23 I saw ?respected men stripped [of arms],
24 and blood that spattered clothing,
25 and a mustering, resharpened and severe for battle.
26 It was not flight that the battle protector contemplated.
27 The lord of Reget, I am astonished that he dared.

28 I saw a splendid (?hundred-man) division about Uryen
29 when he fought with his foes in Llech Wen.
30 The scatterer of enemies delighted in fighting.
31 Shields of men were borne towards doom.
32 May battle lust reside in Uryen.

[33 *And until I grow old*
   34 *in the dire compulsion of death's allotment,*
   35 *I shall not be happy,*
   36 *unless I praise Uryen.*]

◆ ◆ ◆ ◆ ◆ ◆ ◆ ◆ ◆

§119. *Uryen Erechwyð* Uryen of Erechwyð BOOK OF TALIESIN 57

𝐔RYEN OF ERECHWYÐ[22]
most generous man in Christendom,
plentifully do you give
to the human beings of the terrestrial realm.
As you gather,
so do you scatter.   5
Joyous are the bards of Christendom
so long as you live.
[And] greater is the delight
in the high and free-flowing praise.

---

22 Erechwyð, also Yrechwyð: the place-name means 'Land before the Fresh Water' and is likely to refer to what is now 'the Lake District' in Cumbria, north-west England.

There is greater glory 10
while Uryen and his offspring exist.

And he rules as chief
as the most exalted sovereign lord,
as a long-streeted citadel,
as foremost champion. 15

The people of England know it
so they tell of it:
it is death they got
and frequent provocation,
burning of their settlements, 20
and bearing off their finery,
oppressive losses,
and mighty tribulation,
and they get no deliverance
against Uryen of Reget. 25

Reget's defender,
lord of praise, anchor of the realm,
my spirit turns to you
for all that is heard.
Severe is your spear play 30
whenever battle is heard.

When you make for battle,
you do vengeance.
There is fire in houses before daybreak
because of Yrechwyδ's chieftain. 35

Fairest Yrechwyδ
with its most generous people,
it is usual for the Angles to have no protection
because of the most courageous king.

Possessing most courageous nature, 40
the choicest man is yourself.
Of all who were and will be,
there is not your equal.

When one beholds him,
the terror is enormous. 45
Courtesy is usual around him,

around the provocative chieftain.

Courtesy surrounds him
and plentiful wealth,
golden chieftain of the North,
foremost of kings.   50

> *And until I grow old*
> *in the dire compulsion of death's allotment,*
> *I shall not be happy,*
> *unless I praise Uryen.*

◆   ◆   ◆   ◆   ◆   ◆   ◆   ◆   ◆

§120. Canu Taliesin V   BOOK OF TALIESIN 59

THROUGH A SINGLE YEAR,
one man has poured out
wine, and malt, and mead
with unrestrained vigour,

for a troop of singers   5
and for a swarm around spits,
with their neck rings
and fine resting places,

and all of them for their food
went to the battle.   10

With his horse under him,
set to raid Manaw,
seeking spoils
and plentiful plunder,

160 of one colour   15
of both cows and calves,

milch cows and oxen,
and all sorts of fair luxuries.
I would not be happy
if Uryen were slain.   20

He is most dear [to us] because he has gone off
shaking his spear-shaft.

With his whitewashed head of hair,

and a bier would bear him,
and a bloody cheek,   25
splattered with a hero's blood.

A stout steadfast hero,
whose wife would be widowed.
Mine is a true chief;

mine is a true hope   30
for fate, for support, for a chief,
against the rising anguish.

Go to the door and look, boy!
Listen, what is the sound!

Does the earth shake?   35
Or is there an incursion of the sea?

[Rather] a growing chant
from the foot soldiers.

 'If there is fighting on the hill,
Uryen will shake them.   40

If there is fighting in the vale,
Uryen will run them through.

If there is fighting on the mountain,
Uryen will surmount them.

If there is fighting the slope,   45
Uryen will break them up.

If there is fighting on the earthen rampart,
Uryen will strike them.

Fighting on the road, fighting on the height,
fighting in every cranny.'   50

Neither one settlement nor the second
can give protection from him.

There would be no famine
with the spoils all about him.

With his armoured retinue   55
in dark blue mail.

His spear is like death
slaying the enemy.

> *And until I grow old*
> 60 *in the dire compulsion of death's allotment,*
> *I shall not be happy,*
> *unless I praise Uryen.*

◆ ◆ ◆ ◆ ◆ ◆ ◆ ◆ ◆

§121. *Gweith Argoet Llwyfein* The Battle before Elmwood Forest

BOOK OF TALIESIN 60

1 ON SATURDAY MORNING, THERE WAS A GREAT BATTLE,
2 from when the sun rises, lasting until it turns dark.
3 The Flame-bearer invaded leading his four hosts.
4 Goðeu and Reget were mobilising.

5 'Let [the folk] come from the lands by the woods and from as far as the lands
     by the mountains!
6 They will not get a postponement for even the span of a single day!'

7 The Flame-bearer called across loudly, with great bluster:
8 'Have my hostages come? Are they ready?'
9 Owein[23], at the earthwork of the East, answered,
10 'They have not come. They were not, and are not ready.

---

23 Owein is Uryen's son, at least that is how Welsh tradition comes to view him by an early
   date. From the point of view of the history of literature, the introduction of dramatic
   dialogue into a heroic praise poem is interesting.
       My understanding of the battle, as described in this poem, is that the chieftain called
   'the Flame-bearer' has advanced west in full force to the boundary of Uryen's kingdom.
   'Flame-bearer' is probably the nickname of the Anglo-Saxon king of Bernicia, but this is
   not certain. He seeks hostages in a confrontation at a boundary check-point, as a formal
   token of Uryen's submission to Flame-bearer's overlordship. Owein meets Flame-bearer
   with a small party at the border rampart. He surprises Flame-bearer by rejecting the
   demand for hostages with little visible force to back his defiance. Uryen then appears with
   a large army that has been lying in wait, out of sight, behind the ridge of a hill or
   mountain overlooking the scene. Uryen leads a charge immediately and his large force
   surprises, defeats, and kills the Flame-bearer in the ensuing battle. According to a poem in
   memory of Owein's soul below, Owein was remembered for having personally killed Flame-
   bearer. But that conclusion might be no more than an inference drawn from the present
   poem.

11 A whelp of Coel's descent would be a broken chief
12 before he would pay even one hostage to anyone.'

13 Uryen Lord of Erechwyð called back loudly,
14 'If there is to be a meeting to make a peace settlement,
15 let us raise the shafts on the mountain top!
16 And let us turn our faces up over the ridge!
17 And let us raise up spears, men!
18 And attack the Flame-bearer in the midst of his hosts!
19 And kill both him and his comrades in arms!'

20 And from the battle of Argoet Llwyfein, there was many a corpse. Crows were
   reddened from warriors.
21 And the war-band that went forward with the most senior chieftain,
22 for a year I shall prepare poetry for their success.

   23 *And until I grow old*
   24 *in the dire compulsion of death's allotment.*
   25 *I shall not be happy,*
   26 *unless I praise Uryen.*

   ◆ ◆ ◆ ◆ ◆ ◆ ◆ ◆

§122. *Arðwyre Reget, rysseð rieu*   Arise, Reget, glory of kings!
BOOK OF TALIESIN 61

1 ARISE, REGET, GLORY OF KINGS!
2 It is you that I have chosen, though I am not your own.
3 Blades of battle and shafts of battle groaned.
4 Men groaned under ?fallen shields.
5 White gulls came down onto the plain of carnage.
6 Waging war against the king was ill-fated; it is no good to lie [about this].
7 A rightful sovereign equips himself to oppose fellow kings.

8 The demands of favour seekers do not drive him.
9 The swift horseman glories in the praise of heroic men:
10 from the dragon-like war-leader to the minor hero, the most noble and cultured
   of the Earth pass away.
11 Until Wulf came with violence against his enemy,   (*or* Wuffing)
12 until Urien came, in his day, to Aeron,

13 there was no counter-blow; there was no pressing together.
14 It was ?usual for Urien to be at the front, before Powys.
15 There was no ardent enthusiasm from the race of ?Chester's country
16 Hyfaidd (or the bold men) from Gododdin, moving forward into the clear.
17 Deira suffering torture with the weight of the wood [of spear shafts],

18 acting without disgrace in the blood of Gwyðien,
19 that witnessed the leaders of Llwyfenydd shaken
20 at the outworks of a defended field.

21 A battle in Dumbarton's ford, a battle for [the wearing of] the diadem,
22 battle in the cells of Bremenium, the battle of Hir Eurer,
23 battle in the copse of Catleu, battle in the river mouth—
24 his lifetime in confrontation with the steel of land-owning men—

25 a Great battle at Clyde's rock, combat at Pencoed;
26 a pack of feeding dogs on the excessive blood,

27 All the fierce heroes will wither.
28 ?Æthelfrith's²⁴ Angles make entreaty,
29 bloodied from an encounter with ?Wlff(ing) at the ford

30 Let it be sung excellently to the sovereign to whom it has been sung

31 to Britain's ruler, the gracious chief landholder,
32 to the one who governs. There does not conduct himself in clothing of blue or gold
33 nor red, nor heather-coloured any ?praised man (?fighter) so heroic;
34 There has not placed his thigh over thorough-bred piebald
35 steeds of the speckled breed any [man] so fierce;

36 summer until winter with a weapon in hand,
37 from the ford to the causeway, guarding them,
38 and spending the night under earthworks and rousing themselves,
39 and until the end of the world he will be ?famed
40 sweeping down against an army, without asking
41 the way ?forward into combat
42 around shafts of light. It is I who howled in [my] breast
43 as it swelled, with spears on the shoulder, shield in hand,
44 Goðeu and Reget arrayed.
45 It is I who saw a hero forming a stockade,

---

24 Æthelfrith, Old Welsh *Edilurit*, maunscript *edylgwrthryt*. I tentatitively take this as a reference to the defeat and killing of Æthelfrith, the Angle, king of Bernicia, by Rædwald of the Wuffingas (descendants of Wulf) of East Anglia at the Battle on the Banks of the River Idle in east-central England in 617.

46 a renowned and beautiful serpent who trod the ground.
47 It is I who knows war, what will be lost,
48 and of all that I might loose will be lost.

49 I am the one who was overcome by the intoxication of the mead drink,
50 with the bold (*or* Hyfaidd's) following of well chosen noblemen

51 I am the one who acted as an ambassador, sheltered from combat.
52 He gladly divided grants for his kings.
53 [Other] property holding is but vanity compared to Uryen.

54 *And until I grow old*
55 *in the dire compulsion of death's allotment.*
56 *I shall not be happy,*
57 *unless I praise Uryen.*

◆ ◆ ◆ ◆ ◆ ◆ ◆ ◆

§123. *Yspeil Taliessin. Kanu Vryen*
The Spoils of Taliesin, Poetry for Uryen
BOOK OF TALIESIN 62

IN AWKWARD CIRCUMSTANCES, my audacity seeks attention.
I entreat that I might say what I see to be true!

I saw there, while standing in front of someone who did not see me,
all the favourites, making their immodest demands.
On Easter, I saw the great light and the abundant fruits.   5
I saw the leaves that shown brightly, sprouting forth.

I saw the branches, all together in flower.
And I have seen the ruler whose decrees are most generous:
I saw Catraeth's leader over the plains.
Let him be my lord whose fellow kings do not love him!   10
In exchange for my great poetry, there will be the increase of his gifts—

the leader of soldiers, with extensive plunder ?around ?them.
My blessed inspiration is my ash wood spear,
and my fresh bright smile is like shields [poised] against the commander.
Uryen is the very ready and the singularly most noble of rulers. 15

The cattle lord of the great and resounding
bright blue armoured hosts will not withstand me.

the ?young man will ascend above all,
walking over the ignoble and blackened deadwood in the great hall

of the ruler, while making loud utterance, that may go in whatever way you would
want—   20
?surplus of yellow gold in the hall

of the wealthy defender of Aeron,
who delights greatly in poets and deer,
great is the ferocity of his attack against the enemy,
great is the renown of his heroic strength amongst the Britons, 25

like a fiery wheel across the face of the earth,
like the solid ground of Llwyfenydd,

like a song of equal beauty in prayer and battle,
Urien is like the sea in its vast bounty.

Most pleasing are the wide-coursing rays of dawn,   30
Most pleasing are the boisterous chieftains of the governor.
Most fine are cavalry soldiers on their sleek military horses,
at the beginning of May at the farmlands of the armies

it is very pleasing is at the ?Dee as the war-band arrives,
like the course of the eagle of the country of the long slope   35
I was much pleased, on a spirited steed,
in a unique tribe as payment for Taliesin's spoils.

A fine thing is the attack of a laureate champion on a steed
Fine are a landowner's renders to his lord.
it is very pleasing to slay a herd stag.   40
very pleasing is the ravening wolf in broom thickets.

Very pleasing is the land of Eginyr's son.
and in the same way I had delighted in the battlefield of warriors,
. . . .

and the offspring of Nuð Hael with the long land under him. 45

And if I shall get what will make me happy,
he will make the bards of the world joyous—
that I might not call upon the dead sons of Gwyðien—
Uryen, leader of the blood[line] of the blessed land.

§124. The Saga *Englynion* about Uryen's Head[25]

¶ 7   THE HEAD THAT I CARRY AT MY SIDE was an attacker amid war-bands. It was the proud son of Kynfarch that owned it.

¶ 8   The head that I carry at my side: the head of generous Uryen was wont to guide the host. And on his white breast a black crow.

¶ 9   The head that I carry in my tunic: the head of generous Uryen was wont to guide the court. And on his white breast crows devour him.

¶ 10   The head that I carry in my hand was shepherd of Erechwyб [probably the Lake District]. The princely breast was wont to spend spear shafts.

¶ 11   The head that I carry by [my] thigh was a shield over the land. He was a wheel in battle. He was a pillar of battle and a snare at the border.

¶ 12   The head that I carry at my left: better it live than [go to] its grave. It was a fortress to the elders.

¶ 13   The head that I carry from the region of Pennawc[26] far-ranging his hosts: the head of eloquent Uryen of unrestrained praise.

¶ 14   The head that I carry on my shoulder: I shall <not ?> accept disgrace. Woe to my hand for the slaying of my lord.

¶ 15   The head that I carry on my arm made a load for biers out of Bryneich [Bernicia, a northern Anglo-Saxon kingdom] after the battle cry.

¶ 16   The head that I carry in my arm's hand: the generous chieftain used to lead the land. The chief pillar of Britain has been taken away.

¶ 17   The head that I carry carried (sustained) me. He recognised poetry to my advantage. Woe to my hand, it has done cruelly.

---

25 We do not have a surviving prose narrative (if there ever was one) to explain the peculiar scene implied by this poem. It has been assumed that the poet is carrying his patron's head because Uryen's army has been forced to make a hasty retreat and could not carry the whole body, but did not want to leave it to the advancing enemy. Remember that Brân's followers in *Branwen* did more or less precisely the same thing. Note that as in *Branwen* it is the chief's own followers who decapitate him so that they might return home with his head. In Celtic tradition, the fall of the chief is the end of the campaign. 'Head' and 'chief' are the same word (Welsh *pen(n)* = Old Irish *cenn*). It may be that there was an idea that the followers of the chief still needed his head to lead them safely home. Later, as you will see in the next poem, it looks as though the rest of the body was recovered.

Another thematic pun in the poem is that the word for carry *porthi*, as in carrying a head, is precisely the same word for 'sustain and support' which used to evoke the relationship between lord and dependent follower (including the poet). The speaker is possibly Llywarch Hen, Uryen's first cousin. There are more *englynion* from the Llywarch cycle below.

26 **Pennawc**: a district in coastal Northumberland, near the Northumbrian centres of Bamburgh and Lindisfarne],

¶ 18   The head that I carry from the black hill—on its mouth splattered foam [and] blood; woe to Reget today.

¶ 19   My arm has been caused to tremble. My breast is made to heave. My heart has been broken. I carry a head that carried (supported) me.

◆ ◆ ◆ ◆ ◆ ◆ ◆ ◆ ◆

§125. The Saga *Englynion* about Uryen's Corpse

¶ 20   THE WHITE SLENDER BODY THAT IS BURIED today under earth and stones; woe to my hand for the slaying (or dismembering) of Owein's father.

¶ 21   The white slender body that is buried today in the midst of earth and [an] oak [coffin]; woe to my hand for the slaying of my first cousin.

¶ 22   The white slender body that is buried today: under stones it is left; woe to my hand—disaster has fated me.

¶ 23   The white slender body that is buried today: under turf and the sign [?of the cross]; woe to my hand for the death of my lord.

¶ 24   The white slender body that is buried today: under dirt and sand; woe to my hand—disaster has caught me.

¶ 25   The white slender body that is buried today: under dirt and nettles; woe to my hand—I have been taken by disaster.

¶ 26   The white slender body that is buried today: under dirt and blue-grey stones; woe to my hand—disaster has taken me.

◆ ◆ ◆ ◆ ◆ ◆ ◆ ◆ ◆

§126. Efrðyl (Uryen's sister)

¶ 30   EFRÐYL BECOMES UNHAPPY TONIGHT IN MANY WAYS: the slaying of Uryen in Aber Lleu.[27]

¶ 31   Efrðyl is unhappy from tribulation tonight, and it is from the disaster which caught me: the slaying of her brother in Aber Lleu.

◆ ◆ ◆ ◆ ◆ ◆ ◆ ◆ ◆

---

27 **Aber Lleu** = Ross Low, a small body of water, on the North Sea coast of present-day northern England.

§127. The Soul of Owein Son of Uryen

1 THE SOUL OF OWEIN SON OF URYEN: may the Lord consider its need.

2 The chieftain of Reget that the dense green [grass] conceals: it is not frivolous to praise him in verse;

3 the cist-grave of the hero who was renowned in song, vastly praised, whose whetted spears were like the rays of dawn;

4 for no equal can be found to the lord of Llwyfenyb,

5 the reaper whose custom was seizing the foe, like in nature to his father and grandfather.

6 When Owein slew Fflambwyn [Flame-bearer], it was no more than sleeping.

7 [Now] England's broad host sleeps with light in their eyes.

8 And those of them who did not flee were bolder than was reasonable.

9 Owain punished them severely, like a wolf pack in pursuit of sheep.

10 The splendid hero was wont to give out stallions to supplicants while seated on his multi-coloured horse gear.

11 Though he gathered these harshly, they were shared out for the sake of his soul.

00 (the soul of Owein son of Uryen.)

◆ ◆ ◆ ◆ ◆ ◆ ◆ ◆

§§128-130. Three Welsh Texts Pertaining to Modron, Mabon, & The Kynverching Dynasty

¶NOTE. The three texts in this series illustrate the traditional association of the late sixth-century rulers of the North British kingdom of Reget (Modern Welsh *Rheged*)— Uryen (Modern *Urien*) son of Kynfarch and Owein son of Urien—with the former Celtic divinities Modron < Mātronā 'the divine mother' and Mabon < Maponos 'the divine son'. A brief version of their myth is found amongst the wonders of 'Culhwch and Olwen'; see also Proinsias Mac Cana, *Celtic Mythology*, 1968, rpt. 1983, Peter Bedrick, New York (1983), p. 31.

Reget was situated in present-day north-west England and south-west Scotland and was for a time a barrier against the advance of the Northumbrian Angles. It is chiefly within this region that attestations are found for the Romano-British cults of Maponus and the Matres or mother-goddesses. The place-name *Clochmabenstane* ('Mabon's Stone') probably recollects the Romano-British sanctuary *locus Maponi* 'M.'s cult centre'. The cult was probably first brought to North Britain by the migration of the Parisī in *c.* 400 BC from the vicinity of the Marne (< *Mātronā*, the embodiment of their tribal goddess) to Yorkshire, where the same tribal name occurs in Roman times. Their North British Early La Tène (Iron Age B) culture soon after spread, across the Pennine range (in northern England), to the territory that was to become the post-Roman Reget.

Taking the literary sources together, it seems plausible that the oldest version of §128 had concerned an encounter at the Marne of Mātronā and the king-to-be of the Parisī of Gaul, some 2400 years ago. We see that Modron is equated with the daughter of the king of Annwvyn, the 'Un-world'.

Nevyn, the name of Uryen's mother in §129, corresponds exactly to that of the Irish war-goddess *Nembain*.

In §130, the warfare and cattle raiding of Modron's mortal son Owein are likened to the heroic exploits of her divine son Mabon.

Is *arall vro*, which is translated here as 'the other-realm' equivalent to 'the otherworld', *Annwvyn*?

In §130 *Erechwyð* is Owein's country, the present English Lake District and/or the Yorkshire Dales.

Kalchvynyð in §130 means 'chalk' or 'limestone mountain'. It seems to be used in early Welsh sources for the name of a British kingdom. Various locations have been suggested, including the Cotswolds, Chilterns, or Wessex Chalk Downs, all of which are in south-central England. The present reference would lend some support to this general area as the tidings are said to be coming both from Kalchvynyð and the South.

In §130, *Cymry* is the Welsh name for the Welsh people, etymologically **Combrogī* 'fellow countrymen'. The (pre-1974) English county name *Cumber-land* shows that the Britons of the North also used this self-designation.

In §130 many of the places, persons, and other allusions are unknown to us. The important, and intriguing, point is that praise of the heroic exploits of a historical dynast (Owein) seem to be interlaced with references to the tribal god.

The names are spelled as they occur in the texts themselves and therefore vary somewhat, but should offer little difficulty to the reader.

§128. The Onomastic Tale of Ryd-y-gyfarthfa

A folktale recorded in North Wales in the Early Modern Period, ed. **R. Bromwich**,
Trioedd Ynys Prydein, 2nd ed., Cardiff (1978) p. 459

IN DENBIGHSHIRE [in North Wales], there is a parish that is called Llan-verrys, and it is there that one will find Ryd-y-gyfarthfa ['Ford of the Barking']. And in former times, the dogs from the whole country used to come to that ford to bark, and no one dared to go to see what was the matter until Urien of Reged came. And when he came to the bank of the ford, he saw nothing but a young woman washing. And then the dogs ceased their barking. And Urien grabbed hold of the girl, and he had sexual intercourse with her.

And then she said, 'God's blessing on the feet that brought you here.'

'Why?' said he.

'Because I was fated to wash here until I get a son by a Christian. And I am the daughter of the king of Annwvyn [the Un-world]. Come here at the end of the year and you will get the boy.'

And so he came and he got the son there and a daughter, none other than Owein son of Urien and Morfyð daughter of Urien.

§129. The Three Blessed Womb-Fuls of the Island of Britain

Trioedd Ynys Prydein, **ed. Bromwich**, no. 70 (from Aberystwyth, National Library of Wales MS, Peniarth 50)

URIEN AND EFRDDYL, CHILDREN OF KYNVARCH THE OLD, they were in a single womb-load in the womb of their mother Nevyn daughter of Brychan;

and the second, Owein son of Urien, and Morvyð his sister, who were in a single womb-load in the womb of Modron daughter of Avallach;

the third, Gwrgi and Peredur and Ceindrech Wing-Head, children of Eliffer of the Great Retinue, who were in the womb of Efrddyl daughter of Kynvarch, their mother.

◆ ◆ ◆ ◆ ◆ ◆ ◆ ◆ ◆

§130. *Kychwedyl am doðyw o Galchuynyð*
Tidings Have Come to Me from Kalchvynyð

BOOK OF TALIESIN, 38.11–40.3

TIDINGS HAVE COME TO ME FROM KALCHVYNYÐ:
disgrace in the Southland, praiseworthy plunder
herds of cattle which the violent one of Lleu's world will give to him.
His valley is filled, joyous increase.

The bountiful lord of hosts, [who is] the full [?]measure of the bountiful lord of the other-realm:
oppressor in battle, most ardent of the land
a rarity among the *Cymry* ['Welsh/Cumbrians'], he who would tell it.
Dyfed [south-west Wales] was attacked—the cattle of Iðno's son.
And there was no outcry; no one will come
to pay a hundred cows for a single calf.
Inescapable to the foe on the borders of thy land,
like a flame and hot vapour wherever he would be.
When we sought to penetrate the land of Gwyðno,
there was a slender white corpse between the gravel and the pebbles.
When [the army of] Erechwyð returned from the country of the *Cludwys* [men of Strathclyde],
no cow lowed for its calf.
The [?]manifestation of Mabon from the other-realm,
[in] the battle where Owein fought for the cattle of his country.

Battle in Ryt Al-clut [the Ford of Dumbarton, stronghold of Strathclyde, nr.

Glasgow],
battle in Ygwyn, battle in [?]Gossulwyt, they howled in strife,
battle against the [?]Rodawys of snow-white aspect
black spears and a bright jewel
the host of the brilliant slender-sided oak-strong captain of the oak-strong lineage
the shield for the hand, the fortress in combat.
Whoever saw Mabon on his white-flanked ardent [steed],
as men mingled, contending for Reget's cattle,
unless it were by means of wings that they flew,
only as corpses, would they go from Mabon.

Of encounter, descent, and onset of battle
in the realm of Mabon, the inexorable chopper;
when Owein fought to defend his father's cattle,
white-washed shields of waxed hawthorn burst forth.

It will be booty to no man, to bear off the speckled cattle;
sooner would one bear off rigid blood-stained men
        from against the fiery four-towered fort,
        from against the mighty muster,
        against gore on skin,
        against bitter grieving.

Tidings have come to me from the bright lands of the South,
region of kings, brilliant realm of lords.
Complainants do not entreat you
at the boundary ford, about the alder shields of the men great in battle.
When the king, leader of chieftains [lit. 'dragons'], ordered battle,
    . . . cattle for Mabon.

In the encounter of [?]heroes,
there were stiff red corpses;
it was joy which came to carrion crows.
Men tell of it, after the [?]uproar of battle,
no one escaped the shield of Owein.
The broken shield of a fighter in the adversity of combat;
he would not drive cattle without reddening faces.

The red ones of the cattle-lord whose giving is great.
Blood washed over the crown of a head,
and on a white face, there would be
    . . . bloody . . . [?]clothing
booty from the supplicating men of Gwent [SE Wales], booty . . . booty for battle

. . . spear-shafts against shields,
great wallowing, blades about the crown of the head,
battle before great Owein, whose giving is great.
Early in the morning, men fell fighting for land.
Where Owein attacked for the sake of Erechwyð's blessed land,
he [?]secured his father's battle-gains.

◆ ◆ ◆ ◆ ◆ ◆ ◆ ◆ ◆

§§131–132. Poems about Cadwallon Son of Cadfan *fl. c.* 625–634

§131. *Marwnad Cadwallon ap Cadfan*
The Death-song of Cadwallon son of Cadfan

¶ 1

ᚴATWALLAWN PREPARED OUR TRIUMPH BEFORE HE PERISHED: fourteen chief battles about vast and beautiful Britain (*Prydain*) and 60 musterings.[28]

---

28 The poem is edited with a Welsh modernisation and translation by R. Geraint Gruffydd in *Astudiaethau ar yr Hengerdd: Studies in Old Welsh Poetry*, ed. R. Bromwich, R. B. Jones (Cardiff: University of Wales Press, 1978) 34–41. The manuscripts entitle this poem an elegy, but it is in fact a battle-list. Only the first and second to last verses speak of the honorand as if he were dead. The metre is three-line *englynion*.

   Cadwallon son of Cadfan (< *Catumandus* [cf. §42]) was king of Gwynedd, the most powerful of the early Welsh kingdoms, in north-west Wales, 625–634/5. With his ally Penda (the pagan English king of Mercia in the present-day West Midlands of England), he slew King Edwin of Northumbria in 633 and ravaged North Britain. The Anglo-Saxon historian Bede, a Northumbrian, tells us that Cadwallon was intent on exterminating the English and calls him 'a Christian crueler than any pagan'. Through the following year he was the pre-eminent chieftain of Britain and held the *Imperium Britanniae*, though what practically this honour entailed is not certain. In 634 (or 635), he was killed by Edwin's successor Oswald. Cadwallon's campaigns are viewed by some historians as the last serious challenge by the native Brittonic Celts to English domination of Britain.

¶ 2   Katwallawn's campaign in *Ceint* [Kent, England, or district in Wales of the same name]: the men of England [*Lloegyr*] were overthrown as the birds prophesied. The privileged hand frees and binds.

¶ 3   Katwallawn's campaign on the (River) Eden [*Idon*]—cruel sadness to his foes—, the hero who has defended against the English [*Saesson*].

¶ 4   Famed Katwallawn's campaign at the summit of the Long Mynd [Shropshire, England; *Di-goll Uynyδ*], for seven months, seven battles every day.

¶ 5   Katwallawn's campaign on the River Severn [*Hafren*] . . .

¶ 6   Katwallawn's campaign on the River Wye [*Gŵy*], treasures after a sea voyage brought about by a battle on the border.

¶ 7   Katwallawn's campaign at Ffynnawn Uetwyr ['Bedwyr's Spring']: beside warriors, he fostered generosity . . .

¶ 8   Katwallawn's campaign on the River Taff [*Taf*]: I see him with a great host, the mighty chieftain, the strong lord.

¶ 9   Katwallawn's campaign on the River Tawe [*Tawy*]—a slaughterer's hand in the breech, the strong seeker of praise in battle.

¶ 10 Katwallawn's campaign beyond Chester [*Caer*; now in Cheshire, England]—a hundred war-bands and a hundred bold soldiers, a hundred battles which conquered a hundred strongholds.

¶ 11 Katwallawn's campaign on the River Cowyn . . . the men of England [*Lloegyr*] enduring frequent suffering.

¶ 12. Katwallawn's campaign tonight—across the country in Pembroke [*Penn Vro*; south-west Wales]. Great is his protection, difficult to flee from him.

¶ 13. Katwallawn's campaign on the River Teifi [*Teiui*]—brine and blood blend. The men of Gwynedd kindled battle.

¶ 14. Katwallawn's campaign on the River Dufy—[probably the *Dyfi* in Mid Wales]. He sated eagles. After the battle, a corpse was their gift.

¶ 15. Katwallawn, my brother, campaigned on the highland of Dunoding [*Bro Dunawt*], cruelly pursuing in battle. [There was a district of this name in both North Wales and in what became North Yorkshire, England.]

¶ 16. Katwallawn's campaign at sea—the hero with the numerous army, the great host of the savage onrush.

¶ 17. Due to the counsel of foreigners and unrighteous monks, the water of the spring overflows, there is a wretched and oppressive day for Katwallawn.

The name *Cadwallon*, older *Katwallawn*, is the Welsh form of the singular of the old tribal name *Catuvellauni* (meaning something like 'Excelling in Battle'), the pre-eminent tribe of ancient South-east Britain, who spearheaded the resistance to both Caesar's and Claudius's invasions.

¶ 18. The wood dresses in its beautiful raiment in the summer. Battle is destined to follow. Let us mass for the land of Elmet! [*Eluet* = modern South Yorkshire, northern England].

◆ ◆ ◆ ◆ ◆ ◆ ◆ ◆ ◆

§132. *Moliant Cadwallon* In Praise of Cadwallon[29]

THE SEA RUSHES IN. IT CASTS FORTH A HOST ARRAYED FOR BATTLE
the host of Cadwallon in the triumph of his objective,
an opponent like a furious fiery stag.

---

[29] On the honorand **Cadwallon**, see previous note.

   Some of the allusions in the poem can be understood as referring to the exile Cadwallon in Ireland early in his career when the Anglo-Saxon king Edwin of Northumbria was attempting to annex Anglesey, the heartland of Gwynedd.

   'In the manner of an axle. . .': the idea is that the king/battle-leader is 'exaltedly privileged' (*kynneved* < **com+nemeto-*) vis-à-vis other men as the axle is to the wheel, the rest of the vehicle, and its passengers; he is the pivotal unifier and underpinning support. The semantics of Celt. **wo-ret-* 'deliver, succour' (action of the hero/king), lit. 'run under' (action of the wheel) is also relevant. In the oldest of Hindu hymns, the *Rg Veda*, the hero-god Indra is likened to an axle in that his prowess fixes the places of heaven and earth like wheels on either side. A comparable cosmic theme is found in our text. In considering the lines 'Cadwallon will achieve in combat what the mind will intend, | so long as heaven remains above the face of the earth', one might compare the story of Alexander the Great and the Celts of the Balkans (§§9–10). If those Celts thought of the war-leader as infallible in the same terms as articulated in this poem, then they believed themselves invincible so long as the sky was over the earth.

   Maelgwn ruled Gwynedd in the 6th century and was the most powerful British king in his day. He was condemned for his excesses by his contemporary, the monk Gildas, in *De excidio Britannniae* ('On the Destruction of Britain'). He figures as an evil king in the *Romance of Taliesin* (*Ystorya Taliesin*, recently edited by P. K. Ford).

   Gwallawc was a north British king (ruler of Elmet) in the later sixth century and one of the allies of Urbgen (i.e. Uryen of Reget) mentioned in *Historia Brittonum* §110 ¶62.

   On Catraeth, see *Y Gododdin* §117.

   Porth Ysgewin is in extreme south-east Wales, i.e. far from Gwynedd.

   Einiawn was a 5th-century ruler of Gwynedd and direct ancestor of Cadwallon.

   The text survives only in late antiquarian copies, both the 50 lines of the main texts and the 6 lines of further fragments collected at the end. But the language is Old Welsh. The translation is based upon R. G. Gruffydd's annotated edition in *Astudiaethau ar yr Hengerdd*, ed. Rachel Bromwich and R. B. Jones, University of Wales Press, Cardiff (1978) 27ff.

   In light of the historical allusions in the poem, Gruffydd suggests that it was composed in 633. It is therefore the first text to use the word *Cymry* 'fellow-countrymen' for Wales and the Welsh people.

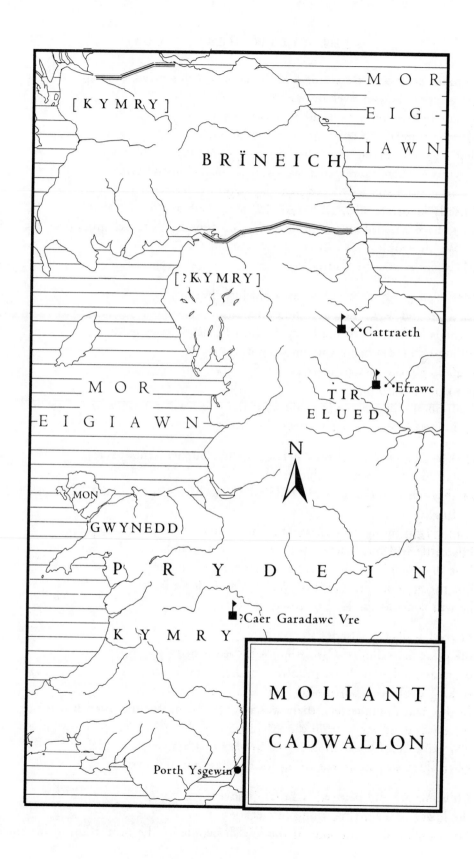

[K Y M R Y]

B R Ï N E I C H

M O R

E I G -

I A W N

[? K Y M R Y]

×Cattraeth

M O R

E I G I A W N

×Efrawc

T I R

E L U E D

N

MON

GWYNEDD

P R Y D E I N

?Caer Garadawc Vre

K Y M R Y

MOLIANT

CADWALLON

Porth Ysgewin

Copious are his battle steeds and the largess of his mead feasting
his praise is known over the vast sea: 5
it sails by the southern wind over the ocean,
like the ship of the chieftain of a foreign host.
The stag who maintains righteousness gives refuge to his men.
Never was there more generous a son so auspiciously born.
As an exalted and privileged axle the valorous one went to feats.
Miserly kings are silenced before the bounteous one.   11
They have groaned since the birth of a profoundly gifted champion of the
    Welsh people
when Christ created Cadwallon.

May God give protection to his bold high hosts;
let wind and waves not overcome them.   15
Tidings have come to me from the broad land of Gwynedd:
killing by heroes in inexorable slaughter.
Unfailingly the numerous tribes of fighters
dealt death with blades.
Cadwallon will achieve in strife what the mind will intend,   20
so long as heaven remains above the face of the earth.

If there is high ground on Anglesey, he has pitched tents on it,
a man like Maelgwn, a noble youth.
He has not negotiated at the bidding of the Bernicians [i.e. the Northumbrian
    English]
with Edwin ruling over them as a chief patriarch in great deception.
His cattle will not bellow; none will make a sound.   26
It is the assembling of an army which suits his nature.
For the honour [lit. 'face'] of Wales, Cadwallon's land,
he will come as the lord of Britain's hosts.

Fierce Gwallawc caused   30
the great mortality of Catraeth, greatly renowned:
overseas foreigners, loyal followers, and rightful lords;
seeking cattle as a portion of great wealth in battle.
In the field headquarters, there was bright feasting for mounted warriors;
there was deliverance from the exhaustion of shipboard, an enclosure of swords.
The advance of Cadwallon to the heights of Caradawc's citadel,
when there was an armed rising for the burning of York.   37

Consummate and beloved is Britain's sovereign,
the image of a lord returning in victory.
He maintained the honour of the Welsh people by the protection of his shield.

Far away may they hear the spears   41
of the man wearing the brooch as he rides in the front rank enclosed in gleaming iron
armour—as far as Porth Ysgewin at the estuary on the border.
A song is sung of the blessed light of heaven:
I praise the generous and bold lord king, whose lineage is illustrious.
The heathen are departed; they have been driven to the briny sea 46
before the great champion. One may not conceive
of that which would be higher than you, noble diademed lord,
if it were not the over-arc of the sky and stars
—Cadwallon, a warlike Einiawn, of the *Imperium* [*Britanniae*].   50

FRAGMENTS:

. . . from Wales, to kindle fire in the land of Elmet [present-day South
Yorkshire, England].
. . . though they would lack bright, bloodstained mail coats,
because of Cadwallon, defender of the Welsh.
. . .the dragon-like chief, defender of the Welsh, Cadwallon.
. . .pillar of the hosts of the Welsh, Cadwallon of Anglesey.
. . .Wales may be so sad for its tribulations. . .

◆ ◆ ◆ ◆ ◆ ◆ ◆ ◆ ◆

§§133–139. Poetry Relating to Cynddylan[30]

§133. *Marwnad Cynddylan* The Death-song of Cynddylan

from Aberystwyth, National Library of Wales, MS 4973b, 108ʳ–109ʳ

I 1 WAR OF UNYIELDING ?menacing noblemen:
2 Rhiau and Rhirid and Rhiosedd
3 and Rhygyfarch, the generous leader, the chariot driver.
4 I shall lament until I lie in my oaken coffin
5 for the slaying of Cynddylan in his greatness.

2 6 Combat of the great ones! Did I think
7 of going to Menai [Strait], though there was no ford for me?
8 I love the one from the land of Cemais who welcomes me,
9 the dynast of Dogfeiling, violator of the descendants of Cadell.
10 I shall lament until I shall be in my unassuming oak
11 for the slaying of Cynddylan, profound loss.

3 12 Combat of the great ones! To think
13 of going to Menai, though I cannot swim!
14 I love the one who welcomes me from Aberffraw
15 the king of Dogfeiling, terror to the descendants of Cadell.
16 I shall lament until I shall be in my much spoken of oak [coffin]
17 for the slaying of Cynddylan with his mustering hosts.

4 18 Combat of the great ones! wine of cultured refinement!
19 [Now] I beseech sorrowfully, old and filled with *hiraeth*.
20 When he raided the cattle of [the region of] Pennawg, I lost
21 a brave, unyielding, unforgiving hero.
22 He used to make campaigns beyond Tren, [into] the prideful land.
23 I shall lament until I shall be where they have up the earth

30 Middle Welsh *Kynδylan*, a mid-7th-century king of Powys [north-east Wales + adjacent parts of present-day England], he belonged to to the Kyndrwynyn dynasty, rivals of the Cadelling 'descendants of Cadell' mentioned in §133 and (favourably) in §116. Cynddylan's death and death, and the deaths of the other heroes mourned in *Marwand Cynddylan* probably occurred at the Battle of Winwæd 15 November 655 (see §110 ¶¶64–65). The ally of the Britons there was Penda of Mercia and their victorious enemy, Oswiu (Osguïd) of Bernicia.

24 for the slaying of Cynddylan, [a hero] of the fame of Caradawg
[Caratācus].

5 25 Combat of the great ones! So good was the destiny
26 that Cynddylan, the battle leader (< centurion), got,
27 700 of a king's host in his provision.
28 When the son of Pyd [i.e. Panna fab Pyd = Penda of Mercia] asked,
he was so ready!
29 He did not go to the wedding feast; he had no spouse.
30 O God! What manner of community fellowship [does he keep now]?
what black interment?
31 I shall lament until I shall be in the plot of ?widowhood.
32 for the slaying of Cynddylan, of majestic fame.

6 33 Combat of the great ones! I am so very well accustomed
34 to all the most pleasing fishes and beasts.
35 Through violence I have lost the most outstanding heroes,
36 Rhiau and Rhirid and Rhiadaf
37 and Rhygyfarch, generous ruler of the host of every borderland.
38 They used to drive spoils back from the dales of the River Taf.
39 Captives would complain and were hurt. Cattle would bellow.
40 I shall lament until I shall be in the most constricted plot
41 for the slaying of Cynddylan, of fame to every extreme.

7 42 Combat of the great ones! Do you see this?
43 My heart burns like a firebrand.
44 I enjoyed the wealth of their men
45 and wives. They could not
46 repay me [enough]! I used to have brothers. It was better when they were
47 the young whelps of great ?Arthur, the mighty citadel.
48 Before Lētocētum's Stronghold [Wall, near Lichfield], they caused
49 gore under ravens and a bloody charge.
50 Lime-washed shields broke before the fair sons of the Cyndrwynyn.
51 I shall lament until I shall be in the land of the resting place
52 for the slaying of Cynddylan, full fame among chieftains.

8 53 Combat of the great ones! Extensive spoils!
54 From the front of Lētocētum's Stronghold, Morial bore off
55 1500 head of cattle from the front line of valorous blows,
56 80 stallions and as much harness.
57 The sleeping-eyed archbishop in his four-sided [. . .].
58 did not protect, [through] the book-clutching monks,
59 those men who fell in their bloody enclosure before the splendid centurion.

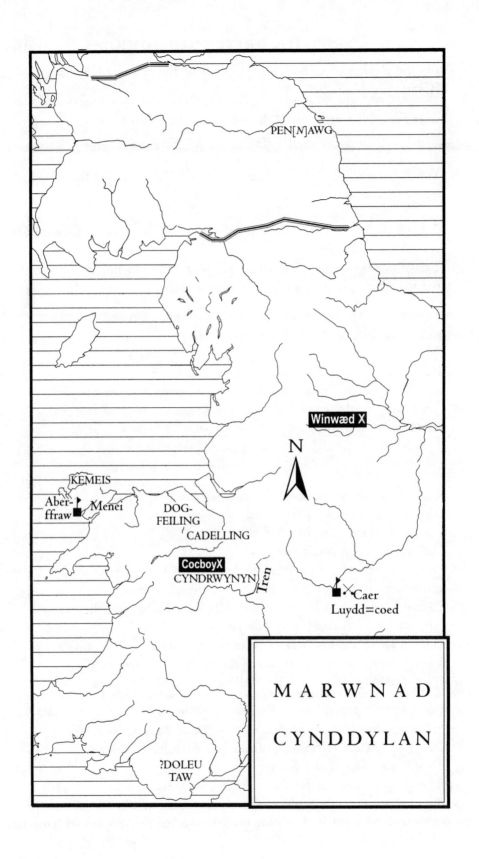

PEN[N]AWG

Winwæd X

N

KEMEIS

Aber-
ffraw ■ Menei

DOG-
FEILING

CADELLING

CocboyX
CYNDRWYNYN

Tren

■ ×Caer
Luydd=coed

?DOLEU
TAW

MARWNAD

CYNDDYLAN

60 No brother escaped from the boundary ditch to his sister.

61 [Rather] they escaped because of their [fatal] wounds, [as] they spun violently.

62 I shall lament until I shall be in a most lowly grave plot

63 for the slaying of Cynddylan, whose is praised freely by every generous man.

9 64 Great men in combat! So ?desirable it was

65 in my soul when I used to visit [the Rivers] Pwll and Alun!

66 [There were] fresh rushes under foot until sleeping time,

67 and feathered [pillows] under me, as deep as my knees!

68 And though I have gone [back] there, to my own country,

69 there is not [now] one kinsman [left]; it is birds that prohibit him.

70 And though I might be brought to God, to the hill of [His] wrath,

71 no one has sinned as I have.

◆ ◆ ◆ ◆ ◆ ◆ ◆

§§134–138. *Canu Heledd*
Poetry Attributed to Heledd, Sister of Cynddylan[31]

§134.

¶ 1 STAND OUTSIDE, O MAIDENS, AND BEHOLD THE LAND OF CYNÐYLAN! The court of Pengwern is ablaze. Woe to the young who long for their brothers!

¶ 3 Cynðylan—O cold heart of winter—who stabbed the wild boar through its head, dearly have you paid for the ale of [the settlement of] Tren.

¶ 5 Cynðylan, fiery pillar of the borderland, wearing mail, obstinate in battle, as he fought for Tren, his father's town.

¶ 6 Cynðylan, wise and fiery mind, a mailed [?]leader of the host used fight for Tren, while he lived.

◆ ◆ ◆ ◆ ◆ ◆ ◆

---

31 Heledd [Middle Welsh *Heleð*], who is the character speaking in these stanzas (three-line *englynion*), is Cynðylan's sister, here surviving his overthrow and that of his kingdom. She is interesting as an example of an early female poet, or, at least, female poetic persona. Like Taliesin, Aneirin, and Llywarch Hen, her story makes her an instance of the theme of poet as survivor and witness of cataclysm. Her name means the 'Salty One' and is found as a river name, so the factor of female personification of the land is possibly and underlying theme.

Many of the persons and places are again not identifiable, but Pengwern is at Shrewsbury (West Midlands England, not far east of the modern Welsh border), the settlement of Tren probably on the River Tern nearby, and *Eglwysseu Bassa* ('Bassa's Churches') are probably at the town of Baschurch (also nr. Shrewsbury).

§135. *Stafell Gynddylan* Cynðylan's Hall

¶ 18   CYNÐYLAN'S HALL IS DARK TONIGHT, without fire, without bed. I shall cry a while. I shall be silent afterwards.

¶ 19   Cynðylan's hall is dark tonight, without fire, without candle. Grief comes to me for you.

¶ 20   Cynðylan's hall is dark tonight, without fire, without light. Except for God, who will give me sanity?

¶ 21   The ceiling of Cynðylan's hall is dark tonight, after its handsome corps. Sorrow that it is not good which comes of it.

¶ 22   Cynðylan's hall, you have become formless. Your shield is in the grave . . .

¶ 23   Cynðylan's hall is without love tonight. . .

¶ 24   Cynðylan's hall is uncomfortable tonight . . . without chieftain, without company, without soldiery.

¶ 25   Cynðylan's hall is dark tonight, without fire, without songs. Tears overwhelm cheeks.

¶ 26   Cynðylan's hall is dark tonight, without fire, without the warband. . .

¶ 27   The vision of Cynðylan's hall wounds me, without roofs, without fire. My lord is dead. I am alive.

¶ 28   Cynðylan's hall is ravaged tonight, after the ready warriors—Elfan and bejeweled Cynðylan.

¶ 29   Cynðylan's hall is grim tonight—after the respect which had been mine—without men, without the women who kept them.

¶ 30   Cynðylan's hall is still tonight, having lost its most senior one. Great merciful God, what shall I do?

¶ 31   The ceiling of Cynðylan's hall is dark, after the English ruined Cynðylan and Elfan of Powys.

¶ 32   Cynðylan's hall is dark tonight, from the children of Cyndrwynyn, Cynon and Gwion and Gwynn.

¶ 33   Cynðylan's hall smites against me ceaselessly, after the great celebration which I saw before your fireplace.

◆ ◆ ◆ ◆ ◆ ◆ ◆

§136. *Eryr Eli* The Eagle of [the River] Eli

¶ 34   THE EAGLE OF ELI, its shriek is piercing tonight. He would drink a stream of blood, the heart's blood of fair Cynðylan.

¶ 35 The eagle of Eli was calling loudly tonight. It was splattering the blood of men. He is in the wood. Oppressive grief comes over me.

¶ 36 I hear the eagle of Eli tonight. He is bloodstained. I shall not dare him. He is in the wood. Oppressive grief comes over me.

¶ 37 The eagle of Eli, most oppressive tonight. In the vale of praiseworthy Meisir, the land of Brochfael [Kynan Garwyn's father, see §116 above] has been deeply injured.

¶ 38 The eagle of Eli clutches the walls. He does not pierce the fish in the river mouth. He cries for the blood of a hero.

¶ 39 The eagle of Eli moves over the wood tonight. . .

◆ ◆ ◆ ◆ ◆ ◆

§137. *Eryr Pengwern* The Eagle of Pengwern [now Shrewsbury, England]

¶ 40 THE EAGLE OF PENGWERN, GRAY-TALONED TONIGHT, his reply is piercing. [He is] eager for the flesh that I loved.

¶ 41 The eagle of Pengwern, gray-taloned tonight, his call is shrill, eager for the flesh of Cynðylan.

¶ 42 The eagle of Pengwern, gray-taloned tonight, his claw is raised, eager for the flesh I cherish.

¶ 43 The eagle of Pengwern shall call afar tonight, for the blood of a hero he shall wait. One can call Tren a devastated town.

¶ 44 The eagle of Pengwern calls afar tonight, for the blood of a hero he waits. One can call Tren a dead town.

◆ ◆ ◆ ◆ ◆ ◆

§138. *Eglwysseu Bassa* The Churches of Bassa

¶ 45 EGLWYSSEU BASSA ARE HIS RESTING PLACE TONIGHT, his final greeting, pillar of battle, heart of the people of Argoed.

¶ 46 Eglwysseu Bassa are crumbling tonight. . . They are red. My *hiraeth* ['longing, nostalgia, grief'] is excessive.

¶ 49 Eglwysseu Bassa lost their privilege [*breint*], after the English overthrew Cynðylan and Elfan Powys.

¶ 50 Eglwysseu Bassa are ruined tonight. Its warriors have not survived . . .

◆ ◆ ◆ ◆ ◆ ◆

§139. *Bryein Eccluys Teliau* The Exalted Privilege of St Teilo's Church[32]

HERE IS THE LAW [*cymreith*] and the exempt status [*breint*] of the church of Teliau of Lanntaf which these kings and princes of the Welsh gave to Teliau's church and to all the bishops after him forever confirmed by the authority of the popes of Rome. All the law [shall be granted] to it [the church] and to its lands [*tir hac dï dair*] free from every service [*guasanaïth*] royal and secular [*breennin bydaul*] from mayor [*maïr*] and councilor [*cygühellaur*], from the public legal disputes [*cyhoïth dadlma*] within its sovereign domain [*gulat*] and without, from military service [*lüyd*], distraint [*gauayl*], and keeping watch. Jurisdiction [shall be] to it completely, over thief and theft, violence [or rape, *treis*], homicide [*dynnyorn*], ambuscade [*cynluyn*], and arson, brawling with and without bloodshed—two sorts of fines [*y dirûy ha'y camcul*] [shall be given over] to it completely—over breach of protection within the church enclosure [*lann*] and without, over ambush in the woods and outside, and over public assault in every place on Teliau's land: right and judgement to the people of the church of Teliau's *Gundy* at Lantaf and in his court; water and pasture and woods and meadow [be granted] equally to Teliau's people; trade and mint at Lanntaf, and harbourage on Teliau's land for the ships which may disembark on its land, wherever it may be. [It shall be] free from king and everyone except Teliau and his church of Lanntaf and its bishops. For any disgrace, insult [*sarhayt*], wrong, and injury which the king of Morcannhuc [Modern *Morgannwg*, English *Glamorgan*] and his men and servants might do to Teliau's bishop and his men and servants, the king of Morcannhuc and his men and servants shall come to Teliau's *Gundy* at Lanntaf to do right and justice and suffer judgement for the wrong that may be done to Teliau's bishop and his men and servants. Its lands [shall be] without military service, overlord, distraint. And every law which the king of Morcannhuc may have in his court, Teliau's bishop shall have completely in his court likewise. He shall be cursed and excommunicate who shall break and diminish this privilege, both he and his children after him; [he shall be] blessed, both he and his children, who honours this privilege and keeps [it].

AMEN.

• • • • • • •

---

32 This Late Old Welsh legal text illustrates the important concept of *bryein* < **briganti* 'exalted privilege'. This legal text explains the loss of *breint* by a church described in the preceding poem: *Eglwysseu Bassa collassant eu breint* 'The Churches of Bassa lost their *breint*'. This word is the cognate of the Old Irish saint's and goddess's name *Brigit*, also the Romano-British tribal goddess *Brigantia*, from whom the tribe the *Brigantes* (North Britain and County Kildare, Ireland) took their name. The name is cognate with the Sanskrit feminine divine epithet *brhati* 'the exalted one' and is also the source of the Germanic tribal name 'Burgundian'. *Breint* is thus a key concept in the hierarchical ideology of the early Celts and one which the early church adapted to its advantage.

§140. The Poetry of Llywarch Hen[33]

TRANS. PATRICK K. FORD

The ancient one bewails his fate and the loss of his sons . . .

¶ 1

MY MIND YEARNS TO BE SITTING ON A HILL,
    And yet it moves me not.
    Short is my journey; my dwelling desolate.

¶ 2   Keen the wind, cow-herds in the open;
        When trees dress in crisp summer
        Colours, I am extremely ill today.

¶ 3   I am not nimble, I hold no host,
        Nor can I freely roam.
        Let the cuckoo sing as long as it likes.

¶ 4   The clamorous cuckoo sings at daybreak
        A piercing plaint in the meadows of Cuawg;
        Better generous than mean.

¶ 5   In Aber Cuawg cuckoos sing
        Upon flowering branches;
        Clamorous cuckoo, let him sing on a while.

¶ 6   In Aber Cuawg cuckoos sing
        Upon flowering branches.
        Woe to the sick one who hears them constantly.

¶ 7   In Aber Cuawg are cuckoos singing;
        It saddens me
        That those who heard them hear them no more.

¶ 8   I listened to a cuckoo on an ivy-covered branch.
        My shield-strap has slackened;
        Grief for what I loved grows.

---

33 The proper names in this section are consistently regularised into Modern Welsh spelling.

¶ 9   From the top of the mighty oak
    I listened to the voice of birds.
    Lusty cuckoo, each remembers what he loves.

¶ 10   Singer of deathless song, longing in its voice,
      Soaring with the motion of the hawk;
    Eloquent cuckoo in Aber Cuawg.

¶ 11   Loud are birds; streams wet.
    The moon shines; midnight is cold.
    I am wasted from painful disease.

¶ 12   White are the hilltops; streams are wet; midnight long.
    Every wise one is honoured.
    I deserve sleep in old age.

¶ 13   Loud are birds; gravel is wet.
    Leaves fall; sad is the homeless one.
    I will not deny it, I am ill tonight.

¶ 14   Loud are birds; wet is the shore.
    Sky is bright; wide
    The wave. Heart withered from longing.

¶ 15   Loud are birds; wet is the shore.
    Bright is the wave with its wide motion.
    That which youth believes
    I would love to get it again.

¶ 16   Loud are birds on Edrywy hill.
    The howl of dogs is desolate.
    Loud are birds again.

¶ 17   May, and every growth is lovely.
    When warriors rush to battle,
    I do not go; a wound prevents me.

¶ 18   May, and it is beautiful at the border.
    When warriors rush to the battlefield,
    I do not go; a wound torments me.

¶ 19   Grey is the mountain top; tender the tips of ash.
    From estuaries flows a shimmering wave.
    Laughter is far from my heart.

¶ 20   Today is the end of a month for me

In the shelter that he left.
I am wasted, disease has seized me.

¶ 21   Clear the sentry's eye;
            Pride causes indolence.
         I am wasted, sickness enfeebles me.

¶ 22   Cattle in sheds; a cup for mead;
            The fortunate abhor adversity.
         The bond of acquaintance is patience.

¶ 23   Cattle in sheds; a bowl for beer
            Slippery the paths; the shower fierce,
         And deep is the ford; the mind plots treachery.

¶ 24   Treason brews wicked work;
            There will be grief when it is atoned;
         Selling a little in exchange for much.

¶ 25   A cauldron will be readied for the wicked
            When the Lord judges on that long day;
         The false will be in darkness, the true shining.

¶ 26   Danger is glorious, the warrior ready;
                Men merry over beer.
            Reeds withered; cattle in sheds.

¶ 27   I have heard the surf, thudding heavily
            Among sand and gravel;
         I am wasted from melancholy tonight.

¶ 28   Dense are the tops of oaks; bitter the taste of ash,
            Sweet the cow-parsnip; a wave laughs;
         The cheek does not conceal a heart's hurts.

¶ 29   Often a sigh envelops me,
                According to my custom.
            God allows no good to the wretched.

¶ 30   Let not good come to the wretched,
            Only sadness and anxiety.
         God does not undo that which he does.

¶ 31   The wasted one was noble once, a bold warrior
                In a king's court;
                May God be gentle to the outcast.

¶ 32   What is done in an oratory,
            Wretched is he who reads it;
            Hated of man below and hated of God above.

¶ 33   Before I was decrepit, I was an eloquent speaker:
                My feats were honoured;
            The men of Argoed always supported me.

¶ 34   Before I was decrepit, I was bold.
            They welcomed me in the taverns of
            Powys, paradise of Welshmen.

¶ 35   Before I was decrepit, I was splendid;
            My spear was foremost, was first in attack.
            Now I am hunched over, I am weary, I am wretched.

¶ 36   Crutch of wood, it is harvest time
            Ferns are reddish brown, stalks yellow;
            I have rejected that which I love.

¶ 37   Crutch of wood, this is winter
            Men are noisy at drink;
            My bedside is not visited.

¶ 38   Crutch of wood, it is spring
            Reddish brown are the cuckoos, bright is their cry;
            I am unloved by a maiden.

¶ 39   Crutch of wood, it is May-time
            Brown is the furrow, wrinkled are the sprouts;
            It is sad for me to look at your bird-like beak.

¶ 40   Crutch of wood, constant branch,
            May you support an old man full of longing
            Llywarch, the steadfast talker.

¶ 41   Crutch of wood, hard branch,
            God of protection will welcome me.
            You are a loyal walking companion.

¶ 42   Crutch of wood, be constant;
            Support me still better.
            I am Llywarch, from afar.

¶ 43   Old age is mocking me
            From my hair to my teeth,
            And the rod the young cherish.

¶ 44   Old age is mocking me
        From my hair to my teeth,
      And the rod women cherish.

¶ 45   Wild is the wind; white on
        Tree stumps; bold the stag, the hill lacks growth;
      Feeble the ancient one, ambling slowly.

¶ 46   This leaf, the wind whips it away.
          Alas for its fate
      Old, born this year.

¶ 47   That which I loved since a lad I despise:
          A lusty maid, and a spirited horse;
      They do not suit me.

¶ 48   The four things I have always hated most
        Have converged on me at the same time:
      A cough and old age, disease and grief.

¶ 49   I am old, I am alone, I am disfigured and cold;
        After an honourable family,
      I am wretched, I am terribly bent.

¶ 50   I am bent with age, a wayward fool,
        I am simpleminded, quarrelsome;
      Those who loved me love me not.

¶ 51   Maidens do not love me, no one visits me,
        I can't get about.
      O death! that it does not come to me.

¶ 52   Neither rest nor rejoicing comes to me
        Since Llawr and Gwen were killed;
      I am mean and feeble, I am old.

¶ 53   A wretched fate is Llywarch's lot
        Since the night he was born:
      Long labour without release.

                   ✦ ✦ ✦ ✦ ✦ ✦ ✦

On Gwen and other sons of Llywarch . . .

¶ 54   DO NOT TAKE ARMS AFTER A FEAST; BE NOT SAD OF MIND
   Sharp is the wind, poison bitter.
  My mother declares that I am your son.

¶ 55   I know by my *awen* [poetic inspiration]
   That we are a noble line;
  It has endured a good while, O Gwen.

¶ 56   Sharp my spear, bright in battle;
   I am gearing to guard the ford,
  Though I may not escape; good-bye.

¶ 57   If you escape, I shall see you;
   If you are killed, I shall lament you.
  Do not lose the honour of warriors in spite of adversity.

¶ 58   I will not disgrace you, O war-worthy one,
   When the brave arm for the border:
  I'll bear the brunt before I yield.

¶ 59   A wave runs along the shore;
   A resolution breaks by chance.
  Under cover of battle, swift flight.

¶ 60   I mean what I say:
   Though spears shatter where I stand,
  I'll not cry out nor shall I flee.

¶ 61   Swamps spongy, hard is the hill;
   The river's brink breaks under horse's hoof.
  A promise not accomplished is no promise at all.

¶ 62   Streams spread about the fort's ditch;
   And I intend to have
  A shattered shield before I flee.

¶ 63   The horn that Urien gave you
   With the gold baldric tied around its tip,
  Sound it if you must.

¶ 64   Despite the dread of battle with the treacherous English,
   I will not mar my dignity
  I will not awaken maidens.

¶ 65   When I was the age of the lad yonder

Who girds on golden spurs,
Swiftly would I rush the spear.

¶ 66   No doubt you speak truly:
You alive and your witness dead.
The ancient one was not feeble as a lad.

¶ 67   Gwen watched at the river Llawen last night;
Despite the attack he did not flee,
Sad is the tale at the green dike.

¶ 68   Gwen watched at the Llawen last night,
With the shield upon his shoulder.
Since he was my son, he was ready.

¶ 69   Gwen watched at the Llawen last night,
With the shield facing the battle.
Since he was my son, he did not escape.

¶ 70   Gwen, warrior, my soul grieves.
Great is the pain of your death;
It is no friend who killed you.

¶ 71   Gwen of the mighty thigh guarded last night
Beside the ford of Morlas.
Since he was my son, he did not flee.

¶ 72   Gwen, I knew your nature:
Like the rush of an eagle in estuaries were you;
Had I been fortunate, you would have escaped.

¶ 73   A wave thunders, breakers cover the coast,
When warriors engage in battle;
Gwen, alas! the ancient one grieves for you.

¶ 74   A wave thunders, the tide covers the coast,
When warriors go on an expedition;
Gwen, alas! the ancient one has lost you.

¶ 75   A man was my boy, fearless in justice,
And nephew to Urien.
At Morlas Ford was Gwen killed.

¶ 76   Fierce in spear-fight, daring in valour,
He arrayed a disciplined host against the English.
This is the grave of Gwen son of Llywarch.

¶77   Four and twenty sons had I;
      Gold-torqued leader of a host,
      Gwen was the best of them.

¶78   Four and twenty sons were mine;
      Gold-torqued battle prince,
      Gwen was the best of his father's sons.

¶79   Four and twenty sons I used to have;
      Gold-torqued prince of chiefs,
      Compared to Gwen they were but lads.

¶80   Four and twenty sons in the family of Llywarch
      A family of men brave and battle-fierce
      Treachery comes from too much praise.

¶81   Four and twenty sons nurtured from my flesh;
      Through my tongue they were killed.
      Good comes from a little [praise]; they are lost.

¶82   When my son Pyll was killed, there were broken planks,
      And blood on tangled hair;
      And on the banks of the Ffraw, a bloody flow.

¶83   Planks of shields enough for sheds
      Were shattered on the hand of Pyll
      As he stood in battle.

¶84   My choice of my sons,
      When each attacked his foe:
      Fair Pyll, like fire through a chimney.

¶85   Well did he throw a thigh over the saddle
      Of his steed, near and afar;
      Fair Pyll, like fire in a flue.

¶86   Generous was the hand of battle, opposed to parley;
      He was a fort on the border.
      Fair Pyll, the wounds were grievous.

¶87   When he stopped in the door of tents
      Atop a spirited steed,
      Pyll's woman could boast a man.

¶88   Skulls of the strong were shattered before Pyll;
      Rare is the refuge where one might hide.
      The feeble are reduced to nothing.

¶ 89   Fair Pyll, far-reaching his fame.
         You brought me joy from being my son,
             And delight in knowing you.

¶ 90   The best threesome under heaven
             Who defended their dwelling:
             Pyll and Selyf and Sanddef.

¶ 91   The shield I gave to Pyll
             Was riddled with holes before he closed his eyes;
             Sad to leave it neglected.

¶ 92   Though there came to Cymru [Wales and/or Cumbria] an
         English host,
                 And many from afar,
             Pyll would show them his mettle.

¶ 93   Neither Pwyll nor Madog could be long-lived
                 From the custom they kept;
             Whether they gave or not, truce they would not seek.

¶ 94   Behold here the grave of a faultless
             And warlike one. His bards would have spread
             His fame where Pyll couldn't go
             Had he endured longer.

¶ 95   Maen and Madog and Medel,
             Brave men, vigorous brothers;
             Selyf, Heilin, Llawr, Lliwer.

¶ 96   The grave of Gwell in Rhiw Felen,
             The grave of Sawel in Llangollen;
             Llorien guards Llam y Bwch.

¶ 97   Sod conceals the reddish-brown grave;
             The earth brings him no shame
             The grave of Llyngedwy son of Llywarch.

¶ 98   Far from here is Aber Lliw;
             Farther is reproach.
             Talan, you deserve my tears today.

¶ 99   I caroused in wine from a bowl;
             He leads the attack before Rheinwg.
             Like wings of dawn were the spears of Dwg.

¶ 100 I am sorry that when Dwg asked me
                    I did not strike with them,
          Though that would not have stretched his life.

¶ 101 I know the sounds of Ceny
                    Whenever he dismounted at a tavern:
          A chief of men deserves a cup of wine.

· · · · · ·

On Urien and the Gogledd [(Men of) the North][34]

¶ 102   UNHWCH THE FIERCE WOULD TELL ME
                    Furious in fights
              Better to smite than sue for truce.

¶ 103   Unhwch the fierce would tell me
                    The spoil of outrage is tribulation;
              I shall lead the hosts of Llewenydd.

¶ 104   Unhwch the fierce would tell me
                    They said at Drws Llech:
              Dunod son of Pabo does not flee.

¶ 105   Unhwch the fierce would tell me
                    Bitter and harsh is the laughing sea;
              Terror in battle, victorious lord.

¶ 106   Fiery Urien Rheged, eagle's grip,
                    Enemy of Unhwch, daring and noble,
              Savage in war, a victorious chief.

¶ 107   Fiery Urien Rheged, eagle's grip,
                    Enemy of Unhwch, great provider:
              Mead for men with the bounty of Llŷr.

· · · · · ·

¶ 133   Friday I saw a great sadness
                    Upon the armies of the world;
              A swarm without a queen is so.

---

34 See also §§124–126 above.

¶ 134   Rhun the Wealthy gave me
       A hundred war-bands and a hundred shields;
       And one war-band was better   a great protection.

¶ 135   Rhun, pleasing prince, gave me
       A hundred dwellings and a hundred bullocks;
       And one that was better than those.

¶ 136   With Rhun, warlord, alive
       The false mended their ways;
       He was a fetter on the horses of the false.

¶ 137   How conscious am I of my wound.
       Each goes to war every summer;
       No one knows anything wrong with me.

¶ 138   Dunod, knight of battle, intended
       To make a corpse at Erechwydd
  Against the rush of Owain [son of Urien].

¶ 139   Dunod, lord of the world, intended
       To do battle at Erechwydd
       Against the rush of Pasgent [son of Urien].

¶ 140   Gwallog [= Guallauc §110 ¶ 63], knight of battle, intended
       To make a slaughter at Erechwydd
       Against the rush of Elphin [?son of Urien].

¶ 141   Brân, son of Ymellyrn, intended
       To banish me, to burn my hearths;
       A wolf who howled at the pass.

¶ 142   Morgan [= Morcant §110 ¶ 63 above] intended, he and his men,
       To banish me, to burn my homestead;
       A shrew who scratched at a rock.

¶ 143   I was wary when Elno was killed;
       He brandished a sword over the rampart
       Of Pyll and a tent from his homeland.

¶ 144   Again I saw after the din of battle,
         A shield on the shoulder of Urien;
       Elno Hen was also there.

¶ 145   Upon Erechwydd has come neglect
       For fear of a knight under javelins.
       Will there ever be another Urien?

¶ 146   My lord is a leader, bold in his manner,
                Warriors do not like his malice;
         Many a chieftain has he dispatched.

¶ 147   The passion of Urien fills me with sadness.
                He was an attacker in every region,
         On the trail of Llofan Law Ddifro.

¶ 148   Silent the wind along the slope;
                Rare is he who may be praised:
         Except Urien's kind there is none.

¶ 149   Many a brave hound and powerful hawk
                Were fed on its floor
         Before this place was in ruins.

¶ 150   This hearth, with its gray covering,
                Was more accustomed to see
         Mead and mead seekers.

¶ 151   This hearth, nettles conceal it.
                While its keeper was living
         It was more accustomed to suppliants.

¶ 152   This hearth, grassy sod conceals it.
                When Owain and Elffin were alive
         Its cauldron bubbled with booty.

¶ 153   This hearth, brown stalks conceal it.
                It was more accustomed to fierce and
         Fearless swordplay around its food.

¶ 154   This hearth, splendid briars hide it.
                A burning wood-fire was once inside;
         The people of Rheged were accustomed to generosity.

¶ 155   This hearth, thorns conceal it.
                Its retinue was more accustomed to
         The favour of the fellowship of Owain.

¶ 156   This hearth, ants conceal it.
         It was more accustomed to glowing tapers
                And loyal mead mates.

¶ 157   This hearth, the dock-leaves cover it.
                It was more accustomed to see

Mead and mead drinkers.

¶ 158   This hearth, a pig burrows in it.
            It was more accustomed to the revelry
            Of men and carousing around cups.

¶ 159   This hearth, a chick scratches in it.
            Want did not harm it
            While Owain and Urien were alive.

¶ 160   This pillar here and that one yonder
            Were more accustomed to see
            The joy of a host and generosity.

                    ✦ ✦ ✦ ✦ ✦ ✦

On Maen, son of Llywarch . . .

¶ 161   FAIR MAEN, WHEN I WAS YOUR AGE
            My cloak was not trampled with feet;
            My land was not ploughed without bloodshed.

¶ 162   Fair Maen, when I was like you,
            With my young men following me,
            The enemy did not violate my border.

¶ 163   Fair Maen, when I was like you,
            In pursuit of my youth,
            The enemy did not like my wrath.

¶ 164   Fair Maen, when I was strong,
            I was fierce in slaughter.
            My deed was a man's though I was a lad.

¶ 165   Fair Maen, consider prudently:
            The need for counsel is neglected.
            Let Maelgwn [king of Gwynedd †547] seek another steward.

¶ 166   My choice is the prince with his armour
            About him, sharp like a thorn.
            Whetting this stone is no vain act.

¶ 167 I have been robbed of a gift from the valley of Merfyrniawn,
                Concealed in a pitcher;
                With sharp iron Odwrn was killed.

¶ 168   Blessed be the distant hag
        Who said from the door of her hut,
      Fair Maen, do not leave your blade behind.

＊ ＊ ＊ ＊ ＊ ＊

Gnomes . . .

¶ 169   SHARP THE WIND, BARE THE HILL, DIFFICULT TO FIND SHELTER.
        The ford spoils, the lake freezes;
      A man can stand upon a single reed.

¶ 170   Wave upon wave washes the land;
        Shrill are the outcries before the mountaintops;
      One can hardly stand outside.

¶ 171   Frigid the lake from the onslaught of winter;
        Withered the reeds, stalks broken;
      Fierce is the wind, trees bare.

¶ 172   Frigid the fish bed in icy shade;
        Lean the stag, reeds are bearded;
      Evening is short, trees bowed down.

¶ 173   Snow falls, white mantle;
        Warriors do not go on their expeditions.
      Lakes cold, their looks want warmth.

¶ 174   Snow falls, white hoarfrost;
        Idle the shield on an ancient's shoulder.
      Fierce the wind, grass is frozen.

¶ 175   Snow falls upon ice;
        Wind sweeps the top of thick woods.
      Mighty the shield upon a brave shoulder.

¶ 176   Snow falls, it covers the vale;
        Warriors hurry to battle.
      I do not go, a wound restrains me.

¶ 177   Snow falls along the hill;
        The steed a captive, cattle are lean:
      Not like a summer's day today.

¶ 178   Snow falls, white the mountaintops;

Naked the masts of ships at sea.
A coward plans many schemes.

¶ 179   Gold handles on drinking horns, horns among the host;
        Seas are cold, lightning in the sky;
        Evening is brief, treetops bent.

¶ 180   Bees in fodder, feeble the cry of birds;
        A dewless day;
        White-cloaked the hill crest, crimson dawn.

¶ 181   Bees in shelter, frigid the ford's covering;
        It freezes when there is ice.
        Despite every evasion, death shall come.

¶ 182   Bees in captivity, the sea green;
        Reeds withered, the hill hard.
        Cold and raw the land today.

¶ 183   Bees sheltered from winter's wetness;
        Pale the stubble, cow-parsnips hollow.
        Cowardice in a man is an evil possession.

¶ 184   Long the night, the moor bare, the slope grey;
        Green the shore, seagull in sea's spume,
        Rough are the seas; there will be rain today.

¶ 185   Dry is the wind, the path wet, the valley treacherous;
        Vegetation cold, the stag lean,
        Smooth is the river; fair weather will come.

¶ 186   Foul weather in mountains, rivers raging,
        Flood drenches dwelling floors;
        It is the sea—seeing the world.

¶ 187   You are not a scholar, you are not grey-haired, lord,
        You are not called in the day of need;
        Alas, Cynddilig, that you were not a woman.

¶ 188   The bowed stag seeks a snug glen;
        Ice ravages the bare countryside.
        The brave escape from many a strait.

¶ 189   The thrush's breast is speckled.
        Speckled is the breast of the thrush.

¶ 190   The bank breaks under a lean, bowed stag's hoof;

Shrill the wind's loud cry.
Scarcely, it is true, can one stand outside.

¶ 191   First day of winter, brown and black the heather tips;
Spuming sea's wave, day is short.
Let your counsel be carried out.

¶ 192   Armed with shield and spirited steed,
And men both bold and brave,
Fair is the night to pursue a foe.

◆ ◆ ◆ ◆ ◆ ◆

On the sons of Urien and Llywarch . . .

¶ 193   SWIFT THE WIND, TREES RAW AND BARE;
Stalks withered, the stag swift.
You who are called Pelis, what land is this?

¶ 194   Though the snow reach the cruppers of Arfwl Melyn,
Darkness would not dishearten me;
I would lead a host to Bryn Tyddwl.

¶ 195   Since you hit upon the rampart so easily
Though snow falls on ford and slope
Pelis, whence is your skill?

¶ 196   I feel no care in Britain tonight,
Attacking the home of the Lord of Nuchain
Upon a horse, following Owain.

¶ 197   Before you bear arms and shield,
Defender of the army of Cynwyd [ancestor of the
dynasty of Strathclyde],
Pelis, in what land were you raised?

¶ 198   The man whom God deliver from dire captivity,
A red-speared kind of chieftain,
Owain Rheged reared me.

¶ 199   Because the lord has gone into the rampart of Iwerydd,
O war-band, do not flee;
After mead, seek not disgrace.

¶ 200   In the morning at daybreak
Mwng Great-Towns was attacked;

The horses of Mechydd were not pampered.

¶ 201   Beer brings me no joy;
From the reports they bring me,
Mechydd, a cover of wood is over you.

¶ 202   They fought a battle at Cafall,
Bloody corpses ignored;
Rhun's encounter with the other brave one.

¶ 203   Since Mechydd killed Mwng's spearmen,
Brave lad, he cannot understand it;
Lord of heaven, you have caused me grief.

¶ 204   Men in war; the ford frozen;
Chilly is the wave, sea's surface flecked.
May the Lord give profound counsel.

¶ 205   Mechydd, son of Llywarch, dauntless chieftain,
Comely and fair in his swan-white cloak
Was first with bridle-tied horse.

◆ ◆ ◆ ◆ ◆ ◆

The Names of the Sons of Llywarch Hen

¶ 206   FAIR SINGS THE BIRD
On a sweet bough above Gwen; before he was set
Under sod, the arms of the ancient could wound.

¶ 207   The best threesome in their land,
Defending their dwellings
Eithir and Erthir and Argad.

¶ 208   Three sons of Llywarch, three fierce bands,
Three joyless champions:
Llew and Araf and Urien.

¶ 209   Complaints are easier for me
On account of leaving him upon the bank of the river
Amid clusters of mildewed cow-parsnips.

¶ 210   Bull of battle, desiring combat;
Pillar in battle, candle of communion;

Lord of heaven, guide the soul of Rhun.

¶ 211 The best threesome under heaven
Defending their home:
Pyll and Selyf and Sanddef.

¶ 212 In the morning at daybreak
Mwng Great-Towns was attacked;
The horses of Mechydd were not pampered.

¶ 213 They fought a battle at Cafall,
Bloody corpses ignored;
Rhun's encounter with the other brave one.

¶ 214 A cry rings out atop Mount Llug
Above the grave of Cynllug;
My fault, I have done it.

¶ 215 Snow falls, covers the vale;
Warriors rush to battle.
I do not go, a wound restrains me.

¶ 216 You are not a scholar, you are not grey-haired, lord,
You are not called in the day of need;
Alas, Cynddilig, that you were not a woman.

¶ 217 Far from here is Aber Lliw,
Farther is reproach.
Talan, you deserve my tears today.

◆ ◆ ◆ ◆ ◆ ◆ ◆

Llywarch seeks shelter . . .

¶ 218 GLORIOUS THE RIDER ON A PLAIN;
While God willed my fortune,
I did not consume acorns like a pig.

¶ 219 Llywarch Hen, do not be sad,
You will get a welcome, friend;
Dry your eyes, be silent   do not weep.

¶ 220 Ancient am I, and do not comprehend you.
 Give me counsel   whither shall I seek?
 Urien is dead, I have need.

¶ 221   It is your counsel to go to Brân,
 With a smooth song full of high praise?
 Dead are all the sons of Urien.

¶ 222   Trust not Brân, trust not Dunod,
 Seek nothing from them in hardship.
 Let the cowherd make for Llanfawr.

¶ 223   There is a Llanfawr across the ocean
 Against which the sea crashes.
 My friend, I do not know if that's it.

¶ 224   There is a Llanfawr beyond Bannog,
 Where the Clwyd flows into the Clywedog.
 And I do not know if that's it, friend.

¶ 225   Seek along the river Dee,
 From the river Meloch to the Treweryn;
 Cowherd, they flow to Llanfawr.

¶ 226   A wretched fate is Llywarch's lot
 Since the night he was born:
 Long labour without release.

¶ 227   Thin is my shield of my left side;
 Though I am old, I can do it.
 I will stand guard at the rampart of Morlas.

¶ 228. It happened that the horse of Gwen ap Llywarch was killed in a battle at ——————— and after the horse was killed, Gwen himself was killed. And a long while after that the horse's skull was used for a stone in a causeway over an estuary that was near the spot where the horse had been killed. And after that Llywarch Hen happened to pass along that road, and there Llywarch's servant said to his master, 'Yonder is the skull of the horse of Gwen ap Llywarch, your son!' And then Llywarch sang this englyn about that:

 I saw this horse in his prime,
 Head of a stag, tosser of turf;
 No one would tread upon his jaw
 When he was under Gwen ap Llywarch.

 Llywarch Hen sang it.

An old englyn on the rugged land of Eifionydd

¶ 229   How suddenly Maen's horse stumbled
          In the sand and sharp stony land
          At accursed Eifionydd mountain.
          Maen goes where there is no marsh.

          ◆ ◆ ◆ ◆ ◆ ◆ ◆

Llywarch Hen on his children

¶ 230   I had, though they were generous,
          It will be sad being without them,
          Many fair and merry children;
          But tonight, I am alone.

          ◆ ◆ ◆ ◆ ◆ ◆ ◆

§§141–142. Two Breton Foundation Legends

From Early Eleventh-Century Latin Texts

TRANS. J. T. KOCH

§141. *Vita Sancti Uuohednouii* The Legend of St Goueznou

giving accounts of the origins of Britain, Brittany, & England

TO THE VENERABLE lord and father in Christ, Bishop Eudo, and to the brothers who work with him in the service of Christ, Guillelm, a priest of their number, gives salutations, in year 1019 of the incarnation of the Lord, and the 24th of your episcopate, my Lord Bishop.

¶ 1. We read in the *Ystoria Britanica* that the Britons, under the command of Brutus and Corineus, subjugated *Albidia*[35] which they renamed 'Britania' together with its adjacent islands by virtue of their martial valour. Seeing their numbers grow and their realm prosper, Conan Meriadoc[36]—a warlike man and an orthodox Christian—crossed the sea to the Armorican gulf of Gaul with a multitudinous and infinite number of Britons, their number having then grown to greater than one small country could contain. His first seat was on the River Guilidon within the limits of Plebis Columbae [Plougoulm], in the place which is still called *Castrum Meriadoci*. He with his Britons conquered the whole land, from sea to sea and as far as the *civitas* of the Andegavi, with all of Bro Naoned and Bro Roazhon [*cum omni territorio Nannetensi et Redonico* '. . . all the country of Nantes and Rennes'], by means of praiseworthy heroism. He killed all the indigenous men, who were still pagan; for this reason they were called *Pengouet*, which means 'wooden heads' [?]. As for the women, he cut out all of their tongues, lest the Breton language [*lingua Britannica*] be changed by them. [The Britons] took the women as wives and for other purposes as the circumstance required. They then built churches for the praise of God in

---

35 Cf. Old Welsh *elbïd* 'habitable surface of the world' < British **albijū* 'ditto, Britain'.

36 Conan Meriadoc in Breton tradition has a counterpart in the Welsh, Kynan son of Eudav who, in the prose tale, *Breuðwyt Maxen Wledic* ('The Dream of Prince Maximus'), leads the Britons to Brittany. This episode is there, as here, used to account for the identity of the Welsh and Breton languages, complete with the episode of the cutting out of the tongues of the indigenous Armorican women, as in a later recension of *Historia Brittonum*. Vortigern is one and the same as the Guorthïgïrn of *Historia Brittonum* §110 above, the 5th-century Brittonic high king of ill repute.

various places. They divided the land into holdings called *Plou-* and *Treb-* [*plebes et tribus*], [and] by the grace of God, it was called 'Lesser Britain' [*minor Britannia*]. And thus, the Armoricans and the insular Britons use the same laws, maintaining a fraternal link, and had formerly for a long time been ruled by a single ruler as one people.

¶ 3. Time passed, Vortigern [i.e. Guorthïgïrn], the usurping king, sought support for his unjust rule, inviting warlike men from Saxonia, and made them his allies. These men, as pagans, brought many ills upon the Britons. Their arrogance was later on repressed by Art[h]ur the Great, king of the Britons, who repelled them from the greater part of the island and constrained them to servitude. But this same Art[h]ur, after achieving numerous glorious victories in parts of both Britain and Gaul, was finally summoned from human endeavour, and the way then lay open for the return of the Saxons. Then came a great oppression of the Britons, destruction of their churches, and persecution of their saints. And this persecution continued through the reigns of many kings, during which the Britons and Saxons fought one another with mixed results. Those Saxons then imposed the name 'Anglia' on Britain, for 'Anglia' was an ancient tribal kingdom [*civitas*] in Saxonia. And they called themselves 'Angli' or 'Anglici' [i.e. 'English'], but to this day they have been called 'Saxones' by the Britons [cf. Welsh *Saeson*, Breton *Saozon*]. In this tempest, many saints offered themselves for martyrdom. Others, heeding the advice of the evangelists, left Great Britain   which is now the land of the Saxons [cf. Breton *Bro Soaz* 'England'] for Brittany—thus to escape the tyranny of pagans. Still others abandoned all their goods, to become the willing and devoted slaves of the Lord in solitary places.

◆ · ◆ · ◆ · ◆ · ◆ · ◆ · ◆

§142. *De sancto Iudicaelo rege Historia* The History Iudicael, Sainted King
featuring Taliesin in Brittany

ONE NIGHT, IUD-HAEL, most noble king, then yet of but youthful years, weary after hunting, slept in the house of his subject Ausoc in Trefles, which is at the end of the long coastline on the west, within the limits of Bro Leon [north-western Brittany] and Kemenet Ili. In a dream he saw a most lofty mountain standing in the middle of his kingdom, i.e. in its very centre [*umbilicus*]. It was difficult to reach by way of a stony track. And there, at the summit of that mountain, he saw himself seated in an ivory chair. And within his view there was a wondrous huge post in the form of a round column, founded by its roots in the ground, its mighty branches reaching the sky, and its straight shaft reaching from the earth up to the heavens. The lower half of this shaft was iron, bright as the whitest [?]unmixed tin, and infixed and inserted into its entire surface there were round iron pegs, of the same colour as the shaft. These pegs held mail coats, metal helmets with plumed crests, quivers full of arrows, short swords and long swords, lances, short spears, javelins, spurs, bridles, saddles, [?]pipes, trumpets, and shields. The upper half of the same shaft was of gleaming gold, an angelic beacon [or candelabra]. And on it, over its whole surface, just as with the aforementioned, were infixed and inserted round pegs of gold, coloured not unlike the shaft, upon which hung candlesticks, censers, sacramental vessels, vestments, and books of the Evangelists. And at the end of each peg, both those of iron and of gold, there stood bright burning candles, shining like stars perpetually. (As, then, he was praying to the Lord, heaven was opened to him.)

[27] And just then, he saw next to him the daughter of his subject Ausoc. She was named Prïtell, a lovely girl, as yet unknown by man, whom he had seen the previous day and had desired in his mind. Immediately, she saluted him in the manner of a subordinate, saying, 'Hail, lord Iud-hael!' [32] Then, turning to look at her, he said, 'Girl, what are you doing here?'

[33] She answered him: 'My king Iud-hael, in some manner it has been fore-ordained by our maker that you and I should come to this place, and that the custody of this ornamental pillar should be handed on for a time from no man in the world but yourself to no woman but myself and that after that it be passed on from no woman other than myself to no man but yourself.'

[38] And after these words were said, the heavens closed. And in the morning, Iud-hael awoke from his dream and rose. He reflected upon his vision and marveled at it. And forthwith he sent a certain loyal attendant to Bro Gueroc [the Vannetais country in southeast Brittany], to the monastery of Gildas, where there was a certain overseas traveller and exile for religion, namely Taliösin the bard[37], son of Dôn[38], [*Taliosinus bardus filius Donis*], a prophet who had great foresight through the interpretation of portents; one who with wondrous eloquence, proclaimed in prophetic utterances the lucky and unlucky lives of lucky and unlucky men.

[47] And the messenger entreated Taliösin with this pleading message and speaking out as if he himself were Iud-hael: 'O greatest of all interpreters of visions! I have beheld a wondrous dream, which I have told to many but none

---

37 The tradition that Taliesin travelled to Brittany and studied there under St. Gildas (whose death is placed in 570 by the *Annales Cambriae*) is found also in the *Vita Merlini* of Geoffrey of Monmouth, published c. 1145.

38 On filius Donis 'son of Dôn' and the Brittonic myth of *plant Dôn* in the 4th Branch of the Mabinogi, cf. Book of Taliesin 25.26ff.: *Am swynnwys i Vath . . . Am swynwys i Wytyon . . . . o Euron o Vodron . . . A nu ym gowy namyn Goronwy* 'Math created me by enchantment . . . Gwydion made me by enchantment . . . no one (?) struck me down except Goronwy' [*Euron* = *Gwron* < *Uûron* < **Wironos* 'the divine man, husband, hero' consort of Mātronā; *Dôn* (always occurring in semantic genitive) < **ghdhõ(n)*, **ghdhonos* 'earth'.

could explain.' And the messenger retold the whole story of the dream of his lord Iud-hael, as I related before, of the pillar and its ornaments.

[53] And then Taliösin responded to him saying: 'The dream that I hear is marvelous, and it signifies and proclaims a wonder. It concerns your good and capable lord Iud-hael as he sits and reigns in his kingdom. And from the daughter of Ausoc (who was mentioned before), he will have a better and far more capable son to reign on earth and in heaven, from whom, by God's gift, will descend the strongest sons of the entire race of the Bretons; from these men will arise royal counts and heavenly priests. Their father's subjects, from the least to the greatest, will obey and serve them, across all the realms of the Bretons. And the first-born son, whose origin is the subject [of the dream], greatly will he prevail amongst the hosts of the world and afterwards likewise amongst the host of heaven. He will thus begin holding worldly office and consummate his career in holy orders. The lay warrior serves the world; the cleric serves God.'

[67] And, as these prophetic words were pronounced by Taliösin as he interpreted the dream, and as they were then related to king Iud-hael by his servant, so subsequent events confirmed them. For, the royal count Iud-hael, having heard these words, rejoiced and took control of all of vast Letau [Brittany; MSS *leticiam*, or for *laetitiam* 'fertile land' ?] and more extensively than he expected. He loved the aforementioned girl, [which was to bring about] the planting of the renowned and noble vine. And demanding her from her parents, the famous and exalted ruler in the flower of youth took her away to sleep with her. And when Iud-hael had known her, as they say, from her first virginal wedding night, the precocious girl Prïtell conceived St Iudic-hael.[39] After some months, she bore the noble [conception], which she had received from the aforementioned count, safely and without difficulty.

[80] Good land, well ploughed;
    productive or fallow under hoes,

---

39 Iudic-hael was the ruler of Armorican Domnonia (northern Brittany) *c.* 600–*c.* ad 640. The tale is translated from the Latin saint's life written by the Breton monk Ingomar (Incomaris Grammaticus), who is known to have been active between 1008 and 1034. The text survives in two manuscripts of *c.* 1400 of *Chronicon Briocense* (the Chronicle of Saint-Brieuc), and a better version is found in the 16th-century Bibliothèque Nationale Latin MS 9889. There is also a French epitome of 1505 by the historian Pierre Le Baud. Both the Latin and the French were published in R. Fawtier, 'Ingomar, historien Breton', in *Mélanges d'histoire du moyen âge offerts a M. Ferdinand Lot* (1925). Breton tradition remembers this king as both a saint and a great warrior-king who extended his frontiers against the Frankish king Dagobert.

Incidentally, the name *Iudic-hael* is the diminutive of his father's name *Iud-hael*, which means 'Generous Lord', and survives in Welsh as *Ithel*. Old Breton *Iudic-hael*, via Middle Breton *Jezikel*, is the source of the English surname *Jekyll*.

adequately fertilised with manure,
seeded with white wheat,
brings forth the fair awn.
The awn, then, at the appropriate time, [brings forth] the ears, and the ears, after they have shed their flowers, produce ripened grain by which both the humble countrymen and their betters survive from year to year.

[88] By this [account] I understand that divine love, and not vain lust, created Iudic-hael, he who was to our fathers a secure place of protection, a vast forest, and a bountiful legacy, and presently to ourselves is a mighty refuge, a well-defended city, and a most skilled physician; whom we, his servants, the Bretons, honour from generation to generation forever.

AMEN.

◆ ◆ ◆ ◆ ◆ ◆ ◆

§143. The Martial Eulogy from *De sancto Iudicaelo*

following the edition and French translation of L. Fleuriot, *La lttérature bretonne dans ses rapports avec l'Histoire* (Toulouse, 1988).[40]

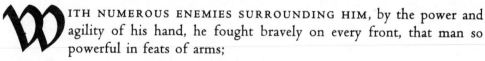ITH NUMEROUS ENEMIES SURROUNDING HIM, by the power and agility of his hand, he fought bravely on every front, that man so powerful in feats of arms;

Or, in the manner of farmers in their fields, sewing seed, Iudic-hael scattered his javelins, each landing wherever he intended;

And when, in the manner of strong warriors fierce in combat, he led the way to war against adversaries,

With his armed men advancing in high spirits in front of him, he shared out many horses equipped with war harness;

And so, many spearmen, who beforehand had gone out as infantry, returned home with plentiful spoils, as cavalry;

And from the many corpses strewn over the earth behind him, dogs, vultures, crows, blackbirds, and magpies were sated;

And many were the towns in which there resided wailing widowed wives;

---

40 The text is Latin, but as Fleuriot argued, the close thematic correspondences to *Y Gododdin* suggest a basis in vernacular praise poetry. Iudic-hael of Domnonia was a contemporary of the Frankish king Dagobert (his enemy) and Cadwallon of Gwynedd. He died in the 630s.

For like the virile bull amid unbred heifers or the boar amongst unfamiliar swine, or the eagle amongst geese, the falcon amongst cranes, or the swallow amongst bees, so did Iudic-hael—king of the Armorican Britons, the swift and agile, the steely-hard man of war—make short work of the enemies arrayed against him;

And he made many great slaughters of the Franks and many times laid waste their provinces, because the Franks sought to subjugate the Bretons.

◆ ◆ ◆ ◆ ◆

SPECIAL NAMES AND TERMS

adgarios (Gaulish): 'invoker' of a deity §1.

áes dáno (Irish): 'the skilled class' of society, especially the poets but also including smiths, jurists, and presumably, in pre-Christian times, druids.

Amaethon (Welsh): the son of **Dôn**. His name means 'divine farmer' or more generally 'the divine underling', < *ambaχtonos, from the *ambaχtos* 'farmer, &c.' literally 'he who is sent around'. This Celtic word is the source of English *ambassador*.

Amairgen: (Irish): There is more than one character with this name: (1) chief poet of the Gaels during the legendary conquest of Ireland and (2) chief poet of Conchobor's court.

Annwvyn (Welsh): Literally the 'un-world', it is the otherworld in Welsh tradition. It is often thought of as underneath the habitable surface of the earth (**elfyð** < *albijū).

baile (Irish): 'frenzy, madness', as in the title of the tale *Buile Shuibne* 'The Madness of Suibne'. Hence 'ecstatic utterance, prophecy'.

bard (Irish) and Welsh **barð**; Modern Welsh **bardd** = Gaulish plural **bardī**: in the classical authors, the term refers to a poet of the learned class; in medieval Ireland, it refers to a less prestigious class of poets than the **filid**.

Beltaine (Irish): a principal sacred day, falling upon the first of May and marking the beginning of summer, corresponding to Welsh **Kalan Mei**, 'May Eve'.

Berneich, Bryneich (Welsh): Southern Gododdin (roughly the present-day English counties of Northumberland and Durham), later English kingdom of *Bernicia*, later the northern part of the composite Anglo-Saxon kingdom of Northumbria which was to conquer and supersede the Celtic kingdom of Gododdin *c.* AD 638.

Boand (Irish): originally a water-goddess, mother of Oengus and eponym of the river Boyne. The form in Ptolemy's Geography (2nd century AD) is *Buvinda*, correctly **Bouvindā**, the sense of which is 'white cow'.

brenin (Welsh): 'king', originally 'he who is possessed by (or possesses) the exalted goddess *Brigantī*'; see §49 above.

brichtu ban (Irish): 'spells of women', cf. Gaulish **bnanom bricton** occurring in the late 1st century AD coven inscription from Larzac in southern France, meaning 'a magical incantation of women'. See §2.

Brigit (Irish): goddess and saint, associated with the sanctuary of Cill Dara (meaning 'Church of the Oak') = Kildare. Cognate with the British goddess ***Brigantī**, Romano-British **Brigantia**, tribal goddess of the **Brigantes** who resided in both North Britain and South Leinster in Ptolemy's world geography. The word also survives in the Welsh common noun **braint** 'exalted and invulnerable privilege'. See §49 above.

Brittonic or **Brythonic**: the ancient Celtic language of Britain and the family of closely-related mediaeval and modern Celtic languages descended from it—Welsh, Breton, and Cornish.

Brug na Bóinne: supernatural dwelling-place of the goddess **Boand**, and an enormous (*c.* 100 metres diameter) megalithic chambered tomb of the Neolithic Age (later fourth millennium BC) known now as Newgrange.

Brython (Welsh): name used by the Celtic Britons for themselves. The ancient form, **Brittones**, first appears in Roman sources in the later first century AD.

Caball (Welsh): Arthur's dog, literally 'horse' < Celtic **caballos* (whence Vulgar Latin *caballus*, whence the word for 'horse' in most of the Romance languages). The modernised Welsh spelling is **cafall**, related to the more common word **ceffyl** = Ir. **capall**. See §110 ¶ 73.

cairde (Irish): 'peace, treaty', especially between tribes but also between gods and men. The exact cognate is Welsh **kerennyδ** (< Common Celtic **karantiom*), which is the word used for the 'friendship' or 'truce' concluded between Pwyll and the Unworld's king Arawn in the First Branch of the Mabinogi.

Cartimanduā (British): queen of the Brigantes, AD 43–70. See §49.

Cisalpine Gaul 'Gaul this side of the Alps'. The plain of the Po river in Northern Italy, conquered by Celtic tribes coming from north of the Alps in the 5th and 4th centuries BC, Early and Middle La Tène times.

coíced (Irish): traditionally thought to mean literally 'a fifth', hence 'province': in the medieval period, early Ireland was thought of as having been divided into five provinces *Ulaid* 'Ulster' (the North-east), *Laigin* 'Leinster' (the South-east), *Muma* 'Munster' (the South-west), *Connacht* (the North-west), and (often) *Mide* 'Meath' (the middle).

Colum Cille or **Columba** (Irish): saint of the 6th century, founder of the monastery of Iona (*c.* 563) and, according to later tradition, protector of the Irish poets at the assembly of Druim Cett in 575.

Connacht (**Connaught**) (Irish): North-western province of early Ireland; originally a dynastic/tribal name; rather than a territorial designation, the descendants of *Conn Cét-chathach*, 'Conn of the Hundred Battles'. This Conn was reckoned as the ancestor of the legendary king Cormac mac Airt and the paramount historical dynasty, the Uí Néill.

Cruachan, older **Cruachu** (Irish): legendary seat of Queen Medb and Ailill of Connacht in the *Táin*. This is the extensive complex of earth works and ringforts at Rath Cróghan, Co. Roscommon.

cú (Irish) genitive and compounding form **con(-)**: 'dog, wolf', a frequent epithet of warriors, corresponding to Welsh **ci**, **Cyn-**, **-gwn** in names.

Culhwch (Welsh): Arthur's cousin in the story of early Welsh wondertale *Culhwch and Olwen*, the protagonist of the frame story.

Cumulative Celticity: a theory of gradual, piecemeal, and largely peaceful establishment of Celtic cultures in British Isles, opposed to the 'Invasion Hypothesis', first proposed by C. F. C. Hawkes, ' "Cumulative Celticity" in

Pre-Roman Britain', *Études Celtiques* 13 (1973), 606-28.

Cunedda (Welsh) (Archaic Welsh **Cunedag**): chieftain of the northern region of Gododdin, legendary founder of the North Welsh kingdom of Gwynedd in the late fourth or early fifth century. See §110 ¶¶ 14, 62, §111.

Cú Roí (Irish): Irish king and hero associated with the province of Munster (South-west Ireland) and famous for his magical powers. He assumes the guise of a giant churl (*bachlach*) in the story *Fled Bricrenn* (§81), also a central character in *Mesca Ulad* (§82).

curadmír (Irish): the champion's portion, the choicest portion of meat due to the boldest warrior. This trophy is a key element in the Ulster Cycle stories *Scéla Muicce Meic Dá Thó* (§80) and *Fled Bricrenn* (§81). The same concept is probably behind the Welsh *kyuran clotuan* 'portion of fame' of the Gododdin. The same idea is found in the ancient account of Gaulish feasts provided by Athenaeus (§17).

Cyfarwyddiaid (Welsh): the 'story-telling' class, they functioned as historians and popular poets; they also kept track of boundaries as is shown in the Old Welsh charters in the Lichfield Gospels.

Dagda, Dagán, Eochaid Ollathair (Irish): literally the 'good god', one of the chief beings of the the Tuatha Dé (Danann/Donann).

dán (Irish): 'gift', cf. Latin *dōnum*, Welsh **dawn**, develops the sense 'poem' in both Irish and Welsh; i.e., a gift to one's patron.

Deur (Old Welsh): the English kingdom of Deira, later the southern part of Northumbria, roughly present-day East Yorkshire (this is where the chariot burials had been some centuries previous to the Anglo-Saxon settlements).

díbergach (Irish): 'outlaw, bandit' or 'banditry'. This is the term used to describe the raiding activities of the descendants of Donn Désa and their British allies led by Ingcél the One-Eyed in *Togail Bruidne Dá Derga* (§90).

domun (Irish): 'world', < Common Celtic **dubno-*, containing the same root as Welsh *Annwvyn* 'Otherworld' < **an-dubno-* 'not world'. The cognate English word is 'deep'; thus the etymological sense of the Celtic is 'the earth' in the sense of what is below.

Donn (Irish): in *Lebor Gabála* 'The Book of Invasions' (§108), the chief of the invading sons of Míl (Maic Míled) who insults the land goddess, *Ériu* 'Ireland', and is subsequently drowned off the south-west coast of Ireland. Buried in *Tech nDuinn* 'the House of Donn', which he inhabits elsewhere in Irish tradition as god of the dead.

Druid (Irish **Druí** and Welsh **Dryw** and **Derwy**): In the classical authors, he functioned as a priest/ philosopher; in the medieval Irish and Welsh material he tends towards a wizard/ prophet.

Dyfneint (Welsh): roughly modern *Devon*-shire, part of Arthur's kingdom, along with **Cernyw**, which signifies in early Welsh tradition Britain south of the Bristol Channel, including the westernmost region of Cornwall which takes its name from that of the old Celtic tribal region.

Eber, Eremón (Irish): the sons of Míl, ancestor figure of the Gaels in the

Lebor Gabála, and from whom the southern and northern Irish respectively were descended.

echtra(e) (Irish): 'journey, adventure', often a generic name for the Irish Otherworld and voyage tales (the latter also known as *immrama* [pl.]).

Elcmar (Irish): Irish deity who is tricked by the Dagda when the latter made the sun stand still for nine months so that Oengus was conceived and born on the same day. See *Tochmarc Étaíne* (§89).

Em(h)ain M(h)acha (Irish): the legendary capital of pre-Christian Ulster, identified with the Bronze-/Iron-Age site at Navan Fort, nr. the associated town of Armagh, which figured importantly from the 7th century AD as Ireland's 'primatial see', i.e. the church of the most important bishop. The founding of the church of Armagh has been credited to St Patrick going back at least to Muirchú and Tírechán in the later 7th century.

Emrys (Welsh), Old Welsh **Embreis**: Latin *Ambrosius (Aurelianus)*, a 5th-century Romanised British leader who, according to the 6th-century British writer Gildas, fought the English between 450–480. Connected with the legend of the red and white dragons and the downfall of the unking Guorthïgïrn (Vortigern). This story is first found in *Historia Brittonum* (§110 ¶¶31, 39–42) and later entered the mainstream of Arthurian tradition by way of Geoffrey of Monmouth's *Historia Regum Brittaniae*. The Welsh wonderchild Emrys is one component of Geoffrey's composite character Merlin.

enech (Irish): literally 'face', but in terms of law and status it means 'honour'. The Welsh cognate, **wyneb**, also conveys both these senses.

eneit (Welsh), Gaulish **anatia** (§2), originally 'life' (thus in *Y Gododdin*) from the same root of Welsh *anadl* 'breath', OIr. *anál* (cf. Latin *animus*, *anima*). In the Christian tradition, this comes to be the word for the soul.

englyn (Welsh): a type of metre based on a stanza of three lines. A younger type has four lines and remains popular in present-day Welsh poetic composition. Often used for dramatic dialogues and monologues in character.

Ériu (Irish): the Irish name for Ireland, attested in a 2nd-century Latin source as *Iveriō* (= Celtic **Iwerijū* probably < IE **piHwerjoH* meaning 'fat, fertile country').

Fedelm (Irish): seeress/poetess in the *Táin Bó Cuailgne*. Based on IE root **weid-/wid-* 'to know' (cf. Old Irish *ro-fitir*, 'knows' and Welsh *cyf-ar-wydd-iaid* above), probably cognate with Gaulish **uidluā** 'seeress', which occurs in the first-century AD inscription found in the sorceress' grave at Larzac, southern France; see §2 above.

fenian (anglicized Irish): adjective pertaining to the Irish hero Find mac Cumaill and his followers in the **fían** (pl. **fíanna**), signifying roughly a warband of landless young men.

filid (Irish): etymologically 'seers', the higher class of poets in early Ireland. They took over many of the ceremonial functions of the pre-Christian druids. The word is probably equivalent to the name *Veledā* (§48).

Findabair (Irish): the daughter of Medb and Ailill, a sovereignty figure whose name is cognate with the Welsh

Gwenhwyfar (i.e. Arthur's wife, Guenevere). Both names are compounds of 'white' (**Find-**, **Gwen-**) and 'phantom' (**siabair**, **hwyfar**).

fír (Irish): 'right, truth, truthful utterance', through which a king ensures the welfare of his tribe and their land; cognate with Welsh **gwir** which has the same range of meanings.

Fomóire, Fomoiri (Irish) 'Fomorians': the Otherworld opponents of the Tuatha Dé in the *Second Battle of Mag Tuired*. They also figure at more than one point in Irish legendary history as presented in *Lebor Gabála Érenn* §108.

Gododdin (Welsh): the ancient form of the name being **Votādīnī**, a tribe that lived in what is now South-east Scotland and North-east England in Iron Age, Roman, and early post-Roman times. They appear on Ptolemy's geography as *Otadinoi*. Also the traditional name of a collection of poems thought to have originated among that tribe in the 6th century (§117).

Goidelic or **Gaelic**: the Celtic language sub-family including Irish, Scottish Gaelic, and Manx; essentially synonymous with **Q-Celtic**.

gonas géntar (Irish): 'he who kills shall be killed', an old Irish proverb occurring in the laws. The Welsh equivalent, **a wanei gwanet** 'he who was wont to slay was slain', is found in the *Gododdin* (§97) and other early heroic verse.

gormes (Welsh): 'oppression, invasion, plague': a key text for this concept is *Lludd and Lleuelys* in the *Mabinogi* (using this title in its wider sense).

Guorthemïr (Welsh): Anglo-Latinized **Vortimer**, the son of the Brittonic over-king Guorthïgïrn (Vortigern). He was supposed to be buried with his body facing the Continent. His name is a title or epithet 'supreme king' < *Vortamo-rīχs*, so it is not impossible that he could be Arthur himself or some other sub-Roman 'Arthur-like figure'. See §110 ¶¶42–43.

Gwynedd (Welsh): the kingdom in North-west Wales which, according to its own foundation legend, was founded by Cunedda of Gododdin in the early fifth century. See §110 ¶62.

Hallstatt: a central-European Late Bronze Age and Early Iron Age culture extending from *c.* 1200 BC down to *c.* 475 BC, with the transition to iron at about 800–700 BC, named for an Austrian type site. The users of this material culture are now generally agreed to have been speakers of Celtic languages. Some Hallstatt-type metalwork reached Britain, less reached Ireland. The earlier, pre-700 BC, pre-iron, portion of the Hallstatt culture is equivalent to 'Urnfield'.

Invasion Hypothesis: a lately unfashionable concept of Insular prehistory as a series of invasions, not unlike those of the Romans, Anglo-Saxons, Vikings, and Normans of history.

Íth (Irish): the first Milesian (i.e. descendant of Mil, i.e. ethnic Gael) to see Ireland from Bregon's Tower in Spain in *Lebor Gabála*. The name means 'fat, lard', < *pītu-, the same root as in *Ériu* 'Ireland' < Indo-European *(p)īwerijō 'the Fertile Land'.

Laigin (Irish): the dominant tribal group of pre-Christian and Early Christian South-east Ireland, from whom the province 'Leinster' is named. Settlers of this group in North Wales are recollected in the place-names *Llŷn* (Peninsula), Ma*llaen*, and Porthdin*llaen*.

La Tène (French) 'The Shallows': Later Celtic Iron Age material culture, named for a Swiss type site, scene of long-term watery ritual depositions. Material in the distinctive La Tène curvilinear decorative style of metal work penetrated Britain extensively, and more thinly, the northern half of Ireland. The La Tène style persisted in Gaul and Southern Britain until their respective Roman conquests. As what is sometimes called 'Ultimate La Tène' the style was to continue in Ireland and Pictland till Early Christian times, when it contributed to the eclectic Insular 'Hiberno-Saxon' style.

Lebor Gabála Érenn §108 (Irish): the 'Book of Invasions', the great work of Irish pseudo-history, aiming (in part at least) to give the Irish as ancient and venerable a history as that of the Greeks or Jews. *Gabál* means 'taking, settling, conquering, reigning'. Welsh *gafael*, OW *gabail* can gave this sense.

Lía Fáil (Irish): 'the Stone of Fál', talismanic stone set on the hill of Tara which shrieked when it came into contact with the true king, or, more especially, his chariot.

Lloegr (Welsh) originally the 'land east of Wales'. It comes to mean 'England', but originally did not include Cernyw, Rheged, or Gododdin.

Lóegaire mac Néill (Irish): legendary king of Tara, credited with meeting St. Patrick in the 7th-century life of the saint of Muirchú (§98).

lóg n-enech or **eneclann** (Irish): functionally cognate with Welsh **wynebwerth**, 'face-price' and Old Breton *enepuuert*, compensation due an injured party, its magnitude determined on the basis of social rank.

Lug(h) (Irish): Gaulish **Lugus**, Welsh **Lleu**, **Lleu-elys**. Pan-Celtic god, with links both to kingship and to the skilled professions. Caesar possibly equated him with the Roman Mercury (§20 ¶17).

Maelgwn (Welsh): descendant of Cunedda and king of Gwynedd in the first half of the 6th century. Antagonist of Taliesin in the *Ystorya Taliesin* 'Legend of Taliesin'.

Manannán mac Lir (Irish): sea-god figure that has probably influenced the name of the Welsh character **Manawydan fab Llŷr**. Both share the same patronymic 'son of the sea' (Irish *ler*, Welsh *llŷr*). The first element may contain the name of the god's home, Irish *Manu*, Welsh *Manaw* 'Isle of Man'. See *Tochmarc Étaíne* (§89 ¶1).

Medb (Anglicized *Maeve*): the queen of the Connachta and consort of Ailill in *Táin Bó Cuailnge* and other Ulster Cycle tales. Other traditions connect her with Tara. Her name is etymologically connected with the Celtic word for 'mead', Old Irish *mid* < **medu* and means 'she who intoxicates'. Her functional origin has been understood as an aspect of the sovereignty goddess who offered the ritual libation to the chosen mate of the deified land.

Mid(h)e (Irish): Anglicized *Meath*. Ideologically significant as the central province of early Ireland containing the ritual site of Tara and Uisnech, derived from Celtic **medio-* 'Middle', cf. *Medio-lanon* 'Middle of the Plain', modern Milan, centre of the Cisalpine Gauls.

Modron (otherwise **Madrun**) (Welsh) = British and Gaulish **Mātronā**: female mythological figure, originally the divine mother and eponym of the River Marne in Gaul, mother of the divine son **Mabon** (Welsh) = British and Gaulish **Maponos**. See §§1, 114, 128–130.

Mongán (Irish): historical 7th-century king of an area in the north of Ireland whom mediaeval tradition was to credit with a supernatural conception, recall of previous lives (including an incarnation as Find mac Cumaill), and magical powers. See §§102–105.

Mumu: Anglicized *Munster*, South-west Ireland.

nemed (Old Irish): Gaulish, Galatian, and Ancient British **Nemeton**, Welsh **nïuet** (in the *Gododdin*). It means 'sacred privilege' and anyone or anything possessing it. In ancient times, this term was first recorded as a designation of the druidical sanctuaries and ritual tribal meeting places of Gaul, Galatia, and Britain. Cf. *Drunemeton* 'Sacred Oak Wood', intertribal meeting place of the Galatians of Asia Minor.

Nera (Irish): protagonist of an otherworldly adventure set on Samain (Hallowe'en) night, enters the *síd* of Cruachu in the ancillary Ulster Cycle tale *Echtrae Nera* (§83).

Newgrange, see **Brug na Bóinne**.

Nuadu Necht (Irish): in Leinster tradition, ancestor of Finn mac Cumail and a leader of the *fíana* 'tribeless warbands'. **Nuadu** is etymologically related to the Welsh fairy king **Nudd** and to **Lludd**. The ancient form is **Nōdons**, a god whose elaborate 4th-century temple was situated at Lydney

on the lower Severn near the present-day Welsh-English border. See §68.

óenach (Irish): ceremonial assembly of the *tuath* 'tribe', convened by its *rí* 'king', often translated as 'fair' under the influence of Mod.Ir. *aonach*.

ogam (Irish), Modern **ogham**: Irish inscriptional alphabet employed in Ireland and Gaelicised areas of Britain, probably from as early as the 4th century AD.

Ogmios (Gaulish): according to Lucan (2nd century AD) the Gaulish equivalent of Hercules. Cf. Irish **Ogma**, Welsh **Eufyδ fab Dôn**.

Ordovices: British tribe 'Sledge-hammer Fighters', occupied North-west Wales in Iron Age and Roman times, before the founding of Gwynedd.

Peir Pen(n)-Annwvyn (Welsh): 'Cauldron of the Chief of the Otherworld', sought by Arthur in the *Preiδeu Annwvyn* (§113); cf. also **Peir Dadeni**, 'the cauldron of rebirth', in the Mabinogi of *Branwen*.

Posidonius: see p. 5 note.

Pritanī: ancient native name for the British, first attested *c.* 325 BC (whence Welsh **Prydein** 'Britain'), probably originally meant 'the people of the forms'; cf. Welsh *pryd*, 'form'.

Pwyll (Welsh): hero of the First Branch of the Mabinogi, and the father of Pryderi. His name means 'sense, care, consciousness, intelligence', cf. Irish *cíall*, both from Celtic *$k^w\bar{e}llo$-.

Pytheas of Marseilles: a Greek explorer who probably sailed to Britain, Ireland, and Scandinavia *c.* 325 BC.

Rhiannon (Welsh): < *Rigantonā*, 'great, divine queen', wife of Pwyll in the First Branch of the Mabinogi.

Rhun (Welsh, Old Welsh **Rün**): son of Uryen of Reget (Urien Rheged), brother of Owein, converted the Northumbrians to Christianity according to *Historia Brittonum*. See §110 ¶¶ 57, 63.

rí (Irish), Welsh **rhi**, Ancient British **rīx**, Gaulish **-rīx**; cf. Latin *rēx*.

Saeson (Welsh), **Sachsain** (Old Irish), **Sauson** (Old Breton): 'the English', originally the tribal group of the Saxons, < *Saxones*.

Samain (Irish): principal Irish feast, tribal assembly time, and new year; the night of 31 October and the day of 1 November, a time of otherworld activity in the mortal world and vice versa = Welsh **Kalan Gaeaf**.

scál (Irish): 'phantom, hero'.

síd (Irish): related to Welsh **gor-sedd** 'pagan burial mound', conceived as a portal to the Otherworld, also means 'peace', for which the Welsh is the related word *hedd-wch*. The Welsh Otherworld fort *Caer-sidi* (named in *Preideu Annwvyn*) probably shows a borrowing of the Irish word.

sírechtach (Irish): used of fairy music with the idea of 'provoking longing, nostalgic'. The corresponding Welsh word is **hiraethog** both from Celtic ***sīraxtāko-**.

synchronic: the study of a phenomenon at a given point in time, the analysis of factors affecting a story or tradition when the text assumed its surviving form. For the Irish and Brittonic material here, synchronic analysis considers the literary culture of Late Antiquity and Early Middle Ages.

Tálc(h)enn (Irish): 'Adze-head' or 'Shaven-head', epithet of St Patrick, more generally 'cleric, priest', in an assumed unsympathetic pagan view of the tonsure. (Irish *tál* 'adze' + *cenn* 'head'). See §98.

Taliesin (Welsh): the 6th-century Welsh poet who became the archetypal bard/druid as culture hero in medieval Welsh tradition, comparable to the Irish Amairgen.

talu medd (Welsh): 'paying for mead', an important theme in the *Gododdin* and elsewhere in Celtic literature. The hero is obligated to pay with martial valour and possibly his life in return for the hospitality of his lord.

Teyrnon (Welsh): < **Tigernonos* 'divine lord', foster father of Pryderi in the First Branch of the Mabinogi.

Temair, Anglicised *Tara*: ancient complex of earthworks in the Boyne Valley, once a cult site, place of the inauguration of one of the most important kingships of Ireland; retrospectively the Irish *literati* of the Christian Period came to view Tara as the seat of an ancient national High King (*ard rí*).

Tírechán (Irish): 7th-century cleric who wrote an 'Account of Patrick's Churches' (§99).

Transalpine Gaul or simply **Gaul**: roughly coterminous with modern France, Switzerland, Belgium, and Germany west of the Rhine. The ancient Celts of Bavaria, Bohemia, and Austria may also be considered as inhabitants of Gaul in some sources.

Tristan and Iseult: a love-triangle story of Celtic origin, tangentially connected to the Arthurian Cycle, attained widespread popularity in 12th- and 13th-century Europe, with versions in several non-Celtic languages.

tuath (Irish): Welsh tud, Gaulish toutā, 'tribe, people' the basic social unit of early Celtic society. The ruler of this group was the rí (Irish; with corresponding forms in the other languages).

Tuatha Dé (Danann) (Irish): 'Tribes of the Gods', used in Irish literature for the old native gods. The third term, signifying 'of the goddess Danu' or 'Danann', does not appear in the oldest texts.

uasal (Irish): 'high, noble' (corresponding to Welsh uchel, Old Celtic Ouxel(l)o-), but in áit uasal 'a fairy place'.

Ulaid (Irish): Ulstermen, dominant tribal group in North-eastern Ireland during the pre-Christian heroic age, central social entity of the 'The Ulster Cycle'. Their territory was greatly reduced from the 5th century.

Uth(e)r Pendragon (Welsh): Arthur's father in later tradition, Vthyr Penn 'the awesome/awful head' in earlier Welsh tradition was perhaps an epithet of the weirdly decapitated Brân. §115.

vātes: term used by several classical authors for a class of Celtic prophets. The Irish fáith used for both poets and poetry and the Welsh gwawt 'inspired poetry', later 'satire', correspond to this term.

Vortigern (Old Welsh Guorthïgïrn): major Brittonic leader of the 5th century who reputedly brought the Anglo-Saxons to Britain. His 'name' (more probably a title in origin) means 'supreme lord'.

INDEX

Maps

J. T. Koch

Ériu, Īveriō
EARLY IRELAND
some places mentioned in the text

KENELCUNILL

ULAID
ULSTER

MAG LENA

AIRGIALLA

■ Emain Macha
Navan Fort

MAG TUIRED   BREFNE

L E T H   C U I N N   CUAILNGE

CONNACHTA

MAG N-AÍ   TETHBA

MAG MUIRTHEMNE

■ Cruachu
Rath Cróghan

MIDE   Tailltiu ■   ■ Dubad *Dowth*
                        ■ Síd in Broga
MEATH   Temair   Brug na Bóinne
             Tara ■   *Newgrange*

■ Uisnech

■ *Clonmacnoise*   Boand *Boyne*   BREGA   *Howth*

                        Liffey ■ Áth Cliath
                        Mag Life

MÚSCRAIGE TÍRE   ■ Kildare
                        ■ Ailenn

                        LAIGIN
                        LEINSTER

MUMU
MUNSTER

■ Temair
Luachra

■ Sliab Mis   DÉSI

CORCU DUIBNE   ■ *The Paps
                    of Anu*

ÉRAINN

Ancient Celtic Europe

The regions within heavy borders show substantial amounts of La Tène material culture together with ancient Celtic place- and tribal names.

The regions within the heavy broken borders show ancient Celtic place- and tribal names but little or no standard La Tène material.

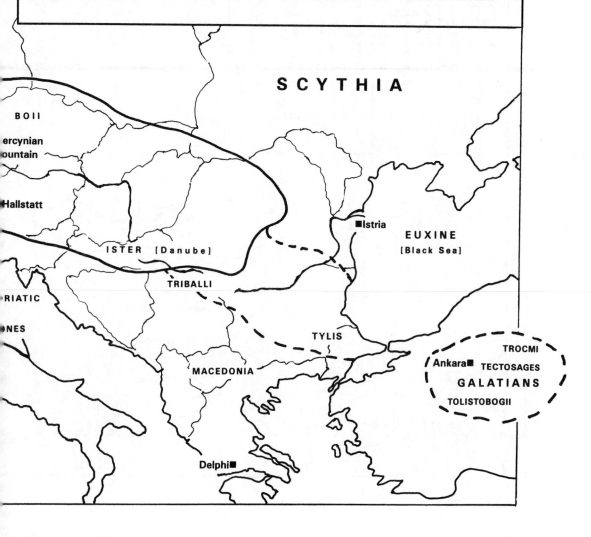

SCYTHIA

BOII

ercynian
ountain

Hallstatt

Istria

EUXINE
[Black Sea]

ISTER [Danube]

TRIBALLI

RIATIC

NES

TYLIS

MACEDONIA

TROCMI

Ankara TECTOSAGES

GALATIANS

TOLISTOBOGII

Delphi

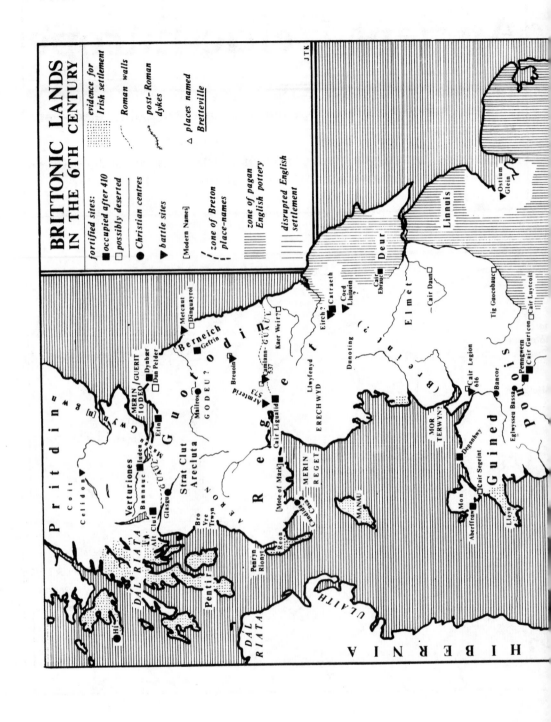

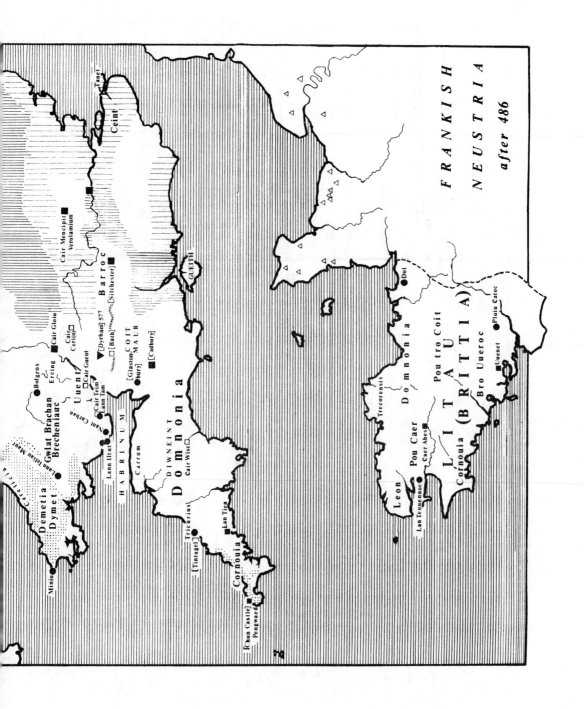

FRANKISH

NEUSTRIA

after 486

Tanet

Ceint

Cair Mencipit
Verolamium

B a r r o c

[Silchester]

GUEITH

COIT
[Dyrham] 577
[Bath]
MAUR
Cair Ceri(o)
Cair Gloiu
Cair Guent
Cair Teim
[Glaston-
bur] [Cadbury]
Ercing
Lann Tam

U e n t

Dol

Bolgros

D o m n o n i a

Gwlat Brachan
Brecheniauc
Nant Carban
Lann Iltut

H A B R I N U M

Pou tro Coit

Demetia
Dymet

Lann Telun Maur

Catrum

D I W N E I N T

D o m n o n i a

Trecorensis

Pou Caer
Caer Ahes

L I T A U

Miniu

C e r e t i c a

Cair Wisc

Cornouia (B R I T T I A)

Bro Ueroc

Uuenet

Pluiu Catoc

Tricurius

Lan Tica

Leon

Lan Teugennoc

[Tintagel]

C o r n o u i a

[Chun Castle]
Pengwaed

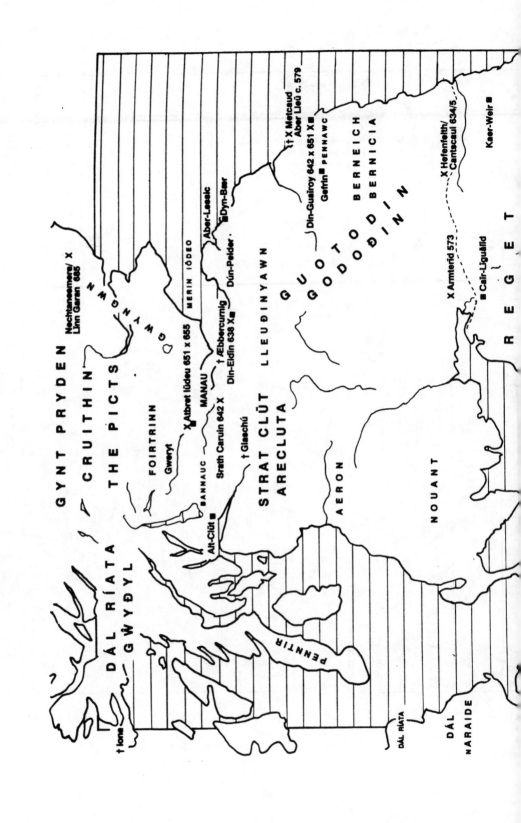

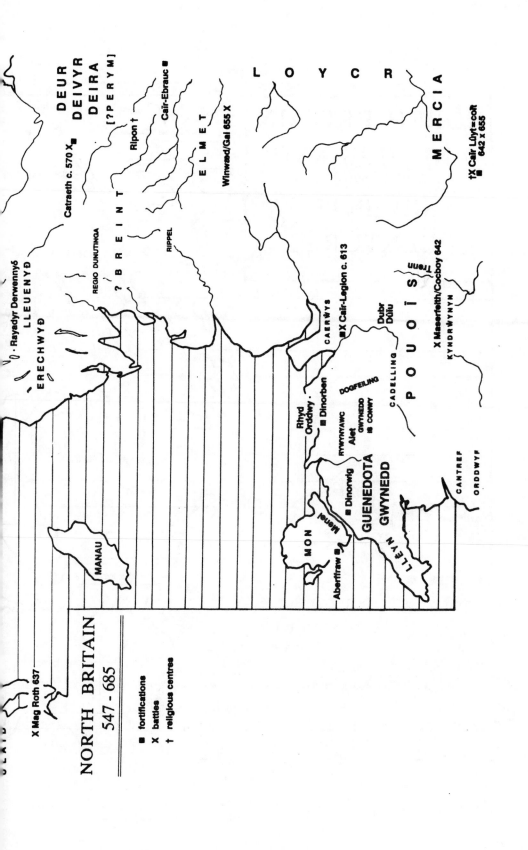

NORTH BRITAIN
547 - 685

■ fortifications
X battles
† religious centres

X Mag Roth 637

· Rhaeadyr Derwennyð
ERECHWYD
LLEUENYD

MANAU

REGIO DUNUTINGA
? B R E I N T

Catraeth c. 570 X■

DEUR
DEIVYR
DEIRA
[?PERYM]

Ripon †
Cair-Ebrauc ■

E L M E T

Wilnwæd/Gai 655 X

L O Y C R

RIPPEL

M E R C I A

†X Cair Llŷt=coit
■ 642 x 655

CAERWYS

■X Cair-Legion c. 613

Dubr
Dŵu

Trenn

X Maserfeith/Cocboy 642
KYNDRWŶNYN

P O U O I S

CADELLING

DOGFEILING

GWYNEDD
■ CONWY

Rhyd
Orddwy ·
■ Dinorben

RYWYNYAWC
Alet

MON
Menai

Abertfraw ■ ▼

■ Dinorwig

GUENEDOTA
GWYNEDD

LLEYN

CANTREF
ORDDWYF

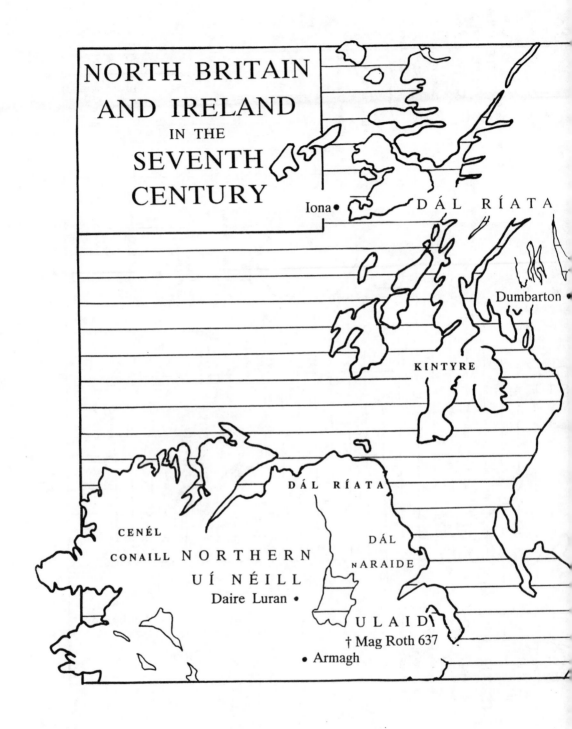

NORTH BRITAIN
AND IRELAND
IN THE
SEVENTH
CENTURY

Iona •

DÁL RÍATA

Dumbarton •

KINTYRE

DÁL RÍATA

CENÉL
CONAILL NORTHERN
UÍ NÉILL
Daire Luran •

DÁL
N ARAIDE

U L A I D
† Mag Roth 637
• Armagh

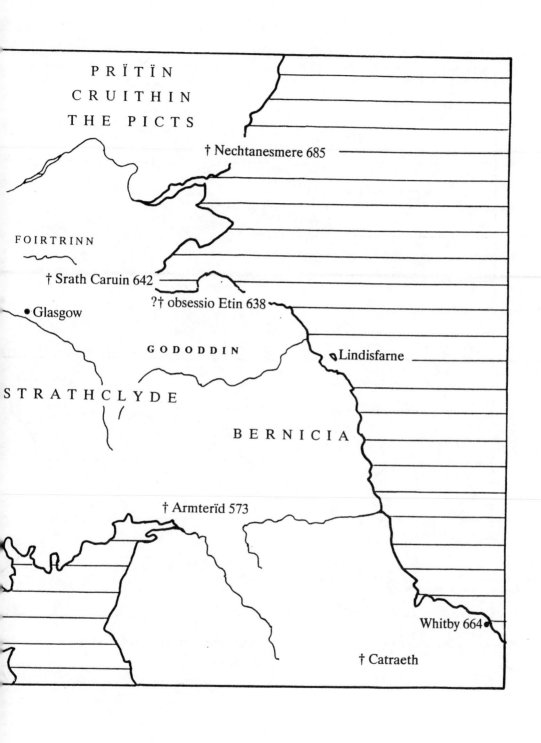

PRÏTÏN
CRUITHIN
THE PICTS

† Nechtanesmere 685

FOIRTRINN

† Srath Caruin 642

?† obsessio Etin 638

• Glasgow

GODODDIN

◖Lindisfarne

STRATHCLYDE

BERNICIA

† Armterïd 573

Whitby 664•

† Catraeth